A CONCISE HISTORY OF JAPAN

To this day, Japan's modern ascendancy challenges many assumptions about world history, particularly theories regarding the rise of the West and why the modern world looks the way it does. In this engaging new history, Brett L. Walker tackles key themes regarding Japan's relationships with its minorities, state and economic development, and the uses of science and medicine. The book begins by tracing the country's early history through archaeological remains, before proceeding to explore life in the imperial court, the rise of the samurai, civil conflict, encounters with Europe, and the advent of modernity and empire. Integrating the pageantry of a unique nation's history with today's environmental concerns, Walker's vibrant and accessible new narrative then follows Japan's ascension from the ashes of the Second World War into the thriving nation of today. It is a history for our times, posing important questions regarding how we should situate a nation's history in an age of environmental and climatological uncertainties.

BRETT L. WALKER is Regents Professor and Michael P. Malone Professor of History at Montana State University, Bozeman.

CAMBRIDGE CONCISE HISTORIES

This is a series of illustrated 'concise histories' of selected individual countries, intended both as university and college textbooks and as general historical introductions for general readers, travellers, and members of the business community.

A full list of titles in the series can be found at:
www.cambridge.org/concisehistories

A Concise History of Japan

BRETT L. WALKER
Montana State University

CAMBRIDGE
UNIVERSITY PRESS

CAMBRIDGE
UNIVERSITY PRESS

University Printing House, Cambridge CB2 8BS, United Kingdom

Cambridge University Press is part of the University of Cambridge.

It furthers the University's mission by disseminating knowledge in the pursuit of
education, learning and research at the highest international levels of excellence.

www.cambridge.org
Information on this title: www.cambridge.org/9780521178723

© Brett L. Walker 2015

First published 2015
7th printing 2018

Printed in the United Kingdom by TJ International Ltd. Padstow, Cornwall

A catalogue record for this publication is available from the British Library

Library of Congress Cataloguing in Publication data
Walker, Brett L., 1967–
A concise history of Japan / Brett L. Walker, Montana State University.
pages cm
Includes index.
ISBN 978-1-107-00418-4 (Hardback) – ISBN 978-0-521-17872-3 (Paperback)
1. Japan–History. I. Title.
DS835.W333 2015
952–dc23   2014031651

ISBN 978-1-107-00418-4 Hardback
ISBN 978-0-521-17872-3 Paperback

For

LaTrelle

うたた寝に
恋しき人を
見てしより
夢てふものは
たのみそめてき
小野小町『古今集』より

CONTENTS

15 Natural Disasters and the Edge of History   283

      Glossary   305
      Further Reading   310
      Index   323

ILLUSTRATIONS

xi

MAPS

PREFACE

While I was writing the final chapters of this book in the autumn of 2013, Super Typhoon Haiyan smashed into the Philippines with all its fury. With sustained winds at 315 kilometres per hour (195 miles per hour) and highs hitting 380 kph, many observers called it the most powerful storm ever recorded. As people in the Philippines fended for their lives, I was writing a chapter on Japan's 'bubble economy' and 'lost decade', covering the stagnant years between 1990 and 2010. But the Pacific 'monster storm' changed my plans. I had seen enough. I had already decided to cover the tragic events of 11 March 2011, when Japan suffered the 'triple disaster' of a catastrophic mega-thrust earthquake and tsunami, and then a dangerous nuclear meltdown at the Fukushima Daiichi plant. Watching Super Typhoon Haiyan throttle the Philippines made me realize that the symptoms of climate change, not tepid economic growth and disgruntled youth, or even international disputes over the Senkaku (Diaoyu) Islands, represented the most serious challenge facing East Asia. In the end, I scrapped the last chapter and drafted a new one that included a history of climate change, sea level rise, Pacific super storms, and natural disasters in the context of what many geologists have come to call the Anthropocene Epoch. It represents an important departure from the conventional manner of telling Japanese history – that is, it required fully embracing the idea that the physical islands called 'Japan' are geologically and historically unstable.

Of the Anthropocene Epoch, the Geological Society of London has stated, 'A case can be made for its consideration as a formal epoch in that, since the start of the Industrial Revolution, Earth has endured changes sufficient to leave a global stratigraphic signature distinct from that of the Holocene or of previous Pleistocene inter-glacial phases, encompassing novel biotic, sedimentary, and geo-chemical change.' Earth has indeed undergone 'novel' changes, ones whose occurrences coincide with the advent of the Industrial Revolution. The important difference between the changes driving the Anthropocene and the previous Holocene Epoch, however, is that the principal causes of those changes are no longer wind, erosion, volcanism, or other naturally occurring forces. Rather, human beings are causing these changes. Though the naturally occurring forces that etched Earth's surface were morally inert during the Holocene, moreover, basically valueless changes that just happened, there is an intent and design behind the forces of the Anthropocene. The Industrial Revolution, and all its assembled values, has served as the engine behind the bio-stratigraphic and litho-stratigraphic changes being carved onto our planet. If climate, elevation, and geographic location determined plant distribution during the Holocene, for example, as the famed Prussian scientist Alexander von Humboldt (1769–1859) famously observed, then our agricultural needs have determined it in the Anthropocene.

Therefore, rather than write a conventional national history, one that concludes with the economic, political, and foreign policy challenges facing Japan, I decided to conclude this book with the global threat of climate change. I came to believe that with the spectre of climate change looming so large on our collective plan-etary horizon, it would be equivalent to being in a state of denial to write a national history of a major industrial power, one that has contributed significantly to greenhouse gas emissions, without sus-tained attention to the short- and long-term environmental conse-quences of that country's industrial decision-making. Think of it this way: Japan industrialized at the end of the nineteenth century, meaning that it has enjoyed the fruits of an industrial society for about a century and a half. If we look ahead a century and a half, that same duration of time, Earth is projected by some to warm by as much as ten degrees or more, making much of it uninhabitable by contemporary standards. Suddenly, in the Anthropocene, geo-logic time has accelerated. Japan has significant coastal development, with millions of people and trillions in investments scattered along its low-lying areas. In a century and a half, Japan will be a very different place than it is today, with much of those low-lying areas submerged or routinely flooded by storm surges and tsunami. Because of its roots in Fernand Braudel's (1902–85) context of the historical *longue durée*, one lesson of environmental history is that the physical stage on which our past unfolds is unstable and dynamic, just like the human societies it supports and sustains. But climate change threatens to amplify that trans-formative process several fold.

That being said, this book is not an environmental history per se. Rather, this book is what I imagine history should look like in the twenty-first century, as ice sheets and glaciers melt and sea levels and storm intensities rise. It is a history written in the Anthropocene. I offer serious consideration of Japanese political, social, and cultural changes because they represent the values that drive Japan's interaction with the world, including the rapid indus-trialization in the late nineteenth century. This book blends many different approaches to history – social, gender, cultural, environ-mental, political, and biographical – in an attempt to tell a more complete story that enables a better understanding of Japan's development. Even though Japan, and a handful of other industri-alized nations, must claim the lion's share of greenhouse gas emissions and hence anthropogenic climate change, the burden of Earth's change will be shared globally, and by every species, even those traditionally viewed as without histories. Think of it this way: the moose of the Greater Yellowstone Ecosystem, where I call home, have played virtually no role in Earth's climate change, but as their ecosystem warms and becomes uninhabitable by them – as declining moose numbers around Yellowstone sug-gest it already is – they will share in the dire consequences. The moral weight of assuming responsibility for these changes to Earth, maybe not for regional moose extinction but perhaps for relentless flooding in Indonesia, and coming to understand the challenges they pose to our children, should be included in our historical narratives, at least at the meta-level of national and global histories. Hence my decision to make environmental change a key part in Japan's story.

To do so, I have built this book from the outstanding scholarship of many of my colleagues in Japanese and environmental history. One of the great thrills of writing this book was reviewing and reacquainting myself with much of this scholarship, which was largely collecting dust on my bookshelves. Thanking all of these gifted scholars would consume pages in an already less-concise history than the Cambridge's Concise Histories series editors probably imaged, but many will see their contributions and ideas rehearsed in these pages. As always, I appreciate the generous support of the Department of History, Philosophy, and Religious Studies at Montana State University, Bozeman; Nicol Rae, Dean of the College of Letters and Science at Montana State University, Bozeman; and Renee A. Reijo-Pera, Vice President for Research and Economic Development at Montana State University, Bozeman. Their commitment to creating new knowledge makes projects such as this one possible. Three people read this manuscript closely: my graduate student, Reed Knappe; my colleague in the Department of English, Kirk Branch; and my partner LaTrelle Scherffius. I am grateful for their many corrections and suggestions, which undoubtedly made this book stronger. Despite their combined efforts, however, mistakes no doubt remain, and I claim those for myself alone.

BRETT L. WALKER
BOZEMAN, MONTANA

CHRONOLOGY

Chapter 1: The Birth of the Yamato State, 14,500 BCE – 710 CE

2.6 million– 11,700 YBP	Pleistocene Epoch
11,700–100 YBP	Holocene Epoch
14,500–300 BCE	Jômon archaeological phase
12,700 YBP	Advent of pottery on Japanese islands
9,500 YBP	Dogs on Japanese islands
3,000–2,400 BCE	Advent of agriculture on Japanese islands
300 BCE–300 CE	Yayoi archaeological phase
57 CE	Eastern Han dynasty dispatched envoys to Wa kingdom
107 CE	Eastern Han dynasty dispatched envoys to Wa kingdom
238 CE	Wa envoys visited Wei emperor Cao Rui
247 CE	Wa envoys visited Korean commanderies
297 CE	*Wei zhi* described Wa kingdom
300–700 CE	Tomb archaeological phase
250–710 CE	Yamato confederacy
604 CE	'Seventeen-article Constitution'
645 CE	Taika Reforms
669 CE	Wa kingdom becomes 'Nihon'
689 CE	Kiyomihara Codes
702–718 CE	Taihô-Yôrô Codes

Chapter 2: The Courtly Age, 710–1185

Chapter 3: The Rise of Samurai Rule, 1185–1336

1192	Minamoto no Yoritomo became shogun
1192–1333	Kamakura *bakufu*
1221	Jôkyû War transfers Kamakura *bakufu* to Hôjô family
1223	Pirates plunder coast near Kumajo
1227	Pirates beheaded in front of Korean envoy
1232	Jôei Codes drafted
1274	First Mongol invasion
1281	Second Mongol invasion
1333–36	Emperor Go-Daigo's Kenmu Restoration
1336–92	Period of North and South courts

Chapter 4: Medieval Japan and the Warring States Period, 1336–1573

1336–1573	Ashikaga *bakufu*
1337–1573	Muromachi culture
1338	Ashikaga Takauji became shogun
1368	Ashikaga Yoshimitsu became shogun
1401	Ashikaga *bakufu* enters tributary relationship with Ming China
1467–77	Ônin War
1467–1573	Warring States period
1532	Ikkôshû launched 'Uprising of the Realm under Heaven'

Chapter 5: Japan's Encounter with Europe, 1543–1640

1542	Portuguese landed at Tanegashima
1570	Padre Francisco Cabral headed Society of Jesus
1579	Padre Alexandro Valignano headed Society of Jesus
1580	Portuguese given administrative authority over Nagasaki
1587	Toyotomi Hideyoshi's first expulsion edict
1596	*San Felipe* Incident
1597	'Twenty-six Saints' of Nagasaki executed
1607	*Santa Buenaventura* travelled from Japan to Mexico
1623	Fifty Christians burned at the stake in Edo
1637–38	Shimabara Uprising

Chapter 6: Unifying the Realm, 1560–1603

1551	Oda Nobuhide died
1555	Oda Nobutomo killed
1557	Oda Nobuyuki killed
1560	Battle of Okehazama
1571	Oda Nobunaga defeated Tendai monks of Mount Hiei
1573	Ashikaga Yoshiaki exiled

1644	Edo *bakufu*'s first *kuniezu* orders
1669	Shakushain's War
1683	Tokugawa Tsunayoshi's sumptuary regulations
1689	Matsuo Bashô travelled to the northeast
1696–1702	Edo *bakufu*'s second *kuniezu* orders
1701	Akô vendetta
1732	Kyôhô famine
1749	Hachinohe's 'wild boar famine'
1782–88	Tenmei famine
1808–10	Mamiya Rinzô maps Sakhalin and Amur Estuary
1821	Inô Tadataka scientific map of Japan completed
1833–37	Tenpô famine
1835–38	Edo *bakufu*'s third *kuniezu* orders

Chapter 8: The Rise of Imperial Nationalism, 1770–1854

1652	Sakura Sôgorô directly petitioned shogun
1751	Yamawaki Tôyô conducted dissection in Kyoto
1771	Sugita Genpaku oversees Kozukapara dissection
1837	Ôshio Heihachirô's rebellion
1853–54	Commodore Matthew C. Perry arrived in 'black ships'
1858–60	Ansei purge
1858	Harris Treaty signed
1860	Ii Naosuke killed by imperial zealots in Sakuradamon Incident
1860	Edo *bakufu* launched *kôbugattai* policy
1861	Hendrick Heusken killed by imperial zealots
1862	Charles Richardson killed by Satsuma samurai
1863	Shogun Tokugawa Iemochi held hostage in Kyoto
1866	'Smash and break' uprisings in Shindatsu
1868	'World renewal' uprisings in Aizu
1868	Matsuo Taseko travelled to Kyoto with other imperial supporters
1868	Edo *bakufu* collapsed after Boshin War

Chapter 9: Meiji Enlightenment, 1868–1912

1858	Keiô University established
1868–1912	Meiji period
1868	Imperial Charter Oath
1869	*Daimyô* relinquished domains
1871–73	Iwakura Mission
1871	Household Registration Law established
1871	Abolishment of early modern status system

1871	Liberation of outcastes
1872	Tokyo–Yokohama railway line opened
1872	Ginza brick quarter built
1872	*María Luz* Incident
1872	Liberation of prostitutes
1872	Women forbidden to bob hair
1873–74	Meiji Six Society founded
1873	Universal conscription
1875	School for Commercial Law established
1875	Kajibashi prison built
1877	Tokyo University established
1881	Matsukata Masayoshi's deflationary policies undertaken
1882	Bank of Japan established
1883	Rokumeikan pavilion completed
1889	Meiji Constitution promulgated
1890	Imperial Restrict on Education promulgated
1890	Law on Associations and Meetings passed
1900	Security Police Law passed

Chapter 10: Meiji's Discontents, 1868–1920

1868	'Separation of Buddhist and Shinto deities' ordered
1868	Meiji switch to fossil fuel energy
1872	Miike coalmine nationalized
1873	Land Tax Reform
1873	Mimasaka Blood-Tax Rebellion
1873	Fukuoka riots
1874	208,000 tons of coal yielded
1876	Mie prefecture protests
1877	Satsuma Rebellion
1877	Furukawa Ichibei bought Ashio copper mine
1881–85	Deflationary policies caused massive rural bankruptcies
1881	Jiyûtô formed
1884	Chichibu Uprising
1884	Ashio Japan's leading copper producer
1889	Hokkaido wolf extinct
1890–91	Watarase River flooded spreading Ashio's toxins
1890	Mitsui takes over Miike coalmine
1890	3 million tons of coal yielded
1890	Tanaka Shôzô elected to Diet
1896	Watarase River flooded spreading Ashio's toxins
1897	Hôjô coal vein discovered

1899	Gas explosion killed 210 at Hôkoku coalmine
1902	Tanaka Shôzô moved to Yanaka Village
1905	Japanese wolf extinct
1907	Gas explosion killed 365 at Hôkoku coalmine
1909	Explosion killed 256 at Ônomura coalmine
1914	Hôjô coalmine explosion killed 687
1917	Explosion killed 365 at Ônomura coalmine

Chapter 11: The Birth of Japan's Imperial State, 1800–1910

1770–71	Russians and Ainu killed in Iturup Incident
1778	Russians attempted to trade with Japanese in eastern Ezo
1802	Edo *bakufu* established Hakodate magistracy in Ezo
1857	Edo *bakufu* sponsored smallpox vaccinations among Ainu
1869–82	Kaitakushi oversaw colonization of Hokkaido
1872	Model silk factory opened in Tomioka
1872	Central Sanitation Bureau created
1875	Japanese ship fired on in Un'yô Incident
1875	Korea 'opened' by Japanese diplomats
1876	'Japan–Korea Treaty of Amity' signed
1876	Sapporo beer founded
1878	Ainu categorized as 'former aboriginals'
1885	Tientsin Convention signed with Qing China
1885	Kitasato Shibasaburô entered Robert Koch's German lab
1890	Kitasato Shibasaburô involved with Koch's tuberculosis cure
1895	Sino-Japanese War
1895	Japan suffered 'Triple Intervention'
1898	School hygiene system created
1899	Hokkaido Former Aborigine Protection Act passed
1902	Japan signed international agreement with England
1903	Government studied tuberculosis in textile industry
1905	Russo-Japanese War
1905	Treaty of Portsmouth
1910–11	Great Treason Incident
1913	800,000 workers involved in silk industry

Chapter 12: Empire and Imperial Democracy, 1905–1931

1875	Treaty of St Petersburg
1896	Shinpotô established
1898	Kenseitô established
1899	US affirmed 'open door policy'

Chapter 13: The Pacific War, 1931–45

Chapter 14: Japan's Post-War History, 1945–Present

1947	Post-war Constitution enacted
1947	US occupation cancelled general strike
1947	Labour Standards Law passed
1949	Joseph Dodge arrived in Japan
1950	National Police Reserve created
1951	San Francisco Peace Treaty signed
1952	'Treaty of Mutual Cooperation and Security' signed
1954	Police Reform Bill
1954	*Lucky Dragon 5* Incident
1955	Jimintô established
1967	Basic Law for Pollution Control passed
1969	Suit filed against Osaka's Itami Airport
1971	Niigata 'Minamata disease' court ruling
1971	Environment Agency established
1972	US relinquished control of Senkaku/Diaoyu Islands to Japan
1972	'Yokkaichi asthma' court ruling
1972	Toyama cadmium pollution court ruling
1973	'Minamata disease' court ruling
1978	Fourteen 'Class A' war criminals interred at Yasukuni shrine
1985	Privatization of tobacco industry
1987	Creation of JR Group
1991	'Bubble economy' burst
2001	Ministry of Environment replaced Environment Agency

Chapter 15: Natural Disasters and the Edge of History

1854	Ansei Earthquake
1891	Nôbi Earthquake
1896	Meiji-Sanriku Earthquake
1900–93	Global sea level rose 1.7 millimetres annually
1923	Great Kantô Earthquake
1958	Typhoon Ida
1959	Typhoon Vera
1993	Global sea level rose 3 millimetres annually
1995	Hanshin-Awaji Earthquake
2005	Japan produced 1,390 megatons of greenhouse gases
2011	Japan's 'triple disaster' on 11 March

Introduction

Writing Japanese History

THE RELEVANCE OF JAPANESE HISTORY

To this day, Japan's national ascendancy challenges many assumptions about world history, particularly theories regarding the rise of the West and why, put simply, the modern world looks the way that it does. It was not China's great Qing dynasty (1644–1911), nor India's sprawling Maratha empire (1674–1818), that confronted the US and European powers during the nineteenth century. Rather, it was Japan, a country, at 377,915 km² (145,913 mi²), about the size of the US state of Montana (Map 1). Not only did this small island country hold the Great Powers of the nineteenth century at bay, it emulated them and competed with them at their own global ambitions, as contemptible as those often were. Then, in the second half of the twentieth century, after the Pacific War, Japan rebuilt and became a model for industrialization outside the US and Europe, with wildly successful companies such as Honda and Toyota, now household names. Soccer mums in the US drive Toyotas, as do Jihadists in Afghanistan. But today, Japan finds itself in the eye of a different global storm. In the early years of the twenty-first century, Japan is embroiled in concerns over industrial economies and climate change because, as an island country with extensive coastal development, it has much to lose from rising sea levels and the increasing number of violent storms in the Pacific. Japan remains at the centre of the modern world and its most serious challenges.

1 Japan

To help us acclimatize to the pace of Japan's history, take the lives of two prominent figures. Fukuzawa Yukichi (1835–1901), a prideful samurai born in Osaka and raised on the southern island of Kyushu, exemplified many of Japan's early experiences in the modern age. In one lifetime, he watched, not as a passive observer but as one of its principal architects, his country transformed from a hotchpotch of domains to a nation with vast military reach and global economic aspirations. As a samurai urchin patrolling the dusty streets of Nakatsu domain, Fukuzawa entertained lofty dreams of shattering the chains of backward Confucian practices and travelling the world in order to discover what made the Western world tick.

At the mischievous age of twelve or thirteen, Fukuzawa stole a sacred paper talisman from his home, which supposedly protected his family from calamities such as theft and fire. He then did what to many would have been utterly unthinkable: 'I deliberately stepped on it when nobody was looking. But no heavenly vengeance came.' Not satisfied that he had done enough to irritate local Shinto deities, he then took the talisman and stomped it into the filth of the toilet. Still no divine Shinto retribution came. Always one to challenge Japan's beliefs, the recalcitrant Fukuzawa then tempted the deities even further by replacing the sacred stones at an Inari shrine in his uncle's garden with sundry stones of his own choosing. When the season of the Inari festival arrived, people came to the shrine to worship, putting up banners, beating drums, and chanting. Fukuzawa chuckled under his breath, 'There they are – worshipping my stones, the fools.' For most of his life, Fukuzawa had nothing but disdain for Japan's traditions, underpinned as they were by conservative Chinese philosophy rather than Western progressive individualism. But his rejection of tradition, exemplified by mocking Inari folkways, as well as his embrace of modernity, exemplified by rationally determining the Inari deities were not paying close attention, are emblematic of Japan's nineteenth-century experience.

In this fashion, Fukuzawa trampled over one sacred assumption after another and in his lifetime witnessed Japan's rise from a country run by sword-wielding men in skirt-like *hakama* pants and *chonmage* shaved pates to the only Asian country to successfully challenge US and European imperialism. When Fukuzawa departed Nakatsu domain for the last time, he 'spat on the ground, and walked quickly away'. In some respects, this is precisely what Japan tried to do in the mid-nineteenth century after the Meiji Restoration (1868): Fukuzawa and his entire generation spat on centuries of political and cultural assumptions and, with a rare sense of national rebirth, charted a new course to global supremacy and, ultimately, national destruction and eventual post-war renewal. At present, Japan faces a new set of national challenges that even the clever Fukuzawa could never have foreseen. Some of these, such as climate change and rising sea levels, dwarf the threats of the US's nineteenth-century 'black ships'. But by studying Japan's past, perhaps we can gather how this island nation, so gifted at the art of rebirth, might tackle these new global threats. Perhaps Japan might find a model of rebirth for us all.

Ishimoto Shidzue's (1897–2001) life began where Fukuzawa's ended, at the beginning of the twentieth century; she had similar experiences, though she struggled with Japan's new brand of nationalism and the fascist 'emperor system ideology'. She lived in a different age of rebirth. Raised in a conservative family not quite prepared to spit on all traditions, Ishimoto was not only burdened with the legacies of samurai rule, but also with Confucian attitudes towards women. Like any well-heeled young woman, her mother dutifully taught her: 'man first, woman to follow'. Though she was raised in a 'purely Japanese fashion', she remembered that 'Western influences crept into our life little by little'. But a conservative reaction was growing in Japan. While in school, Ishimoto astutely detected that, whereas teachers taught boys to be 'great personalities', they trained girls to become 'obedient wives, good mothers and loyal guardians of the family system'. In the early twentieth century, women's bodies became battlegrounds on which political activists, public intellectuals, and government policy-makers fought pitched battles over the legacies of Meiji reforms. In one telling story, she recalled a visit to her school by the Meiji emperor. 'Being homogeneous in racial traditions', she remembered, 'we are one big family in the island empire with the imperial rulers at the head.' She mused: 'How could a girl like myself born in the Meiji era, when the restoration of the Emperor was the main political excitement, and reared under his spell, fail to be moved by the spiritual force which the Emperor symbolized?' When General Nogi Maresuke (1849–1912), hero of the Russo-Japanese War (1905), dutifully committed suicide, along with his wife, following the death of the Meiji emperor in 1912, Ishimoto showed quiet reverence. 'I sat in my own quiet room where I had placed the general's picture on the table and burned incense', she remembered, 'praying to his noble spirit without a spoken word.' Like so many, Ishimoto sometimes rebelled against the spirit of Meiji nationalism, but she also worshipped at its altar.

Emperor worship anchored Japan's emergence as a nation in the early twentieth century, but so did forms of global engagement with modernity. While Ishimoto visited the US in 1920, she met feminist Margaret Sanger (1879–1966) and became an activist for women's causes, particularly reproductive rights. But the Pacific War (1937–45) temporarily derailed her campaign for women's rights. Ishimoto mused in the 1930s, on the eve of the catastrophic war, 'A nationalist reaction against liberalism has recently swept all else before it in the Island Empire. Fascism with its strong militaristic flavour is no defender of feminism with its strong humanistic flavour.' It was during Ishimoto's lifetime that Japan launched its battleships and aircraft carriers to wage a 'sacred war' against the US and its Allies, determined to create a 'new order' in Asia. At stake in the Pacific conflict, argued many Japanese thinkers, was the 'salvation of the world'.

Ishimoto was a little girl when Fukuzawa died, but she admired him. She saw Japan's empire crumble, its cities burned to the ground; she also saw, however, Japan embrace defeat and rise from the ashes to become an economic superpower. From *hakama* pants and *chonmage* hairstyles to the *Yamato* battleship and Toyota's full-sized Tundra pickup trucks, the rise of Japan has punctuated world history. Fukuzawa and Ishimoto, in their own ways, were architects of that world.

JAPAN IN WORLD HISTORY

By placing Japan in the context of world history this history displaces one persistent myth: that Japan has a special, non-intrusive, more subjective, and often-benign relationship to nature, one that views the natural world as alive with Shinto deities, interlaced with Buddhist continuums of life, and bounded by Confucian rites. The myth insists that the Japanese did not render nature as a lifeless, objectified resource for industrial exploitation. Rather, the Japanese conformed to nature by creating holism between cultural and natural spheres. The natural environment sprang to life for Japanese, which limited soulless industrial development and shaped their rarefied national culture.

This stereotype has been centuries in the making. Early on, the sociologist Max Weber (1864–1920) argued that unlike European philosophy that sought to adjust the world to meet human requirements, Confucianism, the core philosophy of East Asia, sought 'adjustment to the world, to its orders and conventions'. In other words, Western Europe adjusted the natural world to suit it, while Confucian societies passively adjusted themselves to suit the natural world. As a Confucian society, early modern Japan, too, is often viewed as conforming to the natural environment, a society in harmony with nature rather than forcing the environment to bend to its economic needs. As a result, Weber insisted that, 'Systematic and naturalist thought ... failed to mature' in Confucian societies. For Weber, this predisposition to defer to nature retarded development and allowed Confucian societies to be victimized by Western predators.

As this history demonstrates, Japan's relationship to the natural environment was often intrusive, probing, exploitative, and controlling, similar to post-Enlightenment Europe. Satô Nobuhiro (1769–1850), an eclectic early modern thinker, understood nature to be driven by creative forces, ones animated by Shinto deities. But when describing the role of economics in the context of state development he sounded more like the Scottish economist Adam Smith (1723–90) than a native Shinto philosopher. When describing the role of government, for example, Satô pronounced, in *Keizai yôryaku* (Summary of economics, 1822): 'The development of products is the first task of the ruler.' Humans organize into states, Satô suggested, in order to better exploit resources and control energy.

Importantly, the environment that Satô sought to develop was of largely human design, Japan's contribution to the early signatures of the Anthropocene Epoch, which is characterized by the pervasiveness of human-induced change on Earth. In their early history, Japanese began discovering and engaging the natural environment through engineering their islands. Indeed, Japan might be seen as a built archipelago, a string of islands envisioned as a controllable, exploitable, legible, and almost technological space. This process began early in Japanese history. With the advent of agriculture came a 'fundamental change in the relation between humans and the natural world', argues one historian. Humans began to 'affect other organisms' and 'remake the nonliving environment' to better control access to nutrition and energy. Agriculture means removing undesirable species, creating artificial landscapes, and increasing the productivity of desirable species through better access to water and sunlight. Humans remade organisms around them, genetically engineering crops and exterminating threatening species, such as Japan's wolves. As they created this agricultural landscape, humans 'may have experienced a growing sense of separation between the "natural" and "human" worlds', or a sense of 'alienation' from natural conditions.

Ultimately, this alienation objectifies nature and facilitates its indifferent exploitation. Historians have identified this objectifying 'death of nature' hypothesis with post-Enlightenment European culture, but, as we shall see, Japanese culture undertook a similar process of alienation. In Japan nature was slowly killed over historical time, but then philosophers and theologians stitched it back together and injected it with the anthropomorphic life of Shinto and Buddhist deities. Nature became a marionette of the human craving for resources and energy, even though observers have long mistaken this raggedy, natural puppet for a living, freestanding nature.

WRITING JAPAN'S HISTORY

'Historical consciousness in modern society has been overwhelmingly framed by the nation state', writes one historian. Even though the nation is a contested entity, it manipulates history and secures the 'false unity of a self-same, national subject evolving through time'. It is the nation 'evolving through time' that claims prehistoric Jômon (14,500 BCE – 300 BCE) hunters and Yayoi (300 BCE – 300 CE) agriculturalists as 'Japanese' because apparent evolutionary development can also be read in reverse order. National history narratives, such as this one, nearly always impose an evolutionary chain on the past. Speaking to this point, one historian insists that, 'the nation is a collective historical subject poised to realize its destiny in a modern future'. In other words, we are conditioned to read national histories as anticipating the rise of the modern state, as if its emergence is inevitable. 'In evolutionary history, historical movement is seen to be produced only by antecedent causes rather than by complex transactions between the past and the present.' This is an important cautionary note for narrating national histories such as this one. Rather than viewing history as a clean linear movement from one cause to another, reaching steadily and inexorably towards the emergence of the modern nation, this history is more sensitive to contemporary political and cultural debates and the nuances that frame questions imposed on the past. Of course, history is often more about present political and cultural debates than it is about the past. Therefore, a major theme in this history is environmental change because that is the challenge of our time.

This concise history does not dismiss outright the reality of the time-travelling power of the modern nation or its ability to sculpt the identities of people it claims as its earliest members. Jômon hunters did not see themselves as 'Japanese', nor did their Yayoi replacements. Heian courtiers viewed courtly positions as far more meaningful than 'Japan', as did later samurai, who moved according to the rhythms of a hierarchical status system. In this respect, the modern nation is a recent 'imagined community', one that is invented through museums, school curricula, holidays, and other national events. As one anthropologist writes, the nation 'is imagined because the members of even the smallest nation will never know most of their fellow-members, meet them, or even hear of them, yet in the minds of each lives the image of their communion'. In modern nations, citizens and subjects are taught that they share affinities with people whom they have never met. As we shall see, Japanese imagine their communities through discourses of a shared natural environment, one neatly delineated by surrounding seas, as well as a common history, language, and cultural practices. Many of these are rehearsed in the pages of this history because they are important in the making of Japan.

This concise history does not necessarily see nations as entirely 'imagined', however. Nations are not merely figments of the cultural imagination. Because one theme in this story is people's relationships to the natural environment, this concise history uncovers the material imprint of Japan's populations throughout its history. It tracks a presence shaped by generations of bodies rotting in the soil, men and women pulling fish from the same rivers and coastal waters, engineered landscapes that reflect shared subsistence values, and transitory ideas heaped on one another for centuries and that shape a distinct manner of being. Viewed from this vantage point, early Jômon inhabitants, though they did not know it themselves, really can be viewed as the earliest 'Japanese'. The nation, for all its time-travelling hegemony, is built, in a fundamentally material way, on the people that preceded it. In this sense, 'tradition' is not necessarily the invented whipping boy of modernity, as some historians have submitted. Modernity, it has been argued, necessitates the 'invention of tradition' in order to demarcate itself historically. But earlier inhabitants of Japan, people we might call 'traditional' for convenience, had traceable material practices, ones imprinted on Japan in material ways and that inform modern life. These practices shaped the evolutionary development of Japan's modern nation, not vice versa. To label a Jômon hunter with the title 'Japanese', and then to pin on him the future horrors of Japan's Nanjing Massacre (1937), is to saddle him with burdens that would have been unimaginable to him. But Jômon hunters died and rotted in Japan's soil. Their progeny and Yayoi replacements adopted ideas, made choices, and imprinted those choices on themselves, their social organizations, their political systems, and on the landscape. These material imprints shaped their progeny, and then their progeny, and so forth. Eventually, those people, guided as they were by generation upon generation of material and cultural drivers, decided to ransack the city of Nanjing during what they trumpeted as the 'Greater East Asian War'.

The nation might be in part imagined, but not out of thin air. It is not entirely an unnatural phenomenon, either. And so it is for Japanese history. For this reason, even in the face of new global predicaments such as climate change, the modern nation remains an important category of historical analysis.

I

The Birth of the Yamato State,
14,500 BCE – 710 CE

Japan's environment proved much more than simply a sculptor of Japanese civilization, where wind and rain painstakingly chiselled, over the centuries, the intricate contours of Japanese life. Rather, the environment was a product of Japanese civilization. Early inhabitants of the Japanese Islands, from the Yayoi archaeological phase (300 BCE – 300 CE) onward, carved, sliced, burned, and hoed their subsistence needs and cultural sensibilities into the alluvial plains, forests, mountainous spine, and bays of the archipelago, transforming it, like some colossal bonsai tree, into a material manifestation of their needs and desires. This is the most profound disjuncture between the Jômon archaeological phase (14,500 BCE – 300 BCE) and the Yayoi: the introduction of East Asian culture and its transformative effect on the archipelago. This chapter explores the emergence of the earliest Japanese state, and how state development was intimately connected to environmental transformation.

EARLY FORAGERS AND SETTLERS

The Pleistocene Epoch, about 2.6 million to 11,700 years before present (YBP), witnessed the first wave of early hominid, non-human animal, and incidental plant migrations across Eurasia and onto the Japanese archipelago. Japan was not an archipelago at the time, however. Rather, it was connected to the continent at both the southern and northern sections by coastal lowlands that formed a terrestrial crescent with the Sea of Japan serving as what must have been an impressive inland sea. Whether modern hominids came from Africa and displaced earlier hominids, or the earlier arrivals evolved into modern hominids, is still debated, but by 100,000 YBP many palaeolithic foragers roamed Eurasia, and some of them wandered onto this terrestrial crescent in pursuit of game and other foraging opportunities. The 1931 discovery of a left pelvic bone first suggested palaeolithic habitation of the terrestrial crescent, but air raids destroyed the bone during the Pacific War (1937–45) and the bone's discoverer was only vindicated with the later unearthing of other palaeolithic remains throughout Japan.

These palaeolithic and, later, mesolithic hunters tracked and killed large game, including Palaeoloxodon elephants and giant deer. They and their prey watched, across generation upon generation, Japan's geographic character transform as fluctuating climates and ocean levels allowed the continent to claim the crescent and then lose it around 12,000 YBP, when oceans poured into coastal lowlands and created the string of islands. As for the early foragers, linguists trace three distinct language groups among these humans, ones that indicate routes of migration: Ural-Altaic (Japanese, Korean, Northeast Asian, and Turkic languages), Chinese (Tibet and Burman languages), and the Austro-Asiatic (Vietnamese, Khmer, and several minority languages in China). With the final stages of the Pleistocene, Japan's early foragers had overhunted most of the archipelago's giant mammals, now geographically confined with hungry hominids, in the so-called 'Pleistocene extinction'.

Hominid foragers, whatever languages they spoke, were not the only hunting tribes that wandered onto this crescent. Wolves arrived there, too. Siberian wolf skulls have been discovered throughout Japan. In the late Pleistocene, these large wolves hunted and foraged in the coniferous forests of northern Honshu, where they brought down large game such as steppe bison. These bison were big, with horns spanning some one metre across their bony skulls; but the Siberian wolf was big, too. It loitered opportunistically among the herds, searching for injured stragglers. We can surmise that hominids were not the only hunters pushing the Pleistocene extinction, or at least picking up the pieces from it. As the archipelago separated from the continent, about 12,000

YBP, coniferous forests yielded to deciduous growth, devouring precious grasslands for large bison and their hungry pursuers. This climate shift and the accompanying changes in forest composition also contributed to the Pleistocene extinction. Now isolated with its large game extinct, the Siberian wolf dwarfed into the smaller Japanese wolf that would become extinct in the early twentieth century. This period also witnessed the emergence of Japan's common species, such as Japanese deer, wild boar, and a variety of other smaller animals. At this juncture, Japan's tumultuous geography, its transformation from a terrestrial crescent to an archipelago, did drive history – in the case of modern hominid foragers, their settlement patterns, dwelling arrangements, and hunting circuits; for the wolf, the very shape and size of its skull – but later human settlers, particularly after the Yayoi phase, proved better at transforming their island home to suit their subsistence and cultural needs.

About 12,700 YBP, while the terrestrial crescent transformed into an archipelago, foragers discovered, or were introduced to (the verdict is still out among archaeologists), a monumental technological breakthrough: pottery. The oldest fragments come from the Fukui cave in northwest Kyushu, an area that served as a conduit for exchange with the continent. Vexingly, nothing this early has been unearthed in China, or anywhere else for that matter. Archaeologists refer to these people as Jômon (cord pattern) because the pottery is often adorned with elaborate cord markings imprinted around the rim and elsewhere on the jars. This techno-logical advance allowed these foragers to become more sedentary, as they could now prepare formerly inedible vegetables and shell-fish, as well as boil seawater to produce salt for consumption and trade. Cultigens became a feature of later Jômon life, but simple agriculture proved more limited than other neolithic groups. The first Jômon man, Japan's 'Adam', discovered in 1949 buried in a flex position at the Hirasaki shell mound, stood 163 centimetres tall, which is about three centimetres taller than average, with women being considerably shorter. Unused wisdom teeth and other evidence suggest a short life expectancy, at some twenty-four years for women and perhaps a decade longer for men. Over the centur-ies, the styles of Jômon pottery changed, but it remained ornate, with swirling patterns and imprints, elaborate handles and other forms of decoration, and delicate shapes with impractically narrow bottoms. The relatively pointy bottoms would have been great for nomadic life, holding the jar upright in loose soil or sand, but impractical for life in a hardened-floor home. Nonetheless, the increasing sophistication of the pottery hints at ritualistic purposes and regular home use, offering a possible first glimpse into the religious life of the archipelago's earliest settlers.

Jômon hunters developed bows, which hurled deadly projectiles at much higher velocities than earlier spears. Wolfish dogs that probably migrated onto the terrestrial crescent with earlier palaeolithic foragers hunted alongside the Jômon for smaller game. Skeletal remains of dogs from the Natsushima shell mounds in Kanagawa prefecture date to 9,500 YBP. Archaeologists have uncovered elaborate systems of pit-traps, no doubt used to trap and impale boar and other game. Jômon also subsisted on fruits and nuts, bulbs and starchy tubers, shellfish such as molluscs, clams and oysters, fish such as seabream, and other food sources as well. Bone harpoon heads and fishhooks from the Numazu shell middens suggest that they became reasonably skilled fishers. But all this was not good enough: skeletal remains demonstrate that the Jômon lived in a nearly constant state of malnutrition, on the cusp of reproductive instability. A diet of high-calorie nuts meant that the teeth of most rotted painfully from their heads. Larger Jômon settlements situated their houses in a circular pattern, with a central communal space for burials, food storage, and ceremonial functions. Better homes with inner posts supporting pitched roofs allowed Jômon to accumulate more possessions, including *dogû*, or earthenware figurines (Figure 1). Often, figurines depicted buxom women, suggesting that their ritual purpose was aimed at reproduction and safe childbirths. Phallic items point to fertility rituals. Snakehead motifs offer tantalizing evidence of snake-related ceremonies, perhaps conducted by village shamans. Skeletal remains with missing adult teeth indicate forms of ritualized teeth pulling, probably as a form of coming-of-age ritual. Some of the larger pottery jars, called 'placenta pots', contain placental remains and even the remains of infants, demonstrating elaborate forms of burial and ceremony.

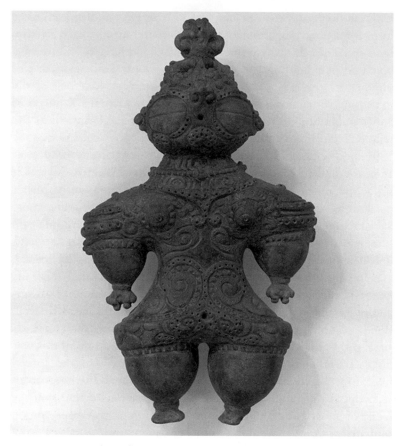

1   Jômon phase figurine, Miyagi prefecture.

As sophisticated as Jômon life became, these souls always survived on the edge and their society proved ill-prepared for environmental changes and disappearing game. Some 4,500 YBP, a drop in global temperatures sparked a herbaceous cascade that led to declines in mammal populations and nut orchards and Jômon people soon found themselves vulnerable to food shortages and famine. With deer and boar harder to find, even with the keen noses of trusted hunting dogs, Jômon foragers took to killing smaller game and many inland settlements relocated to coastal areas to improve foraging and fishing. Some insist that Japan's 260,000 inhabitants in 4,500 YBP might have declined to 160,000 over the course of the

next millennium. Jōmon people had reached the limits of conforming to the changing nature of their home.

Strictly speaking, since the Middle Jōmon (3000 BCE – 2400 BCE),
evidence of incipient neolithic agriculture has survived in the archaeological record. Jōmon cultivated yams and taro, which probably
came from southern China; they also manipulated the growth of
lily bulbs, horse-chestnut, and other plants critical to their survival.
Starch from taro and lily bulbs steamed on wicker trays produced
simple bread, the preserved remnants of which archaeologists have
unearthed in Nagano prefecture. On Late Jōmon (1000 BCE – 250
BCE) pottery, archaeologists observe traces of rice grain imprints.
So Jōmon people raised simple crops, but they did not engineer the
environment for agriculture, other than, for example, through
localized deforestation. Engineering the environment for agriculture was the culture of the Yayoi phase (300 BCE – 300 CE). The
first Yayoi sites were excavated in 1884 on the University of Tokyo
campus; later finds in 1943 in Shizuoka prefecture clarified the
distinctiveness of the Yayoi phase.

Initially, Yayoi agriculture was probably confined to buckwheat
and barley cultivated on the southern island of Kyushu. Both grains
are believed to have originated on the continent, brought over by
Yayoi migrants who, judging from skull remains, appear to have
represented a new wave of migration onto the archipelago, either
living alongside or slowly displacing neolithic Jōmon settlers. They
appear to have been of North Asian descent, whereas most Jōmon
settlers are believed to be from Southeast Asia. Yayoi migrants were
taller and had longer faces, but over the course of the Yayoi phase
lost some of their stature, probably as a result of persistent nutritional deficiencies. Once on the archipelago, however, they repro-
duced at a higher rate. Indeed, Yayoi reproduction rates were such
that, 300 years after their arrival on the archipelago, some estimate
they constituted around 80 per cent of the population. They simply
proved healthier and more fecund than earlier foragers.

These new settlers also brought the knowledge and technical
skills of paddy rice farming. The Yayoi phase corresponds to the

two Han dynasties in China (206 BCE – 220 CE), which, in their records, referred to the archipelago as the 'Wa kingdom'. With new Yayoi migrants, rice cultivation techniques spread throughout the Wa kingdom, encompassing approximately western and central Japan. Early Yayoi paddy engineering was relatively sophisticated: elaborate systems of irrigation canals, dams, paddy walls, and intake/outlet gates ensured that rice was properly irrigated. With rice agriculture, archaeologists estimate that the Yayoi population might have reached between 600,000 and 1 million by the first centuries of the Common Era. Of interest to us, some historians have argued that between 221 BCE and 907 CE, the genesis of the East Asian cultural sphere occurred as Confucian humanism, Buddhist theology, and Chinese *kanji* writing spread on the continent and beyond. We might also include paddy agriculture as a defining characteristic of East Asian civilization. Although Confucianism had yet to restructure Japanese views of family, society, and governance, with the advent of paddy agriculture Japan was already caught up in East Asia's gravitational pull.

Yayoi cultural influence entered the archipelago via the Korean peninsula as an outcome of the Han dynasty's conquest of the Korean kingdom of Gojoseon (233 BCE – 108 BCE). In 108 BCE, Emperor Wu of the Han dynasty built four outposts on the Korean peninsula to govern the region and its people and the archipelago benefited from this newly opened conduit with China. Chinese bronze mirrors, Korean artefacts, and fragments of bronze and iron weapons, hint at the relatively robust trade with the continent. Japanese rice cultivation practices can be traced to the Yangtze Delta. Rice probably proved attractive to Yayoi cultivators because it could be stored and toasted and eaten when required. It was Yayoi cultivators that designed elevated storehouses to tackle the threats of mould, moths, and mice in stored rice supplies. Early in the Yayoi phase, rice was one of many food plants cultivated in northwestern Kyushu, at sites such as Itazuke in Fukuoka prefecture; by the middle and late Yayoi it ranked among the dominant crops. At Itazuke, wooden stakes identified the boundaries of rice fields and the site is inundated with distinctive pits for storage and burial. Dogs and some small horses roamed these settlements, while deer and boar bones provide testimony to flesh in the Yayoi diet.

The ditch that surrounds the Itazuke site was either for irrigation of paddies or, perhaps, served as a defensive moat. Itazuke has also revealed jar burials, mostly containing children. In the middle Yayoi, jars were laid horizontally during burial; in the later Yayoi, they were set vertically with the mouths facing downward. Obviously, some of these jars were rather large and suggest high degrees of specialization. Near jar graves archaeologists have discovered Chinese and Korean artefacts in such abundance that some have speculated that northwestern Kyushu was the centre of legendary Yamato, Japan's first kingdom. We will turn to this question in a moment.

Toro, another developed Yayoi site, is a village along the Abe River and contained some fifty elaborate paddies until the river's flooding abruptly erased them. This highly engineered site contained sluice gates, irrigation canals, wells, and storage facilities of a type that resembled what later came to be Shinto shrines. Archaeologists speculate that life at Toro was relatively communal, with one excavated house yielding a variety of wooden tools and suggesting cooperative ownership of some kind. But competition over attractive sites incited warfare, and skeletal remains – one woman from Nejiko in Nagasaki prefecture has a bronze arrowhead lodged in her skull – attest to the violent struggles. Some Yayoi remains from Yoshinogari, a fortified Yayoi settlement in northern Kyushu, suggest that people were possibly decapitated (though this evidence has been disputed). Bronze became a critical import and, later, domestically produced metal, forged into weapons and valuable heirlooms such as bells. Sandstone bronze moulds demonstrate local production of weapons, and even bells, in the first century BCE. Local bronze production presents interesting logistical problems, not the least of which is the source of copper. Archaeologists believe Yayoi artisans recycled continental bronze and imported lead ingots, as little evidence exists of local surface copper mines on the archipelago until the seventh century.

YAYOI LIFE IN DOCUMENTS

Observations from Chinese envoys provide a window into the life, rituals, and governance of the late Yayoi phase. In 57 CE, the Eastern Han dynasty dispatched envoys to the Wa kingdom and did so again in 107 CE, despite significant turmoil within the Chinese dynasty leading to the loss, and eventual recapture, of the Korean outposts that had once proved a gateway for the flow of bronze, cultigens, and paddy engineering techniques onto the archipelago. The most revealing of these Chinese descriptions is the *Wei zhi* (Wei records, 297 CE). By the third century of the Common Era, the Eastern Han had collapsed and the Cao Wei (220–65) governed much of China from their capital at Luoyang. Not only did Wei missions visit the Wa kingdom, but in 238 Wa dignitaries, specifically Grand Master Natome and his attendants, returned the favour. They paid tribute to the Wei emperor Cao Rui and received a gold seal in return, which read, 'Himiko, Queen of Wa, is designated a friend of Wei', an obvious clue to where Chinese officials believed the Wa kingdom fit in its tributary order. 'We truly recognize this loyalty and filial piety', explained the *Wei zhi*. Wei generals urged Grand Master Natome to 'do your best to bring about peace and comfort for the people and strive for filial piety'. Obviously, East Asia's gravitational pull was becoming harder to resist for the archipelago's inhabitants.

The principal conduit for Wa diplomatic travel was through another Han outpost, Daifang, also on the Korean peninsula, which is from where the Wei envoys began their journey to the Wa kingdom. By 297, representatives from some thirty Wa chiefdoms had travelled between the archipelago and the Cao Wei capital. The Wei envoys recount visiting several chiefdoms during their journey, including the Wa queen's, called the 'Yamaichi chiefdom' in the text. Many believe this rendering is a Wei clerical error, however, and that the name was actually closer to 'Yamatai'. The queen's name was Himiko and she offers us the first glimpse of Japanese kingship.

It is important to keep in mind the cultural lens, defined by the tributary order, through which Chinese envoys would have viewed the dwarfish Wa kingdom, but the descriptions are highly valuable all the same. They confirm, for example, the archaeological evidence of Yayoi warfare, both in reference to the 'chaos as they fought each other' and a palace 'resembling a stockade, normally heavily protected by armed guards'. In 247, Himiko, the Wa queen, dispatched envoys to the Korean outposts to report a conflict with 'Himikoko, the male ruler of Kona'. The Wa queen occupied herself with 'the Way of Demons, keeping all under her spell'. There is also this morsel about co-gendered rulers: 'A younger brother assisted her in governing the domain.' Indeed, co-gendered governance became common among Japan's early 'great kings', called *ōkimi*.

One is struck by the Wei envoy's palpable admiration for the Wa kingdom. 'Their customs are not indecent', the envoy writes. The envoy explains: 'Aristocrats and commoners all [have] tattoo patterns on their faces and bodies.' Wa divers, the envoy continues, 'decorate their bodies in patterns to prevent being annoyed by large fish and water fowl'. Over time, tattooing became more 'decorative', with distinctions across chiefdoms, with 'some [on] aristocrats and some [on] commoners, according to rank'. That no distinctions existed 'between fathers and sons or between men and women by sex' flew in the face of Chinese Confucian norms, which stressed filial piety and hierarchy. Even when greeting, that 'aristocrats clap their hands instead of kneeling or bowing' probably raised the Wei envoy's eyebrows. Yet, even without these Confucian norms in social relations, 'Women are not morally loose or jealous.' The Wa kingdom is portrayed as a thriving place, with full granaries and bustling markets under state supervision. Class distinctions existed – we also know this from Yayoi burial practices – and so did forms of vassalage.

Finally, the *Wei zhi* portrays a rich spiritual life, one expressed in divination practices and elaborate burials, the most prominent of which was Himiko's burial. Divination portended the future: 'It is the custom on the occasion of an event or trip, whatever they do, to divine by baking bones so as to determine future good or bad fortune. The words are the same as those for tortoise shell divination. The fire cracks are examined for signs.' The reference places Wa divination practices in an East Asian context, as divination of this variety was practised in China as early as the Shang dynasty (1600 BCE – 1046 BCE). Quite possibly, this practice migrated along with the many bronze items and agricultural techniques transmitted between the Korean peninsula and northwestern Kyushu. The practice proved critical to determining the outcomes of wars, journeys, and agriculture; the ability to conduct divination was probably part of Himiko's kingship and, consequently, political legitimacy.

The *Wei zhi* also delves into Yayoi burial practices:

> At death they use a coffin with no outer sealing box. Earth is built up like a mound. At death they observe more than ten days of obsequies, during which time they do not eat meat. The chief mourner wails, and others sing, dance, and drink saké. After interment the family assembles to go in water for purification, just like ablutions.

The archaeological record evidences jar burials in Yayoi communities, but the *Wei zhi*'s 'coffins' were probably wooden. What is tantalizing is the reference to 'water for purification' immediately following mourning because the practice resembles later Shinto rituals. With raised storage houses, and now baths of purification, some of the early elements of what would later be referred to as Shinto evolved in the context of Yayoi ritual life.

When Himiko died, 'a large mound was built more than 100 paces in diameter. Over 100 male and female attendants were immolated. Then a male ruler was installed, but in the ensuing protests within the domain bloodshed and killing exterminated more than 1,000 people . . . To replace Himiko a 13-year-old relative named Iyo was made ruler of the domain.' The Wa kingdom's political strength had reached the point where, on her death, the Wa queen's life was celebrated with an elaborate tomb, one that spoke to her triumphs on Earth, as well as her coming life beyond. The construction of the Wa queen's tomb ushered in the next major archaeological phase on the archipelago: the *kofun*, or Tomb phase (250–700).

TOMBS AND THE YAMATO STATE

Himiko emerged onto the strife-ridden, late Yayoi scene as a unifying queen, quelling years of fighting and initiating formal tributary relations with China. Scholars posit many theories regarding the advent of the Tomb phase and the ascendancy of the Yamato confederacy (250–710), which was solidified sometime around Himiko's death. One compelling theory refers once again to climate change and the environment. Historians know from Chinese records that convulsive climate shifts of the late Yayoi and early Tomb phase, specifically around 194 CE, caused famine,

2 Tomb phase bronze mirror, Gunma prefecture.

cannibalism, and, possibly, widespread disillusionment with pro-
tective deities. Himiko could have been on the forefront of such a
religious insurrection of native deities, casting away weapons and
smashing bells associated with older deities, in favour of new
deities associated with mirrors (Figure 2). At least this is how some
of the archaeological evidence can be interpreted. Himiko and the
new deities she spoke to through theurgy – her practice of sorcery
and the 'Way of Demons' – became a focal point. People erected
tombs and worshipped mirrors and, we might speculate, anticipated the promise of better days. In Hyôgo prefecture, for example,
archaeologists discovered a bell that had been shattered into 117
pieces. Somebody broke the mirror so carefully that archaeologists
strongly suspect it was done on purpose, as a rejection of old,

powerless deities associated with them. Himiko, we might again speculate, practised her sorcery as a medium to communicate with new deities, the chief of which emerged as the Sun Goddess Amaterasu Ōmikami, the tutelary deity of the imperial household.

Himiko also represented the emergence of a new military class, one forged by late Yayoi warfare. This military elite thrived on Yamato society's increasing agricultural surplus, which translated into breathtaking burial mounds in the shape of keyholes. Blacksmiths forged iron into better weaponry, much of which followed its owners to their graves. Tomb phase settlements are more elaborate than Yayoi ones, often with larger wooden structures with moats or stone barricades. The groupings of houses and pit dwellings suggest that extended families cohabitated together. In these households, women played a particularly important role in politics and production: nearly half of the tombs excavated contain the remains of women, testimony to their access to resources, including iron weapons, and political clout, perhaps deduced from forms of mirror sorcery. Tombs also contain gold jewellery, including earrings and belt buckles.

Himiko also represented the birth of a new kind of king, one that became the centrepiece of the Yamato state and, as we shall see, the earliest emperors of Japan. The Yamato state is best described as a kind of confederacy, in which the kings wielded control over vassal chiefdoms and where symbolic gift-giving and ceremonial homogeneity cemented relations between core and periphery. Scholars still debate the exact whereabouts of Yamato's centre, but it was most likely in western Honshu or, less likely, in northern Kyushu, perhaps with the militarized settlement of Yoshinogari as its capital. Keyhole-shaped tombs, the namesake of the Tomb phase, provide conflicting evidence for the centre of political power in Yamato; less conflicting is the evidence they provide as to the manner in which Yamato kings manipulated burial rituals to assert control over the realm and, one presumes, the afterlife. One historian has labelled this the 'keyhole-tomb hierarchy', one in which the largest, most elaborate tombs were built in Yamato's centre, and smaller, less elaborate tombs were built on the periphery. The critical point, however, is that the keyhole-tomb style was used fairly consistently across the archipelago, suggesting some degree of burial homogeneity asserted from the political core. These early tombs, such as the Makimuku Ishizuka tomb in Nara prefecture, provide testimony to the archipelago's social stratification, intensification of trade, and emergence of kings. Indeed, these tombs dramatized local authority and power within the Yamato confederacy and they strongly suggest that Nara prefecture, more than northern Kyushu, emerged as Yamato's political core.

A succession of Yamato kings strengthened the power of the centre and tombs were not the only means by which this was accomplished. Yûryaku, who ruled in the fifth century, wrote in a letter to the Chinese emperor that he was the Wa king and boasted of his martial exploits at home and on the Korean peninsula. 'From of old our forebears have clad themselves in armour and helmet and gone across the hills and waters sparing no time for rest', he wrote. 'In the east, they conquered 55 countries of hairy men; and in the west, they brought to their knees 65 countries of various barbarians. Crossing the sea to the north, they subjugated 95 countries.' Yamato kings and their ancestors had become military leaders. Inscriptions on swords unearthed from tombs in central Japan, such as the Inariyama sword, reveal the nature of Yûryaku's vassalage relationship with local chiefdoms. 'When the court of Great King Wakatakeru was at Shiki', reads this particular inscription, 'I aided him in ruling the realm, and had this hundred-times-wrought sword made to record the history of my service.'

Along with martial culture and vassalage, co-gendered rule in the Wa kingdom highlights the scripts for kingly behaviour in Yamato. Not only did Queen Himiko rule with her brother, but later great kings, such as Kitsuhiko and Kitsuhime, Suiko and Prince Shôtoku, and Jitô and Tenmu, all governed together. Presumably, such co-rulers placed the Wa kingdom in geomantic conformity with competing yin-yang elements of the Chinese-inspired cosmos, which, as contact with East Asia grew, slowly crept into the Wa political mentality. It appears that women such as Himiko fulfilled sacred duties for the Wa realm. Increasing ties to East Asia translated into more male definitions of kingship, however.

One compelling piece of evidence of the Wa kingdom's move towards male dominance is Suiko's early seventh-century deployment of Buddhism as a tool to combat patriarchy. Suiko studied Buddhism, in particular such texts as 'True Lion's Roar of Queen

Srimala', which taught of a pious and brilliant Indian queen and explained that a Bodhisattva could inhabit the body of a woman. She also oversaw the construction of the Hôjôki Buddha (608), a five-metre (fifteen foot) representation of Shakyamuni (the Indian prince who transformed into the Buddha). The text would have been appealing to a woman whose confederate rule – the 'sacred court' she presided over – fell under the influence of Confucian values, which rearticulated notions of political and sacred power to be more patriarchal. Suiko also erected the Wa kingdom's first capital at Oharida (603), with an elaborate marketplace, highways to the hinterland, and port facilities.

Simultaneous to Suiko's exploration of Buddhist notions of female kingship, Prince Shôtoku, with whom she co-ruled the Wa kingdom, imported Confucian notions of governance to strengthen the Yamato hold on power. It was this trend that Suiko struggled with. Famously, Prince Shôtoku drafted the 'Seventeen-article Constitution' (604), which stressed bureaucracy and Confucian principles. Importantly, it also legitimized Yamato authority with the moral authority inherent in nature. 'The sovereign is likened to heaven', explained Prince Shôtoku's Constitution, 'and his subjects are likened to earth.' The Constitution also stressed 'decorum' and 'public good' as commensurate with bureaucratic office. This document, combined with the later Taika Reforms (645) and Taihô-Yôrô Codes (702 and 718), cemented the formation of the *ritsuryō* state in Japan, which refers to a legal bureaucracy defined by penal and administrative codes. The seventh and eighth centuries witnessed the advent of this rule of administrative bureaucracy in the Wa kingdom.

Tenmu, who ruled in the mid-seventh century, was likened to a deity – or 'a very god', as one *Man'yôshû* (Collection of ten thousand leaves, eighth century) poem describes. Another poem says, 'He ruled as a god at the Kiyomihara Palace in Asuka' – underscoring the slowly emerging divinity of Yamato rulers, a legacy that would persist into the twentieth century. The Yamato kings transformed from mere controllers of the sacred into the sacred. Tenmu erected the grandest ceremonial centre to date at Kiyomihara, which contained a garden of ministries, a throne hall, a reception hall, and an inner pavilion. In 689, Tenmu promulgated the Kiyomihara Codes, which outlined oversight of monastic orders, a judiciary, vassalage relations, and official promotions. Jitô, who ruled at the end of the seventh century, was the first king to be referred to as 'Heavenly Sovereign', or *tennô*, the name for the Japanese emperor. Jitô transferred the ceremonial centre to a new capital just west of Kiyomihara, at Fujiwara, a city modelled after the great Chinese capital cities and one that conformed to philosophical principles in the classic *Zhouli* (The rites of Zhou). The palace stood in the centre of Fujiwara and was approached by the massive Red Bird Boulevard. In the new capital, such ceremonies as New Year celebrations, the annual Rites for Tasting New Fruits, and other rituals could be performed in grand theatrical style. Then, in 669, the Wa kingdom became known as 'Nihon', the present name for Japan.

CONCLUSION

At the beginning of the eighth century Japan and its Heavenly Sovereigns emerged from the engineered lands of a settled agricultural society. But they also developed from wrenching climate shifts, food shortages, inter-chiefdom war and chaos, and even religious upheaval. Likewise, they evolved from sustained contact with East Asia and the titular legitimacy that accrued from contact with the Chinese court. They then adorned themselves with myths, bejewelled headgear, and other regalia; they surrounded themselves with armed guards and fortifications. Their followers buried them and their treasures in massive keyhole-shaped tombs, an extravagant display of wealth. Eventually, they called themselves Heavenly Sovereigns and their realm Nihon ('originates from the sun'). The early codes discussed in this chapter, such as Taika's 'equal field system', established state ownership of property and control of its transference, all of which led to the formation of the first state bureaucracies. In the next chapter, we will revisit these codes briefly, as well as cover the planning of the first elaborate courts and their commensurate court cultures, because they are critical to the foundation of the Nara (710–794) and Heian (794–1185) regimes.

2

The Courtly Age, 710–1185

With the emergence of the Yamato state and the advent of its imperial line, Japan entered the Nara (710–94) and Heian periods (794–1185). The fledgling imperial regime's history shares much in common with other nascent monarchies around the world: frontier war and conquest, implementation of judicial and administrative bureaucracies, capital planning, elite monopolization of surplus, and the flowering of a rarefied court culture. In Japan, this courtly age served as the domain of the fictional Prince Genji, a literary creation of writer Murasaki Shikibu (c.978–1014). A fictional master of his artful age, Prince Genji writes exquisitely learned poetry, romances such tragic beauties as Yûgao (Evening Face), croons with acquaintances about singing warblers and chirping insects, and moves through the social intricacies of the Heian court with dexterous grace. His mood is perennially sensitive and melancholic, always touched by the sadness of this fleeting world: a Buddhist aesthetic inspired by the transience of things. Importantly, the natural aesthetic of the Heian period, particularly as preserved in poetry, shaped enduring Japanese attitudes towards the natural world.

The development of Japan's courtly age began with the Nara court's conquest of the Emishi, a tribe of hunter-gatherers in the northeastern section of the archipelago, people largely removed from the Chinese-inspired changes that had swept Japan since the fourth century. They are best described as Jômon remnants: people who stood outside the *ritsuryô* (penal and administrative) codes that incrementally defined life in Japan's core provinces by the seventh century. The Nara court constructed an elaborate Buddhist theocracy and Chinese-style administrative bureaucracy, which it relied upon for managing the affairs of state. The Heavenly Sovereigns, following their earlier Yamato trajectory, developed into chief priests and imperial 'living gods', who shared, at least in the pages of the *Kojiki* (Record of ancient matters, 712), divine ancestors with the Sun Goddess. The *Kojiki* brushes over genealogical discontinuities among Japan's emperors, which was its principal purpose in narrating the land's creation myth. Other eighth-century sources, such as the *Nihon shoki* (Chronicles of Japan, 720), resemble Chinese dynastic histories, drafting a record of events from the advent of the Yamato emperors forward. Dynastic genealogies proved important because they, along with the *ritsuryô* codes, cemented and legitimized political power. By the end of the eighth century, Heian culture had become an amalgam of elements from Buddhist theocracy and *ritsuryô* governance.

EMISHI AND THEIR YAMATO RIVALS

The advent of the Yamato state was anything but uniform because not all early Jômon foragers yielded to the gravitational pull of East Asian sensibilities, nor did they buckle under the better-fed Yayoi settlers who carried those ideas to the archipelago. Two distinct civilizations emerged in these formative years, ushering in an age of courtly conquest that occurred over the seventh century and shaped Japanese identity in striking ways. Though much is made of the myth of Japanese homogeneity, the country was, as we shall see, forged in the fires of cultural difference and imperial conquest.

On the archipelago, competing histories complicate the rise of Japanese rule because a northern cultural sphere existed outside the Yamato imperial base, one that waged armed resistance to the changes that swept the Kinai region. The northern sphere did not immediately embrace Buddhism, Confucianism, dynastic history, *ritsuryô* bureaucracy, and, generally speaking, Chinese-style statehood. In the northeast, what archaeologists call the Epi-Jômon (300–700 CE) peoples resisted the centripetal pull of Chinese-style governance and continued their foraging and hunting lifestyles into the eleventh century. China did not shape their cultural milieu, as it had for Yayoi migrants and Yamato kings. Rather, other peoples to the north did, such as the Satsumon and Okhotsk cultures of Hokkaido, as well as more distant people on Sakhalin Island and even in the Amur River Estuary. These distant people, not the celebrated Tang dynasty (618–907) of China, shaped life rhythms in the northern sphere.

In court documents and histories, Nara and Heian officials labelled these Epi-Jômon remnants the 'Emishi' – a pejorative name meaning something like 'toad barbarians' – and mobilized to conquer them with military campaigns in the eighth century. It is important to point out that other clans had resisted Yamato ascendancy – such as the Tsuchigumo, Kuzu, and Hayato – but the Yamato labelled none with the derogatory title of 'barbarian'; they, to a certain degree, participated in the East Asian order, but simply rejected Yamato supremacy within it. Theirs was a political, rather than civilizational, affair. There was something completely different about the Emishi: they repudiated something bigger and more structural. When in 659 the Yamato court dispatched envoys to Emperor Gaozong (628–83), an Emishi couple accompanied the entourage as curiosities. Interested in them, the Chinese emperor enquired about their origins. The envoys explained that they came from the 'land of the Emishi' in the northeast, that they had no settled villages, and that they foraged and hunted. Elsewhere, we learn that they spoke a 'barbarian language', suggesting that the Emishi were distinct Epi-Jômon remnants that had, through remoteness, evasion, or force, avoided the waves of East Asian culture, starting with Yayoi agriculture, that had swept north from Kyushu and into the Kinai region.

The price for repudiating the *ritsuryô* codes, however, was conquest. The vigorousness of the Nara subjugation of the Emishi testifies to the notion that partial compliance with the East Asian order was out of the question. In the Nara period, the northernmost military outpost was Fort Taga (near Sendai), erected sometime around 724 and razed in 780 by Emishi fighters. Its mission was to subdue and then order Emishi villages according to the new *ritsuryô* logic. Its commander was the *chinju shôgun*, or 'peacekeeper general', the earliest predecessor of later samurai shoguns who ruled in the medieval and early modern years. Between

701 and 798, essentially the whole duration of the Nara period, fourteen generals served in this capacity. Nara and early Heian officials constructed other forts, such as Akita and Okachi (both in Akita prefecture); Emishi resistance was tenacious in these areas, however, and the military campaigns often proved cruel and indecisive. Only with the ascendancy of Emperor Kanmu (737–806) in the closing years of the eighth century, and the relocation of the capital from Nara to Kyoto, did Kinai leaders redouble their efforts against the Emishi in what is called the 'Thirty-eight Years War' (773–811). In preparation, generals built up food and weapon stockpiles at Taga. In 789, however, Emishi fighters routed the newly fortified Kinai forces north of the Koromo River. Not deterred, in 800, after the Heian transition, the court dispatched a newly appointed general. Sakanoue no Tamuramaro (758–811), a courtly warrior with ties to the emperor, proved militarily triumphant: after vanquishing Emishi fighters and beheading the Emishi general Aterui in 802, he constructed several additional forts and the Emishi wars came to a close in 805.

Though the Emishi wars ended at the dawn of the ninth century, the northern sphere retained a blended frontier flavour: northeastern Japan marched to a different set of cultural drummers. Even as late as the eleventh century, prominent northeastern families such as the Hiraizumi Fujiwara retained many Emishi idiosyncrasies, such as ritual mummification at death (unknown among Japanese, but practised among groups on Sakhalin Island) at their luxuriant Konjikidô pavilion. In the medieval years, the region became famous for its horse farms, also indicative of earlier connections to the northern sphere. Other historical legacies of the Emishi conflict include the advent of Ainu culture in the twelfth century, and the emergence of the samurai. Those peacekeepers had fought in the Emishi wars and settled in the hinterlands, and would eventually usurp Heian court governance and rule the country for centuries through a series of *bakufu* (shogunal) governments.

NARA AND THE THEOCRATIC COURT

Rather than view the Emishi wars as something new – an invigorated Nara court waging frontier wars against an emergent Emishi

enemy – historians need to view them as the bloody conclusion of
the unfinished business of state formation. Indeed, the conflict
surrounding Yayoi migration and dispersal, and Chinese documentation of the chaos that accompanied Yamato ascendancy, only
concluded with the Heian court beheading Emishi generals. In
Japan, the implementation of an East Asian order required centuries of skull cracking because such regimes function poorly with only
partial compliance.

In 710, when the Emishi wars had heated up, the Yamato capital
was moved to Nara (or Heijô-kyô), where an elaborate court
evolved. As emphasized, the Emishi wars were an extension of the
strengthening of courtly rule at Nara, a ripple effect caused by the
waves of bureaucratic logic sweeping the archipelago. Modelled
after China's Tang capital of Chang'an, Nara became a spatial
dramatization of the *ritsuryô*'s geomantic order, court power, and
theocratic authority. Just as in the court bureaucracy, where proximity to the emperor meant political power, so too did geographic
proximity to the imperial palace signal power. At the centre of
Nara's theocratic order was the Tôdaiji (Great Eastern Temple),
built on the outskirts of Nara between 728 and 752. Just as
keyhole-shaped tombs had, to a certain degree, homogenized burial
rituals under earlier Yamato kings, the Tôdaiji temple served as the
hub in a network of Buddhist temples erected in the provinces.
Though the giant statue of the Vairocana Buddha housed in the
temple exhausted the realm's supply of bronze, it came to symbolize
the theocratic union between the Nara court and Buddhism.
Emperor Shômu (701–56), who initiated the Tôdaiji's construction,
saw in the enormous temple the promise that the 'entire land may
be joined with us in the fellowship of Buddhism and enjoy in
common the advantages which this undertaking affords to the
attainment of Buddhahood'.

To step back one moment, the development of a Buddhist theocracy was far from a foregone conclusion. Even though Empress
Suiko (554–628) had patronized the Indian religion, Buddhism had
a slow start after its initial importation in 552. As the *Nihon shoki*
explains, when envoys of the Korean Paekche king presented a
statue of the historical Buddha Shakyamuni, and sutras and other
artefacts, they explained:

This doctrine is amongst all doctrines the most excellent. But it is hard to explain, and hard to comprehend ... This doctrine can create religious merit and retribution without measure and without bounds, and so lead on to a full appreciation of the highest wisdom. Imagine a man in possession of treasures to his heart's content, so that he might satisfy all his wishes in proportion as he used them.

With such a billing, it is hardly surprising that Buddhism, with its promise of treasure, wisdom, and power, became integrated into Yamato life. With the outbreak of plague after its importation, however, the introduction of the new faith clearly required care. Shortly after the introduction of Buddhism, 'a pestilence was rife in the Land, from which the people died prematurely. As time went on it became worse and worse, and there was no remedy.' On the advice of the Nakatomi and Mononobe families, the emperor ordered that the statue be discarded in the 'currents of the Canal of Naniha' and that the temple be burned to the ground.

Imperial advisers thought that the statue had offended the native Sun Goddess, mythic ancestor of the Yamato emperors. After the bronze statue of the Buddha was discarded, however, 'a sudden conflagration consumed the Great Hall [of the Palace]'. The court found itself in the unfortunate position of being wedged between two jealous gods. The Nakatomi and Mononobe families continued to oppose Buddha worship, despite the smouldering cinders at the Great Hall of the palace. Only the Soga family sought to worship the Buddha, particularly under the patronage of Soga no Umako (551–626). His niece was the tenacious Suiko. From this point forward, under Soga patronage, Buddhism found a secure foothold in court politics and eventually the religious traditions of Japan. We turn to the intricacies of Buddhism later in this book, as many competing sects require separate treatment.

FOREIGN AFFAIRS AND THE *RITSURYŌ* ORDER

The importation of the *ritsuryō* codes (like Yayoi agriculture and Buddhism) was related to continental affairs. When civil war broke out on the Korean peninsula between the three kingdoms of Silla, Baekje (through which Buddhism had entered Japan), and Goguryeo, Yamato intervened and established an outpost at

Mimana, on the southernmost tip of the Korean peninsula. When in 562 Silla forces defeated the Baekje allies of Yamato, the Japanese evacuated Mimana. In 661, Yamato again dispatched forces to assist Baekje, but at the Battle of Baekje River in 663, Tang warships trounced Yamato forces. At this time, many Baekje Koreans evacuated the peninsula with their Yamato allies, which led to a veritable revolution in Yamato life. Many Koreans became Japan's new elite, and the skilled hands of Korean craftsmen accomplished many of the grandest technological achievements, including architectural feats such as the crafting of the Tôdaiji temple. As with the story of Epi-Jômon resistance, Japan's cultural diversity, rather than its mythologized homogeneity, drove its historical development.

Immediately following Yamato's defeat at the hands of the Tang navy, the Chinese dynasty dispatched several embassies to visit the Yamato court. Guo Wuzong arrived in Japan on at least three occasions (664, 665, and 671). Frightened that such official visits heralded reprisals for Yamato's military involvement on the Korean peninsula, the Yamato court built fortifications and a system of signal fires to guard the home front. The most important product of Tang visits, however, was the strengthening of the *ritsuryô* order: the court reasoned that only a strong, centralized state could counter the threat posed by China's robust Tang dynasty.

One critical aspect of the *ritsuryô* order was the place of the emperor. In the Nara period, not only did the emperor rule, but he or she served as supreme priest and, as we have seen, as a 'very god' in the courtly imagination. The Nara bureaucracy, as outlined in the Taihô-Yôrô codes, reveals the *ritsuryô* system's administrative thrust: heading the bureaucratic structure were the Department of Religion, mainly concerned with Shinto rituals, and the Great Council of State. In theory, Nara administration appeared like concentric rings of command and tribute collection, with 'towns' and 'districts' overseen by 'provincial headquarters'. Linked to provincial headquarters was the theocratic authority emanating from the Tôdaiji temple, serving to coordinate Buddhist practice and to calibrate local rites with the rhythms of the Nara court. However, the strengthening of the *ritsuryô* order was not the only consequence of closer interaction with the continent.

Smallpox illustrates the epidemiological consequences of Japan's entanglement with Korea and the disease ecologies of Eurasia. Shortly after these embassies, Japan's first smallpox epidemic erupted. Dazaifu, a port city in western Kyushu, first suffered from the virus that we are told Korean fishermen imported. One dynastic source explained in 737: 'In the spring of this year, an epidemic disease characterized by swellings raged wildly. It came first from Kyushu.' Smallpox wreaked havoc among even the courtiers of Kyoto. Later, in the Heian period (794–1185), a woman whom historians know only as the 'mother of Michitsuna' (c.935–95) wrote in her last entry of *Kagerô nikki* (The gossamer years, c.974): 'In the eighth month there was an epidemic of smallpox. It spread to this section of the city toward the end of the month, and my son came down with a severe case … The epidemic continued to grow worse … I was saddened and at the same time grateful that my own son had recovered.' Michitsuna's surviving smallpox meant that he had developed immunity and would, most likely, survive the periodic outbreaks of the disease. His mother is believed to have died in the epidemic, as her melancholy diary ends with this entry.

The integration of the Japanese archipelago, excepting the northern island of Hokkaido, into Eurasia's disease pools proved one critical consequence of Japan's engagement with the Tang court. It was especially important because when Japan encountered Iberian missionaries for the first time in the sixteenth century, the diseases these Europeans carried, such as smallpox, proved already endemic to Japan, and thus failed to decimate Japanese as they did Amerindians. This allowed Japanese to resist the initial waves of European imperialism and enter a period of relative isolation during the seventeenth through mid-nineteenth centuries.

THE HEIAN COURT

Emperor Kanmu, who concluded the Emishi wars, ordered in 784 that the court be moved to Kyoto (then Heian-kyô). The decision to relocate the capital related to Shinto purification rituals and death, exhaustion of nearby timber supplies (the capitals, with their elaborate palaces, required enormous amounts of timber), and the infamous Dôkyô Incident (760s). At the capital of Nara,

Buddhist institutions had become far too influential. When the monk Dôkyô (700–72) sought to expand his influence in the court through his relationship with an empress – she awarded him the title 'King of the Buddhist Law', which was reserved for abdicated emperors – court officials banished him in 770. The court evidently learned its lesson, however, and officials in the new capital of Kyoto relegated most Buddhist temples to the outskirts of the city, removing them from easy access to the halls of power.

Capital construction had long been intertwined with state formation. We saw that Emperor Tenmu, in order to add grandeur to his reign, began construction of the Kiyomihara Palace at Asuka, but his death delayed its completion. Later, Empress Jitô revived the Asuka project, overseeing the construction of the Fujiwara capital. It possessed many of the spatial characteristics of later capitals at Nara and Kyoto: a prominent boulevard running northward through grand gates, flanked by palaces and office buildings and ending at the emperor's palace. The Fujiwara complex required timber from distant Ômi province, suggesting that loggers and carpenters had depleted nearby stands in earlier palace construction projects. With Empress Genmei's (661–721) succession, officials relocated the capital to Nara, following the examples, as Genmei mused, of the Chinese kings of Zhou. In 710, Genmei had relocated to her new Nara capital, called Heijô-kyô, thus ushering in the Nara period. With Emperor Shômu's death in 756, politics in the Nara court slowly eroded. With the ascendancy of Emperor Kanmu, the desire to once again relocate the capital became overwhelming. After a false start at Nagaoka, Kanmu occupied Kyoto in 794. Though more sprawling than previous capitals, the spatial configuration of Kyoto replicated the geomantic order of Chinese cosmology. Its grand main boulevard, the Suzaku Ôji, ran northward from the Rajô gate to the palaces at the north end of the capital. The main palace, the Daidairi, contained the administrative buildings for the affairs of the expanded imperial government.

COURT LIFE

Kyoto became the home of a rich courtly culture. Such Buddhist sects as Tendai (805), Shingon (806), and Amidism flourished, and courtiers, perennially aggrieved by the impermanence of life, wrote poetry that celebrated life's fragility. Courtiers cavorted while they exchanged poems, wrote letters, judged scents, listened to music, and dressed according to the seasons and their carefully trained emotional sensibilities. Fujiwara no Michinaga (966–1028), whose family held the powerful 'regent' (*kanpaku*) advisory position during the height of the Heian years, epitomized the culture of the day with his graceful movement in elite circles. It helped considerably that he was also a master at marriage politics, having sired four empresses; he was also the uncle of two emperors and the grandfather of three more. Men outmanoeuvred in Heian politics, such as the otherwise talented Sugawara no Michizane (845–903), found themselves exiled to such outposts as Dazaifu, capital of the western provinces. At this time, the emperor radiated with divine energy, in which courtesans eagerly basked. During an imperial procession, Sei Shônagon (966–1017), one of the keenest observers of her times, wrote that, 'When the Emperor passes in his palanquin, he is as impressive as a God and I forget that my work in the Palace constantly brings me into his presence.' To live in the capital of Kyoto was to be in the midst of gods and shining princes.

The Heian court was remarkably detached from the rest of the country, most of which worked the soil. When Sei Shônagon visited the Hase temple near Kyoto, she was overcome by a 'herd of common people', whose clothing was not up to the occasion. Once, when on a pilgrimage, a 'throng' of commoners again spoiled her experience. She wrote, 'They looked like so many basket-worms as they crowded together in their hideous clothes, leaving hardly an inch of space between themselves and me. I really felt like pushing them all over sideways.' Not only in the countryside, but also in the urban environments of Kyoto, the poor walked alongside the courtiers, often begging at temples. In *Kagerô nikki*, the mother of Michitsuna recalled that, 'The beggars at the temple, each with his earthen bowl, were most distressing. I recoiled involuntarily at being brought so near the defiling masses.' Kyoto was a dense city replete with courtiers, beggars, timber merchants, and ravenous gangs of wild dogs that fed on corpses decomposing along the Kamo River.

Courtiers such as Sei Shônagon lived and died by the rhythms of a cosmology imported from China centuries earlier. Japanese measured time according to the Chinese zodiac, which diagrammed the cardinal compass directions, the hours of day and night, and articulated the 'twelve branches'. These twelve branches told time: the Hour of the Boar, for example, corresponded to sometime between 10.00 a.m. and noon. The direction Boar-Sheep represented northeast. According to Chinese cosmology, the substance of the universe, based as it was on the balance of yin and yang elements, was comprised of wood, fire, earth, metal, and water. A whole new science emerged based on these material building blocks. Japanese months related to social occasions instead of solar cycles: the fifth month of the lunar calendar, for example, was the 'rice-sprouting month' and the sixth was the 'watery month', referring, of course, to Japan's monsoon rain season. Countless festivals also ordered courtly time, all of which were highly anticipated by Heian courtiers because they usually involved the emperor.

Other elements of Chinese science permeated people's personal lives. The Chinese zodiac told of auspicious times to have a child and explained how the year it was born (say, the Year of the Dragon) influenced the child's character. Giving birth was followed by a period of defilement because of the blood and afterbirth involved. In *Kagerô nikki*, when the mother of Michitsuna gives birth, the father explains: 'I know that you will not want to see me until after the defilement has worn off.' Certainly, such notions of Shinto purity and defilement can be traced to the 'bath of purification' after Yayoi mourning rituals, as documented by the Chinese mission in Chapter 1. Typically, wet-nurses raised most children in the Heian court. In Japan's increasingly patriarchal society, male children became highly valued, and a woman's inability to have a male heir, at least according to the eighth-century Taihô-Yôrô Codes, qualified as grounds for divorce. Powerful families usually orchestrated weddings in order to build alliances. As we have seen, Fujiwara no Michinaga rose to the zenith of Heian influence through the careful art of marriage politics.

However, just as Chinese cosmology determined the rhythms of life, it also determined rhythms of illness and death. Often, Heian courtiers interpreted disease as spiritual possession. The mother of Michitsuna explained that, 'For some time I had been troubled by a painful cough, some sort of possession it appeared, against which incantations might be effective.' It was a possession, but probably a virus not a ghost. Heian courtiers also employed elaborate medicines, from pharmaceuticals to moxibustion (burning dried mugwort on the patient). The Five Evolutionary Phase theory, which originated from Chinese science, determined the type of medicine used by a physician. Afflictions associated with an internal organ related to fire, for example, could be treated by medicine associated with a competing element such as water. Thus, it was mainly about restoring balances within the body. Courtiers also viewed death as a period of defilement and took appropriate steps during mourning.

HEIAN AESTHETICS

This Chinese science notwithstanding, Heian courtiers observed the natural world around them through a carefully ground aesthetic lens. They savoured poetry about chirping insects, barking deer, and turning leaves because they synchronized insect and deer calls, as well as autumn decay and spring rejuvenation, with their own fickle, melancholic emotions. In nature they discovered disquieting change: relationships made and broken, as well as lives created and terminated. When Murasaki Shikibu penned 'Can I remain indifferent to those birds on the water? I too am floating in a sad uncertain world', she linked her emotions, her unsettling existential transience, to the undeniable transience of the changing world around her (Figure 3).

Significantly, the late ninth and tenth centuries witnessed the rise of the *kana* syllabary, a written language based on imported *kanji* characters from China. Most men wrote poetry, prose, and political treatises entirely in Chinese script, but women, in particular, began to forge more vernacular traditions of literature and poetry written in the *kana* script. In large part, *kana* rose to popularity with thirty-one-syllable *waka* poetry, which developed into the principal means of dialogue between the sexes of Heian society. *Waka* also became central to larger social events, ones requiring public mastery of poetry. In the Heian period, *waka* poetry was collected into imperial anthologies, the first of which was the *Kokinshû* (Collection of ancient and modern Japanese poems, *c.*905). *Waka* became so

3 Depiction of Murasaki Shikibu, Edo period (1600–1868).

popular as a medium that when writers told autobiographical stories, travel narratives, and other forms of writing, they heavily interspersed *waka* poems (Figure 4).

The emergence of Japan's vernacular also led to the rise of women poets and writers. As we have seen, such women as Murasaki Shikibu, Sei Shônagon, mother of Michitsuna, and Izumi Shikibu (b. 976) became literary stars over the centuries. For most men, writing Chinese continued to engender prestige, but the emergence of *kana* script opened a new literary space for women, one that came to symbolize Heian's courtly culture. Whether written by men or women, however, the dominant themes of Heian poetry were love, separation and longing, and natural imagery, often carefully woven together to evoke melancholic sensibilities. In the *Kokinshû*, one gifted *waka* poet, Ono no Komachi (*c.*825–900), wrote: 'The colour of the flowers / has faded – in vain / I grow old in this world, / lost in thought / as the long rain falls'. Such poets evoked natural imagery to communicate their feelings. As this selection from the *Tosa nikki* (Tosa diary, *c.*935) evokes: 'Louder than the roar of the / white-crested waves / rising in your path / will my cries resound / when you depart'.

4 Selection from the Wakashû, Heian period (794–1185), National Treasure.

For Heian poets, cherry blossoms became a popular topic because the life-cycle of the flowers captured the radiant impermanence of Heian's aesthetic. One anonymous poem from the *Kokinshû* reads: 'Are they not like / this fleeting world? / Cherry blossoms: / no sooner do they flower / than they fall'. The short, beautiful life of the cherry blossom is strongly associated with the transient world. A poem from the *Ise monogatari* (Tales of Ise, *c.*947) illustrates the power of cherry blossom imagery: 'It is because they fall soon / that the cherry blossoms / are so admired. / What can stay long / in this fleeting world?' For Kamutsuke no Mineo, cherry blossoms were called on to reflect the sorrowful emotions following the death of a Heian chancellor, whose cremated remains were interred at Mount Fukakusa: 'If cherry trees indeed / have feelings, may those / of the fields of Fukakusa / this year, at least / shroud themselves in black blossoms'. Given the short-lived beauty of cherry blossoms, and its pervasiveness in Japanese poetry, it is not surprising that one twenty-two-year old kamikaze pilot, before his suicide mission in 1945, evoked the cherry blossom in his final *haiku* poem: 'If only we might fall like cherry blossoms in the spring – So pure and radiant!' This tiny, radiant, and short-lived flower has, through the ages, loomed large in the often-melancholic world of Japanese aesthetics.

Not only cherry blossoms, but the seasonal cries and barks of animals also captured the ever-changing quality of nature and, consequently, human life. For example, the bush warbler remained a popular theme in Heian *waka* poetry. An anonymous poem in the *Kokinshû* reads: 'To each meadow where / the warbler cries / I come and see / the wind blow / fading flowers'. All was transient in the Heian world, a viewpoint influenced by the Buddhist tenets of impermanence and the 'four noble truths' of suffering. Indeed, another anonymous *Kokinshû* poem elegantly captures the material impermanence of life: 'Should I pluck the drops of dew / to thread as jewels / they'd vanish: / best see them as they are, / set on bows of clover'. As a selection by the master Ki no Tsurayuki (872–945) illustrates, autumn leaves also captured the pervasive theme of natural transformation: 'They must fall / with no one to see them: / red leaves of autumn / deep in the mountains / like brocade worn by night'.

Although Genji's shining world might seduce us into thinking otherwise, courtiers were not the only people watching the natural environment and searching for meaning. Early farmers had discovered the environment as well, though they viewed it through the prism of labour: growing cycles, the rich soil in their hands, the irrigation channels they dug, insects, blight, the weather they fought, and the crops they harvested and threshed. When discovering nature, the gulf between Heian courtiers and nearby farmers proved a vast one. On one occasion, when Sei Shônagon and fellow courtiers ventured outside Kyoto to write poetry on the cuckoo, a relished spring pastime, they encountered farm women singing and threshing rice with a 'machine of a type that I had never seen before'. The farm women were interacting with the environment as farmers did. However, as Sei Shônagon recalled, the farm women's song was so alien to the courtiers that they 'burst out laughing', and 'completely forgot to write our *hototogisu* poems'. It is a telling encounter: Heian women sought to celebrate nature through *waka* poetry and travel narratives, while farm women sought to do so through threshing and song. Neither, however, understood the other, making it difficult for the historian to isolate a particular 'Japanese' attitude towards the natural world in this encounter.

A selection from a slightly later collection evidences the chasm that separated attitudes towards nature between farmers and courtiers. Encountering a melancholic boy, a priest asks the youth if the symbolic power of the cherry blossoms falling is what grieves him. The lad replies, 'That's not what grieves me.' He continues, 'The reason I am sad is that I am thinking how the flowers will be knocked off my father's barley and the grain will not set.' Barley flowers, or the small pollen receptors that lead to the plant's ovary, are all but invisible to the naked eye. But this young lad had deep knowledge of nature only acquired through agricultural labour. He was not distraught because of the symbolic value of falling cherry blossoms, as were poets in the *Kokinshū*, but because of the damage the weather posed to his father's barley crops.

For the past millennium, Heian's natural aesthetics, largely born in *waka* verse, have shaped popular perceptions of Japan's views towards nature. In truth, Japanese had engaged nature in a variety of capacities, but the least gritty, most distant from the physical environment, the most stylized, the most ethnocentric, and the least widespread manner, that of the Heian courtiers and their *waka* poetry, happens to be the one most strongly associated with the Japanese today. As recently as 2011, internationally acclaimed writer Murakami Haruki (b. 1949), in his Catalunya Prize acceptance speech after the 11 March 'triple disaster', mused on the relationship between impermanence, cherry blossoms, autumn leaves, and the 'ethnic consciousness' of the Japanese. He explained:

> Cherry blossoms, fireflies and red leaves lose their beauty within a very short time. We travel very far to watch the glorious moment. And we are somewhat relieved to confirm that they are not merely beautiful, but already beginning to fall, to lose their small lights and their vivid beauty. We find peace of mind in the fact that the peak of beauty has passed and disappeared.

For Murakami, Japanese associations with a living and dying nature are preserved in the writing of Heian poets, whose literary corpus and other artistic forms have been resurrected countless times in service of Japan's ongoing synchronicity with nature, even after nuclear calamity has befallen the seismically vulnerable country.

Heian's natural aesthetic did not remain static in Japanese history: it was not perfectly preserved in amber, like some DNA-filled mosquito. Writers, thinkers, and policy-makers continued to invoke it through the ages, resurrecting it to do the political and cultural work of articulating Japan's relationship to its surrounding natural world.

CONCLUSION

The Nara and Heian periods were formative ages in Japanese history. By the end of the twelfth century, Japan had conquered, and administratively controlled, if tenuously, much of the southern islands. The Emishi, though still connected to Northeast Asia, paid tribute to Japan's court, a process that slowly integrated them into the East Asian rhythms of Japanese life. The court asserted its *ritsuryô* logic throughout the realm, enmeshing the country within the concentric circles of territorial and administrative bureaucracies. But administrative form far outweighed the importance of administrative function during the Heian period, and courtiers fussed over *waka* verse and clothing choices more than they did the affairs of state. The aesthetic forms of this courtly age proved far more enduring legacies than did its administrative accomplishments. In the late twelfth century, imperial centralization succumbed to the centrifugal forces of feudalism, and Japan entered an age of local rule.

Regardless, the Heian aesthetic notion of a Japanese synchronicity with the natural world, one expressed in the verses of *waka* poetry, gained enormous traction in explaining Japanese connections to the land and cultural sensibilities. When ultranationalists sought to articulate Japan's 'national essence' in the pages of the *Kokutai no hongi* (Principles of the national body, 1937), they evoked Heian sensibilities more than any other. The document offers poetry on cherry blossoms as evidence of Japan's special relationship to nature, insisting that Japanese 'love nature', and that they have demonstrated their 'exquisite harmony with nature from ancient times' through poetry, daily practices, and ceremonies. Indeed, as the *Kokutai no hongi* states, 'there are many poems that sing of this harmonious mind toward nature, and deep love toward nature forms the principal theme of our poetry'. In sum, when Japanese nationalists sought to define the country's 'national essence', it was to the Heian natural aesthetic that they turned.

3

The Rise of Samurai Rule,
1185–1336

The transition from court to samurai rule permanently reconfigured Japan's political and cultural landscape. Samurai notions
of honour gave rise to a society that balanced notions of competition with collaboration, one that has detectable sociological
resonances to this day. Early samurai, such as those who fought
against the thirteenth-century invading Mongols, sought honour
and reward through acts of heroism, while later samurai, domes-
ticated through years of vassalage, had to discipline their pursuit
of honour to concrete public needs. As with the Mongol invasions, samurai fought valiantly in order to better their personal
reputations, and this established a culture of entrepreneurialism.
But, countering this trend, vassalage encouraged the organizational conformity that evolved into Japan's famous tendency
towards corporatism. Throughout their centuries of rule,
samurai balanced the pursuit of honour with their collective
obligations, making them enduring heroic figures for many
around the world.

Samurai sought documentation of their success in battle
through witness reports, just as Meiji entrepreneurs sought
visible financial successes. The samurai Takezaki Suenaga, before
engaging Mongol 'pirates', reportedly exclaimed, 'The way of the
bow and arrow is to do what is worthy of reward.' Samurai
found ways of building individual reputations within a constrict-
ing vassalage system, just as contemporary Japanese have found
means of individual creative expression within Japan's stifling

corporate culture. In some respects, this is one of the most enduring legacies of samurai rule in Japanese society.

LAND, ENVIRONMENT, AND WAR

It is helpful to view the development of samurai rule in three stages. During the early Heian period, approximately 750–850, the court was at the centre of the realm and dominated the *ritsuryō* bureaucratic state and its lands. At this time the military, under the control of the emperor, developed alongside other imperial bureaucratic institutions. From approximately 850 to 1050, the Fujiwara family and, later, a succession of retired emperors, ruled matters in the capital. The military, though no longer conscripted and increasingly represented by provincial samurai families, continued to operate more or less within the imperial structure. After 1050, however, provincial samurai became increasingly powerful and, eventually, wrested administrative and fiscal power from the court. But the court and its emperors never disappeared entirely, and they came to play an important role in legitimizing samurai rulers by granting titular authority; samurai, however, came to control much of the land and its revenue during the so-called 'age of widespread land clearance'. The transfer of governance to samurai paralleled a privatization of control over land, producers, and tax collection, which saw land slip from the court's grip into the hands of temples and shrines, aristocrats, and, eventually, provincial warriors. In essence, public lands controlled by the court evolved into feudal manors. This represented a decay of the earlier imperial Taika Reforms (645), which had declared most lands public with the advent of the 'equal field' system.

'Estates', called *shōen*, served as the keys to the transference of the Taika lands to private hands. During the eighth century, *shōen* mostly referred to feral or otherwise uncultivated fields and woodlands that the court authorized aristocrats or Buddhist temples to develop. Because these lands were public, in principle, the court claimed rights to monitor the *shōen* and limit the revenues generated from them. By the tenth century, however, such feral lands had become less common and aristocrats and temples expanded their reach to cultivated lands as well. As they did so, aristocrats and temples, through increasingly elaborate *shiki* – court documents that described the boundaries and crops of the *shôen*, as well as the rights of the people involved in their cultivation – acquired tax immunity and freedom from the court's public oversight. In time, the court's control over *shôen* became so negligible, so mired in elaborate *shiki*, and in essence so paper thin, that for all intents and purposes these once-public lands had become private manorial holdings. As aristocratic manoeuvring denied court-authorized tax farmers access to more and more land, the court lost valuable tax revenue for the government's coffers. By the twelfth century, around half of Japan's arable land was clustered in such *shôen*.

Important demographic shifts paralleled these landholding and usufruct trends. Specifically, between the eighth and twelfth centuries, Japan's population remained mostly stable at around 6 million souls, as a result of low life expectancy and high infant mortality rates that hovered around 50 per cent. Historians point out that what little population expansion Japan experienced occurred in eastern Honshu, home to the emergent samurai clans, as opposed to western Japan, home to the courtiers and Buddhist clergy. Given that these centuries witnessed the rise of samurai governance, such population trends certainly portended the shifting power dynamics to come.

Wresting control of *shôen* from the court and taxing rice production were not the only means by which samurai generated revenue to fuel their political rise. Iron mining drove Masakado's rebellion (939–40) in the mid-tenth century, illustrating a diversification of provincial economics. Taira no Masakado's (d. 940) aspirations represented a canary in the mineshaft of Japanese power, an early indication that some samurai were not content in their role as mere provincial toughs. Earlier, in the ninth century, most iron mining had occurred in western Japan, but in the tenth century, with the advent of new technologies that produced iron from iron sand, eastern Japan witnessed more mining. For example, archaeologists have discovered an elaborate iron mining site near Masakado's base, with multiple smelters and significant residual iron traces. New technologies enabled mining in previously unproductive places, providing a financial base for the restless Masakado. Indeed, mining and raising horses were as important as rice farming to his war-making capabilities.

Epidemic disease also created restlessness in the countryside. There is a strong correlation between samurai rebellions, which intensified in the tenth and eleventh centuries, and social upheaval caused by infectious diseases and famines. In some respects, disease weakened the authority of the court and paved the way for the rise of the samurai. Taira no Tadatsune's (975–1031) rebellion (1028–31) provides one such example. A seasoned tax evader, 'lawless rat', and basic troublemaker, Tadatsune staged a rebellion in 1028 in his home base of Kazusa and Shimôsa. Not coincidentally, a cluster of epidemics and famines broke out at approximately the same time as Tadatsune's rebellion. Virulent smallpox epidemics occurred in 993–5, 1020, and 1036. Measles hit Japan in 998 and again in 1025. Intestinal diseases, caused by various microbes that can symbiotically evolve with humans but that also cause disease, killed significant numbers in 1016, 1025, and 1027. Other unknown diseases occurred in 1030 and 1044. These epidemics combined with droughts for a double punch in 1030 and 1043–7.

In the period between 1025 and 1030, during Tadatsune's violent rebellion, occurrences of measles and dysentery proved particularly troublesome. Measles is a respiratory infection caused by the morbillivirus, while bacterial or protozoan infections or parasitic worms cause dysentery. In 1025, seven district magistrates died of disease in eastern Japan and the roads to Kyoto were by some accounts littered with the sick and dying. Measles killed in 1026, while intestinal diseases exacted their grim toll in 1027. In 1030, while Tadatsune's rebellion raged, an unknown disease erupted throughout Japan. The combined effects of these micro and macro killers, microbes on the one hand and samurai on the other, proved disastrous for agricultural production and confidence in the court. The shifts in the weather that had sparked the droughts had multiple causes: one was volcanic activity on the Japanese islands. After Tadatsune's rebellion, between 1108 and 1110, Mount Asama (2,568m or 8,425ft) and Mount Fuji (3,776m or 12,389ft) erupted several times, discharging large amount of ash and debris into the atmosphere. This, in turn, led to years of surface cooling.

The influenza virus thrives in cold, damp weather, and volcanic activity likely contributed to the outbreaks of influenza in 1134–5.

There was little the imperial court could do about volcanism and infectious disease. One response, however, was to commission the *Yamai no sôshi* (Scroll of diseases and deformities, late Heian period), compiled from a Tang Chinese dynasty (618–907) index of some 404 afflictions. The scroll represents an important medical technology, as an early *Merck Manual* of sorts, and an effort to understand and treat afflictions (Figure 5). It provides a window into the epidemiological and medical landscape of Japan in the late Heian period. It is unknown how many depictions the original possessed, but by the eighteenth century some seventeen screens existed that depicted afflictions ranging from pyorrhoea (gum disease) to conditions such as hermaphroditism. Textual descriptions range from precise descriptions of diseases and their symptomology to elaborate patient histories. As a window into the past, the *Yamai no sôshi* provides an index of some of the diseases that plagued Japan in the early medieval years. But it also casts some light onto the social lives of the populace and their medicines. Among the

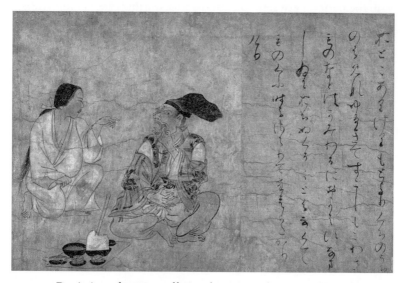

5 Depiction of a man suffering from gum disease and loose teeth in the *Yamai no soshi*.

diseases listed is halitosis, which is produced by the bacterial fermentation of food particles lodged in the gum tissue and teeth, producing nasty sulphuric odours. Uvula disease and colds, two other afflictions included, suggest that a host of viruses such as influenza afflicted Japanese at this time. Hermaphroditism is extremely rare, but obviously existed in medieval Japan. Some of the treatments mentioned seem medically reasonable, at least by medieval standards, though the story of a man from Yamato province with an eye disease concludes with a quack visiting his house and painfully blinding the poor man with misplaced lances and acupuncture pins.

IMPERIAL COMMAND AND UNEASE IN THE PROVINCES

Epidemic disease, land-use patterns and practices, demographic shifts, and rebellion were accompanied by important bureaucratic changes that reconfigured the court's military and, over time, further strengthened samurai control over the provinces. Initially, the imperial bureaucracy included a Tang-style conscript military. Indeed, in conjunction with the establishment of public lands, between 672 and 697 the emperor Tenmu and his wife and successor, Jitô, had taken concrete steps towards the creation of an imperial military. In particular, Tenmu demonstrated an interest in an imperial conscript military because it corresponded with other aspects of the *ritsuryô* bureaucratic system, but also because he had seized power by the sword during the Jinshin civil war of 672. Thus he sought to secure command of the country's military. 'In a government', he explained in 684, 'military matters are the essential thing'. Though Tenmu successfully deprived regional strongmen of horns, fifes, drums, flags, and other accoutrements used for directing troops, he left the creation of drafting 'records of the population', or census taking, for the purposes of conscription, to Jitô. In 689, she ordered that provincial soldiers 'be divided into four groups, one of which was to be designated [in rotation] for training in the military arts'. In 702 the imperial military was cemented in the *ritsuryô* system by the Taihô codes and organized under the command of the Military Ministry. The Taihô codes also specified that governors should establish horse pastures for military purposes and oversee breeding. The horse, an allied organism in humanity's conquest of the planet, became critical to the emergence of samurai rule in Japan, just as they had been for Sundiata (*c*.1217–55) and the Mali empire in Africa and Genghis Khan (1162–1227) and the Mongols of Eurasia.

By 792, however, the imperial military had become a serious burden on the government's treasury. In response, the court ordered that the 'regiments shall be abolished in the capital region and the provinces of the seven circuits, thereby eliminating an onerous burden', effectively abolishing the conscript military. In exchange, the court became increasingly dependent on the provincial elite for law enforcement and other military matters. This created incentives for the organization of armed, military clans in the provinces; it also created incentives for men to polish their martial skills. These men, we are told, became 'highly skilled in the conduct of battles'.

The imperial court knew trouble was brewing in the countryside when Taira no Masakado (d. 940) staged a rebellion in 935. Beginning as a family tiff, Masakado's rebellion quickly metastasized into a serious threat to court authority. Masakado had expelled the Heian-appointed governors from several provinces and, after a shaman designated him as such, he flamboyantly declared himself the new emperor (*shinnô*) of the Kantô plain (the area around present-day Tokyo) in 939. This declaration, and his capture of government headquarters in Hitachi and seven other provinces in rapid succession, represented the most direct threat to imperial authority thus far. Fujiwara no Hidesato, the regent at the time, appointed Masakado's cousin and arch-enemy, Taira no Sadamori, to crush the rebellion. In northwestern Shimôsa, Masakado confronted Sadamori's government-sanctioned troops in fierce fighting. 'Struck by an arrow from the gods', chronicles tell of Masakado's death, 'in the end the New Emperor perished alone'. But the legacies and power of such aristocratic samurai families as the Taira and Minamoto persisted and the next two centuries witnessed the gradual rise to prominence of provincial military strongmen.

Another such strongman was Fujiwara no Sumitomo (d. 941). After having 'heard rumours of Masakado's treason from afar', he and his ruthless bands of maritime buccaneers marauded the Inland Sea littoral. Sumitomo had been born into a powerful Iyo family but abandoned a government career to devote his life to maritime banditry. His base was Hiburi Island, off the coast of Iyo province, from where he deprived imperial and merchant ships of their treasures. Upon attacking Bizen province, he learned that the governor, Fujiwara no Kodaka, had fled with his family to warn the court. Sumitomo tracked down Kodaka. 'In the end', sources tell, 'they captured Kodaka and cut off his ears and sliced his nose. They stole his wife and carried her off; the children were killed by the pirates.' Sumitomo reigned with terror over the Inland Sea until his defeat by imperial forces at Hakata Bay on the west coast of Kyushu. Although Sumitomo escaped, imperial forces captured some 800 of his vessels and killed hundreds of pirates. Sumitomo was later apprehended in Iyo province and beheaded. In suppressing both Masakado's and Sumitomo's rebellions, provincial samurai chiefs, not court generals, became the court's principal law enforcement agents. Working under imperial directive, they had replaced the 'public' conscript military of the Taihô order.

The law enforcement situation in the provinces festered over time, however. In the eleventh century, under Minamoto no Yoriyoshi (998–1082), the Minamoto and its allied families received court sanction to quash a disturbance led by Abe no Yoritoki (d. 1057), a warlord who was described as a 'native chieftain of the eastern barbarians'. The Abe claimed as their dominion the Six Districts of Mutsu and they acted as district magistrates, collecting tribute from other pacified Emishi tribes. In 1051, Yoritoki and the Abe received amnesty from the court and surrendered to Yoriyoshi; they resumed fighting in 1056, however, and Yoriyoshi decided to crush the Abe once and for all. In battle, he engendered fierce loyalty among his troops. 'Our bodies shall repay our debts', they reportedly said to him. 'Our lives shall count for nothing where honour is at stake.' In 1057, despite the loyalty of his troops and the death of Abe no Yoritoki, Sadatô, Yoritoki's son, defeated Yoriyoshi at Kinomi; but in 1057, after gathering more northeastern allies, Yoriyoshi finally crushed the Abe family. Yoriyoshi's soldiers killed Sadatô and another of Yoritoki's sons, Munetô, promptly surrendered to Yoriyoshi's government-sanctioned troops. Both Yoriyoshi and his son, Yoshiie, were adorned with higher court ranks for their service.

Though many historians point to the Former Nine Years War
(1051–63) as an example of the rise of private military forces in
the provinces, in fact Yoriyoshi, the court-appointed commander,
always sought government sanction for his campaign. In principle,
he still operated within the *ritsuryô* bureaucratic system.

Despite Yoriyoshi's successful campaign, the north remained a
tinderbox. The Latter Three Years War (1083–7) started as a fight
between two members of the Kiyowara family of northern Dewa
province, Sanehira and Iehira. Like the Abe, the Kiyowara might
have been of Emishi descent, but there is also evidence that they
heralded from distant aristocratic origins. After suffering a chilling
defeat at the Numa Stockade in the winter of 1086, Minamoto no
Yoshiie, Yoriyoshi's son, laid siege to the Kanezawa stockade the
next year, where Iehira and his uncle had fortified themselves.
Though Yoshiie never received imperial sanction for the conflict –
he applied for it and was denied – he pursued Iehira anyway,
sacrificing both personal treasure and reputation. Yoshiie
concluded the campaign by destroying the Kiyowara family and
collecting forty-eight of their severed heads. These trophies,
however, proved small consolation. One year later, in 1088, the
court removed Yoshiie from his post as governor of Mutsu.

Unlike the Former Nine Years War, during which Yoriyoshi had
received court sanction and, subsequently, troop reinforcements
and elevated court rank, Yoshiie never received such sanction for
the second conflict and, ultimately, was dismissed from his official
post. Even though the court played an important role in these two
conflicts, the feudal aspects of these northeastern conflicts are hard
to ignore. Private forces, or retainers of the Minamoto, far outnumbered public court forces on the battlefield. Clearly, Japan was in
the throes of a major historical transition.

GENPEI WAR (1156–1185)

The historical transition occurred quickly. In the century after the
Latter Three Years War, the court continued to mobilize the military for its law enforcement needs, often to crush religious riots
sparked by temple appointments, provincial policies, tax burdens,
and squabbles between religious institutions. In 1081, for example,

more than 1,000 Enryakuji monks from Mount Hiei, along with their military allies, descended on Kyoto while the court deployed troops to defend the capital. Similar episodes involving warrior-monks occurred on at least five separate occasions in the eleventh and twelfth centuries, and the court often called on the Taira and Minamoto families to guard Kyoto. In 1113, the temples Kôfukuji (Nara) and Enryakuji became embroiled in a dispute over an appointment at Kiyomizu temple in the capital. The court caved to Kôfukuji demands on the matter, only to invite the anger of Enryakuji's warrior-monks, who ransacked buildings at Kiyomizu-dera (a branch temple of Kôfukuji). On this occasion, the court called on the Taira and Minamoto families to defend the capital. 'Warriors formed a line and went on guard throughout the night', one chronicle explains, despite the fact that the 'voices of the monks calling out shook the heavens'.

But inviting warriors to Kyoto was risky business, as the Hôgen-Heiji Disturbance (1156–60) demonstrates. In 1155, with the death of Emperor Konoye, a succession dispute erupted in the Heian court. The reformer Fujiwara no Yorinaga (1120–56) supported the retired-emperor Sutoku (1119–64), while Fujiwara no Tadamichi (1097–1164) supported cloistered-emperor Toba's favourite son, Go-Shirakawa (1127–92). When Go-Shirakawa became emperor, Yorinaga allied himself with the Minamoto family and marched on Kyoto, forcefully enthroning Sutoku as emperor. Tadamichi responded by allying himself with the Taira family, who smarted for a fight with the Minamotos. When the Taira defeated Sutoku's forces, a wholesale slaughter of the Minamoto family commenced. For days the blood of once-proud Minamotos flowed in the streets of Kyoto. In one of the great historical mysteries, however, the Taira left a handful of Minamotos alive, including Minamoto no Yoritomo (1147–99) and Minamoto no Yoshitsune (1159–89). The tragic story of these two brothers and their later rise to power is surely one of the most compelling in Japanese history.

Once the Minamoto were out of the picture, Taira no Kiyomori (1118–81) began the slow insinuation of the Taira family into courtly life. In fact, it is fair to say that he adored Kyoto. The Taira family – somewhat like the Fujiwara family – became adept at orchestrating political marriage and his daughter married into the imperial family and gave birth to a potential future emperor named Antoku (1178–85). In the countryside, however, Yoritomo gained strength and allies, and by 1180 felt confident enough to mount a challenge to the Taira hold on Kyoto. It started when Minamoto no Yorimasa's (1106–80) plot to oust the Taira was discovered, and he fled to the Onjoji monastery on the shores of Lake Biwa (near Kyoto). When he realized the monastic forces there could not protect him from the Taira warriors, he again fled, this time towards Nara, the ancient capital, where he met up with Prince Mochihito (d. 1180). En route to the Tôdaiji and Kôfukuji temples Taira warriors forced an engagement at the Tatsuta River, and the two emerged victorious, at least temporarily. At this juncture, Yoritomo and his allies entered the conflict. With his brother Yoshitsune in command, the hardened Minamoto forces outmatched the softened Taira samurai, who had grown comfortable at the court, as explained in the *Heike monogatari* (Tale of Heike). Of the Taira forces, or the warriors of the western provinces, this chronicle explains,

> If their parents are killed they retire from the battle and perform Buddhist rites to console the souls of the dead. Only after the mourning is over will they fight again. If their children are slain, their grief is so deep that they cease fighting altogether ... They dislike the heat of summer. They grumble at the severe cold of winter.'

Ominously, as if describing a dark cloud on the eastern horizon, the *Heike monogatari* explains that, 'This is not the way of the soldiers from the eastern provinces.' Indeed, it was not.

In the rematch between the Taira and Minamoto families, called the Genpei War (1180–5), the eastern Minamotos proved victorious. The final scene of the war, the Battle of Dannoura (1185), featured the remnants of the Taira family fleeing onto the Inland Sea by boat. The Lady Nii, the daughter of Taira no Kiyomori, was in the vessel, along with her emperor son Antoku. When they realized the war was lost, the Lady Nii embraced Antoku in her arms and prepared for death by flinging herself into the sea. 'Where are you taking me?' asked the seven-year-old. With tears on her cheeks, she replied, 'Japan is small as a grain of millet, but now it is a veil of misery. There is a pure land of happiness beneath the waves, another capital where no sorrow is. It is there that I am taking my Sovereign.' She then leapt into the sea and with her died the future of the Taira family.

Immediately after the Genpei War, Yoritomo placed his brother, Yoshitsune, in charge of the capital. While in Kyoto, Yoshitsune received the title of 'steward' (*jitô*) from Emperor Go-Shirakawa, who had come to power during the disastrous Hôgen-Heiji Disturbance, which, as we have seen, had precipitated the Taira ascendancy. By accepting the title, however, Yoshitsune appears to have recognized an authority other than his brother's in Kamakura, the new Minamoto stronghold. Incensed, Yoritomo had his brother and his sidekick Saitô Musashibô Benkei (1155–89) hunted down. When Yoshitsune and Benkei could run no more, the younger brother committed ritual suicide in epic fashion. 'Seizing the sword', one account explains, 'Yoshitsune plunged it into his body below the left breast, thrusting it in so far that the blade almost emerged through his back. Then he cut deeply into his stomach and, tearing the wound wide open in three directions, pulled out his intestines.' His wife and son also died by his side. Interestingly, even though Yoritomo, the elder brother, lived to subdue the realm and establish the Kamakura *bakufu*, it is Yoshitsune who is more celebrated in Japanese lore. As one scholar aptly called it, this is the 'nobility of failure' in Japanese culture, as to die for a cause suggests sincerity, which is revered in Confucian cultures.

THE KAMAKURA *BAKUFU*

With the violent death of Yoshitsune, his elder brother Yoritomo began the process of consolidating a system of governance in Kamakura. Though samurai certainly marched to a different cultural drummer than Kyoto aristocrats, the Kamakura *bakufu* bears a striking resemblance to the early imperial bureaucracy in Kyoto. In 1192, Go-Toba (1180–1239), the emperor, granted Yoritomo the imperial title *seii taishôgun*, or 'Barbarian Subduing General'. Typical of past governance, the emperor reigned but did not rule, serving more as a legitimizing figure that, in his 'gilded cage', transcended the messy day-to-day affairs of administration. As with the Fujiwara regents, Go-Toba retained imperial prerogative as giver of titles, while Yoritomo, in accepting the title, could claim the mantle of not just military supremacy but imperial, and hence divine, authority. This system dictated the intricacies of Japanese politics for centuries.

When Yoritomo died in 1199 without an heir, his wife, the clever Hôjô Masako (1156–1225), masterfully orchestrated a Hôjô take-over by placing her father as chief of the Kamakura bureaucracy. In the Jôkyû War (1221), the Hôjô finally wrested control of the realm from the clutches of the remaining Minamotos. In 1232, the Hôjô family drafted the Jôei codes, which clarified the duties of the provincial governors and stewards, and protected the interests of the court. In essence, the document outlined the basics of medieval law.

Under samurai rule, Japan slowly entered its medieval age and witnessed a restructuring of society at every level. Marriage patterns shifted from the visiting and uxorilocal patterns of the Heian court to the co-residential patterns of the samurai patriarchy. This shift solidified the patrilocal and patrilinear household system as the basic social unit of society. In the household, the husband–wife duo stood at the centre of the patriarchal union. The husband served as head of the household, while the wife's principal duty was to give birth to a male heir. Importantly, the shift, generally speaking, witnessed women transformed from people who could have property (most prominent Heian women, such as Lady Murasaki, owned property and had hereditary access to it) to people that both were and could have property. In resolving rape cases, for example, the Kamakura and later Ashikaga *bakufu* (1336–1573) demonstrated an interest in the mediation of property transmission and the maintenance of the social order, rather than individual justice for women. In one interesting case from 1479, a samurai from the Akamatsu family had illicit sex with the wife of a prominent Kyoto saké merchant. The merchant avenged himself by cutting down the Akamatsu samurai in the streets of Kyoto. It just so happened that the son of the Kyoto merchant served the Itakura family, a rival of the Akamatsu, which raised the spectre of the conflict broadening into inter-clan warfare. The Ashikaga *bakufu* ruled that if the wronged husband avenged the violator inside his home, then the wife could be spared. If the husband killed the violator outside the home, however, then the wife must be killed, to demonstrate that it was a genuine act of revenge. This legal precedent – that 'both the man and the woman must be killed by the husband' – was upheld through the sixteenth century. It demonstrates that women had come to serve as property, or something that could be vandalized, in the samurai order.

As Japanese society shifted under samurai rule, agriculture blossomed and the population grew. It is estimated that in 1200 (immediately after the Genpei War) Japan's population stood at approximately 7 million souls. By 1600, on the eve of the early modern transition, Japan's population stood at 12 million. Rural villages proved fiercely independent, with village heads overseeing members of village associations. Buddhist theologies continually penetrated Japan's spiritual life. In accordance with certain Buddhist calendars, many believed that the world had entered a kind of 'latter age', and that salvation required new paths. Old sects, such as Amidism, persisted, and new sects, such as Pure Land (*Jôdo*, founded by the monk Hônen in Japan), True Pure Land (*Jôdo shin*, founded by the monk Shinran in Japan), the monk Ippen and his 'Timely School', and even schools of Zen Buddhism, such as Rinzai Zen and Sôtô Zen, blossomed. With the exception of Zen Buddhism, which is a sect that depends on the individual for salvation, most other sects relied on the power of a benevolent Buddha. In the Pure Land sects, by either constantly uttering the *nenbutsu*, 'I Take Refuge in the Amida Buddha', or doing so once with sincerity, brought salvation. For a medieval world on the edge of an historical abyss, achieving salvation through the supernatural power of the other had a compelling appeal.

Kamo no Chôme's (1155–1216) *Hôjôki* (An account of my hut, 1212) captures the gestalt of the medieval transition, with its ruminations on Buddhist impermanence, environmental upheaval, and political transformation. After turning 50, Kamo no Chôme rejected the hustle and bustle of the materially driven life in Kyoto and, after a brief trip to Kamakura, settled in a small, rustic hut near Mount Hino in the Kinai region. 'Dead in the morning and born at night', he ruminated, 'so man goes on forever, un-enduring as the foam on the water'. Such Buddhist statements of impermanence abound in *Hôjôki*, but his thoughts on the correlation between environmental upheaval and political transformation are instructive. In 1181, as the Genpei War raged and warriors stood at the brink of ruling the realm, famine caused by bad weather savaged the land and its already malnourished people. 'The spring and summer were scorching hot, and autumn and winter brought typhoons and floods, and as one bad season followed another the Five Cereals could not ripen.' After prayers failed to fertilize these cereals, farmers deserted their land. Respectable citizens became barefooted beggars. The dead lingered and a 'terrible stench filled the streets'. In a morbid scene, some babies 'continued to feed at their mother's breast, not knowing she was already dead'. The medieval transition had become a time of widespread dying.

In the medieval mind, riverbeds and the waters that flowed through them became the shores that separated this world and the next. The water purified because tides surged and swept away the corpses that collected there. Medieval Japanese used riverbeds as graveyards and shunned the Kyoto outcastes who lived there because the rotting dead permanently dirtied them. They neither buried nor cremated decomposing bodies, but rather let the waters of the Kamo River flush these impurities away. For this reason, officials also executed the condemned along riverbanks. Lepers and other diseased people, reclusive monks, and miscellaneous pariahs sought shelter along the transitory banks of the Kamo River. Outcastes butchered animals and tanned hides in this impure, fluctuating space, where waters rose and fell. In time, outcastes found employment as gardeners and groundskeepers, and became pervasive parts of Kyoto's vibrant social scene. It is not surprising, then, that the 1181 famine became particularly visible along the Kamo's riverbanks.

Three years later, in 1184, Kamo no Chôme records a large earthquake, which further exacerbated the social and political turmoil. In scenes reminiscent of 11 March 2011, the hills crumbled and 'sea surged up and overwhelmed the land'. Landslides plummeted into the valleys while 'boats at sea staggered in the swell and horses on land could find no sure footing'. On the occasion of such natural disasters, remarks Kamo no Chôme, people become 'convinced of the impermanence of all earthly things, and ... talk of the evil of attachment to them, and of the impurity of their hearts', but such feelings rarely lasted very long. Pointing to the connection between upheaval in the natural world and social hardship he says, 'Thus it seems to me that all the difficulties of life spring from this fleeting evanescent nature of man and his habitation.'

Seismic activity in the Earth's crust paralleled seismic shifts in Japan's political landscape. Japanese lore explained that the archipelago balanced on the back of a giant catfish and whenever it shifted Japan quaked. Neither malignant nor benign, the catfish became the subject of woodblock prints and stories of devastation and good fortune. This giant catfish's wiggling notwithstanding, Japan's earthquakes are also the result of its position on the 'ring of fire', or circum-Pacific seismic belt. As we shall discuss further in Chapter 15, volcanic and earthquake activity in Japan is directly related to the subduction of the Pacific Plate in the larger process of plate tectonics. Subduction refers to the process whereby one tectonic plate dives under an oceanic or continental plate and into the Earth's mantle, constituting a 'subduction zone'. For this reason, Japan experiences somewhere in the neighbourhood of 1,500 earthquakes annually, many of them substantial. Given their frequency and magnitude, their role in Japanese history is irrefutable.

THREATS OF INVASION

The Kamakura *bakufu* had more than simply a Buddhist 'latter age' to contend with. Throughout the twelfth and thirteenth centuries, Japan maintained ties to China's Southern Song dynasty (1127–1279) and Korea's Goryeo dynasty (918–1392), while Chinese merchants emerged as instrumental in the strengthening of several western Kyushu shrines and temples. Ports such as Dazaifu and Hakata became hubs for these Chinese merchants, who constructed temples, such as the Jôtenji in Hakata and Sôfukuji in Daizaifu, solidifying Tendai Buddhism's gains in southwestern Japan. The exchange functioned both ways, however; the monk En'in, who founded the Jôtenji temple, travelled to China in 1235 and when he returned established the Tôfukuji temple in Kyoto, which facilitated the rise of Zen Buddhism in Japan.

Relations with the continent were not always so lofty and benign, however. One endemic problem in the medieval years was pirates, who looted the southern coast of Korea. In 1223, pirates plundered the coastline near Kumajo. Four years later, officials from Korea would complain of coastal raids from pirates originating in Tsushima. Throughout the thirteenth century, Korean officials complained bitterly of Japanese pirates and burned several ships in response. Concerned that pirates might cool the vibrant trade with the continent, Japanese beheaded some ninety pirates in 1227 in front of Korean envoys. The reason Dazaifu officials worried about pirates was the nature of the Korean trade. Whereas Japan mostly imported raw materials from Korea, the Goryeo dynasty imported value-added, manufactured products from Japan. Thirteenth-century trade also included the importation of copper coins, which became essential to currency reform under the Kamakura *bakufu*. In 1242, for example, a Japanese vessel belonging to Saionji Kintsune returned from Song China with holds weighted down by copper coins, as well as exotic parrots and oxen. It was later determined that the amount of copper coins in Saionji's holds was roughly equivalent to the entire amount minted by the Song dynasty (960–1279) that year.

The Mongol invasions proved the most serious threat to Japan's trade and cultural interaction with the continent. In 1206, Genghis Khan (1162–1227) unleashed his horse-driven war machine and brought parts of Europe, the Islamic world, northern Asia, and much of East Asia under Mongol domination. After the death of Genghis Khan, Kublai Khan (1215–94) triumphed in battle over his brother, Ariq Böke (1219–66). After succeeding his grandfather, Kublai Khan established the Yuan dynasty (1271–1368) in China, which became his base of operations. Once in China the Mongols attempted invasions of Japan on two occasions, in 1274 and 1281. Though the Japanese, with the help of timely typhoons, managed to resist the Mongol invasions, these episodes did have the long-term effect of transforming relations with the continent, hastening the collapse of the Kamakura *bakufu*, and sparking an emergent sense of realm-wide national consciousness in Japan.

Kublai Khan began diplomatic wrangling with the Kamakura *bakufu* in 1265 with the intent of cutting off trade to the Southern Song dynasty (1127–1279), which had yet to be fully subdued by the Mongols. The Kamakura *bakufu*, under regent Hôjô Tokimune (1251–84), decided to ignore early Mongol overtures. Tokimune was heavily influenced by Song Chinese priests who, not incorrectly, viewed the Mongols as invaders and, hence, illegitimate rulers of China. Likewise, Tokimune, following Japanese precedent, refused to acknowledge the diplomatic centrality of China in East Asia, under Mongol control or not. Though never executed, Tokimune made plans for a pre-emptive strike against Mongol fortifications on the Korean peninsula. He also began construction of a defensive wall along the coastline of Hakata Bay. It is conventionally assumed that foul weather vanquished the invading Mongol 'pirates', not battle-hardened samurai, but there was some fierce fighting as well (Figure 6). In battle, samurai sought to demonstrate their individual success through witnesses and rewards for bravery. Before entering battle with Mongol forces, Takezaki Suenaga proclaimed, 'I have no purpose in my life but to advance and be known [text missing]. I want [my deeds] to be known by his

6 Depiction of a mounted samurai fighting the Mongols in Takizaki Suenaga, *Môkoshurai ekotoba* (Mongol invasion scrolls, 1293).

lordship.' How military service was made known to lords was through 'battle service reports', 'records of witness', and 'verification reports'. In recognition of their service, lords granted medieval samurai rewards based on conduct.

One reason the Mongol invasions are cited as precipitating the fall of the Kamakura *bakufu* is that many samurai felt that they were rewarded inadequately for their fighting. But the Mongol invasion also represented new challenges for samurai governance. Unlike internecine warfare between competing groups within Japan, such as the Taira and the Minamoto families, the Mongols represented a foreign threat. Japanese therefore fought more collectively for their country. But as no territory was taken at home or abroad, samurai rewards and spoils were modest indeed. How to reward samurai for service to their nation, as opposed to their clan, had yet to be ironed out, and the Kamakura *bakufu* suffered the consequences.

KENMU REVOLUTION

It was imperial politics, however, that triggered the demise of the Kamakura *bakufu*. In 1259, the *bakufu* intervened in an imperial succession dispute between branches of the royal family, eventually devising a precarious settlement that alternated succession between the two branches. This functioned reasonably well until the Bunpô Compromise (1317) when it was determined that the successor to the imperium would be Go-Daigo (1288–1339) from the junior line because of lack of fitness in the senior line. Because he was neither a direct heir nor an imperial insider, officials also decided that Go-Daigo could only serve for ten years. Go-Daigo, however, had other plans: his education in the Confucian classics and Chinese history had shaped his thinking about imperial rule. Unlike in Japan, where emperors reigned alongside ruling Kamakura shoguns, the dynastic cycle governed Chinese imperial succession and attracted Go-Daigo's attention. He bought into the notion of the dynastic cycle and the direct rule of emperors. Indeed, the idea of a new regime in Japan, one that has received the 'mandate of heaven', was deeply seductive for Go-Daigo.

Go-Daigo's orientation towards Chinese historical paradigms was not the only ingredient working in his favour. On seizing the throne, he immediately surrounded himself with loyal ministers with limited independent power bases, such as Kitabatake Chikafusa (1293–1354). These men fit the ideal Chinese mould, as ministers of merit and not hereditary power. Go-Daigo later wrote on the matter: '[I] have been instructed that the *Huainan [zi]* states that "to have few with virtue and to rely much on affection is the first danger of governing".' Documents describe Go-Daigo's ministers as 'maintaining lifelong loyalties to their sovereign' and 'proffering sound advice', rather than guarding their own family interests in the capital. Go-Daigo also meddled in the commercial affairs of Kyoto and levied taxes where they had not been traditionally levied, such as on saké brewers and residents in the Tôji temple areas. Go-Daigo sought to tap into the commercial potential of Kyoto to strengthen his hold on the throne.

The 'dual polity', or situation wherein emperors reigned and shoguns ruled, continued to be a thorn in Go-Daigo's side. Affairs finally came to a head with the Shôchû Incident (1324). Having devised a half-baked plan to overthrow samurai governance, Go-Daigo's men perpetrated a disturbance during a festival at the Kitano shrine in order to distract the *bakufu* and move against Rokuhara (the Kamakura *bakufu*'s outpost in Kyoto). The plan backfired, however, and Go-Daigo's men were captured. Immediately, Go-Daigo drafted a letter that outlined in no uncertain terms his views of imperial authority. 'The imperial wrath is severe', he wrote. The Kamakura shogun is 'not lord of the realm yet has succeeded to powers of government ... What is fitting for the eastern barbarians is that [just like] the people of the realm they look to the just government [of the emperor] and respectfully bow their heads.' Go-Daigo also possessed an acute sense of Mencian natural imagery. In a particularly poignant sentence that demonstrates Go-Daigo's keen understanding of the historical relationship between emperors and shoguns, he wrote, 'I am the lord of this entire country. All below are in receipt of the favours of the court. To constrict [me] is certainly equivalent to dwelling in the shade and snapping off the foliage, or to drawing water from a stream and forgetting the source.' Go-Daigo's use of natural imagery – 'drawing water from a stream and forgetting the source' – served to naturalize imperial power and position shogunal rule as the product of human artifice. Go-Daigo upped the ante when he appealed to Buddhist magic to curse the Kamakura *bakufu*, participating in esoteric Tachikawa rituals, for example.

In 1331, Go-Daigo mobilized disgruntled samurai from the Kantô and Kinai regions, many still chafing from slim rewards in the aftermath of the Mongol invasions, and moved against the Kamakura *bakufu*. But forces loyal to the Hôjô family proved well prepared and Go-Daigo fled to Kasagi temple, with its massive cliff-face image of the Maitreya (Future) Buddha. Go-Daigo fancied himself as a 'future' king of sorts, so the location was carefully selected, even though it proved a lacklustre hiding place. Kamakura samurai quickly captured Go-Daigo. He was exiled to Oki Island from where he escaped in 1332, hidden under heaps of dried fish. Samurai families that felt slighted by the Hôjô proved eager to aid Go-Daigo in his designs to seize power. With the aid of Ashikaga Takauji (1305–58) and the militant monks of Mount Hiei (Enryakuji temple) Go-Daigo finally overthrew the Kamakura *bakufu* and declared the 'Kenmu restoration'. Dramatic and short-lived, the Kenmu regime established a new judiciary, rebuilt the imperial palace, revived imperial rituals, and patronized such powerful Buddhist temples as the Daitokuji and Nanzenji.

Go-Daigo's grip on power depended heavily on the continuing blessings of Ashikaga Takauji, which he did not receive. In 1336, Takauji rebelled against Go-Daigo. In the ensuing struggle for the realm, the forces of Takauji met Go-Daigo's loyalists at the famous battle of Minato River. The fierce loyalists Kusunoki Masashige (1294–1336) and his brother, Masasue, led Go-Daigo's men in battle, but they committed suicide together in a modest farmhouse when the day had been lost. The final conversation between the two brothers, before they slit their bellies and laid their 'heads on the same pillow', is famous in the annals of imperial devotion. Masa-shige asked his brother for his last wish. Masasue replied, 'I should like to be reborn seven times into this world of men ... so that I might destroy the enemies of the court.' Fifty of their closest followers quickly disembowelled themselves as well and 'all cut open their stomachs at the same time'. Go-Daigo fled southward to Yoshino and established the Southern Court, while Ashikaga Takauji placed Kômyô, of the Senior Line, in power, establishing the Northern Court. The division between the Southern and Northern courts would not be resolved until 1392.

CONCLUSION

Inherent in the feudal system set up by samurai were the seeds of political disintegration. As Japan inched towards the fifteenth century, centrifugal forces began tearing its domains asunder, bleeding into a tumultuous period known as the 'Warring States period' (1467–1582), named after a similarly chaotic period in ancient China. 'Japan', as a unified political entity, disintegrated and the country emerged as a hotchpotch of domains that viewed themselves as independent 'states'. In other words, the 'state' that emerged in the fifteenth century scarcely resembled a nation, but rather localized domains under the control of ruling samurai households. This is not to discount the importance of the medieval transition. Samurai knit a new social fabric in Japan, one that emphasized Confucian patrilocal and patrilinear households, and which became the core of Japanese society for centuries. The samurai also walked a thin line between personal honour and vassalage obligations, setting the tone for Japanese individual life and civic participation to this day. The samurai ruled Japan until the Meiji Restoration of 1868, placing their contribution to Japanese history at the centre of the next several chapters.

4

Medieval Japan and the Warring States Period, 1336–1573

In the fourteenth and fifteenth centuries, political authority migrated outward into the provinces and away from the centre. If the Kyoto court, prior to the twelfth century, managed to consolidate authority in the *ritsuryô* bureaucracy, then with the advent of samurai governance influence became more decentralized and more feudal in nature. As the political authority and military might of the Ashikaga *bakufu* (1336–1578) waned, alliances external to the state began to take shape, between powerful samurai families, well-armed Buddhist monasteries, and even Kyoto neighbourhood associations. Under pressure from such groups, the Ashikaga *bakufu* eventually weakened to the point where it became ineffective and Japan descended to a socio-political condition best captured by the expression *gekokujô*, or the 'low rising against the high'. In the political vacuum left by the weakened *bakufu*, new alliances formed as domain lords, known as *daimyô*, consolidated their power at the local level. The legacy of the domains and their *daimyô* is an important and lasting one. When the country was finally reunified at the end of the sixteenth century, many domains retained much of their autonomy, even as the Edo *bakufu* (1603–1868) consolidated its power in the new capital. In fact the legacy of regionalism survives to this day: even though Japan is a relatively small country, it retains a strong sense of local identity, today expressed benignly through local foods, literary traditions, and gifts. In the medieval period, regionalism proved far more malignant, often taking the form of predatory warfare.

THE ASHIKAGA *BAKUFU*

Emperor Go-Daigo survived the slaughter at Minato River and fled south to Yoshino, where he set up a parallel imperial court, inaugurating the confusing period of the North and South Courts (1336–92). Legitimized by the Northern Court, Ashikaga Takauji became shogun in 1338 and established the Ashikaga *bakufu* in Kyoto. Takauji's son, Ashikaga Yoshiakira (1330–67), ruled in the footsteps of his father until his untimely death at 37. This left his young son, Yoshimitsu (1358–1408), in the hands of his powerful retainer Hosokawa Yoriyuki (1329–92). While on his deathbed he said to Yoriyuki, 'I give you a son', and to his son he said, 'I give you a father'. Ashikaga authority reached its zenith under Yoriyuki and, later, Yoshimitsu, in part fuelled by a creative 1371 tax levied on saké brewers and their associated pawn brokerages. The Ashikaga family, unlike their predecessors in Kamakura, had always been poor in land and the alcohol tax provided much-needed revenue streams. He also developed the Deputy Shogun (*kanrei*) position to strengthen the *bakufu* bureaucracy. Eventually, Yoshimitsu took the reins of power in 1379 after Yoriyuki's forced resignation. Yoshimitsu oversaw the *bakufu* until his death in 1408, successfully negotiating the stormy political waters of the fourteenth and early fifteenth centuries. Principally, Yoshimitsu had to contend with three powerful blocs: religious institutions, loyalists to Go-Daigo's Southern Court, and provincial governors (*shugo*). He arranged a settlement with the Southern Court in 1392 through a promise of alternate succession and handily crushed dangerous governors such as the tenacious Ôuchi Yoshihiro (1359–99) at the close of the fourteenth century.

The weak spot of the Ashikaga *bakufu* was in its system of bifurcated rule, wherein governors simultaneously served as Kyoto bureaucrats and governors of the provinces. Fourteen governor families represented branches of the Ashikaga family, while the remaining seven lived far from Kyoto and governed in exchange for land. (This number fluctuated. In 1392, there were about twenty governor households administering some forty-five provinces.) Underneath the shogun, the most important position was the Deputy Shogun, usually occupied by one of three families:

Shiba, Hatakeyama, or Hosokawa. They became the core of Ashikaga hegemony: when functioning together they wielded effective power over the governors, when divided they ripped the country apart at its loosely knit seams. As we shall see, it was conflict among these three families that led to the outbreak of the vicious Ōnin War (1467–77), in which the capital burned in over a decade's worth of urban door-to-door combat.

Governors were in a tricky position because of the manner in which they divided their time between Kyoto, as *bakufu* bureaucrats and retainers, and the provinces, as local overseers. When in the provinces, governors competed for control with local stakeholders called 'provincial men', whose authority emanated not from Kyoto but from local hereditary alliances. Over time, the authority of these governors waned in the provinces, particularly in the aftermath of the Ōnin War that destroyed the remaining vestiges of Ashikaga power. As the *bakufu* withered and governors lost local legitimacy, 'provincial men', who generated their legitimacy locally, moved easily into the power vacuums.

Trouble started for the *bakufu* with the assassination of Ashikaga Yoshinori (1394–1441). Following the assassination, the *bakufu* hit back hard with a military campaign against the perpetrators in Harima province. The assassin, Akamatsu Mitsusuke (1381–1441), committed suicide during the campaign, but his death failed to improve the fortunes of the *bakufu*. Yoshinori's successors were young, feeble-minded men. Infamously, Ashikaga Yoshimasa (1436–90) was the worst of the shoguns and is roundly condemned for his clownish extravagance. It is said that he 'governed solely by the wishes of inexperienced wives and nuns'. He and his adviser, Ise Sadachika, are often held responsible for the decay of the *bakufu*, even though institutional problems and natural disasters were mainly to blame. Under Shogun Yoshimasa, a series of successional disputes jarred the Hatakeyama and Shiba families and, eventually, spilled over into the Ashikaga family and caused the Ōnin War, from which the *bakufu* never fully recovered. But before we turn to the man-made mayhem of the Ōnin War, we must turn our attention briefly to the cataclysms that helped push the *bakufu* over the edge.

Between 1457 and 1460, a series of natural disasters rocked the archipelago. Making matters worse, during the calamities

Yoshimasa was at the height of his extravagant behaviour. Hardship was widespread: one observer wrote in 1460 that he had seen a woman cradling a child at Rokujô, in the capital, while walking home. 'After calling the child's name over and over', he recalled, 'she finally ceased and began to wail. I looked closely and saw that the child was already dead.' People began asking where the woman was from. She replied that she was a refugee from Kawachi. She continued, 'The drought there has lasted for three years and the young rice plants no longer sprout ... As it is I have not been able to provide for this child and now it has come to this.' Juxtaposed to this hardship the observer witnessed another scene, one of elite extravagance. 'While still in a mood of sorrow over this experience, I came across a group of lords out viewing flowers ... They looked down haughtily on pedestrians and railed at the soldiers in front of their horses. They were in a frolicsome mood, stealing flowers, and some had drawn their swords and were singing drinking songs.'

Such was the environmental and social backdrop of the Ônin War. In 1464, Ashikaga Yoshimi (1439–91) became shogun when Yoshimasa unexpectedly stepped down. The influential Hosokawa family bolstered Yoshimi's new position. But tensions flared when Yoshimasa's wife, Tomiko, gave birth to a male heir, Yoshihisa, who had the backing of the competing Yamana family. The stage was now set for a successional bloodletting. The two families rallied massive armies by the standards of the period (about 110,000 with the Yamana and 160,000 with the Hosokawa) and, with hellish fury, descended on wooden, tinderbox Kyoto. The war between these factions lasted a devastating eleven years, with neither side celebrating a decisive victory. Kyoto was shattered and scorched during the clashes and the *bakufu* emerged mortally wounded, but still managed to limp along ineffectually for over a century.

Even as political authority decentralized and further gravitated to the domain level, however, signs of change appeared in local attitudes towards law and governance. Warring states lords drafted 'household codes' that aimed to preserve their extended families and its domain territory; they also rendered earlier, medieval laws, such as the Jôei codes (1232) issued by the Kamakura *bakufu*, obsolete. What is interesting about the Warring States 'household codes' is the slow erosion of private ethics, such as samurai principles, in favour of public law. In 1536 codes designed by Date Tanemune (1488–1565), acts of revenge were trumped by domain law, which forbade vendettas. This was 'law that overrides principles' and it served as a cornerstone of Warring States politics. Indeed, although a samurai would be tempted to seek revenge for a sword cut, for example, law forbade him from doing so. As one 'household code' read, 'It is forbidden for anyone wounded by a sword cut in a quarrel to take private measures of retaliation ...' It continued, 'Although such acts of revenge may be in keeping with the principles of a *bushi* [samurai], because they break the law [forbidding private vendettas], those guilty of such illegal acts should be punished.'

Domain law forbade samurai from building alliances outside the lord's sphere of influence because such 'leagues' were the source of disorder. Samurai demonstrated their loyalty through 'military service' and loyalty to the domain 'state'. This system lured many samurai into cohesive political spheres, but still other groups resisted *daimyô* power. One group that emerged after the Ônin conflict, and that posed a serious challenge to the *bakufu*, was the armed Buddhist sectarians.

BUDDHIST SECTARIANS

In Chapter 3, we discussed the rise of several Buddhist sects. During the twelfth and thirteenth centuries, the Pure Land, True Pure Land, and other Buddhist monasteries began re-sculpting Japan's religious and cultural landscape. They altered the military and political landscape as well. In 1532, Ikkô sectarians, members of Shinran's True Pure Land sect, instigated the 'Uprising of the Realm under Heaven' by launching a military attack against Miyoshi Motonaga in Kawachi and Settsu provinces with forces that may have ranged as high as 200,000 men. Thousands were killed. Reprisals against the Kasuga and Kôfukuji temples in Nara quickly followed. Alarmed, Hosokawa Harumoto (1519–63) enlisted the support of other armed Buddhist sectarians, the Hokke of Nichiren Buddhism, who rapidly moved against Ikkô strongholds and burned down several temples, including the Ikkô headquarters at Honganji in Yamashina province. In military spectacles called 'circular processions', Hokke sectarians rode through Kyoto's charred streets, repeating, 'all praise the marvellous law of the lotus sutra'. They descended on Ikkô sectarians marching to drums and flutes, and rode astride horses with large banners adorned with Buddhist mantras. 'Do not give, do not take' and 'Break what is bent, widen the path', served as the Hokke's guiding slogans. With the number of large Nichiren Buddhist temples in Kyoto, which with moats and watchtowers more resembled stockades than sites of devotion, the Hokke spectacle resonated with Kyoto's population.

The urban justice hammered out by Hokke sectarians illustrates the degree to which vigilantism had replaced Ashikaga law and order. One diarist wrote in 1533, 'I hear that members of the Nichiren sect have apprehended several arsonists. Because there was no formal assembly of the community [to decide their fate] . . . [t]hey brought forward the three arsonists and immediately executed them.' The same diarist observed, 'In order to enforce judgment and apprehend the two foot soldiers who had pillaged the fields of Shôgôin and eastern Kawara, about 5,000 people of northern Kyoto set out for an attack. They apprehended both men, I hear, and put them to death.' Another writer summarized the pervasiveness of Hokke influence when he wrote, 'The Hokke sectarians have taken power in Kyoto. The government of Kyoto and its environs, which underlies the control of the shogun and the [Deputy Shogun], is entirely an affair of the Hokke sectarians.' Militant religious sectarians, through judicial activism, had become judge and executioner in the imperial capital. It is little wonder that, when powerful warlords unified the realm with force in the latter half of the sixteenth century, they first trained their sights on organized Buddhist sectarians.

In the absence of the *bakufu*, other affiliations arose in Kyoto. Voluntary urban associations in the form of city blocks sought to defend themselves against exploitation by samurai. Often, city blocks were named after local landmarks, shrines or temples, or places of employment. There was the Myôden temple block, the Northern Boat Bridge block, the Fan Guild, and the Leather Workers, and all sometimes fortified themselves against powerful warlords. These stable enclaves of people suggest that new, long-term forms of urban identity were solidifying in sixteenth-century

Kyoto. In time, the *bakufu* even recognize the quasi-authority of these block associations, granting them leave to 'terminate the havoc' should troop encampments in the city become too rowdy.

The capital became a city of contradictions. While Buddhist sectarians throttled each other, city blocks set up barricades, and samurai troops fought sporadically, an uncomfortable new normalcy pervaded Kyoto. In 1506, one courtier observed an official wooden placard explaining that 'theft', 'arson', and 'quarrels' were 'forbidden', as were 'sumô wrestling' and 'dancing'. This was, he thought to himself, just as it 'should be'. Another diarist noted that 'discharging arrows' was forbidden, along with 'pleasure boating' and 'excursions with lanterns'. In the milieu of endemic war and lawlessness, whimsical authority replaced genuine political and social order. The capital struggled to control what few vestiges of social order it could. These were the tangled shreds of order in a city that had been ravaged by decades of fighting. As one traveller noted in 1526, 'Now looking over Kyoto, at the homes of high and low alike, I saw but one building where once there had been ten. The dwellings of the common people are given over to farming. The palace is a tangle of summer grasses. It is too much for words.' It might have been too much for words, but it was not too much to discourage 'pleasure boating' and 'dancing'.

Actually, dancing was dangerous in Kyoto. In 1520, a diarist observed that dancing occurred 'every night this year' and he wondered if it was 'because the realm appears peaceful' or because it has entered a period of 'new commotion'. The spectacle of such nocturnal dancing, when hundreds of people took to the streets to dance, signalled both 'peace' and 'new commotion'. The dancing appeared uncontrolled and the participants, as one diarist noted in 1532, were 'gripped by lunacy'. The dancing became a playful reflection of the politics of disorder; it parodied social and political structure, with status, class, and gender-bending elements. Kyoto had become ground zero of Warring States mayhem, with armed city blocks, militarized Buddhist sectarians, roaming squadrons of samurai toughs, and night-time dancing that parodied the political and social order. In the sixteenth century, Japan appeared on the brink, at least in the imperial capital, of careening into complete social chaos.

WAR AND MEDICAL SCIENCE

In previous chapters, our discussion of disease, public health, and science in Japan mainly explored the introduction of infectious diseases to the archipelago and their demographic, political, and social impacts. With outbreaks of epidemic disease, the bacteriological microcosm intersected with the macrocosm in which Japanese lived, forever altering, at a cellular level, the evolutionary path of the country. Japanese exposure to measles and smallpox in earlier periods spared them the sort of biological holocaust that occurred when Spanish conquistadors set foot on the 'virgin soil' of the New World, infecting and decimating such indigenous populations as the Tainos. On an immunological level, the Japanese, at least south of Hokkaido, found themselves squarely in the infectious disease communities that led to the ascendancy of Western Europe.

Through the international portal of Dazaifu, Buddhist monks and other travellers from the continent also introduced Japanese to the intricacies of early East Asian medicine. In the late twelfth century, Myôan Eisai (1141–1215) made two trips to China, where he studied Zen Buddhism and brought the teachings back to Japan. In his *Kissa yôjôki* (On drinking tea as a means to long life) he offered new information about green tea and its nourishing qualities. In the text, he also listed medical concoctions for treating diabetes, palsy, and other diseases. The monk Enni Ben'en (1202–80), who also travelled to the continent, established a medical library at the Tôfukuji temple in Kyoto, comprising both Japanese and Song dynasty works on pulse, acupuncture, pharmacology, and other topics. Tôfukuji was located in a rather run-down part of Kyoto, and the temple probably practised charitable medicine in the community. Other Buddhist sects, such as the Ritsu Precept, under the guidance of its founder Eison, also practised charitable, community medicine, focusing on the health conditions of such outcaste groups as 'riverbank people' and 'non-persons'. In Kamakura, the Gokurakuji temple became a public welfare centre for treating the underfed, poorly clothed, socially shunned, disease-ridden (often leprous), and demographically expanding 'non-human' outcaste populations of the Kamakura *bakufu*'s capital.

The most important Japanese medical text written before the thirteenth century is the *Ishinpô* (Formulas from the heart of medicine, 984), written by Tanba Yasuyori. But also important are Fukane Sukehito's (898–922) *Honzô wamyô* (Japanese names in natural studies, 922) and Minamoto no Shitagau's (911–83) *Wamyôrui shûshô* (A collection of Japanese names, 931–7), which represent taxonomical catalogues of natural objects, many of them part of Japan's rapidly expanding pharmacopeia. Chinese learning overwhelmingly influenced the texts, rather than empirical observation, but they do reflect an attempt by medieval Japanese to assert some order over their natural world. Obstetrics remained a principal concern of medieval Japanese medical texts. 'Sometimes the foetus is dead but the mother is still alive; sometimes two lives are joined as one', wrote Buddhist physician Kajiwara Shôzan. In many instances, he pondered, there were 'no proscribed medicines' when treating pregnant women. He urged physicians to combine old methods with the newly imported Song Chinese techniques to remedy such problems.

Throughout the medieval period, a steady stream of medical texts, medicines, tools, and techniques travelled to Japan via what one historian has called a 'silk road of pharmaceuticals and formulas'. One main concern was synchronizing Chinese and Japanese names, weights, and measurements, which proved critical in creating the various medical treatments imported from China and Korea. This was one of the principal concerns of the *Honzô wamyô*, for example. In the treatment of newly identified disorders, medical texts listed ingredients of Western origins, such as nutmeg, as powerful new weapons in the medical arsenal. In the medieval years, Japan had become part of a global exchange of medical knowledge. Some ingredients, such as nutmeg, were of Islamic origin; other explanations, such as the karmic origins of disease, were Indian and Chinese in origin.

In the midst of the fourteenth century, as warfare began to rip the Ashikaga *bakufu* asunder, 'wound medicine' became an important part of Japanese medical culture. The first two Japanese works on wound medicine – the *Kinsô ryôjishô* (On healing incised wounds) and *Kihô* (Demon formulas) – are from the fourteenth century. As vicious warfare replaced the epoch campaigns of previous times, close-action combat with swords replaced bows and arrows. Campaigns had once had a seasonal flavour, while the warfare of the fourteenth century was an all-season affair. The fourteenth-century *Taiheiki* (Chronicle of medieval Japan) vividly depicts situations where 'autumn frost ripped their flesh and dawn ice stuck to their skin'. The index of the *Kinsô ryôjishô* includes such topics as 'Putting back in viscera that have come out', 'Insects appearing in a wound', and 'Brains protruding from a wound in the head', illustrating the grisly side of the Warring States period. The authors of such texts accumulated knowledge through experience, through conversations with other physicians regarding their 'secrets', and through consulting Song Chinese texts. Unfortunately, historians are left to speculate how the exposure to maimed and opened bodies might have advanced the understanding of human anatomy and physiology.

THE COUNTRYSIDE

Despite the endemic lawlessness that spilled over into the country-side, Japan's farmlands had entered a period of agricultural intensi-fication. Many of the epidemic diseases of earlier centuries had settled into endemic patterns, with mortality and morbidity largely confined to children. As children were exposed to periodic infections, some lived and developed immunities, others did not and died, but even the dead contributed to the slow establishment of a new, hereditary immunological order in Japan that would prepare it for the arrival of Europeans and their infections in the sixteenth century. The severe famines of the thirteenth century, discussed in the previous chapter, also lessened in intensity. With increasing agricultural surpluses, born of the cultivation of more land and the deployment of better farming technologies, Japan's medieval population grew from about 7 million people in 1200 to about 12 million in 1600, at the close of the medieval period.

Several factors drove the intensification of agriculture, one being the *kandaka* system. *Kandaka* referred to the monetary equivalent of agricultural production, including other resources and services that vassals extracted from their holdings. Surveyors assessed the yield in coins, unlike the later Tokugawa *kokudaka* system that assessed yields in bushels of rice. Moreover, surveyors assessed the *kandaka* equivalent at the village level, rather than at the level of the individual proprietor; they also levied the assessment based on all arable, rather than cultivated, land. In other words, because villages paid 'annual tax' based on arable land, the system incentivized the cultivation of more land. Indeed, peasants might as well put the land to work because they were going to pay taxes on its estimated yield anyway. Warring states *daimyô* were always on the hunt for fresh sources of revenue, due to the high cost of the military build-up and vassal stipends. After 1300, new villages and agricultural fields sprouted in places that had once been characterized as feral or wild lands.

These villages cultivated new lands and rallied around local leaders to create village clusters and protect themselves against bandits, or to build religious communities. Surplus increased with better and more regular tillage with iron tools, improved irrigation, and better fertilizers; and diversified crops allowed village clustering and the establishment of even larger communities. Some agricultural adjustments proved quite simple: field levelling, which allowed an equal distribution of water over the entire crop, proved straightforward. Other advancements were more complicated: elaborate riparian projects that transported irrigation water to rice paddies, for example. Farmers deployed elaborate water wheels, dug holding ponds, and channelled irrigation water through sluice gates and dikes. Double cropping also increased yields and surpluses. One historian estimates that by 1550 farmers double cropped a quarter of the paddies in central and western Japan. In 1420, a Korean envoy observed double cropping in the Hyôgo area. He wrote, 'In the beginning of the fall they cut their rice ... and plant buckwheat, which they cut in early winter. They can plant seeds three times in one year on one paddy field.' With the intensification of agriculture, village clusters became meaningful defences against the ravages of the Warring States period. Some villages even engineered moats that served to define community boundaries.

Agricultural intensification extended both 'downward' and 'upward', a reference by one historian to the ripple effect these changes had on the trophic food web. 'Downward' refers to the impact that agricultural expansion had on non-human biological communities of fauna and flora. Creating more farmland meant clearing more forests, particularly in the alluvial flatlands and less-fertile terrace areas. Crafting villages, homes, and new agricultural technologies meant harvesting more timber. Fertilizer requirements meant gathering grasses and forest leaves and twigs. Villagers required firewood fuel for cooking, metallurgy, and kilns, and timber for riparian works and bridges. Increasing use of slash-and-burn agriculture placed even more pressure on the wooded areas around village clusters, leading to fires, soil exhaustion, and erosion. Unlike the later Edo *bakufu*, the Ashikaga *bakufu* appears to have paid changing conditions in Japan's woodlands little to no attention. Most control over forests was distributed locally, with village clusters often staking claims to nearby woodlands. In 1448, Imabori village, in Ōmi province, tried tackling the problem of deteriorating forest health by prohibiting cutting trees without authorization. The village redoubled its efforts in 1502.

Woodlands suffered the ecological footprint of Japan's endemic fighting. Hardwood charcoal proved essential for making armour, swords, lances, and other metal weapons. As housing improved, the desire for charcoal over firewood (which produced dangerous sparks) led to the harvest of more hardwoods for charcoal. In the thirteenth century, the Kamakura *bakufu* frequently complained of high charcoal and firewood prices. Monument building also required timber. During the Genpei War battles of 1180, Nara's Tōdaiji burned and large trees were required to rebuild the temple. Having 'Tōdaiji' stamped on trees before loggers harvested them identified stands in western Honshu for the reconstruction project. In 1219, documents record that the 'centre of Kamakura was destroyed by fire', which required more timber. In sum, Japan's expanding agriculture, monument and city construction and main-tenance, endemic lawlessness and warfare, and emergence of village clusters placed increasing pressure on Japan's woodlands.

The 'upward' influence of agricultural intensification assumed the form of economic commercialization as resources moved up through the human community. Throughout the Warring States period, *daimyō* traded with other regions throughout Japan. Inland *daimyō* sought marine goods from coastal areas and domains suffering poor harvests sought to import rice. *Daimyō* granted merchant 'guilds' special privileges and a handful even acquired posts as 'official merchants'. Import restrictions, a medieval version of trade tariffs, protected some domestic industries and, therefore, the domain's tax base. As a general rule, goods flowed throughout the country relatively unrestricted because most *daimyô* sought to benefit from robust commercial activity within their domain.

ASHIKAGA FOREIGN RELATIONS

The absence of a strong political centre confused Japanese relations with the continent during the medieval period. Prince Kaneyoshi, son of Go-Daigo and representative of the Southern Court, oversaw relations with China. In 1370, when Ming envoys arrived in Japan demanding subjugation to the Middle Kingdom, Prince Kaneyoshi referred to himself as a 'subject' within the Ming diplomatic order. One year later he sent his vassal to the Ming court to offer tribute, according to the protocol of the Chinese tributary order. The realm of the Chinese international order, or *tianxia*, included all countries unified by the virtuous Chinese rulers, the 'son of heaven'. The Ming court expected tribute from the 'four barbarian regions', which, in the Chinese mind, included Japan. The Ming court granted rulers of countries that presented tribute the title of 'king', which seemed demeaning to the emperors and shoguns of Japan's medieval world.

The Southern Court proceeded to dispatch envoys to the Ming 'son of heaven' on at least seven occasions in the 1370s and 1380s. Most of these the Chinese turned back, either because they desired to see the true ruler of Japan or because of diplomatic tensions caused by pirates. Indeed, the pirate problem became so pronounced that the Ming court referred to the 'king of Japan' as a 'pirate'. Tensions always existed between Japan and China within the context of the tributary system because Japan refused to play a subordinate role to the Chinese in geopolitical diplomacy. Only twice did Japanese rulers briefly enter the Chinese tributary system: as the Wa realm in the sixth century and under Shogun Ashikaga Yoshimitsu in 1401. We have already examined the importance of the first instance, but the second instance requires some explanation because it shaped early modern Japan's diplomatic posture in Asia.

On two occasions, 1374 and 1380, Shogun Yoshimitsu dispatched envoys to the Ming court. Two decades later, in 1401, the Ming court finally agreed to meet with the Japanese envoy. Yoshimitsu had sent tribute and returned Chinese sailors captured by pirates. A Ming envoy returned with the envoy to Japan and addressed Yoshimitsu as 'you, King of Japan'. When envoys returned to the Ming court in 1403 Yoshimitsu addressed the Ming 'son of heaven' by offering himself as 'King of Japan, Your Subject', emphasizing his subordinate place within China's tributary order. Importantly, the Ming court advised Yoshimitsu that Japan was to adopt the Chinese calendar, putting the island country within the rhythms of Chinese dynastic rule. Shogun Yoshimitsu's motivations related to regularizing trade with China through the 'tally' system: Japan received tallies for entering and exiting the Middle Kingdom. When Ashikaga Yoshimochi (1386–1428) became shogun, however, he discontinued the tally trade with China.

Certain cities, such as Sakai, rose to great prominence through the tally trade with China. Sakai merchants who handled the official China trade for the *bakufu* forged powerful relations with samurai in Kyoto and elsewhere. They handled the business side of the tally trade, outfitting ships and cataloguing merchandise headed to the Middle Kingdom. They manned municipal boards in Sakai, creating the impression that Sakai was under bourgeois rule. The economic opportunity engendered by the Ming tally trade allowed merchants to govern Sakai with a surprising degree of autonomy, making it resemble such European cities as Venice or Genoa.

MUROMACHI CULTURE

Writers such as Kitabatake Chikafusa (1293–1354), in his *Jinnô shôtôki* (A chronicle of gods and sovereigns, 1339), famously trumpeted: 'Great Japan is a divine land. The heavenly progenitor founded it, and the sun goddess bequeathed it to her descendants to rule eternally. Only in our country is this true; there are no similar examples in other countries. This is why our country is called the divine land.' Kitabatake's musings on Japan's divine origins and exceptional qualities stand as potent examples of proto-nationalism, underpinned by myths that persisted into the twentieth century and

7 The Ginkakuji (1490), a Zen temple illustrative of the austere
Muromachi aesthetic of the late medieval period. Kyoto, Japan.

provided justification for Japanese empire. In the medieval years,
Kitabatake was part of a growing consensus about certain distinct
Japanese characteristics, one that distinguished the country from its
East Asian neighbours. Japan was different from China and else-
where, submitted Kitabatake, because the 'heavenly progenitor

founded it', a myth that both Meiji reformers and early twentieth-century militarists would draw on extensively.

Within this distinctive Japanese discourse, a new aesthetic also emerged, called the Muromachi culture, characterized by delicate sensibilities, tea ceremonies and Nô drama, Zen Buddhist austerity, and a nearly maniacal adherence to aesthetic simplicity. The term that best captures the nature of the Muromachi culture is the Nô drama vocabulary *yûgen*, a term which evokes something deep, mysterious, unfathomable, and distant. Muromachi culture was a world of meticulously raked white sands surrounding carefully placed stones in gardens, painstaking representations of an orderly cosmos, as well as rustic ink-brush landscape paintings and wooden sculptures. Wooden architectural achievements such as the Kinkakuji (Golden Pavilion) and the Ginkakuji (Silver Pavilion, Figure 7) were products of the fourteenth and fifteenth centuries, and evoke strong Zen Buddhist sensibilities. While rival samurai factions and armed monks tore the country asunder during the Warring States period, artists refashioned their natural world into some of Japan's most lasting contributions to global art.

CONCLUSION

With the decline of the Ashikaga *bakufu*, the Warring States period witnessed a virtual evaporation of central authority in Japan. But it also witnessed the birth of many of the political, social, intellectual, and environmental conditions that would thrust Japan into the early modern period. The wars and rivalries of the fifteenth and sixteenth centuries elevated the domain as the locus of political identity, a situation that persisted, to greater and lesser degrees, until the middle of the nineteenth century. *Daimyô* became the most powerful political figures in Japan, men whose 'household codes' served as early versions of public law. Likewise, Buddhist sectarians flexed their muscles repeatedly during the fifteenth century, and in doing so attracted the ire of unifiers who targeted them as they killed one competitor after another.

Japan also became part of a global exchange of medical knowledge, advancing a cosmopolitan science. As we shall see, with the arrival of Europeans, Japan's cosmopolitan science became even more sophisticated with the importation of many pre- and post-Enlightenment philosophies and practices. Alongside such cosmopolitanism, Japanese intellectuals began a process of defining Japan's distinctive qualities, one couched in the country's divine origins. Finally, Japan also witnessed the birth of the Muromachi aesthetic, which drew from continental and indigenous forms to create a ruthlessly simple beauty that captures the fluid rawness of Japan's medieval years.

5

Japan's Encounter with Europe, 1543–1640

In the late fifteenth century, a handful of small European states began to refashion the world. Prior to that time, most of the world's wealth had been located in Asia, the Middle East, and the Indian subcontinent, where traditional trade networks in luxury items, from spices to slaves, enriched the sultans and emperors of the grand Asiatic empires. With two striking maritime voyages, however, Europe entered the age of discovery and, eventually, the age of colonialism. These voyages explain how Europeans ascended to a position of global domination through command of resources such as silver and sugar, and exchange of such micro-organisms as the smallpox virus. Between the fifteenth and the nineteenth centuries, once-great empires and civilizations crumbled under the pressure of Eurasian microbes, military technologies, colonial rule, and economic rapaciousness. The early modern age witnessed the dispersal of European culture and institutions globally, including to the shores of Japan. Japan survived Europe's age of discovery, however, and did so completely intact, at least compared to the New World, India, and China, for reasons that will be described in this chapter. Importantly, Japan's initial encounter with Europe in the sixteenth century contributed to its relative successes against later Western imperialism in the nineteenth.

ECOLOGIES OF EMPIRE

Two maritime breakthroughs set the stage for European ascendancy. The first occurred when, famously, Christopher Columbus

(1451–1506) set out in 1492 on a voyage of discovery to Asia, which resulted, unbeknownst to him (he continued to insist he was in Asia), in the colonization of the Americas and decimation of the Amerindians. The second voyage of great consequence occurred when the Portuguese explorer Vasco da Gama (1460–1524) departed Lisbon in 1497 and sailed around the Cape of Good Hope into the Indian Ocean. Da Gama sailed with monsoons and arrived at Kozhikode (Calicut) in May 1498. When he set out for home, he sailed against onshore monsoons, and what had taken twenty-three days on the outbound journey took 132 days on the return, and it exacted a heavy toll on his fleet. Half the crew died of scurvy. Nonetheless, in 1499 he returned to Lisbon, having opened up a lucrative spice trade with the Middle East and the Indian subcontinent. In effect these two voyages, once they tapped into pre-existing trade networks, birthed the early modern world, with its increasingly interdependent channels of commerce, forms of political power, technologies, ecologies, and ideas. It also brought Europeans one step closer to Japan.

Traditionally, historians assert that Europe's ascendancy resulted from a unique amalgam of historical developments, such as competition among small European states, the Enlightenment, the Protestant work ethic, the scientific revolution with its technological breakthroughs, or the birth of capitalism. Revisionists now claim that it was good geographic fortune. But the rapid injection of silver and sugar, cultivated in the New World, into the veins of Europe's economies and bodies also explains how Europe transformed from a global backwater into a collection of states that competed for world supremacy. The process was as biological as it was military, political, or economic because particular micro-organisms that had evolved with Eurasians since the advent of agriculture aided them in their endeavours, as did tenacious weeds, calorie-rich agricultural crops, and the meaty livestock they brought with them on their wooden carracks. With livestock domestication, micro-organisms such as smallpox had jumped between cattle and humans and, over the centuries, these once-zoonotic diseases became specific to humans. Throughout Eurasia, these diseases persisted in the human population with mortality occurring mostly in children. Children who survived the micro-organism's assault developed immunities that usually served them for the rest of their lives. As we have seen, smallpox had been introduced to Japan centuries earlier, so unlike the Amerindians, Japanese had already undergone the brutal immunological initiation into Eurasia's disease pools. The Japanese had also produced sugar since the Nara period (710–94 CE), likely Chinese molasses, when the technology was transferred from the Tang dynasty (618–907). Later, sugarcane cultivation was established when Shogun Tokugawa Yoshimune (1684–1751) imported it from the Ryukyu Islands and planted it at Edo castle. Matsudaira Yoritaka (1810–86) later encouraged its cultivation in Takamatsu domain, so Japanese bodies gained this important caloric advantage. Undeniably, the fact that smallpox was endemic, and that Japanese had plenty of calories, served as important factors in the island country's ability to withstand the initial brunt of Europe's age of discovery. As did the fact that Japan's Warring States domains were relatively well organized, politically sophisticated, and armed to the teeth.

In the sixteenth and seventeenth centuries, just under a million Spanish migrated to the New World. In what is now called the 'Columbian exchange', each Spanish ship that travelled from Seville carried not just human passengers, but a biological package that aided European domination. As Spaniards returned from Havana or elsewhere, they carried with them a similar hotchpotch of plants and animals, though the micro-organisms exchanged, with the exception of syphilis, proved far less devastating. The maize and potatoes that travelled with Europeans around the world became globally important crops from the Yangzi Highlands to sub-Saharan Africa. When the Spanish arrived in 1492, Amerindian populations probably stood at somewhere around 54 million people. By the seventeenth century, and some seventeen recorded epidemics later, they stood at a tenth of their former population, probably somewhere between 5 and 6 million. Smallpox and other diseases explain why Amerindian populations crashed so precipitously. When Taino populations of Hispaniola began dying of smallpox, local friars wrote, 'It has pleased Our Lord to bestow a pestilence, of small pox among the said Indians, and that it does not cease. From it have died and continued to die to the present almost a third of the said Indians.' Such plagues evidenced God's preference for the Spanish. With such mortality rates, Amerindians were easily killed, conquered, or impressed into sugar plantations to serve their new masters. Columbus had brought sugarcane to Hispaniola from the Canary Islands on his second voyage in 1493, and the Old World crop thrived in parts of the New. Sugar proved an important source of caloric energy to fuel European conquest.

Silver soon became the main Spanish export. Between 1561 and 1580, historians estimate that approximately 85 per cent of the world's silver came from such New World mines as Potosí, where seven out of every ten Amerindian workers perished. Ultimately, as part of the early modern global economy, this silver largely ended up in Chinese coffers. This was the result of Ming dynastic (1368–1644) monetary and tax policies that will be discussed later. The benefits of conquest to European bodies and economies cannot be overstated; and the promise of riches, bolstered by the divine legitimacy of proselytizing to 'pagans', ultimately brought the Portuguese, Spanish, Dutch, and other European countries to the shores of Japan.

By 1542, the Portuguese captain Francisco Zeimoto had landed on the small southern Japanese island of Tanegashima. Because they came from the south and arrived in southern Japan, Japanese called the Portuguese *Nanbanjin*, or 'Southern Barbarians'. Influenced by the Chinese tributary order, Japan envisioned a world where barbarians inhabited the four cardinal directions; the Japanese, according to this taxonomy of 'barbarians', were among the precious few humans. In Hokkaido (called Ezo at this juncture), for example, the southern tip of the island, where Japanese lived, was sometimes called Ningenchi, or 'Human Land', while the Ainu lived in Ezochi, or 'Barbarian Land'.

Because Japanese proved adept in dealing with their European first encounter, it is worth placing the Portuguese arrival in Japan in some comparative perspective. The experience with Brazil is instructive. In the sixteenth century, at the same time the Portuguese arrived in Japan, the Portuguese monarchy was in the process of settling the Atlantic coast of Brazil. For the colonial project to work, however, the subtropical and tropical forests needed to be emptied of the Tupis people who called them home. In 1500, historians estimate that about 1 million Tupis occupied the region from Natal in Rio Grande do Norte in the north to São Vincente and São Paulo in the south. What made the Tupis different from other Amerindians, and similar to the Japanese that Portuguese encountered in the sixteenth century, was that they were a 'very brave people who esteem death lightly' and were 'daring in war'. Tupi warriors wielded giant sword-clubs, pieces of hardwood with sharp edges, and they were expert archers. What made Tupi warriors even more grisly than the Warring States samurai, at least to the eyes of Europeans, was that they sometimes ate their victims, often with great public hoopla. Despite such formidable adversaries, the Portuguese sought to colonize coastal Brazil and, by the mid-sixteenth century, epidemic diseases such as smallpox had enlisted to aid them.

In the 1530s, the Portuguese monarchy dispatched a fleet of four ships to Brazil carrying colonizers, as well as their biological entourage of seeds, domestic animals, and plants. Then in 1549, only six years after Francisco Zeimoto arrived at Tanegashima, the Portuguese monarch dispatched his viceroy Tome de Sousa (1503–79) with 1,000 settlers, and the commensurate biological retinue of cattle, pigs, birds, seeds, weeds, and diseases. The Tupis had tolerated the early Portuguese and had even cut and hauled brazilwood for trade, but when Portuguese started enslaving Indians to work on plantations they understandably resisted. The Portuguese responded violently, undertaking military sorties that involved 'burning and destroying' villages inhabited by Tupis. By the end of the final campaigns, 'no Tupinikin remained alive'. With the Tupi mostly subdued or eradicated, Portuguese and their African slaves continued colonizing Brazil throughout the sixteenth and seventeenth centuries, until the colonial population reached about 300,000, of which about 100,000 were white Europeans. The colonists harvested brazilwood, laboured at sugar and tobacco plantations, raised cattle, and, after 1695, mined for gold. In 1819, on the eve of Brazilian independence, the population of the country was 4.4 million people, 800,000 of them being unassimilated Indians. Brazil had been transformed into a European ecology, with people, plantations, cattle ranches, gold mines, and other lithographical and biological signatures of the European order.

European colonial politics in Japan proved markedly different. Japan never became a European colony or adopted European ecology. Of course, the Japanese were no less warlike than the Tupis. As a Portuguese missionary observed, 'The Japanese are much braver and more warlike' than other peoples of Asia. They were far better politically organized as well, with powerful Warring States domains in the south where the Portuguese first arrived. The Portuguese had been intrigued by rumours of potential riches in Japan, but lamented that, 'Only the king still works' the gold mines. This was particularly lamentable because 'there are mines everywhere and the metal is of high quality'. But subduing the Japanese by a means that echoed Brazil ultimately proved impossible: the indigenous East Asian ecology of Japan was ensconced and staunchly defended by its human cultivators. The one agent that had most assisted Europeans with the conquest of the New World – disease, particularly the smallpox virus – was already endemic to Japan. Not able to rely on 'Our Lord to bestow a pestilence', the Portuguese instead relied on their Lord in other ways, and pursued conversion of Japanese to Catholicism.

THE CHRISTIAN STORY

The *Krishitan monogatari* (Tale of the Christians, 1639) explains that, when Japanese first set eyes on them, the Portuguese appeared strikingly barbaric. From the Southern Barbarian ship, 'emerged an unnameable creature, somewhat similar in shape to a human being, but looking rather more like a long-nosed goblin … What he said could not be understood at all: his voice was like the screech of an owl.' Portuguese fit squarely into the barbarian taxonomies that Japanese imagined characterized the world beyond their horizons. Every corner of this outside world was filled with fantastic creatures, many of them humanlike, but some far more fantastic than others. In eighteenth-century Japanese encyclopaedias, the reader encounters a world inhabited by Cyclops people, three-armed people, and people with no abdomens, just to name a few, all part of the exotic hominid varieties that inhabited Earth. But also included were other, less fanciful peoples, such as the Ryukyu Islanders, the Ainu of Hokkaido, and Koreans. At this date, in the

Japanese imagination, the potential to encounter screeching goblins on the shores of Japan was quite possible, although no doubt unsettling.

The Portuguese were not goblins, however. They were mostly missionaries and they saw great promise in Japanese they encountered. 'Judging by the people we have so far met', wrote missionary Francis Xavier (1506–52), 'I would say that the Japanese are the best race yet discovered and I do not think you will find their match among the pagan nations.' The Japanese divided the world among humans and barbarians, but the vocabulary of choice for Europeans, influenced as they were by Christianity, was to describe non-Europeans as 'pagans'. Despite the promising circumstances, Xavier's missionary effort ran aground immediately. It started with his Japanese assistant, Yajirô, whom he baptized in 1548 with the name Paulo de Santa Fe. When Xavier asked Yajirô, who was no theologian, to translate the 'Almighty' into Japanese, Yajirô understandably came up with Dainichi (the Japanese version of the Vairocana Buddha), drawing on such Buddhist traditions as Shingon. In essence, Xavier spent his first years introducing jaded Japanese to Dainichi, an all-powerful Buddhist figure they already knew well. When Xavier later phonetically translated Deus as 'Deusu', Buddhist monks mocked the new religion by likening Deusu to '*dai uso*', which means 'great lie'. Despite these humorous setbacks, Xavier made some gains among the pagan Japanese. He converted 150 souls in Satsuma, 100 in Hirado, and 500 in Yamaguchi. Xavier later blamed his overall lack of success in Japan on the 'four sins' of the Japanese: denial of the true God, sodomy, abortion, and infanticide.

But troubles far more menacing than sodomy threatened Japan. The first missionaries witnessed a Japan in the midst of political meltdown – the Warring States period (1467–1590). It was probably inevitable that Portuguese and other Europeans embroiled themselves in the violent intrigues of Warring States politics. Missionary João Rodrigues commented on the political upheaval. He observed that, 'The whole kingdom was full of robbers and highwaymen, and on the seas there were innumerable pirates who continually plundered not only Japan but also the coast of China.' He continued that, 'Men chastised and killed each other, banished people and confiscated their goods as they saw fit, in such fashion that treachery was rampant and nobody trusted his neighbour.' Rodrigues also wrote that, 'Order decays here for everyone acts according to the present moment and speaks according to circumstances and occasion.' It was a tough time to be in Japan, a well-armed country run by entrepreneurial samurai subservient to none, other than themselves.

The Iberian missionaries pressed on, however. In 1570, Padre Francisco Cabral (1529–1609) became head of the Jesuit Society of Jesus, maintaining that the Portuguese should run the Society because Japanese could not be trusted. Created in 1540, the Society brimmed with the missionary enthusiasm inherent in the Counter-Reformation that followed the Council of Trent (1545–63). Cabral remarked, 'If one does not cease and desist admitting Japanese into the Society... that will be the reason for the collapse of the Society, Nay! Of Christianity in Japan.' He explained that, 'I have seen no other nation as conceited, covetous, inconstant, and insincere as the Japanese.' Under Cabral, the mission made few positive gains in Japan, largely because of his refusal to admit Japanese to the Society.

Padre Alexandro Valignano (1539–1606), the Society's next head, experienced greater success after landing in Japan in 1579. He believed that the Society needed to assimilate to Japanese life if it was to be successful. 'Like Children', he wrote, '[the missionaries would have to] learn again'. An interesting example of this cultural encounter related to Europeans, their eating habits, and the biological package they travelled with, particularly pigs and cattle. One can only imagine the hungry padres sitting around the dinner table, beef bones strewn near their plates and tallow lodged in their thick beards, as they lectured polite Japanese on the glory of Christ. Japanese, who ate comparatively little meat at the time, and had even less animal husbandry, must have been appalled and, in a spiritual sense, not enticed by the padres. Seeing this, Valignano ordered that no 'pigs, goats, or cows could be kept at residences, nor could animal hides be cured or sold, because such practices were viewed as filthy and abominable in the eyes of the Japanese'. In such areas as Nagasaki, which already had a cosmopolitan feel because of the Chinese presence, animal flesh 'may at times be eaten in our residences; provided that they accord with Japanese usage'. He stressed that it is important that 'scraps and bones are not let to fall upon the table; and that there be no such large slices as might appear grotesque to the Japanese'. With such efforts, by 1590 missionaries had converted some 130,000 Japanese.

Powerful *daimyô* were among the first converted by the missionaries, and herein lies some of Christianity's early troubles. Ômura Sumitada (1533–87) is one such lord. He was baptized in 1563 and, because of his maritime location in western Kyushu, capitalized on trade with the Portuguese in 1565. It was not long before the terminal point of the Great Ship, which sailed from Macao, became Nagasaki and the city emerged as a European settlement. Ômura's friendship with the Portuguese paid off when in 1574 they came to his aid against his rival, samurai lord Saigô Sumitaka. Six years later, Ômura offered the Portuguese administrative authority over Nagasaki, which assured the lucrative Great Ship hailed in Ômura's domain and provided the Portuguese with a base of operations. Once in Nagasaki, Society members openly spoke of fortifying the city, accumulating weapons for its defence, and colonizing it. Unsurprisingly, the threat of Portuguese incursions into the divine land offended the sensibilities of one of Japan's emerging great unifiers, Toyotomi Hideyoshi (1536–98). Initially, he was amicable toward the new religion. 'I am pleased by everything this law of yours preaches and I feel no other obstacle to becoming a Christian than its prohibition against keeping many wives', he admitted to the padres. 'If you stretched a point for me there', he cajoled them, 'I would turn Christian myself'. But the status of Nagasaki became intertwined with other concerns regarding the Europeans, specifically the nature of economic relations with China and the silver trade.

JAPAN AND THE GLOBAL SILVER TRADE

The arrival of the Portuguese did more than simply alter Japan's spiritual landscape. It had important environmental and scientific outcomes as well. As we have seen, in the New World the Portuguese and other Europeans had developed giant silver mines as part of their colonial projects. Amerindians laboured as slaves in these mines, injecting huge amounts of silver into the veins of the early modern world economy. Warring States lords in Japan, sensing the potential profits from silver, developed these resources for themselves. Interestingly, this became a familiar pattern in Japan's indirect experience of colonization. Until the US occupation (1945–52), Westerners never put military boots on Japan's soil, but the Japanese, persuaded by Western ways, initiated changes on their own. With the arrival of Europeans, Japanese immediately discovered that silver was what made the early modern world go round, and warlords were eager to fund Japan's endemic wars through trading silver with China. The Portuguese, along with a motley crew of other maritime riff-raff, served as middlemen in this sixteenth-century silver connection.

In the early sixteenth century, entrepreneurial Warring States lords opened up several important mine sites. It was not only more mines that increased Japan's gold and silver output, but better cupellation smelting technologies allowed more silver to be extracted and exported to China. The numbers are striking: gold and silver production in Japan in the century after the arrival of the Portuguese was not surpassed until the late nineteenth century, when far better mining technologies were available in the global marketplace. Essentially, the silver and gold trade between China and Japan depended on the exchange ratios of the two metals. Because silver remained about seven to ten times more expensive than gold in China, Japanese exported silver – and China craved silver. During the Ming dynasty, silver had started replacing paper currencies and the Single Whip Reform tax policies of 1581 meant that taxes could no longer be paid in kind, but rather were paid in silver. As a consequence, nearly all Ming revenues were collected in silver of one form or another. Ironically, just as Ming officials began these reforms, output from silver mines in China began declining. Consequently, New World mines picked up the slack, with Dutch arms merchants and English and Italian financiers gainfully serving as middlemen. It is believed that approximately three-quarters of New World silver found its way to China. So did most of Japan's silver.

Making trade matters complicated, from 1371, the only official link between Ming China and Japan had been the tally trade, meaning that only official Japanese emissaries could conduct trade within the context of China's tributary system. However, the chaos of the Ônin War had destroyed the last vestiges of official relations with China, and the last Warring States tribute mission visited Ming authorities at Ningbo in 1549. Shortly thereafter, an illicit trade flourished between Japan and China, with such Chinese pirates as the swashbuckling Wang Zhi becoming rich by smuggling silver and gold between Japan and the Malay Peninsula until his execution in 1557. Because of Ming trade policies, the Portuguese, after their arrival at Tanegashima, quickly became involved in the silver trade with China. Portuguese carracks transported silver, weapons, sulphur, and other merchandise to China, in exchange for silks, saltpetre, porcelain, and mercury. After 1550, usually only one carrack made the journey annually, but controlling the port of call for the so-called 'Great Ship' became paramount to southern Warring States lords.

As we have seen, Nagasaki, formerly a small village under the control of the son-in-law of Ômura Sumitada, had become the port of call for Portuguese carracks by 1571. By 1580, Nagasaki was in the hands of the Portuguese. Quickly, the city became embroiled in competition between southern Warring States lords and, because of this, affairs in Nagasaki caught the attention of Toyotomi Hideyoshi (1536–98) in 1588. He confiscated the port town and placed it under control of his lieutenants. Hideyoshi had become interested in the Great Ship, but he had also come to believe that the newly imported religion was offending Buddhist and indigenous Shinto deities. In a sense, the missionaries represented a national threat, given the strong connections between Japan and its deities. After meeting with Gaspar Coelho in 1587, Hideyoshi issued the first expulsion edict. He wrote that, because of missionary activity, a 'violation of the Buddhist Law in these precincts of the Sun has resulted'. The padres can 'hardly be allowed to remain on Japanese soil. Within twenty days they must make their preparations and return to their country.' Following the *San Felipe* Incident (1596), in which the eponymous Spanish Franciscan galleon, which made the lucrative trans-Pacific run between Manila and Acapulco, was wrecked on the Japanese coast, the situation for Europeans and their converts deteriorated. Among the cargo were weapons, deepening Hideyoshi's suspicions that the friars represented a first wave of Iberian colonialism. After confiscating the lucrative cargo, Hideyoshi, acting under the advice of his confidant Ishida Mitsunari (1560–1600), ordered that the friars and their flocks be executed. Hideyoshi's men mutilated the faces of the twenty-six Franciscans and forcibly marched them to Nagasaki to be crucified. These martyrs became known as the 'Twenty-six Saints'. As the twenty-six marched to Nagasaki, 'they were constantly looking for a miracle from Deus, gazing up at the sky, peering across the mountains – but there wasn't even a dewdrop of a miracle', explained one anti-Christian document.

In a letter Hideyoshi wrote to the Viceroy of the Indies just prior to his death, he accused Europeans of intending to destroy the 'righteous law' of Shinto, Buddhism, and Confucianism, by teaching 'heresies' and the 'unreasonable and wanton doctrines' of Christianity. The letter exposes the warlord's core fears. The padres who had arrived in Japan tried to 'bewitch our men and women', and so 'punishment was administered on them'. If more padres come, he warned, 'they shall be destroyed'. Hideyoshi, by this time lord of the realm, had firmly determined that Christianity was a threat to Japan.

Although Japanese patience with Christian missionaries waxed and waned in the late sixteenth and early seventeenth centuries, the Edo *bakufu* (1603–1868) continued to crack down on both padres and Japanese converts. In 1623, Tokugawa Iemitsu (1604–51), the third shogun, burned fifty Christians at the stake in the capital of Edo. This incident, and others like it, commenced the brutal eradication of Christianity from Japanese soil in the early seventeenth century, characterized by the meticulous hunting down of converts and forcing them into apostasy. In charge of this process was Inoue Masashige (1585–1662), an Edo *bakufu* official, who perfected such methods as *fumie*, or 'stepping on the image', where suspected believers were made to step on a sacred image. Inoue wrote this on the method of exposing Christians: 'Old wives and women when made to tread upon the image of Deus get agitated and red in the face; they cast off their headdress; their breath comes in rough gasps; sweat pours from them.' If they proved reluctant, they were forced into apostasy with such horrific techniques as *anatsurushi*, wherein the victim was dangled upside down in a pit of excrement.

A vent was sliced into the victim's forehead to induce cerebral bleeding. One hand was left free to signal that the victim had given up the faith. At the conclusion of the Shimabara Uprising (1637), where a messianic leader, Amakusa Shirô (1621–38), had led a ragtag group of peasants against the Shimabara lord, Matsukura Katsuie (1598–1638), deploying Christian symbols along the way, the Tokugawa shoguns could declare the country essentially Christian-free except for small underground pockets.

The legacies of Japan's seventeenth-century Christian eradication campaigns are underestimated at the historian's peril. To begin with, one might speculate that, in the late eighteenth and nineteenth centuries, another reason Japan was spared the brunt of European imperialism was the absence of an entrenched missionary presence. At least two of the most brutal and destabilizing events in nineteenth-century China, the Taiping Rebellion (1850–64) and the Boxer Rebellion (1899–1901), events from which the Qing dynasty never recovered, had connections to missionary activity. The Christian suppressions also defined Japan's posture towards the outside world for centuries. Isolation from Europe became one of the cornerstones of Tokugawa authority. Under the Tokugawa shoguns, Japan confined its foreign trade to politically valuable interactions through the four windows to the outside world: Tsushima trade with Korea, Satsuma trade with the Ryukyu Kingdom (Okinawa), Nagasaki trade with the Chinese and Dutch, and Matsumae trade with Ezo (Ainu).

After the expulsion of Christians, Japan was not secluded – or what historians have referred to as *sakoku*, or the 'closed country' – but rather, Japan reconfigured foreign relations in a manner that strictly benefited Tokugawa state formation and commerce. When Korean and Ryukyuan embassies visited Edo, they did so in carefully orchestrated performances of Tokugawa political power. Koreans visited the Tôshôgû shrine, for instance, a mausoleum dedicated to Tokugawa Ieyasu (1543–1616), paying homage to the deified progenitor of the Tokugawa family. Dressed in exotic foreign attire, it was clear to all who witnessed these processional events that Tokugawa power extended beyond Japan's borders to distant countries. The Edo *bakufu* forced envoys to wear exotic attire, even though Ryukyu reformers, such as Sai On (1682–1761), had sought to assimilate the island kingdom to Japanese ideas and customs over a half century after Satsuma domain sacked his country in 1609. These foreign visits proved so valuable that, when Ryukyu embassies visited Edo, authorities made them wear native garb, lest the increasingly assimilated Ryukyu Islanders be confused with Japanese. In other words, encounters with foreigners, whether Iberian missionaries, Koreans, or even the Ainu to the north, drew ethnic boundaries around Japan, ones rooted not in theories of race, but rather in theories of the customary differences that separated people, such as hairstyles, clothing, and language. To this day, these are some of the important ways in which Japanese people define themselves and their culture, and distinguish themselves from others.

INTELLECTUAL LEGACIES OF THE EUROPEAN ENCOUNTER

In 1552, Francis Xavier wrote to Ignatius Loyola (1491–1556), founder of the Society, that recruits for the Japan mission should be 'well acquainted with cosmic phenomena, because the Japanese are enthusiastic about listening to explanations of planetary motions, solar eclipses, and the waxing and waning of the moon'. This is because 'all explanations of natural philosophy greatly engage that people's minds'. Indeed, by the sixteenth century Japanese had engaged with a cosmopolitan complex of sciences, mostly Neo-Confucianism from China and Buddhist renditions of the cosmos from India. Japanese pored over tables related to astrology, astronomy, and calendric studies. Traditionally, calendric studies had been the domain of the Kamo family of Kyoto. In 1414, for example, court astronomer Kamo no Arikata published the *Rekirin mondôshû* (Collection of dialogues on the calendar), an important work that made extensive references to Chinese cosmology, Neo-Confucianism, and Buddhism. Yet the decentralizing forces of the Warring States period witnessed the creation of competing calendars elsewhere in Japan, although most continued to rely on astronomical tables imported from China in the ninth century. Astrology and calendars remained popular in the Warring States period because of their prognostic promise in an era of dire

uncertainty and political chaos, not unlike the philosophical roadmap offered by the *Dao De Jing* during China's own Warring States
period (475–221 BCE).

The year Portuguese arrived at Tanegashima, a scientific revolution was getting under way in Europe. In 1543, the Renaissance
astronomer Nicolaus Copernicus (1473–1543) had published *De
revolutionibus orbium coelestium* (On the revolutions of the
celestial spheres), displacing the Ptolemaic geocentric explanation
of the planets with a heliocentric one. Later, in the early seventeenth century, Galileo Galilei (1564–1642) acquired the tele-
scope lenses required to make his revolutionary discoveries. In
other words, the European science the Portuguese brought to
Japan was rapidly becoming outdated, but it nonetheless had a
lasting impact.

To begin with, it forced Japanese to confront the notion of a
spherical planet. Largely due to Chinese Neo-Confucian science,
Japanese understood Earth to be flat and part of stacked hierarchical planes, like bookshelves. As we have seen, the fact that heaven
was above Earth provided the natural imagery that Prince Shōtoku
deployed in the 'Seventeen-article Constitution'. Later, in a famous
1606 debate between Neo-Confucian scholar Hayashi Razan
(1583–1657) and Fucan Fabian, a former Zen Buddhist, the Earth's
spherical nature was the topic of much discussion. Fabian claimed
that Earth was round, with heavens both above and below, and that
one could sail around the world and wind up where one departed.
Razan, a good Neo-Confucian, articulated an orderly, hierarchical
image of Earth, like empty bookshelves, with heaven above Earth.
Consequently, the Earth could not be spherical. Despite Fabian's
gallant effort, the spherical Earth concept never penetrated the
early modern Japanese consciousness, probably because Europeans, and their rapidly advancing science, had such a short stay
and delimited influence in Japan.

Jesuits published a solar calendar while in Japan, but it mainly
served as a guide to Christian observances. The Portuguese nautical
calendar, with sun declination tables, proved far more valuable,
and Japanese sailors learned how to use them for their own maritime purposes. By 1618, Ikeda Koun, in the *Genna kōkaisho* (Navigational treatise of the Genna era, 1615–24), distilled practical

elements of European navigation into one text. It contained descriptions of how to use an astrolabe, quadrant, and other instruments essential to navigation, as well as instructions for solar nautical calendars and navigational charts. As part of this technological package, Europeans also introduced Japanese to mechanical watches, which, along with quadrants and astrolabes, they began producing (without glass fronts). But watches remained primarily a luxury item for centuries.

Under the supervision of an Englishman named William Adams (1564–1620), who had arrived in Japan in 1600 aboard a Dutch ship, two Western-style ships were constructed by order of the shogun. The larger one, a 120-ton vessel, was loaned to the former governor-general of the Philippines after his ship wrecked in 1606 on the coast near Edo on its way to Mexico. Manned by a skilled Japanese crew, the *Santa Buenaventura* successfully made the journey to Mexico one year later. Later, Date Masamune (1567–1636), lord of Sendai, had a 500-ton ship built under the direction of a Spaniard in order to deliver his retainer, Hasekura Tsunenaga (1571–1622), as an envoy to Rome. The ship successfully crossed the Pacific to Mexico and returned to the Philippines in 1616 where it was purchased by the Spanish and made part of their fleet. The globe-trotting Hasekura found other passage from the Philippines to Japan. Interestingly, the window between the arrival of the Portuguese in 1543, and 1640, when the shoguns enforced strict 'maritime prohibition', has been described as the 'Christian century' by some historians. It would be better described as Japan's global century, with 'Japan towns' sprouting up throughout Southeast Asia and envoys crossing the Pacific. Japan was exposed to a diverse array of religions, ideologies, sciences, and technologies that directly and indirectly shaped its cultural and political development.

During this global century, Japan proved remarkably open-minded to new technologies. In the fifteenth century, after the importation of gunpowder from China, Europeans manufactured the first harquebus, an early musket that, as we will see in the next chapter, played a critical role in the unification of Japan in the late sixteenth century. Immediately after the Portuguese landed at Tanegashima, Japanese bought two harquebuses and swordsmiths began their reproduction. In time, Japanese gunsmiths produced thousands of these muskets and they became export commodities to Southeast Asia. In short, not long after Japanese saw their first harquebus, they became international arms merchants, as well as participating in mercenary activities in Southeast Asia.

Though muskets and early artillery impacted Japan's late sixteenth-century military and political landscape, European glass and glass lenses became an important element of Japanese culture and sparked epistemological shifts in the way Japanese saw the world around them. At this early juncture of European contact, Japan began to construct its own version of Western culture, one that involved fundamentally new ways of seeing influenced by glass lenses. The new manner of seeing proved less synaptic and more dissecting, a fixed and focused analytical gaze. Though earlier Japanese seeing had involved the external connections between things, glass lenses facilitated an early scientific gaze that probed for the internal mechanics of things, exposing their insides for all to see, record and, eventually, exploit. Glass lenses separated the viewer from viewed in new ways, creating objectivity in Japanese seeing (Figures 8 and 9). Glass lenses made visible the heavens and exposed the microscopic world of mosquito larvae, while glass

8 A depiction of a European-designed microscope in *Kômô zatsuwa* (Miscellany on the Dutch, 1787).

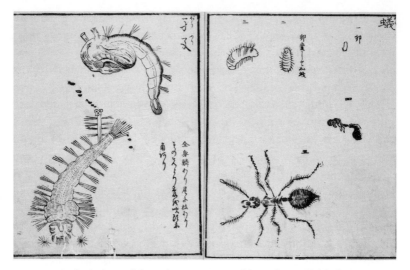

9 A depiction of the microscopic world made available by European-designed glass lenses in *Kômô zatsuwa* (Miscellany on the Dutch, 1787).

bottles preserved pickled alligators and lizards, and spectacles enabled people to see. The cultural implications of the encounter with Europe were multifaceted, but the discovery of the scientific gaze, a radical new way of seeing, had lasting importance for the development of Japanese aesthetics and science.

CONCLUSION

Historians used to see the period between 1542 and 1640 as Japan's 'Christian century', and indeed Christianity proved an important element of the cultural package brought to Japan by first the Portuguese, and later European missionaries, explorers, travellers, and conquerors. Christianity's legacies proved important and lasting ones; and the geopolitical stance Japan took after the expulsion of Christian missionaries defined Japanese foreign engagement until the early nineteenth century, when an even more belligerent wave of European and US encroachment began, from both the north and south. However, the initial encounter with Europeans at Tanegashima and elsewhere sparked Japan's first global century, where Japanese peddled arms in Southeast Asia, planted potatoes from the New World, exported silver to Ming China, and experimented with new technologies ranging from firearms and navigational aids to astronomical theories and glass lenses. Japan's new geopolitical posture, as well as its incorporation of new technologies, particularly military ones, directly shaped the 'age of unification' that recentralized politics and thrust Japan into the early modern period.

6

Unifying the Realm, 1560–1603

What makes the legacies of the Japanese sixteenth-century encounter with Europeans so important is that it coincided with the final years of the Warring States period and the birth of the age of unification (1560–1603). During this time, three ambitious warlords sought to unify the realm. At roughly the same time that the Portuguese strengthened their hold over Nagasaki, a young warrior in central Japan began his improbable climb to supremacy. Oda Nobunaga (1534–82), first of the 'three great unifiers', began the process of breaking down the culture of lawlessness and medieval regionalism to unify the realm under a single, though never completely hegemonic, shogunal authority. Indeed, none of the three unifiers accomplished complete unification, as *daimyô* continued to assert political and economic control in the seventeenth and eighteenth centuries. Nonetheless, their achievements defined Japanese politics for generations to come. The modern Japanese nation was, to be sure, a product of modern forces that swept the world in the nineteenth century, but it was also a product of the brutal labour of the warlord unifiers, as they struggled to reassemble the pieces in the aftermath of the Warring States period and cobble together a unified realm.

JAPONIUS TYRANNUS

Oda Nobunaga was forged in the crucible of Warring States violence (Figure 10). The forging of his character began in his youth.

10 Oda Nobunaga by Kano Motohide, titled *Oda Nobunaga zu* (Oda Nobunaga portrait). Located at Chôkôji, Aichi Prefecture, Japan.

In 1551, his father, Nobuhide (1510–51), lord of Owari domain, died suddenly of disease. When the prayers of Buddhists had failed to save his father, Nobunaga, according to the Jesuit Luís Fróis, locked the monks in a temple, encouraged them to pray harder, and shot some of them with harquebuses from the outside to provide incentive. 'They had better pray to their idols with greater devotion for their own lives', he reportedly said. The Jesuit's account is surely embellished, riddled with his own prejudices about the 'pagan' religion, but Nobunaga's harsh treatment of Buddhist sectarians later became infamous. At his father's funeral, he impetuously 'proceeded to the altar, suddenly grabbed a handful of incense powder, threw it on the altar, and left', leading some in the Oda family to believe he was overly eccentric and unfit to rule Owari domain.

But Nobunaga proved quite fit for rule and expertly dispatched many of his rivals. Chief among them were his uncle Nobutomo (1516–55) and his younger brother, Nobuyuki (1536–57). Nobutomo had challenged Nobunaga's ascendancy to lordship of Owari domain. In 1555, with the aid of another uncle, Nobumitsu, Nobutomo was killed, thus paving the way for Nobunaga to take Kiyosu castle, Owari's stronghold. Then, in 1556, the younger brother, Nobuyuki, rebelled against Nobunaga, with the assistance of two rival Warring States lords. But he was ultimately defeated and then pardoned when their mother intervened. In 1557, hoping to eliminate the threat of Nobuyuki once and for all, Nobunaga feigned illness and then complained to his mother that Nobuyuki 'did not call upon him'. When Nobuyuki finally did visit his supposedly ailing brother, Nobunaga's men ambushed and murdered him. Through such brutal tactics, by 1559 Nobunaga had unified Owari under his authority.

In 1560, the powerful Warring States lord Imagawa Yoshimoto (1519–60), filled with grandiose aspirations of his own, marched through the small domain of Owari on his way to the imperial capital of Kyoto. Yoshimoto claimed to be aiding the Ashikaga shogun, but actually he had ambitions to rule the realm. Yoshimoto's army of 20,000 vastly outnumbered that of Owari's young lord Nobunaga, and he figured to stroll through the domain relatively unimpeded. In what became known as the Battle of Okehazama, however, Nobunaga struck swiftly during a torrential thunderstorm. His forces caught Yoshimoto's men in a narrow gorge, prematurely celebrating their victories. Unaware Nobunaga was stalking him, Yoshimoto was reportedly inspecting severed heads. With little warning, Nobunaga struck and, finding Yoshimoto amidst the chaos, severed his head from his body. By the end of the fighting, 3,100 of Imagawa's elite troops lay dead in the bloodied mud. The unconventional rainstorm attack epitomized Nobunaga's gift for unorthodox warfare.

But his most famous victory came at Nagashino castle in June 1575. By that year, Takeda Katsuyori (1546–1582) had emerged as his principal rival, who continued to make inroads into the domains of Oda's allies, including Mikawa, base of the third great unifier Tokugwawa Ieyasu (1543–1616). Ieyasu had captured Nagashino castle from Katsuyori earlier in 1574, but its recapture by Katsuyori would have served as a launching point into Mikawa. Katsuyori began by deploying 15,000 men, and Nobunaga responded by dispatching a relief force to assist in the defence of the castle. Combined with Ieyasu's forces, Nobunaga's troops numbered around 30,000. As Katsuyori's cavalry laid siege to the castle, they made five charges against a barricade Nobunaga had erected around the castle. Behind the structure hid Nobunaga's men, both archers and harquebus musketeers. In the ensuing charge, Katsuyori's men were torn to pieces. The harquebus played an important role in Nobunaga's victory, and in Japan's age of unification.

As early as 1549, only six years after the arrival of the Portuguese, Nobunaga had ordered 500 harquebuses from Japanese gunsmiths. Other sources explain that, for one Warring States lord, 'All his vassals from far and near trained with the new weapon.' It is not surprising that Japan proved adept at adopting and manufacturing harquebuses, given its brisk arms export business in the medieval years. In 1483, Japanese had exported some 67,000 blades to China alone. A little over a century later, an Italian merchant observed Japan's lively export in 'weapons of all kinds, both offensive and defensive, of which this country has, I suppose, a more abundant supply than any other country in the world'. Indeed, in the Warring States period, Japan was a heavily armed country. Japanese blades were among the finest in the world. As one Dutchman explained, Japanese swords 'are so well wrought, and excellently temper'd, that they will cut our *European* blades asunder'.

Nobunaga used Japanese-made harquebuses at Nagashino. Sources explain of Nobunaga's tactics that 'he deployed 3000 musketeers in three ranks in this action, having trained them to fire in volleys so as to maintain a constant barrage'. As Japan's 1592 invasion of Korea began to bog down, even though many generals requested harquebuses Japan gradually stopped producing muskets for a complex set of reasons rooted in samurai culture. Swords had come to possess crucial symbolic value for samurai, a symbolism that harquebuses, which killed dishonourably at a distance, threatened. Even though guns proved pivotal in Japan's sixteenth-century unification, by the close of the seventeenth century production had all but ceased. Early modern Japan had turned away from the gun, which left it technologically vulnerable in the nineteenth century.

In late medieval Japan, however, Warring States rivals and family members were not the only ones threatening Nobunaga's designs to unify the realm. As we have seen, Buddhist sectarians emerged as powerful non-state actors in the decentralized political environment of medieval Japan. Nobunaga's quarrel with the monks of Enryakuji started in 1569, when he confiscated lands belonging to the Tendai monks, a move that made them obstinate towards the warlord. Nobunaga is known to have feared and despised organized Buddhism; in part, he blamed Buddhist monks for the death of his father. In the chaos of the Warring States period, monasteries rose to political and military prominence and stood squarely in the path of unification. It is also known that the Tendai monks had carelessly allied themselves with Nobunaga's archenemies, Asai Nagamasa (1545–73) and Asakura Yoshikage (1533–73). In 1571, he attacked the Tendai monks of the Enryakuji monastery at Mount Hiei, just outside Kyoto. Nobunaga's 30,000 troops killed 3,000 monks during the engagement. Five days after the attack, Jesuit Luís Fróis (1532–97) recounted the raw brutality of Nobunaga's wrath. After sacking the Enryakuji complex, 'Nobunaga sent many harquebusiers into the mountains and woods to hunt for bonzes [monks] who might be hiding there. The soldiers were to spare nobody, and they executed this order promptly.' Nobunaga was not satisfied with simply hunting down the Tendai monks and their families. 'As he wanted to quench his thirst for revenge still more and thus strengthen his reputation', Fróis continued, 'he ordered his whole army to immediately devastate the remaining houses of the bonzes, and to burn down all 400 or so temples of the very famous' Mount Hiei Enryakuji complex. The elimination of Enryakuji left a power vacuum in its wake that Nobunaga, as vanquisher of the temple, eagerly filled. He confiscated Enryakuji lands and distributed them to retainers, including one of his favourites, Akechi Mitsuhide (1528–82).

Three years later, Nobunaga waged war against the Ikkôshû monks of the Honganji (Truc Pure Land) sect, after they attempted to erect a domain ruled by the peasantry in Echizen. Obviously, this egalitarian vision flew in the face of Nobunaga's designs, as did their provocations, when they mobilized forces and broke a tenuous truce with the short-tempered Nobunaga in April 1574. Nagashima, the Ikkôshû sectarian stronghold, was situated in the network of rivers that drained into Ise Bay on the Inland Sea. In this watery domain, the sectarians had foiled Nobunaga in the past. This time, he erected palisades around the main Nagashima complexes and sealed in the sectarians. He then burned the complexes to the ground, but not before driving some 20,000 men, women, and children into the enclosure to burn. Given that an additional 20,000 had starved during Nobunaga's siege, this put the death toll at about 40,000. Nobunaga appeared determined to exterminate the sectarians. Early in the campaign, he had written that the Ikkôshû sectarians 'make all kinds of entreaties, but as I want to exterminate them root and branch this time, I shall not forgive their crimes'. Once the sectarians were enclosed, he gave his lieutenants orders to 'slaughter men and women alike', which they carried out expertly.

Nobunaga made equally important gains off the battlefield. While in Kyoto, he began slowly undermining what remained of Ashikaga authority by insisting that they consult him regarding national policy. 'In the event that there are matters to be ordered to the provinces through [Yoshiaki's] directives', explained one edict, 'Nobunaga is to be informed and his own letter [of confirmation] appended'. Another edict struck even more to the point: 'Insofar as the affairs of the realm have been fully entrusted to Nobunaga, all judgments shall be rendered – regardless of those concerned – in accord with his perceptions and without consultation of the shogun.' Clearly, Shogun Yoshiaki found himself marginalized from decision-making circles. In 1573, affairs regarding the powerless shogun came to a head when a letter he wrote to Takeda Shingen urged Nobunaga's mortal enemy to 'take military action and exert yourself unremittingly for the peace of the state'.

Simultaneously, Yoshiaki appeared to be making preparation to evacuate Nijô castle, his residence in Kyoto.

Alarmed that his enemies might be taking action, and that Yoshiaki appeared prepared to flee into exile, Nobunaga dispatched an important letter, the famous 'Remonstrance', to the cornered puppet shogun. He berated the shogun for supporting political newcomers, probably a thinly veiled allusion to Takeda Shingen. If the shogun supported newcomers at the cost of old supporters, 'then the distinction between loyal and disloyal disappears. The public does not think well of this.' In the 'Remonstrance' he wondered why the shogun was selling rice in preparation to depart Nijô castle. 'When the shogun stores gold and silver, and leaves his residence at the slightest rumour, it is no wonder that even the lowliest take this as a sign that the shogun wishes to abandon the capital.' What makes the 'Remonstrance' so important is its reference to the 'populace'. Yoshiaki had betrayed the public trust and, thereby, had lost legitimacy to govern the realm. That the 'public' might figure into notions of political legitimacy was new to Japanese political discourse.

By March 1573, Yoshiaki had formed an alliance with Nobunaga's mortal enemies, provoking the warlord's wrath. The next month, Nobunaga tried to reason with Yoshiaki, but was rebuffed. As he wrote to Tokugawa Ieyasu about his next actions, 'I had no other options'. He burned much of Kyoto to cinders. One Kyoto observer wrote, 'the whole of Upper Kyoto was burned down, with not a single house left standing'. The residents of Lower Kyoto paid for their lives by filling Nobunaga's coffers. Nobunaga's forces then surrounded Nijô, persuading the powerless shogun to sue for peace. The decisive encounter came in August 1573, when Nobunaga's forces crossed Lake Biwa and surprised Yoshiaki's garrisons at Nijô. When they witnessed the size of Nobunaga's army, the Nijô garrison 'all went over to Nobunaga's camp' and within days Yoshiaki was tracked down. Nobunaga 'spared his life', and he was exiled from the capital, becoming the 'Beggar Shogun' and ending centuries of Ashikaga rule from Kyoto.

Nobunaga's relationship with the court also proved prickly. He frequently made court envoys wait to have audiences with him, sometimes for days. Often, such delays were caused by Nobunaga's 'resting'. In May 1582, imperial envoys paid Nobunaga a visit, their intention being to bestow on him the title of regent or shogun, in recognition of his conquest of so much territory and ouster of Yoshiaki. 'The conquest of the Kantô is a splendid exploit', the court envoys trumpeted, 'so it has been decided to make [Nobunaga] shogun'. But Nobunaga refused to meet with the envoys for two full days, raising the question of whether he ever intended to work within the traditional framework of Japanese political authority (that is, the acceptance of imperial titles). Powerful men before him – Fujiwara no Michinaga, Minamoto no Yoritimo, and other regents and shoguns – had all accepted imperial titles to legitimize their rule. However, Nobunaga might have aspired to function within an entirely new monarchical framework, one in which he served as the divine centre. An example of this pursuit of divine rule was the construction of Azuchi castle, which Nobunaga had erected in 1579. The castle became the greatest symbol of military might in Japan. As one missionary observed, 'On top of the hill in the middle of the city, Nobunaga built his palace and castle, which as regards architecture, strength, wealth and grandeur may well be compared with the greatest buildings of Europe.' In some respects, Azuchi was Nobunaga's grand theatre to rehearse and project a new kind of political authority, one with religious and military icons that symbolized his burgeoning autocracy.

Nobunaga ruled over his terrified vassals with an iron fist. Often, he spoke of 'regimenting the realm'. He encouraged his underlings to practise the austere 'way of the warrior'. He imposed harsh demands on even his most loyal subordinates, often relocating them like 'potted plants' in order to keep them politically and militarily off balance. His personal stamp, which was affixed to all realm documents, read 'overspread the realm with military might', a phrase that neatly sums up his approach to governance. His harsh treatment of his vassals came back to haunt him, however. In 1582, while staying at the Honnôji temple, one of his vassals, Akechi Mitsuhide, laid siege to the temple, forcing Nobunaga to commit suicide. After burning the Honnôji, Mitsuhide turned his attention to Nobunaga's heir, Nobutada (1557–82), who was staying nearby, killing him, too. With these events, Mitsuhide had hoped to 'slay Nobunaga, and become lord of the realm'.

Consequently, at the age of 48, Nobunaga died in the same flames of violence that had characterized his rule. His vassal and successor, Hideyoshi, though also born in the crucible of the Warring States period, sought a slightly different approach to unification, one that had lasting legacies. Hideyoshi came from a modest family and so his rise to pre-eminence is striking. He, more than any other figure, might be described as a product of the social mobility that characterized the medieval years, a fluidity that he worked tirelessly to coagulate in the late sixteenth century.

BOUNTIFUL MINISTER

When Nobunaga was murdered, Hideyoshi was in the north waging war against the Môri family at Takamatsu castle. Realizing that Takamatsu castle sat precariously just above sea level, he began to engineer dykes and channels, diverting water to the castle in an attempt to drown the Môri out. Hideyoshi's musketeers, teetering on towers supported by floating barges, were made ready for the wet, fleeing enemy. Had he lived long enough, Nobunaga would have rendezvoused with Hideyoshi at Takamatsu castle to command what he viewed as a decisive campaign for western Honshu. It was all planned perfectly, except that Nobunaga was now dead.

When Hideyoshi received word of Nobunaga's death, he quietly concluded a peace deal with the Môri and, in a mere six days, broke camp and force-marched his troops to Himeji, some 113 kilometres (seventy miles). There, with the help of other Oda allies, Hideyoshi defeated Mitsuhide's men southwest of Kyoto. Mitsuhide's head eventually made it back to the smouldering ruins of the Honnôji, where it was placed on public display as a grim lesson. Convened to determine Nobunaga's successor, the Kiyosu conference, held at Nobunaga's original stronghold, followed Hideyoshi's victory in 1582. Most Oda allies were present, minus Tokugawa Ieyasu and Sassa Narimasa (1536–88), who elected to diligently watch over their own territories instead. The death of Nobunaga's designated heir Nobutada (1557–82) had complicated the selection of a successor, and the conference members split between Hideyoshi, who championed Oda Sanbôshi, and Shibata Katsuie who favoured Oda Nobutaka (1558–83).

The Kiyosu conference dissolved with no concrete resolution and the following winter Hideyoshi faced off against the formidable Shibata Katsuie and his allies in the snow-covered fields north of Lake Biwa. The resourceful Shibata soundly defeated Hideyoshi's garrisons at Ômi. In response, Hideyoshi marched his troops fifty-two kilometres (thirty miles) in six hours at night to personally face Shibata in the Battle of Shizugatake. He wrote in a letter, 'This is the time to decide who shall govern Japan.' A masterful tactician, Hideyoshi defeated Shibata who, in the finest warrior tradition, committed ritual suicide as an example for future generations in full view of the enemy, and only after stabbing his wife, who was Nobunaga's sister. As one chronicler described the moment:

> Katsuie climbed to the ninth floor of his keep, addressed some words to those assembled and declared his intentions to kill himself to serve [as an example] to later generations. His men, deeply moved, shed tears, which soaked the sleeves of their armour. When all was quiet to the east and west, Katsuie stabbed his wife, children, and other members of his family, and then cut open his stomach, together with eighty retainers.

With Shibata's grisly demise, Hideyoshi was able to focus his attention on other military matters beyond the boundaries of Nobunaga's territories.

In 1585, Hideyoshi attacked Chôsokabe Motochika (1538–99) on the island of Shikoku, and Sassa Narimasa in Etchû province that same year. Like his predecessor, he also struck out against Buddhist monks, specifically the Shingon monks of Negoro and the Jôdo Shinshû sectarians of Saiga. He cautioned the monks against further militarization: 'The [contemplative] monks, the priests in the world, and others have not been prudent in their religious studies. The manufacture or retention of senseless weapons, muskets, and the like is treacherous and wicked.' In 1587, he launched the largest military endeavour of his generation, excepting his later invasion of Korea, the Kyushu campaign. Hideyoshi overwhelmed Shimazu Yoshihisa (1533–1611) with an estimated 250,000 troops, forcing Yoshihisa to surrender at Hideyoshi's camp and take a priestly name and renounce politics. Three years later, Hideyoshi marched north against Hôjô Ujimasa (1538–90). In only eight years, Hideyoshi had vastly expanded his landholdings and stood *primus inter pares* among Warring States lords.

Victories in battle brought Hideyoshi power. Given his humble background, however, political legitimacy proved harder to conjure. Between 1583 and 1590, Hideyoshi began construction of Osaka castle, a grandiose fortification designed to radiate his power throughout warrior society. He also constructed the sumptuous Jurakudai palace in Kyoto. In 1588, to demonstrate his place at the pinnacle of warrior society, Hideyoshi orchestrated an imperial procession with Emperor Go-Yôzei (1571–1617), who visited the ruler at his new palace. The two exchanged poems on the theme of the pine tree, a symbol of longevity, to celebrate the occasion.

Hideyoshi also slowly dismantled the medieval order, which had propelled him to power and had been characterized by social fluidity. The same year that Hideyoshi hosted Emperor Go-Yôzei at the Jurakudai palace, he ordered the legendary 'Sword Hunt' in order to disarm country samurai and militant peasants, forcing them to choose between living as samurai in the castle towns or as peasants in the countryside. The perseverance of murky boundaries between peasants and samurai was partially to blame for the chaos of the Warring States period, and the 'Sword Hunt' was designed to clarify those boundaries by creating a concrete and hierarchical status system. It stated, 'The farmers of the various provinces are strictly forbidden to possess long swords, short swords, bows, spears, muskets, or any other form of weapon.' Gradually, fighting was placed in the hands of the samurai, a hereditary military class, whom Hideyoshi removed from the land, their independent power base. The samurai were organized into urban armies under the watchful eyes of *daimyô*, who provided them with stipends.

To be sure that the divisions between peasant and samurai remained cemented, Hideyoshi forced the samurai into the castle towns. Peasants, in turn, remained on their farms and permanently abandoned any military ambitions. The swords that Hideyoshi's magistrates confiscated were, as he promised, melted down and 'used as rivets and clamps in the forthcoming construction of the Great Buddha. This will be an act by which farmers will be saved in this life and, needless to say, in the life to come.' The giant Buddha erected at the Hôkôji monastery came to symbolize the growing peace sweeping the realm. In 1591, Hideyoshi essentially froze the social order by restricting geographic and social mobility, the very mobility that had enabled his improbable rise to power. The son of Yaemon, a foot soldier in Nobunaga's army, Hideyoshi had come from a modest family in Owari and had risen through the ranks. Hideyoshi's facial features prompted Nobunaga to give him the name Kozaru, or 'Small Monkey'. But such social mobility would soon be a thing of the past. In a census of 1592, Hideyoshi instructed his magistrates to register the 'military men as military men, farmers as farmers, and the townspeople as townspeople', cementing the populace in their occupationally based status. This status system became one of the linchpins of the new early modern order.

Starting in 1582, Hideyoshi had begun elaborate land surveys designed to tighten his control over the agricultural lands of the realm. Though some Warring States lords had surveyed local hold-ings, Hideyoshi's surveys remained fairly standardized at a national scale, a clear effort to make the realm economically legible to its new master. Hideyoshi based this new legibility on assessing the estimated yield of land under cultivation, which became the basis for domain rankings, tribute and tax amounts, as well as military taxation. Hideyoshi's military taxation created a largely hypothet-ical national military, one based on conscription rates tied to agri-cultural productivity. When faced with the Ainu rebellion of 1669, called Shakushain's War, Tokugawa military planners drew on this system to mobilize northeastern domains, such as Hirosaki, for war in the north. It is easy to overstate how thoroughly Hideyoshi's land surveys standardized survey practices throughout the entire realm, but the surveys did further privatize landholding by officially linking agricultural lands to individual cultivators. The practice of jointly owning lands, a strategy farm communities used to insure themselves against the threat of natural disasters, persisted throughout the early modern years, but the majority of arable land came to resemble private property, an important step in the emergence of Japan's rurally based, proto-capitalistic economic development.

In recognition of his military successes and the new legibility of the realm, the emperor granted Hideyoshi the imperial titles of 'regent' (*kanpaku*) in 1585, as the Fujiwara had been centuries earlier, and 'retired-regent' in 1592. In 1585, the emperor also offered Hideyoshi a new surname, Toyotomi, or 'Bountiful Minister', in recognition of his new-found national prominence (Figure 11). Because of his modest family background, Hideyoshi had gone through life with bestowed surnames, first Hashiba, a name Nobunaga built from characters borrowed from other prominent retainers. In 1585, the emperor bestowed 'Toyotomi',

11 Toyotomi Hideyoshi (1536–98), Imperial Regent, 1585–91; Chancellor of the Realm, 1587–98.

signalling Hideyoshi's national prestige and carrying the divine legitimacy of imperial entrustment. Then, in 1595, Hideyoshi's 'Wall Writings of Osaka Castle' solidified political relations throughout the realm, ordering Warring States lords to 'obtain approval' before entering into marriage and strictly prohibiting them from 'entering deliberately into contracts' with each other. By the beginning of the last decade of the sixteenth century, much of the realm appeared to be within Hideyoshi's grasp, but military aspirations far grander than control over Japan began to enter the warlord's fevered imagination.

UNIFYING THREE COUNTRIES

As early as 1586, Hideyoshi divulged to Luís Fróis (1532–97), a Jesuit confidant of Nobunaga, that once he had placed the 'affairs of Japan in order', he would entrust them to his brother Hidenaga (1540–91) and begin planning the 'conquest of Korea and China'. The next year, still brimming with confidence after his victory in the Kyushu campaign, Hideyoshi penned a letter to his wife, wherein he explained that he had 'sent word by fast ship to Korea ordering them to appear and submit to the Emperor. I told them that if they do not appear I will punish them next year.' He continued, 'And I will also get China in my grasp.' In 1587, Koreans rebuffed Japanese overtures, spearheaded by the Sô family of Tsushima, but later efforts in 1590 proved more successful. That year, Koreans agreed to dispatch envoys as 'friendly neighbours' but refused to include the tribute, which would have been a clear acknowledgement of Japanese superiority. Nonetheless, the envoys returned to Korea with a bombastic letter from Hideyoshi, in which he stated, 'My object is to enter China, to spread the customs of our country to the four hundred or more provinces of that nation.' He elaborated, 'My wish is nothing other than that my name be known throughout the three countries [of Japan, China, and India].'

Shortly thereafter, Hideyoshi dispatched an extraordinary letter to the Viceroy of the Indies, in which he articulated the theological unity of a broader realm, one that he planned to forge by military force. 'Ours is the land of the kami', he explained, referring to the Shinto deities, and kami is mind, and the one mind is all encompassing. No phenomena exist outside it … They are thus the root and sources of all phenomena. They are in India under the name of Buddhism; they are in China under the name of Confucianism; they are in Japan where they are called Shinto. To know Shinto is to know Buddhism and Confucianism.

In other words, on a theological level, Hideyoshi already saw metaphysical unity in the 'Three Countries', essentially the known civilized world. (India was included because it was the birthplace of Buddhism.) In this respect, the invasion of Korea and China represented a kind of restoration, a way of creating political and military unity where theological unity already existed. Moreover, Hideyoshi should create this broader political and spiritual sphere, one that encompassed the 'Three Countries', because of his role in the unification of Japan. 'Tenka, the realm, is not tenka', he wrote,

> I am tenka. Kami and Buddha are not kami and Buddha: I am kami and Buddha. Men are not men: I am mankind … Japan is not my country, China is not my country: China, India, and Japan are all my body. Therefore, if the people of China or Japan are grieved it is as if I am afflicted in my whole body.

In his mind, Hideyoshi had come to physically embody the necessity for global conquest, or at least those parts of the globe worth conquering.

Hideyoshi's troops landed in Korea in 1592, led by Konishi Yukinaga (1555–1600). It would prove to be an invasion that, along with twentieth-century atrocities, poisoned the waters of Korean–Japanese relations for centuries. Within three weeks they had reached Seoul, which had largely been abandoned and burned. On receiving word that his soldiers had entered Seoul, Hideyoshi wrote optimistically to his mother, 'I shall take China about the ninth month.' He then began making plans for an audacious occupation of Ming China. 'Our sovereign shall move to the Ming capital', he wrote of the Japanese emperor, who he imagined would begin relocating to Beijing, 'and there should be proper arrangements for this'. Hideyoshi's nephew, Hidetsugu (1568–95), he slated to be 'regent' of China, and the 'throne of Japan' was to be occupied by a prince. 'Korea and China will be taken without trouble', he trumpeted. Hideyoshi's invasion force, drawn from experienced samurai of the Warring States period, proved able to hold the field during most military engagements. Over the course of the six-year war, Hideyoshi deployed approximately 500,000 hardened soldiers to the Korean peninsula (Map 2).

But even as Hideyoshi penned these phrases, a Korean counter-offensive was under way. When the Japanese attacked the coastal city of Busan, Korea's Joseon dynasty (1392–1897) dispatched the talented naval commander Yi Sun-shin (1545–98) to attack Japanese troops and supply lines crossing the Tsushima Strait. Admiral Yi expertly used the Korean 'turtle ship' to outmanoeuvre the Japanese navy, handing them spectacular defeats in what Koreans call the Imjin War (1592–8). At Okpo (1592), Sacheon (1592), Hansen Islands (1592), and victories late in the conflict such as Myeong-nyang, Admiral Yi harassed the Japanese navy and sent hundreds of ships to the ocean's bottom. Then, Joseon guerrillas began a scorched earth campaign that left the Japanese with few resources or supplies. When Ming troops crossed the Yalu River, Japan started negotiations to end the conflict in 1593. The Ming court rejected Hideyoshi's demands and war resumed in 1597, with Hideyoshi dispatching an additional 140,000 troops to the peninsula. By the end of 1598, however, Hideyoshi and his successors had ordered most Japanese troops home.

The war devastated Korea, burning elaborate Joseon palaces to the ground, as well as causing crop failures, famines, and banditry. In China, Emperor Wanli's (1563–1620) intervention, though militarily decisive, financially burdened the Ming dynasty and ultimately hastened its collapse just over four decades later at the hands of the Manchus. Koreans experienced a veritable brain drain during the war as Japanese abducted countless artisans and scientists and brought them to Japan, where they advanced the pottery and movable type industries. No monument better captures the brutality of the Imjin War than the 'Ear Tomb' in Kyoto, where the mutilated ears and noses of nearly 40,000 Koreans, sliced off by Japanese soldiers as wartime trophies, remain buried to this day. In the grisly world of samurai combat, victors usually brought severed heads to collection stations, where they were counted for remuneration. Hideyoshi, during the second invasion, had ordered his soldiers to 'mow down everyone ... and send the heads'. With the

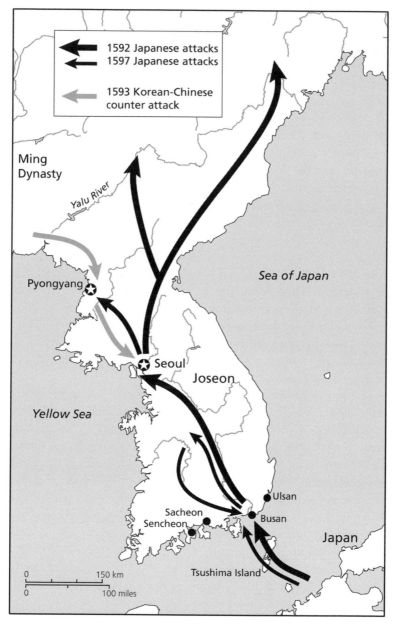

2 Toyotomi Hideyoshi's invasion of Korea, 1592–1598

Korean invasion, however, the cramped quarters aboard Japanese naval vessels crossing the Tsushima Strait dictated that ears and noses, rather than complete heads, were counted, catalogued, and salted for the journey back to Japan.

ENTER IEYASU

Hideyoshi died in 1598 during the second Korean invasion. The first three lines of his death poem, 'My life / Came like dew / Disappears like dew', belie the monumental consequences of a man whose ephemeral existence, dreamlike in its improbability, had reshaped his world. After Hideyoshi's 'Sword Hunt', his freezing of the social order, the Korean invasion, and other policy decisions, the once-fluid social and geographic milieu of the medieval world had crystallized, and precious few could follow his path upward. Social, political, and geographic immobility became hallmarks of early modern stability, or what eventually came to be called the 'great peace'.

Hideyoshi's choice of a successor proved less enduring, however. He originally chose Hidetsugu, his twisted and mercurial nephew. One missionary claimed that Hidetsugu 'opened and ripped up women to see their entrails and place of conception' for sheer entertainment. In 1593, after Hideyoshi's son, Hideyori (1593–1615), was born to his mistress Yodogimi, the malevolent Hidetsugu was conveniently implicated in a treasonous plot and executed in 1595, along with thirty-one members of his family. Their tomb reads: 'The Tomb of the Traitors'. With Hidetsugu out of the picture, Hideyoshi, while on his deathbed, implored his allies, in particular the wily Tokugawa Ieyasu, to watch over the young Hideyori until he was old enough to govern the realm and continue the vulnerable Toyotomi line. 'I depend upon you for everything', he reportedly said to his assembled vassals.

However, the future of Toyotomi rule had more of a dreamlike character than Hideyoshi ever imagined. With Hideyoshi dead and the young Hideyori ensconced in Osaka castle, the realm divided into two well-armed camps. The outcome of the impending conflict would determine the direction of modern Japan. Domain lords that gathered under Ishida Mitsunari (1560–1600), known as the 'Western Army', faced Tokugawa Ieyasu's 'Eastern Army' at the Battle of Sekigahara in 1600. Ieyasu's forces emerged victorious, and leading Western generals such as Mitsunari, Konishi Yukinaga, and Ankokuji Ekei (1539–1600), had their heads severed and placed on pikes on the Sonjô Bridge in Kyoto. Emperor Go-Yôzei, whom Hideyoshi had entertained at the Jurakudai, granted Ieyasu the title of shogun in 1603, and the warlord quickly took steps to secure the realm and fortify Tokugawa rule. Ieyasu manoeuvred in a volatile environment, where even allied warlords such as Ikeda Terumasa (1565–1613) at Himeji castle reportedly stored 1,200 harquebus muskets at his stronghold. However, Ieyasu handsomely rewarded those warlords who had sided with him in the confrontation at Sekigahara, distributing over 6 million *koku* of land (one *koku* had the potential to produce about 176 litres, or five bushels, of rice) to his allies.

The violence that characterized the Warring States period bled long into the seventeenth century. In 1615, Hideyori was killed at Osaka castle by Ieyasu's armies, and the heads of his allies were placed on pikes that lined the highway between Osaka and Kyoto. That same year, the 'Laws for Military Households' laid out a basic framework for the conduct of warrior families, including provisions against unauthorized marriages, new castle construction, and unauthorized alliances. It also set the moral tone for samurai conduct, admonishing them to practise frugality because displaying wealth corrupted public values. The Edo *bakufu* (1603–1868), located in the new capital of Edo (present-day Tokyo), also dispatched 'inspectors' and 'provincial censors' (essentially spies) to keep careful watch over the domain lords, both allies and enemies alike.

To maintain political stability and military superiority, the *bakufu* divided the realm's domain lords into three categories to better monitor them; a domain's categorization determined its access to decision-making circles. 'Vassal lords' (*fudai*) were those men who had fought on the side of Ieyasu at Sekigahara. These men took blood oaths to the Tokugawa family and could serve in the government, for example, as 'senior councillors'. Those men who could trace their lineage to the Tokugawa family (*shinpan*) retained a special place in the Tokugawa order, and relatives could attain the status of shogun. Finally, the 'outside lords' (*tozama*) were those unfortunate men who had fought against Ieyasu's allies at Sekigahara. They were excluded from decision-making circles, and scattered throughout the realm in a manner that isolated and ostracized them. In the first fifty years of Tokugawa rule, 213 lords lost territories and titles and 172 saw their holdings increase.

The capital city of Edo was erected from the wetlands of eastern Japan, an area known as the Kantô plain, between 1603 and 1636. Originally, Ieyasu had decided on Edo, at the time a derelict, earthen-walled fortification on a bluff partially encircled by small creeks, because of its defensibility as a military fortification. The name Edo referred to the village of some 100 homes along the Edo River. Ieyasu began transforming the marshy site immediately. Labourers cut forests, levelled hills to reclaim the brackish wetlands, re-engineered rivers, erected bridges, built massive rock walls to guard the castle, and erected the many wooden structures sheltered within. It constituted one of the largest land reclamation projects in Japanese history and the outside lords carried much of the financial burden.

The unification of Japan and the construction of such 'castle towns' as Edo had severe consequences for the environment, particularly Japan's forests. In the sixteenth century, military fortifications required timber and, over the decades, warlords had repeatedly built them, ripped them down, or torched and toppled them. Nobunaga's 42 metre (138 feet) wooden keep at Azuchi near Lake Biwa, built in 1576, necessitated staggering amounts of lumber to complete. Town construction was similarly intensified by the wars of unification. Nearly as many towns were built in Japan in the eighteen years between 1572 and 1590 as in the preceding century. Temple construction also consumed large quantities of timber because warlords such as Ieyasu sought to curry favour with abbots by promising lumber for temple and shrine renovation projects. The premium placed on lumber meant that many Warring States lords sought to tighten control over forestlands in their domains by designating them as the 'lord's forests'. In 1564, for example, the powerful Hôjô family placed the forests of Mount Amagi under its direct administration, as did the Takeda family in the richly forested Kai province. Some Warring States lords, such as those in Sendai, undertook tree planting to guard coasts against erosion.

Despite these efforts, increased timber consumption under Hide-yoshi proved destructive. Erected in 1582–3, Osaka castle consumed vast quantities of timber, as did the wooden armadas so skilfully sunk by Admiral Yi during the abortive invasion of Korea. Opulent monuments to Hideyoshi's rule included the Jurakudai palace in Kyoto, the Hôkôji temple in Kyoto (housing a 50 metre [164 feet] statue of the Buddha outsizing the Tôdaiji temple in Nara), and elaborate reconstructions of Enryakuji on Mount Hiei and other temple complexes torched by Hideyoshi's predecessor. After Hideyoshi's death, Ieyasu kept up timber consumption, building monumental castles at Edo, Sunpu, and Nagoya, and aiding the construction of others at Hikone and Zeze (Ômi province), Sasayama and Kameyama (Tanba province), Takada (Echigo province), and Nijô in Kyoto. He also restored sections of the imperial complex in Kyoto, including construction of the Katsura Detached Palace. One historian estimates that the construction of the three large castles at Edo, Sunpu, and Nagoya required felling 2,750 hectares (6,800 acres) of lush conifer stands. Domain lords supplied much of this timber.

In order to properly celebrate Ieyasu's achievements, after his death in 1615 loggers sacrificed even more woodlands. The Tôshôgû shrine complex at Nikkô, Ieyasu's mausoleum, required large amounts of timber, as did more modest efforts to celebrate Ieyasu's life. In 1634, shogun Tokugawa Iemitsu (1604–51), after a procession to Kyoto, ordered the Asama shrine built in Sunpu, the location of Ieyasu's birth and death. To furnish the requisite timber, axemen felled trees along the Ôi River in present-day Shizuoka prefecture, and rafted some 60,000 pieces of lumber down to the ocean, eastward along the coast, and upriver again to Sunpu. These construction projects, from shrines to castles, required endless reconstruction because fire constantly burned down parts of Japan's wooden towns and cities. One historian estimates that ninety-three major fires (each one destroying at least ten blocks) occurred between 1601 and 1866, exerting relentless pressure on Japan's forests. By the late seventeenth century, when Japan was finally unified, much of the country had been clear-cut. As one Confucian scholar lamented, 'eight out of ten mountains of the realm have been denuded'.

Domain lords provided much of this lumber, and also footed the bill for policies such as the crippling 'alternate attendance' system

(1635), wherein Tokugawa shoguns made domain lords travel to Edo every other year. Not only did they pay for the expenses of the elaborate journey to the capital, but they also maintained residences there and left their wives and children behind. This 'alternate attendance' system facilitated national communication and cultural interaction, as well as urbanization and commercialization on such travel routes as the Eastern Sea Circuit. Moreover, the shogun made the entire realm more legible through mapping *daimyô* territories. These 'provincial maps', which proved strategically valuable to Edo military planners, contained information about borders and mountain ranges, as well as the 'village productive yield', which assisted with tax collection.

CONCLUSIONS

At the time of Ieyasu's death, most elements of Tokugawa rule were firmly in place. By the mid-seventeenth century, the role of raw violence and military power had ebbed as innovative strategies for articulating political authority spread over the realm. Domain lords preserved broad swaths of autonomy within their domains, particularly in economic matters, but politically Edo had emerged as Japan's new centre of gravity. Domain lords travelled to Edo every other year within the 'alternate attendance' system, dividing their time between local rule and bureaucratic duties in the capital. As a result of their annual migration, Japan's travel routes underwent widespread commercialization, as eateries, brothels, lodging, and other service industries sprouted up along the well-trodden circuits. Moreover, the shogun had ordered the lords to map their domains, rendering transparent the intricacies of local terrain, from mountains to coasts, as well as their agricultural productive capacities. As the Tokugawa's 'great peace' became a reality, Japan's early modern period was fully under way. Political centralization, proto-capitalist growth, widespread urbanization, secular political ideologies, technological advancements, politicized foreign diplomacy, and other historical developments linked Japan to a global community of nations undergoing similar changes.

7

Early Modern Japan, 1600–1800

Early modern Japan, or the period between 1600 and 1868, witnessed the birth of many of Japan's most enduring cultural and political attributes, as well as the expansion of its basic geographic boundaries. For our purposes, the characterization of this period as 'early modern' is important because it bridges the historical chasm that usually separates the 'traditional' and 'modern' realms of Japan's historical development. Once the three unifiers had completed the military and political labours of uniting the realm, Japan developed in a manner that propelled it into the modern age.

Japan's mid-nineteenth-century entry into the modern period was not exclusively the result of its adoption of Western civilization after the Meiji Restoration of 1868, but also the result of forces pushing from within. These forces caused indigenous changes, such as early forms of capitalism, increasing political centralization, development of science and technology, and the gradual emergence of early nationalism. These developments conspired with the importation of Western institutions and cultures to make Japan a rising Asian power in the late nineteenth century. The implications of identifying an early modern period in Japan are profound. They suggest commonalities in human histories, ones that transcend striking cultural variations. That is, as different from Europeans as Japanese had become over the centuries, with their blackened teeth and *chonmage* (shaven pate) hairstyles, they also developed in a manner that paralleled societies around the globe.

TOKUGAWA RULE

In 1603, the third unifier Tokugawa Ieyasu (1542–1616) had received the title 'Barbarian Subduing General' (*seii taishôgun*) from the emperor and established the Edo *bakufu*. The Warring States lords may have denuded Japan's hillsides in their sixteenth-century quest for military supremacy, but by the seventeenth century the political landscape had become far more orderly than the natural one. With the exception of the Shimabara Uprising (1637–8) and scattered peasant rebellions of varying severity, Japan experienced relative stability throughout the early modern years, encouraging cultural and economic growth. This is all the more remarkable considering that between the seventeenth and the mid-nineteenth century, ceaseless warfare wracked Europe: King William's War (1689–97), Queen Anne's War (1702–13), the Anglo-Spanish War (1739), King George's War (1743–8), the French and Indian War (1755–63), the American Revolution (1763–88), the Napoleonic Wars (1805–15), and the emergence of the German empire (1871–1914). In the same period, Japan avoided such debilitating conflicts. Instead, with an astonishing degree of independence, Japan developed the political, economic, and cultural institutions that drove its later emergence as a modern nation.

The key to Japan's most dramatic changes was seventeenth-century urban growth. When Toyotomi Hideyoshi had relocated 'country samurai' (*jizamurai*) to castle towns during the demilitarizing 'Sword Hunt' (1588), he inadvertently created some of the largest cities in the world. Samurai who, because of the nature of the social order, tended to produce little but consume much, populated these cities. Consequently, cities such as Edo became consumer centres with considerable influence, urban environments that reshaped the political, economic, cultural, and environmental landscape of early modern Japan.

Not only in the shogun's capital of Edo, but also in cities such as Himeji, Osaka, Wakayama, Okayama, and many others, urban populations expanded during the seventeenth century as a result of transplanted samurai. In some instances, samurai constituted 50–80 per cent of urban populations. To build cities and supply them, merchants and townspeople followed the samurai to urban areas, which, in the case of Edo, bulged with about 1 million souls by the early seventeenth century. Neo-Confucian ideologies, made manifest in the status system, created social divisions between samurai and others and determined the contours of Japan's cities. Indeed, over the course of the seventeenth century, the Edo *bakufu* crafted a syncretic ideology, originally consisting of Zen Buddhist and Shinto elements but later heavily infused with the Chinese Neo-Confucian thought of Zhu Xi (1130–1200). Signalling this ideological move, when Ieyasu died in 1616, the *bakufu* built the grand Nikkô mausoleum and Tôshôgû shrine complex in his honour. The Nikkô mausoleum manifested a strategy of legitimizing the *bakufu* not only through military strength, but the otherworldly power of sacred authority. Ieyasu came to be viewed as a 'divine ruler' in the context of the Tôshôgû shrine complex, while smaller individual shrines served as reminders of the earthly reach of the 'divine ruler' and his progeny.

As an ideological superstructure, Zhu Xi Neo-Confucianism was well suited to Tokugawa political ambitions. Neo-Confucianism encompassed the Four Books – *Lunyu* (Analects), *Mengzi* (Mencius), the *Da xue* (Greater Learning), and *Zhong yong* (Doctrine of the Mean) – all Chinese classics that advocated the basic Confucian precepts of 'preserving the heart', 'holding fast to the mean', and 'maintaining quiescence'. Neo-Confucianism was a belief system comprised of Confucian, Buddhist, and Taoist elements, and as such focused more on the metaphysical relationship between people and the universe than traditional Confucianism. In order to discover the 'original nature' of people, which was believed to be benevolent, people clarified their physical being through study and quiet contemplation. Hayashi Razan, (1583–1657), who ran the pre-eminent seventeenth-century institute for Neo-Confucian studies, described the process whereby natural human benevolence was made evil by the material desires of the physical body. 'One may wonder why human nature can be evil when it is inherently good', he wrote. 'Human nature is like water. If it is poured into a clean container, it remains pure; if it is poured into a dirty container, it becomes dirty ... Thus the heart becomes clouded.'

To clarify the cloudy waters of desire, Neo-Confucianism stressed quietness over political action, and as such promised to create harmony in the realm. Importantly, Neo-Confucianism also saw order in the natural world. If people 'investigate moral principle', Zhu Xi wrote, 'everything will naturally fall in place and interconnect with everything else; each thing will have its order'. Presumably, people would see that their place in the social order was a reflection of the natural world. Indeed, an important representation of that natural order was its social manifestation, a natural hierarchy that placed samurai (*shi*) at the top, and then farmers (*nô*), artisans (*kô*), and finally merchants (*shô*) at the bottom. This social hierarchy became the basis of the status system, the logic behind moving samurai to the cities and freezing the social order in the late sixteenth century. This status system drove many aspects of Tokugawa governance, society, economy, and culture, as well as manifesting itself through changes in the natural environment.

The Confucian status system also drove debates over law and private behaviour. In the famous 'Akô vendetta', fictionalized in *Chûshingura* (The treasury of loyal retainers, 1748) and celebrated in kabuki plays, the lord of Akô domain, Asano Naganori (1675–1701), slashed court etiquette master Kira Yoshinaka (1641–1703) with a dagger in the Edo castle compound in 1701 after the latter called him a country bumpkin. After the insult to Asano and his ancestral lands, attacking Kira made sense according to samurai codes of honour, particularly given the history between the two men. The public law of the shoguns, however, forbade drawing a sword in the castle, and the *bakufu* ordered Asano to commit suicide and forfeit his lands, making his retainers *rônin*, or master-less samurai. Led by Oishi Yoshio (1659–1703), the former retainers of Akô feigned drunken debauched lives, but secretly planned to avenge Asano. Two years later, in January 1703, the master-less samurai, led by Oishi, sliced off Kira's head at his mansion in Edo; they then carted the head to Asano's grave, having successfully avenged their lord. By any standard of their time, Akô's master-less samurai proved doyens of loyalty and samurai behaviour, but, once again, they had broken the law. The *bakufu* allowed the loyal retainers to commit ritual suicide, thus salvaging their honour. Ogyû Sorai (1666–1728), a noted Confucian scholar, justified the decision by explaining that the forty-seven *rônin* had broken the law, but they had possessed 'shame' and had retained a sense of 'righteousness', so they deserved honourable deaths. In sum, within the parameters of Confucian ideology modern notions of law and order were evolving under the Tokugawa shoguns and their counsellors.

If Edo served as the political hub for governing samurai, like the unruly Asano and his loyal men, then Osaka, also a large city with some 400,000 people, emerged as Japan's financial centre with a lively merchant culture. It was a city of traders, townspeople, and artisans. Domain lords exchanged their rice for currency in Osaka in order to make the long and expensive 'alternate attendance' (*sankin kôtai*) journeys to Edo. Ihara Saikaku (1642–93), a popular seventeenth-century writer, who narrated the lives of merchants and townspeople, observed that:

> Osaka is the foremost trading centre of Japan, and in the Kitahama rice-exchange five thousand *kanme* in promissory notes change hands within the quarter hour. While rice lies heaped in mountains in the granaries, speculators scan the heavens for signs of a storm this evening or rain tomorrow morning . . . The great merchants of Osaka, the foremost in Japan, are great in spirit, too; and such are their methods of business.

With so much increasing wealth and social clout, merchants could send their children to such academies as the Kaitokudô, where they received a Confucian education not unlike that Hayashi Razan taught to samurai youngsters. The scholar Ishida Baigan (1685–1744) submitted that because of their essential commercial role, merchants contributed to the overall order and prosperity of the realm, even though they ranked low in the Confucian hierarchy. 'Warriors, farmers, artisans and merchants are all of assistance in governing the nation', he insisted. 'If one says to the merchant, "Your profit alone is a sign of greed, and therefore a deviation from the right path," one is hating the merchant and wishing for his destruction. Why should the merchant alone be detested as an inferior being?'

Despite Ishida's logic, many Confucian-educated samurai did detest merchants and consistently identified them as a national pestilence, particularly when coupled with the slowly increasing impoverishment of the samurai over the Tokugawa years. Merchant luxuries chafed scholar Kumazawa Banzan (1619–91), who wrote that, 'in big cities and small alike, on land by rivers and sea which is convenient for transport, urban areas are being built, and luxury is growing day by day without check. Merchants grow rich while warriors are impoverished.' For Kumazawa, the problem was a systemic one: 'The poverty of the samurai also means that merchants have no one with whom they can exchange goods for grain, and only the big merchants become steadily richer.' Famously, Ogyû Sorai identified the dislocation of samurai from the land to the cities as the source of Japan's woes. He appealed to the ancient rulers of China and argued, 'The basis of the social order created by the ancient sages was that all people, both high and low, should live on the land.' In Japan's cities, 'Both greater and lesser people are living like guests at an inn, which is directly contrary to the way of the sages.'

However, Sorai's 'guests at an inn' became the basis for Japan's vibrant urban culture and proto-capitalistic economic growth. It also caused destabilizing changes in Japan's natural environment. Even though the Tokugawa shoguns originally established the capital of Edo to be the 'lord's city', merchants and other towns-people slowly claimed the city's spaces for themselves. The Edo native – who was said to 'receive his first bath in the water of the city's aqueducts; he grows up in sight of the gargoyles on the roof of Edo castle' – epitomized urban life with his cherished sense of sophistication. When together, these townspeople participated in parties where they improvised comic verse, arranged flowers, mimicked kabuki lines, told fortunes, and listened to street music and other performances. Highly literate, they borrowed books from book vendors such as the Suwaraya. They dined at newly built sushi vendors, satisfying their culinary desires with shrimp, egg, and an assortment of fish. Prosperity meant that they built better homes with strong stone foundations, where storage space, in the form of chests and cupboards, was required for the fruits of their conspicuous consumption. Such consumption became so conspicu-ous, in fact, that early modern Japan witnessed its first sumptuary regulations, such as those proposed by shogun Tokugawa

Tsunayoshi (1646–1709) in 1683. These were designed to keep
merchants from publicly flaunting their wealth and causing social
jealousy and chaos.

When books and shrimp failed to satisfy townspeople, they
visited the Yoshiwara pleasure quarters, where they strolled the
Nakanochô Boulevard window-shopping for the courtesans of the
bordellos. If estimates regarding syphilis and gonorrhoea rates are
accurate (somewhere around 30–40 per cent of the inhabitants of
Edo are believed to have had one of the diseases), the sex trade
proved quite widespread and presumably lucrative. Outside the
Yoshiwara, more specialized sex shops, such as 'Children's Shops',
satisfied customers with an appetite for young boys. The German
doctor Engelbert Kaempfer (1651–1716) wrote of teahouses that
catered to such clientele:

> On the chief street of this town were built nine or ten neat houses, or
> booths, before each of which sat one, two, or three young boys, of ten or
> twelve years of age, well dressed, with their faces painted, and feminine
> gestures, kept by their lewd and cruel masters for the secret pleasure
> and entertainment of rich travellers, the Japanese being very much
> addicted to this vice.

Often, fathers sold daughters to bordellos for complex economic
and ideological reasons. Principally, it related to the place of
women in early modern Japan's patrilinear order, wherein young
men, not women, continued family lines and paid respect to ancestral deities. Women were expected to act womanly, which meant,
according to the *Onna daigaku* (Greater learning for women,
1672), aspiring for 'gentle obedience, chastity, mercy, and quietness'. The bizarre story of a young woman named Také illustrates
the complexity of womanly behaviour in Japan's gender roles.
While Také was a little girl she was known to be a tomboy; later
in life, in a decidedly unwomanly move, she cut her hair and
assumed the persona of a young boy named Takejirô. The inn-
keeper she worked for was outraged and raped her in order to
reacquaint her with her womanliness. When she discovered that
she was pregnant, she fled and, when the child was born, promptly
killed it. When she was arrested, *bakufu* officials charged her with
'corrupting moral values', because she dissociated her gender from

her biological sex. In effect, she was arrested for not acting womanly. Just as status expectations proved politically important, wherein merchants were to act like merchants, so did gender roles. Such gender and status compartments governed Japanese society more or less strictly throughout the early modern years.

Despite such cultural obstacles, some women, such as Tadano Makuzu (1763–1825), became prominent scholars. While never debunking the Confucian order that relegated women to a subordinate position, instead, in *Hitori kangae* (Solitary thoughts, 1818), she argued that 'womanly accomplishments', such as those of her grandmother, constituted important contributions to society. The differences between women and men fit the yin-yang balance of Chinese cosmology, as did, she pointed out, the physiological differences between the sexes. Like her father, the scholar Kudô Heisuke (1734–1800), she wrote at length on domestic social problems and the threat posed by Russia.

The important point is that the Neo-Confucian status system provided the moral framework for Japanese society. It positioned samurai at the top of the social ladder and merchants at the bottom. It required little actual policing, other than the largely cultural monitoring that insisted women act womanly and samurai like samurai. But there was stability in such a social order. When the Meiji government abolished the status system, and lumped everybody together as 'commoners', violence ensued between farmers and former outcaste groups because the status categories that had once distinguished and sustained them were removed. In early modern Japan, the status system was manifested spatially in villages and cities, but the Meiji state, which trowelled the new ideological grout into the seams of Japanese social relations, mixed former outcastes and farmers as commoners, sparking violent episodes such as the Mimasaka Blood-Tax Rebellion (1873). The point is that the violence that ensued with the demolishing of the status system evidences the important harmonizing role it played in Tokugawa society.

CHANGES IN THE LAND

The ecological footprint of large early modern cities was considerable. In the countryside, supplying cities with goods transformed many subsistence farmers to cash crop entrepreneurs. In turn, complex kinship relationships in rural households began breaking down. In the medieval years, farm labour had often taken the form of patriarchs adopting sons into their families because they needed more labour; by the eighteenth century, however, farm labour had become more business-like than kinship-based, as seasonal labour replaced adoptions. Seasonal labourers proved less expensive because farmers did not have to support them year round. Rather, they paid them only during the harvest. No longer did adopted sons, elements of Japan's excess rural population, labour and live on farms and worship ancestral deities; they now found themselves dispossessed from the land and vulnerable to food shortages that swept Japan in the eighteenth century, particularly in the northeast. Millions perished in these disasters, which were a product of everything from shifting weather patterns and Icelandic eruptions to Japan's emerging proto-capitalist economy. Four devastating famines occurred during Japan's early modern period, known as the Kan'ei Famine (1642–43), the Kyôhô Famine (1732), the Tenmei Famine (1782–8), and the Tenpô Famine (1833–7), all named for the imperial reigns in which they occurred. A disastrous melding of natural and man-made forces conspired to intensify these famines and their causes, illustrating the environmental echoes of the historical changes that transformed Japan. Such events fore-shadowed generations of natural disasters, such as the 11 March 2011 'triple disaster' in northeastern Japan.

Japan's sixteenth-century unification, the status system, and the ecological footprint of large castle towns worked in conjunction with natural forces to create famines. In this sense, they were as much unnatural disasters as they were natural ones. Of these, the Tenmei (1782–8) famine was probably the cruellest. It witnessed massive food shortages and afflicted many of Japan's provinces, but the northeast experienced the direst consequences. In 1782, Hirosaki domain in the far northeast suffered unseasonably cool tempera-tures, driving wind, ceaseless rain, and other weather anomalies associated with the Little Ice Age, which affected farmers around the world. The eruption of Lakagígar and Mount Grímsvötn in southern Iceland further intensified these conditions. Indeed, the Edo *bakufu* might have successfully isolated Japan from global political currents by evicting missionaries, but it could not isolate Japan from global environmental or climatological ones. To explain, Lakagígar is a system of volcanic fissures that is connected to Mount Grímsvötn. In 1783 and 1784, the fissures erupted in an explosion that lasted for over eight months. During this period, the fissures and volcano belched out some 14 cubic kilometres (3.36 cubic miles) of basalt lava and enormous plumes of deadly hydrofluoric acid and sulphur dioxide that spread around the world. The toxic plume killed over half of Iceland's livestock, and the resulting famine killed a quarter of Iceland's human population. The mayhem of the 'Skaftá fires', as the eruption is called in Iceland, was global in scale, causing deadly famine in Egypt and extreme weather events in Europe.

In Japan, these volcanic eruptions combined with global and local weather anomalies to slash Hirosaki domain's harvest to a quarter of normal. The next year, similar conditions persisted, and when Tsugaru authorities mistakenly transported 40,000 bales of rice to Edo and Osaka as tribute to the Edo *bakufu*, rice scarcity struck the entire domain. Limited supplies meant that rice prices soared and by summer no rice was available for hungry bellies. Family farms were abandoned and riots ensued. By the autumn, people were rummaging for roots and wild plants, as well as eating oxen, horses, dogs, and cats. Reports of cannibalism were also widespread as the situation grew increasingly desperate. In response, the *bakufu* offered Hirosaki loans to build relief huts and rice was purchased from neighbouring domains. By 1784, however, as a result of malnutrition and weakened immune systems, disease struck the famine-ridden areas, and fatalities skyrocketed. By the end of the famine, the death toll in Hirosaki was in the hundreds of thousands. Nationally, the Tenmei famine (Figure 12) killed close to one million souls, largely those made vulnerable by Japan's economic transformations.

What had transformed these natural disasters into decidedly unnatural ones was the proto-capitalization of the Japanese economy. Take Hachinohe's 'wild boar famine' of 1749, which occurred, as did the Tenmei Famine, as a result of local and global weather anomalies, but also as a result of traceable man-made forces. Over the course of the eighteenth century, farmers in Hachinohe, also in the northeast, had started slashing and burning swaths

12 Image from the Tenmei famine.

of new land for soybean agriculture, almost exclusively to supply
Edo and other urban markets. Soybeans are an important part of the
Japanese diet, supplying badly needed protein. Originally, farmers
had raised soybeans closer to Edo, but as farmers replanted those
fields with mulberry for sericulture, a far more lucrative cash crop,
lands further afield were re-engineered to feed Japan's cities. This
upland soybean agriculture required that farmers rotate fields, or let
them go fallow, in order to keep them productive; but fallow fields,
particularly in upland areas, served as prime wild boar habitat.
When farmers cut down acorn trees to make room for more soybean crops, they inadvertently deprived wild boar of an important
food source and the always-hungry ungulates searched for others,
including wild yams and arrowroot. As a result of the turn to
upland soybean farming, Hachinohe's wild boar population
exploded, to the point where the hooved ungulates began competing
with farmers for food. This competition became dire during the
Little Ice Age (*c.*1550–1850), when crops declined. Normally,
farmers could return to their land to dig up wild yams, arrowroot,

and other wild plants, but many of the seasonal labourers, Japan's landless class, did not have access to land to do so. Even those who set out to scour the mountains for wild yams and arrowroot discovered that wild boar had got there first. In the end, thousands of farmers died in the disaster, one caused, at least in part, by the market requirements of Japan's large cities. On a smaller scale, Hachinohe farmers found themselves victims to similar global forces that savaged India during the Bengal famine (1769–73), when Indians starved as the British East India Company shipped grain out of Indian ports. It is not surprising that some historians have likened the integration of domains into Japan's early modern order to internal colonialism, in that it had similarly jarring consequences.

The ecological footprint of Japan's cities manifested itself in the environment in other ways as well. It was not just famished, malnourished bodies that bore the scars of Japan's economic transformations. To build such large cities, the timber industry expanded from subsistence and command logging, wherein lords ordered trees to build their castles, to more entrepreneurial extraction. With entrepreneurial logging, merchant families such as the Yamatoya felled some 8,000 trees near the Tone and Katashina rivers, giving less than half to the shogun and selling the rest on the market. Because of the high value of timber, a tradition of forest management emerged in Japan, keeping the archipelago relatively green in the seventeenth and eighteenth centuries. Nearby seas also underwent changes because of the Japanese economy. Japanese opened up new fertilizer fisheries to fuel cash-crop farms. Herring fisheries expanded to the distant northern lands of Ezo, where Japanese merchants from Osaka and Ōmi employed Ainu to catch fish that they then dried and shipped to the south. In this manner, the urban footprint of early modern Japan extended beyond the traditional borders of the realm. It altered not only timber supplies and forested environments on Honshu, but also fisheries and marine environments around Hokkaido.

THE CONQUEST OF EZO

The trade in Hokkaido led to changes in the land and epidemiological exchanges that undermined the ability of Ainu to resist

Japanese incursions. The herring fishery served as only one com-
ponent of the early modern Japanese intrusion into Ezo. It is
important to remember that the island of Hokkaido, the land
formerly known as Ezo, constitutes about 20 per cent of Japan, so
the conquest of this area demands our attention. Later, it became a
major source of coal, a critical resource that fuelled Japan's early
industrialization, and was transformed into an agricultural bread-
basket with the help of American advisers, well schooled in colonizing lands formerly inhabited by indigenous peoples. Importantly,
the Japanese conquest of Ainu lands started in the political reorganization initiated by the Edo *bakufu*.

After the Battle of Sekigahara (1600), Ieyasu had recognized the
Matsumae family's 'exclusive rights' to trade with the Ainu and,
during the seventeenth and eighteenth centuries, they expanded
trade with Ainu throughout Hokkaido. The Matsumae family
governed a small territory on the southernmost tip of Hokkaido
that they called Wajinchi, or 'Japanese land'. Just like early modern
Japanese, the Ainu of Hokkaido proved anything but unified, and
archaeologists have discerned five major groups – Shumukuru,
Menashikuru, Ishikari, Uchiura, and Sôya – that inhabited
Hokkaido and that proved distinguishable through language,
burial customs, and other cultural practices. Because the Matsumae
family was unable to grow rice, largely due to northern latitudes
and colder sub-arctic/temperate climates, the household relied on a
thriving trade with Ainu, who were in part remnants of the earlier
Epi-Jômon Emishi. In an initially small-scale trade, Matsumae
boats travelled to coastal outposts scattered throughout Hokkaido,
where they exchanged desirable items, ranging from animal pelts
and bird feathers to exotic pharmaceuticals.

The trading posts were built on coastal areas near rivers
because Ainu communities, called *pet-iwor* in the Ainu language,
tended to be located there. This had to do with centuries of
hunter-gatherer heritage. In large part, Ainu identified with their
home through a sacred relationship with local *kamuy*, or deities,
that often took the form of animals. In turn, the sacred relationship with these animals was expressed through hunting: Ainu
hunters liberated the animal's spirit through the kill. Animals
such as brown bear, deer, and salmon were part of Ainu

communities and, as such, Ainu hunters had sacred obligations towards them, just as they did their own ancestors. The *iyomante*, often called the 'bear ceremony', was perhaps the most elaborate expression of these obligations, wherein Ainu raised brown bears from cubs and sacrificially slaughtered them to maintain ties to the land and its deities.

In other words, hunting meant something different to Ainu than it did to Japanese. This is not to say that Japanese had thoroughly objectified animals. It is true that anatomical parts of many animals, such as bear gall-bladder and fur seal penis, possessed pharmacological value; and otter and deer pelts conveyed prestige as gifts in political circles. Moreover, Japanese, like the Ainu, believed animals to have a sacred side as well, in the form of Shinto deities called *kami*. More elaborately, Japanese associated some animals, such as wolves, with not only Shinto messengers, such as the Daimyôjin, but with Buddhist deities as well. In other words, the encounter between the Ainu and Japanese was not simply one between heartless proto-capitalists, who had objectified animals and killed their nature, and spiritual hunters who worshipped them. Rather, trade benefited certain constituencies on both sides and had multiple and competing meanings, even though Ainu ultimately faired far worse. In the end, the roots of Ainu dependency were firmly planted in trade with the Japanese.

Eventually, the competition over trade resources pitted Ainu communities against one another, leading to the largest war in Ezo, called Shakushain's War (1669). In perhaps the only example of the Tokugawa ruler actually having to 'subdue barbarians', as the shogunal title required, the *bakufu* dispatched troops to Hokkaido to crush Shakushain's unified Ainu band. In the aftermath of the conflict, trade intensified, but so did attempts to divide, by customary difference, Japanese and Ainu on Hokkaido. Consequently, the early modern state proved capable of defining, more precisely, what it was to be Japanese in the frontier regions. What it meant to be Japanese, a nascent national identity, had been taking shape over the centuries: Kitabatake Chikafusa, as we learned, had defined Japan as a 'divine land'. This was in the aftermath of the Mongol invasion, when Japanese, in a violent encounter, faced a brutal external threat. Shakushain's War was a violent encounter, too, suggesting that contact with outsiders, whether they were Mongol invaders, Iberian missionaries, or Ainu rebels, contributed to the forging of Japanese identity. The encounter with outsiders forced Japanese to transcend internal divisions, such as the silos inherent in the status system, and create definitions of an increasingly national self.

In elaborate ceremonies, Tokugawa officials made Ainu – like the Ryukyu Island embassies on procession to Edo, discussed briefly earlier – wear traditional Ainu clothing and hairstyles, so that the customary lines between Ainu and Japanese could be policed in the north. This became increasingly complicated over the course of the seventeenth and eighteenth centuries, as more mixing between Ainu and Japanese occurred. Shakushain, who waged war against the Japanese in 1669, had a Japanese son-in-law named Shôdayû, who was executed by samurai along with Shakushain in the aftermath of the war. Because it became increasingly complicated to distinguish Ainu from Japanese, at least in southern Hokkaido, those distinctions had to be manufactured through ritual. The case of Iwanosuke is instructive. Iwanosuke was an Ainu from southern Hokkaido who had thoroughly assimilated to Japanese customs. He had a Japanese name, lived in a predominantly Japanese village, and wore his hair in Japanese fashion. But during New Year's ceremonies, Matsumae officials transformed Iwanosuke into a representative of the Ainu people, forcing him to grow out his hair and wear traditional Ainu clothing. It was through the performance of such difference, a kind of ceremonial diplomacy, that the customary boundaries of the early modern Japanese state were demarcated. In Edo, Ryukyuan embassies from the south, also forced to wear traditional garb, served similar purposes. The important point is that borderlands, the ragged edges of Japan, had come to play a critical role in the formation of a Japanese national identity, one that anticipated the nationalism of the Meiji period (1868–1912).

Over the eighteenth century, trade with Japanese, whether ritualized or others, exacted a heavy toll on Ainu communities. Ainu overfished salmon and overhunted deer for trade with Japanese, while Japanese inadvertently introduced smallpox, measles, and syphilis to Ainu communities. Ainu undermined their own subsistence systems as such Japanese trade items as silks, swords, iron goods, rice, and saké became prestige items in Ainu communities. Ainu chiefs, such as Shakushain, rose to prominence through trade with Japanese, just as Japanese, such as members of the Matsumae family, gained prestige through gift-giving practices with the Tokugawa family; these gifts included pharmaceuticals such as bear gall-bladder, as well as military items such as eagle feathers for arrows, hawks for falconry, and deer pelts for saddles, all obtained in Ezo. Trade required that animals fall from the world of spirits and ancestors to the world of proto-capitalism, and become 'hunted commodities' in the context of interaction with the Japanese. By the nineteenth century, Ainu populations had collapsed from disease, by nearly half according to some estimates, and Hokkaido was ripe for swift incorporation into the modern Japanese state within a matter of decades.

LEGIBILITY AND THE REALM

Early modern Japan also witnessed the most concerted efforts to render legible the emerging nation, to imagine the Japanese community as having common cultural and geographic traits. When the renowned poet Matsuo Bashô travelled north and penned his famous seventeenth-century *Oku no hosomichi* (Narrow road to the deep north), he contributed to establishing a sense of cultural legibility within Japan, one that closely wed time and space to the nascent nation. Each location he plotted in his narrative and evoked through his poetry created an axis of history and geography to describe Japan's national experience. In 1689, Bashô became 'filled with a strong desire to wander', and set out to northeastern Japan to visit locations written about by earlier Japanese poets. He travelled geographically, covering the rugged space of the northeast; but he also travelled historically, exploring how earlier poets had created and recreated locations and, thereby, a cultural commons in the landscape of the northeast. Bashô imagined a cultural community bounded by Japan's geography, and sought to trace that through his own musings and poetic contributions. His writings were indicative of the traces of an early national consciousness coalescing in the early modern period.

Many of the locations he visited on his journey were shrines, but others were natural artefacts. Bashô rested his 'worn out legs' under the shade of a giant willow tree celebrated in the poetry of Saigyô (1118–90). He passed through the ancestral lands of Satô Motoharu, whose family had fought bravely at the side of the tragic Minamoto no Yoshitsune. While stopping at a temple for tea, he viewed treasures such as Yoshitsune's sword and Benkei's satchel. He reminisced about the famous pine of Takekuma, and responded to the poet Kyohaku, who had also written about the twin-trunked evergreen. The pine was the 'most beautiful shape one could possibly think of for a pine tree', Bashô wrote. When at the ancient site of Taga castle, he contemplated a monument dated to the reign of Emperor Shômu (701–56). He evoked the immutability of the Japanese past, and its persistence in the cultural imagination. Bashô wrote, 'In this ever-changing world where mountains crumble, rivers change their courses, roads are deserted, rocks are buried, and old trees yield to young shoots, it was nothing short of a miracle that this monument alone had survived the battering of a thousand years to be the living memory of the ancients.' He remembered, 'I felt as if I was in the presence of the ancients themselves', in the presence of Japan's cultural forebears. On visiting the Myôjin shrine, he was 'impressed by the fact that the divine powers of the gods had penetrated even to the extreme north of our country, and I bowed in humble reverence before the altar'. Through identifying such cultural markers, Bashô contributed to the defining of 'our country', demarcating its cultural limits, boundaries, and characteristics.

Bashô was a contributor to a growing body of cultural knowledge that proved an important building block for the modern Japanese nation. This metaphorical archive of public knowledge, knit together by Tokugawa political forces, linked Japanese living in the south to those in the far northeast. The archive was built over the course of centuries, and it was consolidated through the alternate attendance system, where the capital of Edo became a meeting place that homogenized dialects and dispersed the stories of natural and cultural artefacts that comprised the fabric of the nation.

The early modern period was an important time for other forms of nation building as well. Indeed, more concrete ways of mapping borders were undertaken in the eighteenth and nineteenth centuries. The Tokugawa shoguns took a keen interest in mapping the realm. The shoguns ordered maps from domain lords on three occasions (1644, 1696–1702, and 1835–8). When domain lords submitted such 'provincial maps' (*kuniezu*) to Edo they served important political and military purposes. When domain lords submitted provincial maps in 1700, for example, all the maps were compiled and redrawn. The new map, the *Shôhô Nihonzu* (The Shôhô era map of all Japan), featured the greater realm, with its jagged coastline, meandering rivers, ports and trade routes, and provincial boundaries. For the first time the rulers of Japan could gaze down on a standardized, legible representation of the entire realm and imagine the extent of its geographic and topographic features.

Later, the shogun ordered mapmaker Ino Tadataka (1745–1818) to survey the coastline of Japan, utilizing Western cartographic techniques. In effect, he sought to further define the geographic boundaries of Japan. In 1821, Ino's monumental *Dai Nippon enkai yochi zenzu* (Complete map of greater Japan's coastline) became available to Tokugawa policy-makers. Traditional Japanese maps might contain extensive textual information, taxonomic representations, or religious significance, making them dependent on local knowledge; but Inô built his maps with the new language of Western science, incorporating longitudinal and latitudinal lines, thereby also making Japan legible to a global early modern community. With Inô's map, Japan was placed within the same spatial logic as Europe and its colonies, paving the way for the positioning of the country according to the logic of the modern world. Inô's maps also removed references to human taxonomies and cultures, a practice that, in the cartographic imagination, depopulated regions of future imperial interest. Building on the cartographic work of Inô, Mamiya Rinzô (1754–1836) took Western techniques northward, travelling through Hokkaido, Sakhalin, and as far as the Amur Estuary, mapping the region and documenting the inhabitants and natural resources. He also deployed European cartographic science, placing Sakhalin on a universally recognizable grid and anticipating later Japanese imperial ambitions in the region.

CONCLUSION

Japan's early modern period witnessed the strengthening of an understanding of what constituted 'our country', or Japan, a recognition that transcended specific status, regional, or family categories of identity. As an early form of nationalism, this process started with the centralizing of the realm under the Tokugawa shoguns and the political requirement that all domain lords participate in the alternate attendance system in Edo. While they travelled, domain lords planted the seeds of commercialization along Japan's most trodden travel circuits. While in Edo, they undertook official duties, exchanged stories, homogenized dialects, offered gifts, and began the process of creating, visit after visit, generation after generation, a national political culture revolving around Edo, which in location if not in name, remains Japan's political, cultural, and financial capital. The Tokugawa system never completely erased dangerous individual political ambitions of age-old domain rivalries, or other forces that kept Japan politically fractured, but Japanese rulers clearly began operating under the logic of the existence of a national authority. Nonetheless, the Edo *bakufu* created a system with inherent problems, ones that manifested themselves in the late eighteenth and nineteenth centuries, and eventually led to the collapse of the regime in Edo and the birth of the Meiji Restoration in 1868.

8

The Rise of Imperial Nationalism, 1770–1854

The Tokugawa Peace endured for well over two centuries. Early on, however, cracks began to disfigure the edifice of Tokugawa rule. Over time, these cracks expanded and branched out into a complex web of problems that toppled the Edo *bakufu* in the mid-nineteenth century, ending centuries of samurai rule in Japan. Some of these problems were domestic in nature and included peasant uprisings, disparities between merchant wealth and samurai poverty, bizarre examples of urban millenarianism, and ideological challenges calling for a return to imperial rule. These domestic problems were compounded by external ones, which included Russian encroachment in the North Pacific and the arrival of US Commodore Matthew C. Perry (1794–1858) and his smoke-belching 'black ships' in 1853. Together, these domestic and international forces overburdened the Edo *bakufu* and it collapsed in 1868 in a relatively brief conflict called the Boshin War (1868–9).

CRACKS IN TOKUGAWA LEGITIMACY

Some 2,809 different instances of peasant rebellion occurred during the early modern period, in forms ranging from 'direct petition' and violent 'collective action' to 'smash and break' and 'world renewal'. Though most peasant rebellions occurred for reasons more economic than political – that is, they sought to smash the houses of local wealthy merchants or peasants who had profited from the vibrant cash-crop economy – some rebellions proved politically subversive and carried aspirations of regime change. An implicit 'moral economy' existed in the Neo-Confucian orthodoxy of the early modern years, assuring that 'honourable peasants' were treated fairly by 'benevolent lords'. When domain lords squeezed peasants too hard, as Sakura Sôgorô (d. 1653) and others in Narita experienced in the seventeenth century, they directly petitioned domain lords and, in the case of Sôgorô, even the shogun, to alleviate some of the economic hardships in their villages. They believed they were entitled to live. 'In fear and trembling we respectfully present our statement in writing', explained the petition that Sôgorô delivered in dramatic form to the shogun in Edo. The petition explained that the 'peasants in the villages have suffered many years of privations. Right now they are on the brink of starvation, and they are unable to survive.' Because of exorbitant rice taxes, 'Many people, old and young, men and women, a total of 737, have starved to death by the roadside or have become beggars.' Ultimately, in this episode, Sôgorô and his entire family were executed for directly petitioning the shogun. In a brutal scene, Sôgorô and his wife watched, while tied to crosses, as executioners decapitated their children one by one, before their own violent deaths. Even though Sôgorô became a peasant martyr, the price for petitioning the shogun proved enormous. Regardless, the 'moral economy' that shaped political relations between the Tokugawa state and local village heads began to expose serious flaws in the fabric of Japan's transforming economy.

Later, 'smash and break' uprisings in Shindatsu (1866), largely a result of social changes caused by silk production, and 'world renewal' uprisings in Aizu (1868), proved deadly and disruptive, as angry peasant mobs, dislocated by economic changes discussed in the previous chapter, ransacked the homes of wealthier villagers. As a result of the proto-industrial economy, other peasants had profited handsomely from economic growth. As one observer wrote, 'Now the most lamentable abuses of the present day among the peasants is that those who have become wealthy forget their status and live luxuriously like city aristocrats.' However, the same forces that brought wealth to some brought poverty and starvation to others, and the 'world renewal' uprisings of the later Tokugawa years had the political trappings of revolution. Meanwhile, in large cities such as Edo, a phenomenon called *ofudafuri* reportedly occurred, wherein talismans from the Grand Shrine of Ise, the head shrine of the imperial family, were rumoured to have showered down in cities, prompting dancing in the streets. In a dangerous disregard for the strictures of the status system and gender lines, merry-making townspeople cross-dressed, wore masks, and danced in the streets. While dancing and parading they shouted, 'Isn't it great!' and 'What the hell!' The scene took on the feel of a millenarian moment – clearly, the winds of change were freshening.

EXTERNAL THREATS

The arrival of Commodore Matthew C. Perry in July 1853 at Uraga near Edo brought this domestic turmoil to a head. As yet another foreign encounter that led to nationalistic reactions, Perry's arrival, and his three-part ultimatum to the *bakufu*, tipped the government off balance. President Millard Fillmore (1800–74) asked that Japan initiate diplomatic relations, treat marooned whalers more humanely (many were simply beheaded once they washed ashore), open ports, and, more generally, initiate commercial relations. Flummoxed by the persistent Perry (he left Japan only to return one year later, in February 1854), the Edo *bakufu* inadvertently prompted a national debate by soliciting advice from the domain lords. In doing so, the realm divided into two camps: one seeking to 'expel the barbarians, revere the emperor' (*sonnô jôi*) and the other to 'open the country' (*kaikoku*). Pointing to domestic problems facing Japan, particularly the impoverishment of the samurai and the growth in merchant wealth, the 'expel the barbarians' camp argued that the *bakufu*, by not administering the realm properly and tackling the threat posed by Perry's 'black ships', had failed in its titular duties. After all, the shogun was the 'Barbarian Subduing General'. The shogun served as a kind of manager for the emperor and he had failed, many claimed, in his duty to do so. Their solution: kick the Westerners out and rally around direct imperial rule.

On the other hand, the 'open the country' camp pointed out that to resist Perry and the European powers would be inviting national destruction. Japan should acquiesce to Perry's demands and open the country; after centuries of virtual isolation from Europe and the US Japanese observers knew what was unfolding in China with the Opium War, where the British deployed with customary ruthlessness the technologies of war, such as the steam-powered *Nemesis*, to demolish the Qing navy and coastal defences. As the scholar Sakuma Shôzen (1811–64) wrote, 'According to what I've heard, the situation is that the Europeans [British] have polluted the district Li-yüeh, which had existed since the Tang dynasty. Our country is only a short distance by sea from China, and no country in the East will be able to remain out of the reach of the yearly attacks of British ships.' To Sakuma, the threat of Westerners was quite real.

The 'expel the barbarians' camp drew on decades of debate that had fermented in Japan over whether the emperor should directly rule the realm. 'Nativist' (*kokugaku*) scholars such as Kamo Mabuchi (1697–1769), Motoori Norinaga (1730–1801), and Hirata Atsutane (1776–1843) emerged as influential voices in the debate as they, in different ways, criticized the *bakufu*'s ideological fixation on Chinese philosophy. In essence, they argued that Japan, not China, was the 'Middle Kingdom', because unlike the Chinese emperor who was merely the 'son of heaven', Japan's emperor was heaven itself, or a 'living god'. They often called Neo-Confucianism 'artificial', rather than natural, in the sense that it organized society according to manufactured categories. Only Japan, Kamo submitted, had 'transmitted the language of the gods' through the imperial institution. Kamo then wrote, 'To know the *kokutai* [national essence] is to know the ancestors and, thus, to exhaust loyal intention to the emperor . . .' It is important to note that the term *kokutai* later became a kind of omnibus term for describing cultural and political attributes unique to the Japanese and their nation. Norinaga, too, focused on the 'unbroken succession' of Japan's emperors. Criticizing Neo-Confucian scholars, he argued that they had 'failed to comprehend and realize that the Way of the Gods [Shinto] is superior to the Ways of foreign lands'. These scholars fixated on language as the key to understanding Japan's past, prior to the wholesale importation of Buddhism and Confucianism in the sixth and seventh centuries; they studied ancient songs and the poems of classic literary anthologies. The important point for these men, however, was that what made Japan exceptional was its illustrious imperial line. Ultimately, this would become the basis of imperial nationalism in the Meiji years, as well as the 'Shôwa Restoration' that fostered Japanese fascism in the 1930s.

Even Neo-Confucian scholars began to argue for the restoration of the emperor. In what is known as Wang Yangming (1472–1529) Confucianism, scholars argued that the 'static' nature of the *bakufu*'s ideology had overly stressed 'contemplativeness' rather than 'public action'. Wang Yangming's (he was a prominent Ming philosopher and military general) emphasis on 'public action' threatened the *bakufu* because it was often aimed at the healing of social and political ills, which put the Tokugawa regime in the crosshairs. Practitioners of Wang Yangming, such as Ôshio Heihachirô (1793–1837), focused obsessively on the expression of 'sincerity of will' and 'righteousness of purpose' through 'rectifying public injustices'. One such major injustice, it turned out, was the decaying administrative capabilities of Tokugawa shoguns. In 1834, Ôshio published *Senshindô satsuki* (School to cleanse the inner spirit) and quickly became one of Japan's most prominent Wang Yangming thinkers, a kind of quasi-revolutionary. In 1837 Ôshio launched a failed rebellion in Osaka, in his attempt to rectify society through public action. The rebel's slogans were 'Save the People!' and, important for our purposes here, 'Restore the Emperor!' The rebellion failed and Ôshio committed suicide in his home while fires raged around him, but subversive forces had been set in motion. For Wang Yangming scholars of many stripes, rectifying society meant restoring the emperor and destroying the *bakufu*.

The Mito School also took up the mantle of restoring the emperor. This tack was a tricky one for Mito domain because Mito *daimyô* carried the last name of 'Tokugawa' and could become shoguns. Prominent Mito School scholars, such as Fujita Yûkoku (1774–1826), Aizawa Seishisai (1781–1863), and Fujita Tôko (1806–55), also submitted that Japan needed to follow the 'imperial way'. Aizawa was the most outspoken of the Mito critics. In his *Shinron* (New theses, 1825), he took aim at failed Tokugawa policies, greedy merchants, and menacing foreigners. Many of the domain lords had fallen into debt, explained Aizawa, and 'cunning, tight-fisted profit mongers manipulated the great lords of the land like so many puppets-on-a-string. Clearly, the realm's wealth had fallen into the merchants' clutches.' Drawing on traditional fears of Christianity, he cautioned his readers against Westerners and their insidious religion: 'They all believe in the same religion, Christianity, which they use to annex territories. Wherever they go, they destroy native houses of worship, deceive local peoples, and seize those lands. These barbarians will settle for nothing less than subjugating the rulers of all nations and conscripting all peoples into their ranks.' He then spun his critique into a nationalist discourse that could have come straight from the mouths of propagandists during the Pacific War, writing: 'Our Divine Land is where the sun rises and where the primordial energy originates ... Japan's position at the vertex of the earth makes it the standard for the nations of the world. Indeed, it casts light over the world, and the distance which the resplendent imperial influence reaches knows no limit.'

Sakuma Shôzan (1811–64), who wrote earlier of the Opium War in China, emerged as another critic of moral decline in the Tokugawa years, but embraced a more practical approach. His slogan, 'eastern ethics as base, Western technology as means', straddled the two ideological camps. He believed that Japan needed to restore the emperor to power to stop Japan's moral decline, while also embracing Western technology to defend itself. The urgency of the situation in China necessitated a practical approach, and 'expelling the barbarians', no matter how compelling, was impossible until Japan adopted the requisite military technology to do so. He divided his philosophy in this manner: 'In teachings concerning morality, benevolence, and righteousness, filial piety and brotherly love, loyalty and faithfulness, we must follow the examples and precepts of the Chinese sages. In astronomy, geography, navigation, surveying, the investigation of the principle of all things, the art of gunnery, commerce, medicine, machinery and construction, we must rely mainly on the West.' Ultimately, this practical approach came to characterize Japan during the Meiji years, but only after the dust had settled from the collapse of Tokugawa rule.

It was not only in the arenas of political discourse and nascent imperial nationalism that scholars mounted ideological challenges to the Tokugawa Neo-Confucian orthodoxy. It is important to remember that Neo-Confucianism served as a larger philosophical package, one that encompassed not only political ideas, but also medicine, natural history, and cosmology. At about the same time that nativist thinkers began to attack Neo-Confucianism as 'artificial' and inappropriate for Japan, physicians began to see discrepancies between Chinese anatomical atlases and actual bodies. This was further dramatized by the importation of Dutch anatomical atlases, which Japanese physicians found to be far more accurate than the Chinese ones. It did not take long for Japanese scholars to make broader connections between inaccurate Chinese medical atlases and possible inaccuracies in Chinese political philosophies. Once again, the Neo-Confucian orthodoxy came under fire, this time because of the emergence of empirical observation and Dutch medicine in Japan.

COSMOPOLITAN SCIENCE AND CONFUCIAN DECLINE

The development of sciences in early modern Japan, particularly the influence of 'Dutch learning', thus created another source of cracks in the edifice of Tokugawa authority. On the battlefield of knowledge surrounding the body, understanding human anatomy through dissection became the focus of many physicians interested in European medicine. Whereas Neo-Confucian medicine had favoured a conservative, non-interventionist approach to the body, Dutch learning offered a more revolutionary scientific gaze, one that probed inside the body. Early on, however, certain Neo-Confucianists objected to opening and peering into bodies because of the threat it posed to traditional understandings of anatomy and the established medical sciences. Indirectly, questioning Neo-Confucian medicine came to mean questioning the ideological foundation on which Tokugawa rule rested.

In his scathing critique of the practice of dissection, for example, the physician Sano Yasusada ridiculed the need to open bodies and see human organs. Sano wrote of dissecting the body and observing the internal organs: 'I cannot imagine what is to be gained by looking at them, listening to them, or talking about them.' Other physicians, however, such as Yamawaki Tôyô (1705–62) and Sugita

Genpaku (1733–1817), similar to their European counterparts, believed there was much to be gained by opening and probing the body. For some European and Japanese physicians, execution grounds, with their bird-pecked corpses and sun-bleached bones, proved irresistible hunting grounds for anatomical discoveries.

In *Rangaku kotohajime* (The beginnings of Dutch learning, 1815), Sugita (Figure 13) told the now-famous story of the dissection of an elderly woman, a criminal nicknamed Old Hag Green Tea. Police had executed her at the Kozukapara execution grounds in April 1771. Usually only outcastes, the *eta* or *burakumin*, handled dead bodies because of fears of defilement, which was one social factor inhibiting the empirical study of human anatomy in early modern Japan. Maeno Ryôtaku (1723–1803), another physician, accompanied Sugita, and brought with him a copy of *Anatomische Tabellen*, an anatomy text by the Danzig physician Johannes Adam Kulmus (1689–1745) published in German in

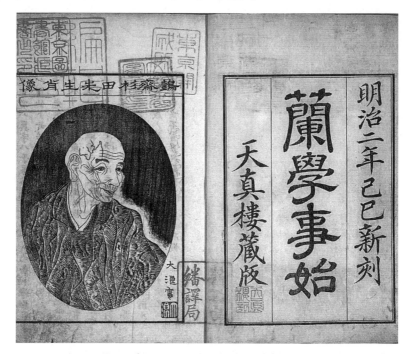

13 Sugita Genpaku as appears in title and frontispiece of *Rangaku kotohajime*, 1869 (The Beginnings of Dutch Learning, 1815).

1725. Japanese knew the text by its Dutch title, *Ontleedkundige tafelen*, published nine years later. Maeno had obtained the copy in Nagasaki, where the Dutch East India Company traded with Japanese from the small, man-made islet of Dejima. Coincidentally, Sugita had acquired a copy of the text as well. Nagasaki continuously provided the conduit through which Dutch learning entered Japan. Both Sugita and Maeno observed how differently the Dutch text depicted the lungs, heart, stomach, and spleen when compared to anatomical images handed down by Neo-Confucian medicine. They initially questioned the accuracy of the Dutch text, but changed their minds with the Kozukapara dissection, when they probed and peered inside the body before them.

Toramatsu, the outcaste slated to perform the autopsy, had been taken ill and his ninety-year-old grandfather substituted for him. He sliced through Old Hag Green Tea's wrinkled skin and pried open the flesh. He commented on the location of several of the internal organs, but also pointed to several organs for which Chinese medicine had no names. Sugita, on comparing them with the *Ontleedkundige tafelen*, identified them as arteries, veins, and suprarenal glands (Figure 14). The old man commented that, in all his times dissecting bodies, doctors had never asked about discrepancies between the actual body, filleted in front of them, and Chinese anatomical depictions. By contrast, Sugita and Maeno were amazed by the similarities between the Dutch text and Old Hag Green Tea's innards. Sugita and Maeno also gathered a few bleached bones from the Kozukapara grounds and noticed that they, too, were identical to those in the Dutch text. The Chinese depictions were revealed to be completely inaccurate. What is more, many Chinese anatomical organs, such as the 'six lobes and double auricles of the lungs' or the 'three left and four right lobes of the liver', appeared to be complete fabrications.

It is tempting to depict this moment as a critical milestone in early modern Japanese history, a revolutionary transition from the deductive, theoretical learning of Neo-Confucian medicine to the empirical observations of the Kozukapara execution grounds and Dutch texts. Indeed, in this sense, the moment is not unlike the dissections and anatomical sketches of the Belgian Andreas Vesalius (1514–64) who, in his *De Humani Corporis Fabrica* (On the fabric

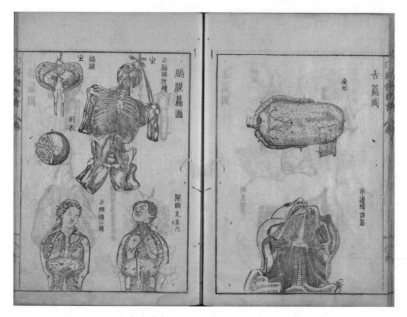

14 Anatomical detail from Sugita Genpaku's *Kaitai shinsho* (New anatomical atlas, 1774).

of the human body, 1543), discredited millennia of anatomical theory, exemplified in the humorism of Aelius Galenus (129–99). Not unlike the Neo-Confucian medical tradition embraced by Sano Yasusada and most of the early modern Japanese medical establishment, humorism, or Hippocratic medicine, viewed the body as comprised of four basic bodily fluids that corresponded to the Aristotelian Four Elements Theory – black bile (earth), yellow bile (fire), phlegm (water), and blood (air). Excesses or deficiencies in these fluids were at the root of human disease. Basically, this theory converged with Neo-Confucianism's Five Phase Theory that reduced the world to the five elements of water, wood, fire, earth, and metal, which in turn corresponded to colours, numbers, directions, and temperaments.

In 1536, accompanied by his sidekick Regnier Gemma, Vesalius travelled to the execution grounds outside Louvain, Belgium, where he discovered the intact skeleton of a thief. Authorities had chained the poor fellow to the gallows and then slowly cooked him alive, leaving the charred flesh for hungry birds. Vesalius carted the remains home for his anatomical studies. At the University of Padua, near Venice, Vesalius performed human dissections and non-human vivisections, replacing barbers (the European equivalent of Japan's outcastes, at least where dissections were concerned) with his medical students. During these years, Vesalius conducted several public dissections, theatrical in design and impact, and the cumulative experience led to the publication of *Fabrica* in 1543. Though colleagues, notably his teacher, Franciscus Sylvius (1614–72), criticized Vesalius for his anti-Galenist conclusions and depictions, his work laid the foundation for the empirical study of the body in Europe and eventually Japan. Indeed, the large spectacles of public lectures and theatrical dissections at Padua epitomized the post-Vesalian era, where students and teachers interacted to produce and disseminate anatomical knowledge.

Though not as groundbreaking as *Fabrica*, and clearly influenced by the diffusion of European ideas and methods, Sugita's translation and interpretation was a breakthrough in Japanese empirical thinking. However, similar breakthroughs had already disrupted Japan's scientific consensus. The new scientific atmosphere led physician Kosugi Genteki (1730–91) to conclude that Chinese anatomical depictions were 'entirely wrong', after a controversial dissection he observed in 1751, conducted by his teacher Yamawaki Tôyô. Yamawaki conducted the dissection of a headless criminal's body at a temple in Kyoto. Yamawaki, in his *Zôshi* (Description of the organs, 1759), published the first Japanese anatomical text based not on Chinese learning but on empirical observations. Sugita later commented on the dissection: 'Judging from what he [Kosugi] saw, he found that all the knowledge handed down by ancestors was entirely wrong: they were all empty fabrications.' Indeed, by the eighteenth century, Japanese physicians had become increasingly sceptical of Chinese anatomical atlases. With few restrictions against opening the body and a ready supply of outcastes to circumvent those taboos that existed, early modern Japanese physicians could begin their empirical discovery of the human body.

Even though traditional physicians decried the 1751 Kyoto dissection, official Neo-Confucian scholars, Tokugawa officials, and most other doctors remained relatively quiet on the matter. Sugita wrote that Okada Yôsen (1722–97) and Fujimoto Rissen (1703–69), official *bakufu* physicians who had observed seven or eight dissections of their own, also noted the difference between the Chinese texts and actual bodies. To reconcile the fact, they speculated on the possible anatomical differences between Chinese and 'barbarian' (in this case Japanese and European) anatomy. Such dubious medical logic is unsurprising, as bogus racial theories of human difference also permeated Western medicine. Sugita's reference to their observations, when combined with Yamawaki's *Zôshi*, suggest that a pent-up exploratory culture blossomed during Japan's eighteenth century, resembling earlier experiences in Europe.

Following the Kozukapara dissection, Sugita hypothesized that ancient Chinese actually knew of dissection because the term appears in ancient medical texts, but that the practice had not been transmitted through the ages. Because of this, he claimed that Japan had received only the dregs of Chinese learning. Sugita emphasized that, given the 'experience' at Kozukapara, he and other physicians should learn the 'true structure of the human body' in order to practise better medicine. In the nineteenth century and at the dawn of Japan's modern age, Sugita looked back at the popularity of Dutch learning and speculated on the reasons why it flourished. One reason was that it 'expressed facts as they were', or an empirical rather than deductive, philological reality. Another reason Dutch learning flourished was that the 'time was right for this type of learning', with its greater emphasis on observations. This empiricism lies at the heart of the 'true medicine' that actually 'saves people's lives', he reflected.

In fact, the 'time was right' for a critique of Chinese science. The fear for Tokugawa authority was, if Chinese Neo-Confucian medicine proved illegitimate and inaccurate, and failed to express 'facts as they were', then so too might the entire fabric of Zhu Xi Neo-Confucianism and its political and social frameworks. When combined with the activities of the 'revere the emperor, expel the barbarians' radicals, it proved just enough to begin weakening the legitimacy of the state. Radical samurai began to wedge open the cracks in the foundation of Tokugawa authority, leading to the *bakufu*'s collapse in 1868.

MEN AND WOMEN OF HIGH PURPOSE

Unsurprisingly, most of the domain lords who embraced the 'expel the barbarians' doctrine were 'outside' lords, the men still smarting from their defeat at the Battle of Sekigahara (1600) two centuries earlier. Increasingly, samurai from 'outside' domains gathered in Kyoto and cautioned the shogun against betraying the wishes of the emperor. Though a woman from a farming background, Matsuo Taseko (1811–94) was one such imperial zealot who travelled to Kyoto to contribute to the energy of impending regime change. In 1852, Matsuo had come into contact with a disciple of nativist Hirata Atsutane, who attacked Buddhism as yet another destructive foreign import. Not surprisingly, many imperial zealots began defacing Buddhist statuary in their support of the native Shinto religion, which worshipped native deities. Matsuo travelled to Kyoto with some 'men of high purpose' (*shishi*) to agitate for an imperial restoration. While in Kyoto, Matsuo was overwhelmed by nationalism, as demonstrated in a poem she penned. She wrote, 'How do you expect me / to stop now? / My thoughts rise / constantly upward / when I am crazy with the Japanese spirit'. The energy of the imperial restoration had permeated all status groups.

Despite the intense political agitating of 'men of high purpose', the *bakufu* set a course for opening the country and signed the Harris Treaty (Treaty of Amity and Commerce, 1858) with the US. Imperial zealots chafed at much in the treaty, but nothing more so than the extraterritoriality conditions. In Article Six, the treaty stipulated that, 'Americans committing offences against Japanese shall be tried in American Consular courts, and, when guilty, shall be punished according to American law.' In other words, US citizens living in the newly designated treaty ports would be subject to US rather than Japanese law, which was viewed as 'Oriental', despotic, and barbaric by Westerners. Most Japanese observers viewed this as a breach of sovereignty. Because of Article Six and others involving unfair tariffs, this treaty, and others like it imposed on China (on which the Harris Treaty was modelled), became known as the 'unequal treaties'.

The architect of the *bakufu*'s 'open country' strategy was the dauntless Ii Naosuke (1815–860). Immediately after signing the

Harris Treaty he purged imperial sympathizers, such as Hotta
Masayoshi (1810–64), from court and *bakufu* circles. In 1860, he
intervened in a Tokugawa successional dispute, ensuring that 'open
the country' supporter Tokugawa Iemochi (1846–66), rather than
the more radical Tokugawa Hitotsubashi (from Mito domain),
became the next shogun. Meanwhile, regent Manabe Akikatsu
(1804–84) applied considerable pressure on the court to acquiesce
to the *bakufu*'s diplomatic position. But imperial zealots pushed
back hard: in reaction to Ii's purge of court sympathizers, radical
samurai struck back in the name of the court and in defence of the
'divine land' with attacks in 1859. Immediately after the Harris
Treaty was signed, zealots brutally attacked a Russian naval officer,
a Dutch merchant captain, a Chinese employee of the French, and a
Japanese in the employ of the British consulate. In January 1861,
samurai cut down the secretary of US Consul General Townsend
Harris in the capital of Edo. Then, in the Sakuradamon Incident, Ii
himself, then the shogun's top minister, was hacked down outside
the shogunal compound in Edo. Like all samurai, the 'men of high
purpose' believed that some things were worth killing and dying for
as honour dictated. This legacy of radical political violence and
honourable self-willed death had a lasting impact on modern Japanese politics, as political assassinations would later become widespread during Japan's tumultuous 1930s.

  In response to samurai attacks, particularly the murder of Ii
Naosuke, the *bakufu* launched yet another series of reforms,
designed to craft a 'union of the court and *bakufu*'. The architect
of the reforms was Matsudaira Shungaku and he dispatched representatives to Kyoto, who officially announced the *bakufu*'s reversal
and adoption of the 'expel the barbarians' position. After Ii's assassination, the Tokugawa reversal led imperial advisers Sanjô
Sanetomi (1837–1891) and Iwakura Tomomi (1825–83) to boast
that the shogun 'quaked' in the presence of imperial authority.
Sanjô delighted in the weakening of the *bakufu* and trumpeted,
'The imperial restoration will soon be here. Oh joy. Oh joy.'
Quaking or not, the *bakufu*'s reversal signalled a loss of political
will and many of the actual and symbolic trappings of Tokugawa
authority began to erode. To accommodate restless domains, the
Tokugawa regime modified the alternate attendance system and

eliminated onerous ceremonial gift-giving during audiences with the shogun. The cannibalization of Tokugawa authority had begun.

Meanwhile, imperial zealots pressed on with dramatic activities designed to restore imperial power, expel the barbarians, and undermine Tokugawa rule. In 1862, samurai from Satsuma domain, a seedbed of the 'expel the barbarians' camp, cut down a British merchant named Charles Richardson (1834–62). The British responded by demanding an indemnity, with which Satsuma was not forthcoming. The British eventually responded by shelling Satsuma. The next two years witnessed even more political upheaval. In 1863, *bakufu* general Ogasawara Nagamichi (1822–91) was dispatched to Kyoto after the shogun, Tokugawa Iemochi (1846–66), was briefly held hostage in the imperial capital. That same year, a group of samurai calling themselves 'patriots of the realm' burned parts of Edo castle, further illustrating the nationalist overtones of Japan's nineteenth-century encounter with the West. In 1864, when *bakufu* official Matsudaira Yorinori (1831–64) defected and led an army against the shogun, national authority appeared to be slipping from the hands of the *bakufu*. When later that same year the British sent a message demanding Satsuma be dealt with in response to Richardson's murder, the challenges facing Tokugawa rule became overwhelming.

Like Satsuma, Chôshû domain had become a thorn in the side of the *bakufu*. Leaders from Chôshû and other outside domains still champed at the bit to avenge their ancestors for the loss at Sekigahara, the battle that had propelled the Tokugawa family to supremacy. In fact, they had even ritualized their animosity towards their ancestral enemy. In one secret ceremony, Chôshû elders asked the domain lord, 'Has the time come to begin the subjugation of the *bakufu*?' The lord then replied, 'It is still too early; the time has not yet come.' Mothers went so far as to instruct Chôshû children to sleep with their feet facing the east, a sign of disrespect to shoguns in Edo. Chôshû became a safe haven for imperial zealots; it had also taken advantage of the weakening of the *bakufu*'s hold on the domains to strengthen its own political and military position. Indeed, by 1865 Chôshû had purchased some 7,000 modern rifles that would be used against Tokugawa allies only three years later. Intellectuals from Chôshû, such as Yoshida Shôin (1830–59), spoke openly of 'destroying the *bakufu*' and promoted the nationalistic loyalty inherent in revering the emperor, as opposed to the compartmentalized, feudal loyalty of the Tokugawa system. When Chôshû allied itself with samurai from Tosa and Satsuma domain, creating the Satchô alliance, the fate of the *bakufu* was sealed. In January 1868, at the battlefields of Fushimi and Toba, the Tokugawa *bakufu* succumbed to its enemies and collapsed.

CONCLUSION

The political discourse of the twilight years of the early modern period structured political discourse during the Meiji Restoration, from the 'Eight-point Plan' of Sakamoto Ryôma (1836–67), a Tosa samurai who articulated a roadmap to imperial restoration, to the derring-do of Yoshida Shôin. Sakamoto chafed at *bakufu* conduct: 'Those rascals in Edo are hand in glove with the barbarians. But although those scoundrels have a good deal of power, once I get together with two or three daimyo [domain lords] they'll have to think about their country … It is my firm desire to clean up Japan.' Architects of Meiji governance, such as Itô Hirobumi (1841–1909), studied with radical samurai like Yoshida Shôin, and this background shaped their approach to imperial rule, Japanese nationalism, and, eventually, empire-building projects in the Asia-Pacific region.

In response to 'unequal treaties' and fuelled by the radical politics of imperial nationalism, Japan began embarking on radically new forms of state building in the Meiji years, ones that put the small island country on near parity with the Great Powers. The cultural encounter with the US and Europe sparked an intensely nationalistic response, characterized by the 'revere the emperor' movement. The activities of imperial zealots illustrate these radical politics, born in the crucible of colonialism, which would have enduring legacies in Japan and elsewhere. But the most immediate result of the political upheaval and nationalist dialogue of the 1860s was the collapse of Tokugawa rule and the Meiji Restoration of 1868.

9

Meiji Enlightenment, 1868–1912

In January 1868, on the battlefields of Fushimi and Toba, the Edo *bakufu* succumbed to the Satchô alliance. After some 268 restive years, the losers at the Battle of Sekigahara (1600), the 'outside' domains that the shoguns had kept so carefully under their thumbs, finally exacted their revenge. If the architects of the Meiji Restoration had extolled the 'expel the barbarians, revere the emperor' doctrine in the early 1860s, however, the reality of governance – and the reality of the threat posed by the Great Powers and their crippling 'unequal treaties' – made such patriotic slogans untenable as actual policy. The radical imperial nationalism of the early nineteenth century surrendered to a *realpolitik* engagement with the US and Europe, in which modernization became the preoccupation of Japanese politics, culture, and society. Meiji reformers sought to thrust Japan into the modern age, with its constitutional governments, powerful steam engines, and twenty-four-hour electrically lit factories. With powerful policies and philosophies guiding them, Meiji reformers reinvented Japan in the late nineteenth and early twentieth centuries. They moulded Japan into a country that, less than a half century later, became a world economic and military power.

MEIJI STATE

The new leadership of the Meiji regime was, as Ôkuma Shigenobu (1838–1922) described it, akin to the 'myriad gods' setting out to build a new state. The Charter Oath of April 1868 laid out the basic framework for the new regime. Although the first four tenets – 'deliberative assemblies', universal male suffrage, the abandonment of the 'evil customs of the past', and open access to entrepreneurial opportunities – proved slow to materialize, the new leadership vigorously pursued the fifth tenet, which stated that, 'Knowledge shall be sought throughout the world so as to invigorate the foundations of imperial rule.' This international engagement transformed Japan at every level, from cultural borrowing to armed conflict.

The Iwakura mission of 1871–3 epitomized the sheer determination of the Japanese to utilize Western culture and institutions to 'invigorate the foundations of imperial rule'. Kume Kunitake (1839–1931), author of the official accounts of the mission, reflected that, 'The Meiji Restoration has led to an unprecedented political transformation in Japan.' When the mission travelled to the US and Europe, it entered a modern world, where many days were 'spent on noisy trains with wheels screaming and whistles screeching, amid the smell of iron and belching flames, careering through billowing clouds of smoke'. The steam-powered locomotive became a potent symbol of the Meiji transformation, as did the Meiji emperor, who, after 1871, dressed in his Prussian field marshal's attire. In 1872, Japan's first railway line opened between Tokyo and Yokohama, and many kilometres of railway soon followed.

Immediately following the Meiji Restoration, reformers eliminated domain registers, an important vestige of feudal power. In the new state, domains became prefectures, and the great *daimyô* became 'governors'. Such Meiji leaders as Kido Kôin (Takayoshi, 1833–77) and Ôkubo Toshimichi (1830–78), from Chôshû and Satsuma domains, respectively, had orchestrated a cohort of domains to issue a statement in March 1869 that relinquished their regional authorities, ones formerly institutionalized by the 'boundless despotism' of the Tokugawa shoguns. 'The lands in which we live are the Emperor's lands', they declared. 'The people we govern are the Emperor's people. How, then, can we lightly treat them as our own? We now surrender our registers to the throne, asking that the Court dispose of them at will.' They submitted that surrendering their land would place Japan 'in the hands of a single authority', and thereby put the country on a 'footing of equality with countries overseas', namely the Great Powers poised to conquer Asia. With such declarations, Meiji reformers, acting through the court, dismantled Japan's early modern order in favour of a newly centralized one. Japan was now nominally under the control of a 'single authority', the Meiji emperor. Indeed, 'personal rule by the Emperor' came to serve as a prominent rallying cry in these early years, even though in reality a small oligarchy of men from former outside domains actually governed the country.

Such men as Kido believed that Japan needed to be centralized along military lines before substantive modernization reforms could be undertaken. Kido observed that, 'today's urgent duty is to sweep away domain practices and firmly establish the military axis without which nothing can be carried out'. Sanjô Sanetomi (1837–91), a court official, believed that time was of the essence when it came to centralizing political and military power: 'The outcome of the Restoration depends on the next three or four or five months', he speculated. In order to expedite and enforce new reforms emanating from the political centre, Meiji leaders established a centralized police force, which they modelled after the *gens d'armes* of France and placed under the directorship of another Satsuma notable named Kawaji Toshiyoshi (1829–79). This police force went through several iterations and eventually was housed within the all-powerful Home Ministry. This represented a dramatic change from the regional and status-based law enforcement practices of the Tokugawa years. By 1873, militarization of the Meiji state took another giant step under Yamagata Aritomo (1838–1922), with the establishment of what commoners called a 'blood tax', or universal conscription into a military utterly loyal to the emperor.

Equally dramatic as these examples of Meiji administrative re-engineering were the examples of social re-engineering. Starting in 1869, the court dismantled the early modern status system and created broad new categories to situate those at the top and bottom of the social heap. The Meiji state granted occupational freedom to former samurai (and most other people), eliminated domain registers, and established direct ties between the state and individuals. In 1871, with the establishment of the Household Registration Law, the court divided society into four broad categories and, one year later, most people were categorized as 'commoners'. Moreover, a 'liberation edict' abolished the outcaste categories of the early modern status system that had been so connected to livelihood. In the Tokugawa years, outcastes worked with corpses and tanned leather; and the association of these livelihoods with 'pollution', mainly in the form of death and blood, officially relegated outcastes, by inheritance, to the margins of Japanese society. In 1871, the government decreed that, 'The names *eta*, *hinin*, and so forth are hereby abolished. Henceforth in their status and occupation [former outcastes] shall be treated as commoners.' Even after the 'liberation edict', it was not uncommon for officials to list, in household registries, former outcastes as 'new commoners' and Ainu as 'former aboriginals', basically perpetuating diluted forms of discrimination. But the symbolism of such shifts is important. As with other Meiji administrative and social changes that revolutionized Japanese life, no longer did status hinge on a person's livelihood. Rather, now it hinged on a person's distance from the emperor. In the meteorological vortex of the Meiji hurricane, the emperor always served as the eye of the storm. But incorporating former outcastes with commoners came at the high cost of murderous social violence. In the early modern status system everyone had a place, and former peasants, who had enjoyed prestige within the Neo-Confucian value system, were now lumped together with outcastes. In the next chapter, we will explore how the 'liberation edict' in fact made many former outcastes more vulnerable to social violence than they had been previously.

THE MEIJI RESTORATION IN HISTORY

Amidst this swirling hurricane of political change, the Meiji period represents one of the most dramatic moments in Japan's history and it is not surprising that arguments still rage over its legacy. Historians debate what the Meiji Restoration – the *Meiji ishin* in Japanese – actually represented. Clearly, the confusion arises from the fact that nobody knew, not even Meiji reformers, what the future actually held. Initially, the Meiji leadership hailed 1868 as 'the restoration of imperial rule', one confirmed by their victory in the Boshin War (1868). But far deeper implications were at stake than an anachronistic return to the imperial rule of a millennium earlier. As we have seen, a central bureaucracy arose to replace the domains of the early modern period, as a new social order emerged from the rubble of the Tokugawa status system. Military service was no longer dependent on samurai heredity, but rather on a national conscription policy. As we will see, the 'industrious revolution' of the early modern period was subsumed under a true industrial revolution; and Western education and science, which drove technological advancement, became the norms. Given the dramatic nature of these changes, the Meiji years came to be seen less as a period of 'restoration' than one of 'renovation', when Japan became one of the 'enlightened' nations of the world. In the nineteenth century, Ernest Satow (1843–1929), a member of the British Foreign Service in Japan, understood the revolutionary nature of these changes. In his memoirs, Satow repeatedly referred to the 'revolution of 1868'. He mused that, 'The revolution in Japan was like that of 1789, minus the guillotine.'

Japanese historians struggled to place these changes in context. Taguchi Ukichi (1855–1905), a Meiji scholar, sought to explain the total 'renovation' of Japan occurring during the first half of the Meiji years, even though the overthrow of the Tokugawa shoguns was originally purported to be a 'restoration' of older imperial institutions. Taguchi viewed history as naturally propelling societies from 'barbarism' to 'civilization'. When Japan shed its 'feudal' Tokugawa authority for the national unity of imperial rule it simply served as one step in the direction of its inevitable historical 'enlightenment'. Similarly, Nishimura Shigeki (1828–1902), another Meiji scholar, argued that history actually 'generates progress', even as regimes, such as the Tokugawa, rise and fall. Influenced by Western intellectuals such as John Stuart Mill (1806–73) and others, these Meiji scholars contextualized the Meiji Restoration in a progression of regimes and states, propelled by forces embedded in history and evolutionary natural law only coming to light in the late nineteenth century. They orchestrated a Meiji temporal revolution, wherein the old cyclical notions of time and history, ones embedded in Confucianism and Chinese cosmology, were replaced by Western progressive ideas.

In 1860, the young Fukuzawa Yukichi (1835–1901), another Meiji scholar whom we met in the introduction, accompanied a mission to the US to ratify the Harris Treaty (1858). His experiences capture the nature of this revolution. Fukuzawa was dazzled by the West, which he described as 'wondrous' and 'powerful'. He and the Meiji oligarchy concluded that it was essential to replicate Western civilization. Led by Fukuzawa and the Meiji Six Society, a collection of thinkers dedicated to bringing Western civilization to Japan, the notion of progress came to dominate the first decades of the Meiji experiment. Fukuzawa believed that the Japanese needed to refashion their temporal perspective and their understanding of what terms such as 'civilization' and 'history' actually meant. In a series of publications, Fukuzawa refined how Japanese should view the past and future. He argued that human civilization, whether in Japan or England, progressed from 'barbarism', 'primitive chaos', and 'semi-civilization', to full-blown 'civilization'. History, for Fukuzawa and his cohort, generated progress and all nations found themselves at some point on this trajectory from barbarism to civilization. This was, as Taguchi had described it, the 'law of historical development'. This temporal perspective was radically different from Neo-Confucian views of history and civilization, which looked to the past and the sages of ancient China for political answers and moral standards. Neo-Confucianism looked to the past; Western progress was fixated on the future.

Briefly consider two key figures in East Asian and European thought. In the *Analects*, Confucius (551–479 BCE), founder of East Asian philosophy, stated: 'I transmit but do not create'. This became the *modus operandi* of Confucianism, with its many attempts, by various interpreters, to retrieve and 'transmit' this moral past through close readings of the core Confucian texts. In this respect, though highly dynamic, Confucianism was principally antiquarian, constantly looking for answers to contemporary challenges in the teachings of sagely figures from China's ancient past. Because of this dependence on looking to the past, Fukuzawa Yukichi believed Chinese philosophy to be a 'retrogressive doctrine' with 'degenerate influences' and, therefore, 'responsible for our obvious shortcomings' when compared to the Great Powers. Meanwhile, Western philosophy taught 'independence' and 'self-respect', important creeds to Fukuzawa. In large part, these ideas were rooted in the philosophy of Georg Wilhelm Friedrich Hegel (1770–1831), one of the architects of modern progressive thought. He argued that, 'The history of the world is none other than the progress of the consciousness of freedom.' In other words, in the Western philosophy embraced by Fukuzawa and his contemporaries, history was not a lost political Eden ruled by enlightened sages, but a wake fanning out and slowly disappearing behind a sailboat, one used to trace civilizational progress as nations slowly glided forward through time.

Guided by such progressive ideals, Japan absorbed Western ideas and material culture at a rapid clip. New vocabularies were even designed to describe imported Western concepts. '*Bunmei*', which traditionally had referred to a Confucian notion of 'Chinese civilization', came to refer to 'Western civilization' in the hands of the Meiji intelligentsia. In other instances, Meiji intellectuals created neologisms such as *jiyû* and *kenri* to describe such Western political concepts as 'freedom' and 'rights', the very concepts tracked by Hegel's developmental model. Some neologisms corresponded to the social engineering described earlier, as when *shakai*, or 'society', replaced the *shimin*, or 'four peoples' of the early modern status system (recall that the 'four peoples' had been samurai, peasants, artisans, and merchants). New words were also needed to describe foreign material objects, such as *shashin*, for 'photograph', and *kokkai*, for 'national assembly'. At the hands of progressive politicians and thinkers, Japan modulated to accommodate a host of powerful Western notions. Examples of Western material culture began sprouting up like daisies. From the Ginza Brick Quarter (1872) and the Rokumeikan pavilion (1883) to beer (1869) and spaghetti (1872), Japanese imported Western material culture at a fantastic pace.

Slowly, however, some Japanese reformers and politicians became disillusioned with the West, particularly after diplomatic setbacks such as the 'Triple Intervention' in the aftermath of the Sino-Japanese War (1895). It became clear that, no matter how modern Japan became, it would still be denied a seat at the table of the Great Powers. The second generation of Meiji thus sought a more Japanese-style nationhood, one increasingly rooted in traditional Eastern values, the very 'evil customs' rejected in the Charter Oath of 1868 and as 'retrograde' by Fukuzawa. The Meiji Constitution (1889) bore the striations and fractures of this transition, as did the Imperial Rescript on Education (1890).

MEIJI POLITICS

Early in the Meiji years, many ex-samurai and wealthy peasants, disillusioned at the direction of Meiji economic and political reform, formed the 'Popular Rights Movement'. Building on Western notions of 'individual liberty' and 'natural rights', Tosa men such as Itagaki Taisuke (1837–1919) and Gotô Shôjirô (1838–97), who had been influenced by Sakamoto Ryôma's earlier call for a 'national assembly', began campaigning for popular participation in governance. In 1881, Itagaki established the Jiyûtô (Liberal Party), which helped apply pressure on the Meiji oligarchy to draft a constitution. For thinkers such as Fukuzawa, the Japanese nation would liberate itself from the threat of Western imperialism through this pursuit of popular rights: 'If we Japanese begin to pursue learning with spirit and energy, so as to achieve personal independence and thereby enrich and strengthen the nation, why should we fear the powers of the Westerners?' But the Meiji Constitution was built on a different foundation than the one pushed by the Popular Rights Movement, one that more reflected the second wave of Meiji reforms.

Itô Hirobumi (1841–1909), father of the Meiji Constitution, described the constitution not as a product of 'natural law' or 'individual rights', but rather as a 'gift of a benevolent and charitable emperor to the people of his country'. That is, the Meiji Constitution's legitimacy came not from a Jeffersonian 'Creator' or inalienable natural rights, but from the Meiji emperor's tireless charity. Itô rejected the notion of a 'separation of powers' and argued that sovereignty rested solely with the emperor. The state is 'like a human body', he concluded, 'which has limbs and bones but whose source of spiritual life is the mind [i.e. the emperor]'. With Meiji's second wave, Japan's exceptionalist history – the fact that, as Itô wrote, 'our country was founded and ruled by the emperor himself since the very beginning of our history' – directly shaped the language and laws of the Constitution. The Imperial Rescript on Education (1890) was even more focused on the moral decay caused by the excesses of the early Meiji years. 'For morality', explained the preamble to the Rescript, 'the study of Confucius is the best guide'.

In sum, the early Meiji years saw the wholesale import of Western ideas and institutions into Japan in order to 'strengthen the foundations of imperial rule'. But the West was anything but monolithic, and Meiji reformers confronted ideas ranging from 'natural rights' and participatory government to Prussian executive monarchism. In the end, the proclaimed need to strengthen the new state in the face of Western imperialism, to avoid the fate of China's Qing dynasty during the Opium War (1839–42), outweighed the need for widespread democratization. By Meiji's second wave, Meiji reformers criticized many aspects of Western culture as excessive, and a slow disillusionment with the Great Powers occurred. In no place was this conflict between democratization and Meiji conservatism more acute than in the arena of women's rights. Early on, many Meiji reformers, such as those associated with the Meiji Six Society, advocated for women's rights and suffrage. But as Meiji's second wave gained hold, women's bodies became the principal battleground on which the fight over the legacies of Japanese modernity was fought.

MEIJI POLICY AND WOMEN

This war over the fate of the Meiji state – whether to forge a Western-style nation or a uniquely imperial Japanese one with an ethos of conservative Confucian values – was waged nowhere more intensely than on the bodies of Japanese women. Initially, for groups such as the Meiji Six Society, the status of women served as a metric of Japan's progress towards civilization. In the first years of the Meiji period, the fledgling government asked women to contribute to the state through frugality, hard work, efficient household management, care for the young and old, and responsible upbringing of children. The Ministry of Education's slogan 'good wife, wise mother' captured early Meiji's expectations of women. But women had ideas of their own, and it did not take long for a women's rights movement to gain traction. In 1872, when American educator David Murray (1830–1905) encouraged Meiji leaders to provide women with better access to education, the Tokyo Girls' School was established, which boasted a demanding curriculum for young women. A handful of women attended the Iwakura Mission, when Meiji leaders toured the world browsing for models to modernize their country. One of them, Tsuda Umeko (1864–1929), eventually established a university for women. For some enlightened Meiji oligarchs, such as Kuroda Kiyotaka (1840–1900), education remained the key to creating progressive and enlightened women, and he consistently advocated sending them abroad.

Women's rights debates broke out in 1872, during the *Maria Luz* Incident. In the incident, a Peruvian-flagged vessel of that name called at the port of Yokohama and several passengers escaped. As it turned out, these passengers were men who had been recruited as labourers and women as prostitutes from throughout Asia. This highly publicized incident prompted reformists and foreign governments to pressure Japan to reform its laws regarding prostitution, specifically by cancelling debts and contracts that shackled women to pimps and bordellos. Consequently, in 1872, shortly after liberating its outcastes, Japan liberated its prostitutes. Yet, while such gains were made, women's bodies continued to serve as battlegrounds over the direction of the Meiji transformation. In 1872, Meiji officials forbade women from cutting their hair short or from bobbing it. Some of Meiji Japan's most prominent thinkers, such as Fukuzawa, Nakamura Masanao (1832–91), and Mori Arinori (1847–89) responded with the slogan 'women are people, too' and hammered at Japan's 'feudal' household system, which relegated women to the home and subordinated them to husbands.

By the late 1870s, the Meiji state had become more conservative in reaction to the Popular Rights Movement. As we have seen, the movement started in 1874, when Itagaki Taisuke and Gotô Shôjirô called for a National Assembly based on the model submitted by John Stuart Mill. By 1880, they organized the 'Association for the Establishment of a National Assembly'. Meiji officials reacted by curtailing rights to political assembly, particularly among women. In 1890, the Meiji government enacted the 'Law on Associations and Meetings', which, among other curtailments, barred women from participating in political gatherings. The government reinforced the law in 1900 with the Home Ministry's 'Security Police Law', which further restricted the political involvement of women. The Home Ministry argued that politicized women were dangerous because political meetings compromised their womanly virtues. The ministry pointed to the French Revolution's food riots (1792) as a case where women had turned from innocents to animals because of radical politics. In the magazine *Shinmin* (The subject), the Home Ministry promoted its version of idealized women. For example, the Home Ministry turned Yamasaki Ichi's private suffering into a public morality play when her story was published in the magazine. 'Ichi cared for her blind father, her younger sisters, and her mad mother. She married in 1891, but only five years later her husband became ill. She nursed her husband and her father until their deaths, and continued to care for her unappreciative mother.' Such stories became models for women's behaviour. In effect, the Meiji government began denying rights to women because the state's claims to the household were critical to its approaches to governance and defining nationhood.

Several women challenged the Meiji state's assault on women's rights. Some challenges, such as that by 'Grandmother Popular Rights', Kusunose Kita (1833–1920), focused on the relationship between property, taxation, and voting rights. After her husband died in 1872, she inherited her husband's property and, consequently, its tax liabilities. She wrote:

> We women who are heads of households must respond to the demands of the government just as other ordinary heads of households, but because we are women, we do not enjoy equal rights. We have the right neither to vote for district assembly representatives nor to act as legal guarantors in matters of property, even though we hold legal instruments for that purpose. This is an enormous infringement of our rights!

Echoing eighteenth-century Bostonians, she continued, 'Most reprehensible of all, the only equality I share with men who are heads of their households is the enormous duty of paying taxes.'

A steady stream of women activists followed the common-sense prose of Grandmother Popular Rights. Kishida Toshiko (1863–1901) was one of the earliest advocates for women. At the tender age of twenty, Kishida wowed a Popular Rights Movement rally in Osaka with a speech on 'The Way for Women'. Kishida came from a well-heeled family; she had even served as a literary tutor to the empress. Another famous women's rights activist, Fukuda Hideko (1865–1927), who heard Kishida speak, described the experience in this manner: 'Listening to her speech', remembered Fukuda, 'delivered in that marvellous oratorical style, I was unable to suppress my resentment and indignation ... and began immediately to organize women and their daughters.' Kishida argued that Japan would never realize the Meiji enlightenment as long as men subordinated women: 'In this country, as in the past, men continue to be respected as masters and husbands while women are held in contempt as maids and serving women. There can be no equality in such an environment.' Kishida's push for women's education and equality between the sexes spawned several important women's rights groups.

The important point is that the ongoing Meiji articulation of Japanese nationhood remained intertwined with the fight for women's rights and equality. Because Meiji nationalism came to emphasize the notion of the 'family state', the role of women in the household, as defenders of traditional values, trumped their access to voting rights and proper citizenship. The fate of women in Meiji Japan serves as an important signifier of the increasingly conservative politics of the late Meiji period. Unlike the first wave of Meiji reforms, which endorsed a wholesale adoption of Western ideas and institutions, the second wave pushed Confucian retrenchment, or a re-emphasis on those 'Eastern ethics' central to Japan's imperial nationalism. This aggressive, top-down style also characterized the Meiji approach to revitalizing the Japanese economy to participate more competitively in world trade.

POLITICAL ECONOMIES

Economic transformation also became a critical element in the Meiji Restoration. Reformers realized that industrial wealth translated into national strength, and they eagerly embraced Western economic theories and practices. But even though Japan was quickly integrated into global capitalist markets, largely under

Western imperial duress, it was not the first time that Japan had participated in overseas trade. As we have seen, fifteenth- and sixteenth-century trade outposts in Southeast Asia opened for medieval Japanese, as did Japan's participation in the seventeenth- and eighteenth-century silver trade revolving around China. It is easy to overstate the historical rupture represented by the capitalization and industrialization of the Japanese economy in the early Meiji years. Some historians, pointing to Japan's rapid industrialization in the late nineteenth century, have labelled the island country a 'late modernizer'. However, widespread evidence exists that the Japanese economy exhibited proto-capitalist and proto-industrial elements far before Japan's Meiji 'opening'. Given Japan's early modern history, the 'late modernizer' characterization does not fit. Whether in the herring fisheries in the north, the Kinai cotton trade in the west, lumber guilds in Edo, or just the sheer power of Japan's consumer culture, from woodblock vendors selling prints of kabuki stars to shops specializing in dried kelp, Japan's economy was already robust, diverse, consumer-driven, and rapidly expanding. Indeed, by the early nineteenth century, Japanese may not have spoken in the language of Western capitalism fluently, but much of the basic grammar was well in place by that time. This fact, as much as Japan's notorious cultural borrowing skills, explains the country's meteoric economic rise in the twentieth century.

Meiji policy-makers were impressed by the power conveyed by industrialization. During the Iwakura Mission, Western industrial sites had caught the attention of the embassy; but Meiji officials were not the first to be impressed by Western economics and industrialism. The Edo *bakufu* had established the Institute for the Study of Barbarian Writings, where some Dutch economic theory was taught. Meiji reformers, however, devoted unprecedented priority to industrialization and in 1877, with the establishment of Tokyo University (which grew out of the aforementioned Institute), Ernest Fenelossa (1853–1908), an art historian by training, travelled to Japan to teach political economy. In 1858, Fukuzawa had founded Keiô University, which emphasized economics, and he lectured on substantial portions of Francis Wayland's (1796–1865) *Elements of Political Economy* (1837).

In 1875, Education Minister Mori Arinori established the School for Commercial Law, which taught economic theory. Simultaneously, a whirlwind of important translations appeared, including Adam Smith's (1723–90) *The Wealth of Nations* (published in Japanese in 1884) and John Stuart Mill's *Principles of Political Economy* (published in Japanese in 1886). The Japanese began adding dynamic Western theories of capitalist development to the rich stratigraphy of their own economic experience.

New economic philosophies precipitated a more exploitative interaction with people and, as we shall see in the next chapter, the natural environment. However, it is easy to overemphasize the rupture between the proto-capitalist economy of the early modern years and the industrial one of the late nineteenth century. Even given early modern views of a natural environment alive with Shinto deities and Buddhist continuums of life, early modern thinkers advocated the exploitation of the environment for economic and political advantage. Satô Nobuhiro (1769–1850), an eclectic early modern thinker, understood nature to be driven by creative forces, ones animated by Shinto deities. However, this animated view of nature did not preclude exploiting the environment. When describing the role of government, for example, Satô pronounced, in *Keizai yôryaku* (Summary of economics, 1822): 'The development of products is the first task of the ruler.' Humans organize into states, Satô suggested, in order to better exploit resources and control energy, basically offering an early modern defence of modern political ecology. Indeed, Satô's linkages between the 'ruler' and the 'development of products' anticipated the political economic thinking and practices of the Meiji years.

Though some economists pushed for a laissez-faire economic model, the prevailing desire was for a Prussian-style political economy, where state interests were closely aligned with private ones. This sort of model began with Friedrich List (1789–1846), the nineteenth-century German economist who advocated 'national economics'. Unlike the 'individual economics' advocated by Adam Smith, which predominantly benefited personal interests, List viewed the individual in a 'commercial union' with the interests of the state. Certainly, many Japanese economists came to see Japan's economic future through this 'national economics' lens.

The National Economics Association, for example, established in 1890, embraced this view of political economy. Its founding manifesto announced that, 'Power is created by wealth. It is unheard of that power can exist where there is no wealth. The competition which is occurring at present between nation and nation is nothing but a competition of strength and productive power.' Wealth served as the key to Japan overthrowing the 'unequal treaties' and wresting national sovereignty from the Great Powers. Initially, such economists as Seki Hajime (1873–1935), a future architect of Japan's interwar economy and mayor of Osaka, subscribed to the 'List boom' and its adherence to national economics. However, he later modified his position into a slightly more laissez-faire 'people's national economy', wherein conservative national economics would be replaced by a 'progressive, energetic, international' economics that relied more on entrepreneurial energy. In some respects, Seki's middle-ground approach, born in Germany and modified on the ground in Japan, characterized the Japanese economy in general as Japan entered the twentieth century.

Building linkages between industrial development and the state meant that most large Meiji industries before 1880 were state owned. But under Finance Minister Matsukata Masayoshi (1835–1924), who was responsible for widespread deflationary policies in 1881 and the establishment of the Bank of Japan in 1882, the government gradually released its industrial holdings to such firms as Mitsui, Mitsubishi, and Sumitomo, which later evolved into the industrial mega-conglomerates known as 'zaibatsu'. The Meiji government planned growth through prioritizing certain industries, building model factories, and hiring foreign advisers to oversee the development of select industries. The policies established in the 1880s fuelled Japan's first stage of economic growth. Between 1885 and 1905, imports and exports doubled; moreover, coal consumption increased from two million tons in 1893 to fifteen million tons in 1913 and steel production, an important indicator of heavy industry, increased from 7,500 tons in 1901 to 255,000 tons in 1913. Entrepreneurs such as Shibusawa Eiichi (1840–1931), who founded the First National Bank, a joint-stock ownership operation, spearheaded the development of Japan's cotton textile industry. By 1888, Shibusawa employed some

1,100 workers at his Osaka Spinning Mills plants. Nationally, in 1900 no fewer than 70 per cent of Japan's factories were involved in textile production. Shibusawa deployed steam engines at his various textile mills, enabling his 10,500 spindles to run day and night with electric lighting.

The electrification of Japan played an important part in the Meiji economy. Shibusawa's electrification of his factories portended the general electrification of the nation, as copper transmission lines stitched across the Japanese islands. Itô Hirobumi wrote of the newly founded Industry Ministry that its purpose was to 'make good Japan's deficiencies by swiftly seizing upon the strengths of the Western industrial arts; to construct within Japan all kinds of mechanical equipment on the Western model, including ship building, railways, telegraph, mines and buildings; and thus with one great leap to introduce to Japan the concept of enlightenment'. Miners dug copper from such mines as the Ashio copper mine, stretching the metal into 4,000 miles of copper transmission lines by 1895. By 1910, some private residences in Kyoto had electric lights. In her diary, Nakano Makiko noted that in January 1910 a new electric light brightened her house. 'It was so bright that I felt as though I had walked into the wrong house.' By 1935, Japan had already become a world leader in electrification by providing 89 per cent of its households with electricity, significantly more than Britain and the US.

CRIME AND PUNISHMENT

Along with economic reform, revising Japan's legal codes was another key ingredient to breaking the shackles of the 'unequal treaties'. Elements of Article Six in the Harris Treaty chafed Japanese the most. In a colonial legal structure known as 'extraterritoriality', the treaty specified, 'Americans committing offenses against Japanese shall be tried in American Consular courts, and, when guilty, shall be punished according to American law.' The reason Americans were immune to Japanese law was because of the perceived barbaric nature of 'Oriental' forms of punishment and incarceration, which in the eyes of most Westerners were feudal and savage. If Japanese were to dismantle the 'unequal treaties' with the Great Powers and enter a period of multilateral global parity, then

Japan's penal codes needed to be rewritten to reflect Japan's newly discovered 'civilization and enlightenment'.

The attention Meiji reformers paid to legal reform was not the first example of a Japanese state exhibiting such an interest. As we have seen, in the eighth century, the court had imported Tang Chinese legal codes, facilitating the creation of the *ritsuryô* state. In 1697, during the early modern period, the Edo *bakufu* sought to bring national uniformity to crime and punishment in an order issued to the domain lords. Later, by the middle of the eighteenth century, Shogun Tokugawa Yoshimune (1684–1751) systematized penal codes with the 'One Hundred Articles'. In early modern towns and cities, signposts communicated these legal codes. On the outskirts of Edo, execution grounds, filled with rotting disfigured corpses, deterred people from committing future crimes. It was at one of these execution grounds that Sugita Genpaku, the intrepid dissector, had, with the aid of an outcaste, dissected Old Hag Green Tea. In 1832, when a Ryukyuan embassy arrived in Edo, the *bakufu* had arranged a special execution to coincide with their arrival. In this way, execution grounds served as disciplinary markers of state authority that adorned the approach to the shogun's capital. Starting in 1610, the *bakufu* also built the jail complex at Koden-machô, which continued to serve Japan's incarceration purposes well into the Meiji years. With such grisly punishments as 'pulling the saw', 'pillorying', 'flogging', 'tattooing', 'stringing up', 'hugging the stones', and crucifixion, some of which took place in such locations as the 'drilling room', there is little wonder why American visitors to nineteenth-century Japan were squeamish about their citizens being punished according to such cruel procedures.

Prison conditions in the US were not much better, however, even though information disseminated throughout East Asia made them out to be enlightened. The Chinese book titled *Haiguo tuzhi* (An illustrated treatise on the maritime countries), written by Wei Yuan (1794–1857), brought circumstances surrounding US prisons to Japanese readers, particularly such nineteenth-century activists as Yoshida Shôin (1830–59). When Commodore Matthew C. Perry had steamed into Edo Bay in his 'black ships', Yoshida and a compatriot had tried to smuggle themselves aboard one of the gunboats in order to travel to the US and see the country for themselves.

Yoshida and his companion were caught, and incarcerated in a Chôshû domain jail. While incarcerated, Yoshida acquired a copy of *Haiguo tuzhi*. He learned that in US jails criminals 'changed their ways and became good people' through positive instruction; in Edo prisons, Yoshida mused, 'I have never yet seen a person who came to have good thoughts' as a result of their incarceration.

With the rumours and realities of 'Oriental barbarism' so closely connected to the 'unequal treaties', Japanese reformers realized that penal reform was critical to regaining total Japanese sovereignty from the Great Powers. Iwakura Tomomi (1825–83) spearheaded efforts to petition the emperor to prioritize penal reform. Shortly after the Meiji Restoration, the court announced that, 'among the hundreds of reforms to be implemented in conjunction with the Restoration of Imperial Rule, the penal laws are a matter of life and death for the multitudes and are thus in urgent need of correction'. Crucifixion was first restricted to perpetrators of regicide and parricide, but then, in the 1871 *Shinritsu kôryô* (Outline of the new code), banned outright, as was being burned alive. Under the urging of prison reformers such as Ohara Shigechika, the Meiji's Justice Ministry built its first modern prison at Kajibashi. Architecturally a cross with an observation point in the middle, the prison resembled Jeremy Bentham's (1748–1832) 'panopticon', where, as Ohara noted, the entire prison could be inspected at 'a single glance'. As one incarcerated journalist remembered of Kajibashi, 'The design follows that of a Western jail and forms a cross shape ... there is a guard in the middle ... who keeps watch in all four directions.' In due course, Meiji officials replicated the successful Kajibashi prison in Sapporo in 1875, and in other major cities. Thereafter, reforms of Japan's penal codes and the building of modern prisons proved critical in demonstrating to the Great Powers that Japan had abandoned the 'Oriental' practices of the early modern period.

CONCLUSION

It is hard to overemphasize the degree to which the Meiji Restoration was shaped by imported fragments of Western civilization. Japan's cultural borrowing at this moment surpassed even the Yamato borrowing of seventh- and eighth-century Tang dynastic institutions. After the Iwakura Mission, Japanese policy-makers, thinkers, and entrepreneurs began the strategic remaking of almost every facet of Japanese life. To defend the nation, Prussia provided the model for the army; the navy, quite naturally, was modelled on British forms. For domestic law enforcement, the police force resembled the one in downtown Paris; Sapporo's agricultural college mirrored US colleges created with the Morrill Act (1862) land-grant legislation. With an eye towards Western political thinkers, Japan reinvented its governing apparatus, social hierarchies, and notions of civil society, while also refashioning the basic nature of the economy and international trade agreements. For the judiciary, the draconian punishments and prisons of the past were replaced by punishments and innovative prison designs borrowed from the US and elsewhere. To entertain and educate, museums, zoological and botanical gardens, and universities came to adorn the Japanese capital of Tokyo and other major cities. Material artefacts such as multi-storey brick buildings hosted newly imported cultural practices such as ballroom dancing. Beer and spaghetti, both of Western origin, appeared alongside traditional Japanese entrées on restaurant menus. For a new pastime, baseball proved a popular and lasting import from the US, as did many other forms of sport and recreation. Indeed, in the name of 'civilization and enlightenment', Japan modernized at an astonishing pace after the Meiji Restoration, placing it on the same historical trajectory as the Great Powers.

But Japan's modernization was also a product of internal historical developments; not everything about Meiji merely mimicked foreign models. Japan borrowed many economic theories and institutions from the West, but after the proto-capitalistic experiences of the early modern years, Meiji reformers found such imported theories and institutions relatively easy to impose onto already receptive Japanese economic contexts. The new Meiji Constitution created a monarchical political system unlike anything Japan had ever seen before, but the idea of a powerful centralized state, with elaborate and influential bureaucracies, was anything but new. Although the emperor entered the Meiji period with traditional imperial garb and a grandiose hat, only a year later he wore Prussian field marshal attire (Figure 15). The notion of an imperial restoration was itself deeply rooted in traditional Japanese imperial

15 Emperor Mutsuhito (1852–1912) of Japan, *c.*1880–1901.

traditions, even if those were largely invented traditions. In other words, the Meiji Restoration grafted old and new, Japanese and Western, in a manner that created new relationships between the state and its subjects. For many, however, these new relationships ushered in hard times, illustrating the degree to which the benefits of modernity were not evenly spread throughout Japan in the nineteenth and early twentieth centuries.

10

Meiji's Discontents, 1868–1920

By the early twentieth century, Meiji reforms had refashioned the island country. Japan's early modern experience, combined with the global trends of the nineteenth century, proved powerful enough to remake Japan into a burgeoning modern nation, transforming politics, society, and culture, along with the environment and many of the non-human organisms that lived on the archipelago. Both people and the natural world became artefacts of modern and industrial life. With bobbed-hair 'modern girls' and urban dandies sporting the newest Western attire, Japan came to share more in common with the modern industrial nations of Europe than it did with its former pre-Meiji self or its immediate neighbours. In this respect, Meiji reforms had reconfigured and rescripted virtually every aspect of the Japanese landscape and life, but often at great social and environmental cost. The Meiji period had a dark underbelly, one characterized by human hardship and early signs of the environmental problems invited by unbridled industrialization and the reliance on fossil fuels.

CHANGES IN THE COUNTRYSIDE

Meiji reforms weighed heavily on Japan's new commoners, particularly those living in the countryside. By the mid-Meiji period, farmers in Japan cultivated about 11 per cent of the total land available in Japan, or approximately 4 million hectares (nearly 10 million acres), and that later rose to nearly 16 per cent, or close

to 6 million hectares (nearly 15 million acres) in 1919. This
contrasts with more contemporary practices: in the post-Pacific
War years, Japan witnessed a precipitous decline in the number of
farmers and farmer households. In 1965, the number of 'core
agricultural workers' stood at 8.94 million people, but that number
had declined to 2.24 million by 2005. In terms of hectares of land
under cultivation, Japan declined from 6 million hectares in
1965 to 4.69 million in 2005, stabilizing around the mid-Meiji
numbers. This is despite the fact that Japan's population increased
from just under 40 million in 1890 to nearly 128 million in 2005.
These numbers suggest that, with Japanese paving over much of
their farmland and rural populations declining rapidly, the island
nation is on the cusp of not being able to feed itself. As we shall
see, much of Japan's rural turmoil can be traced to the Meiji
Restoration and taxation policies.

Although the new era sparked widespread changes throughout
Japan, the actual material conditions in the countryside changed
little from the early modern period. In fact, with the abolishment of
the status system and the liberation of former outcastes, the social
standing of farmers as 'honourable peasants', venerable producers
of grain in the Neo-Confucian order, weakened and these tillers of
the soil found themselves lumped together with former outcastes.
Traditionally, such outcastes had been treated disparagingly:
commentator Kaiho Seiryô (1755–1817) wrote that outcastes were
actually descendants of 'barbarians', rather than the Sun Goddess,
so they differed from Japanese. They looked Japanese, he continued, but they have 'impure hearts'. In his writings, Kaiho went
so far as to advise that adult outcastes should have marks tattooed
onto their foreheads so that people could more easily identify them,
'impure hearts', apparently, being hard to spot from afar. However,
even with such traditions of discrimination, the Meiji government
abolished the outcaste status in 1871, completely disrupting earlier
Tokugawa social hierarchies. In response, two years later the
Mimasaka Blood-Tax Rebellion (1873) erupted, with violence
aimed at former outcaste populations.

In some respects, it is unsurprising that violence broke out in
Mimasaka. The area had a long tradition of tension between farmer
and outcaste communities. In the early nineteenth century, the area

hosted about a 7 per cent outcaste population, higher than Japan as a whole (which was between 2 and 3 per cent) but about the same as other regions of western Japan. Often, outcaste communities were stricken with poverty, even after the liberating legislation of the Meiji Restoration. Meiji reforms, rumours of 'blood taxes', and traditions of outcaste violence shaped the contours of the rebellion. The violence in Mimasaka began when Fudeyasu Utarô, a local resident, launched an uprising against the new Meiji regime, drawing on rumours of marauding figures roaming the countryside to seize blood and fat, reportedly to peddle to Westerners. Initially, Fudeyasu staged the uprising as a resistance to these putative blood-tax collectors, but the uprising quickly spread into the nearby countryside. For six days in May 1873, gangs roamed the Mimasaka area, targeting local officials and recently liberated out-castes. Tellingly, the gangs only destroyed the property of officials, but took the lives of liberated outcastes, killing eighteen and injuring scores more. Initially, the gangs smashed property in the typical early modern rebel fashion of 'smash and break', but in the last days of the uprising, they resorted to the indiscriminate violence of arson. After authorities quashed the uprising and arrested the ringleaders, it became clear from interrogations that farmers felt the liberated outcastes exhibited a lack of deference towards them. As one ringleader put it, 'Ever since the abolition of the label *eta* [outcaste], the former *eta* of Tsugawahara village have forgotten about their former status and have in many instances behaved impertinently.' Even the liberation of outcastes carried with it enormous social weight. The murderous violence at Mimasaka portended further rural disruption and violence caused by the otherwise progressive Meiji reforms.

With the Land Tax Reform (1873), the government recognized the rights of farmers to own land, rather than simply till it for a *daimyô* lord, and this was accompanied by fundamental changes in taxation policies. Under the Tokugawa shoguns, farmers offered 'tribute' of some 40 to 60 per cent of their harvest to local lords, but the Meiji government revised this to 3 per cent of the assessed value of the land. Generally, this translated into about 33 per cent of the harvest, but because farmers paid taxes in currency, the amount of the harvest surrendered depended on the value of rice in the market.

Consequently, the brunt of the cost of the Meiji revolution fell on the backs of farmers. Between 1875 and 1879, over 80 per cent of the Meiji government's revenue derived from brutal land taxes. Between 1882 and 1892, that number increased to 85 per cent. Meiji reformers rationalized this as a necessity to protect Japan's fledgling industrial sector. Because of vagaries in the rice market, the absolute value of the land tax actually doubled, forcing many small landowners to fall into debt and forfeit their property. In many instances they became tenant farmers, a widespread condition that persisted until 1945.

As we saw with the Mimasaka Blood-Tax Rebellion, 'blood taxes', actually military conscription, often accompanied crippling land taxes. In 1873, the Meiji government stressed the importance of service in the military through conscription: 'First there is military service. After that, the people are free to pursue their chosen occupations ... If people want freedom, they must take part in military service.' Despite such lofty rhetoric, farmers in Shizuoka prefecture, much like their counterparts in Mimasaka, believed that the government 'will draft young men, hang them upside down, and draw out their blood so that Westerners can drink it'. With such wild rumours circulating, it is not surprising that anti-conscription riots erupted in several prefectures. The problem was that many farmers, because they often lived in squalid conditions, had not made the transition from Tokugawa to Meiji rule. Once, when Fukuzawa Yukichi encountered a farmer on horseback while on holiday with his children, the farmer quickly dismounted and offered the horse to Fukuzawa, who was a former samurai. 'According to the laws of the present government', an exasperated Fukuzawa explained, 'any person, farmer or merchant, can ride freely on horseback, without regard to whom he meets on the road'. With farmers still seeing themselves as shackled under feudal obligations, it is not surprising that many farmers saw conscription as a form of the despised corvée labour; or worse, they imagined it as bloodletting for parched Westerners. As one leader from the anti-conscription movement protested, 'If we are conscripted into the military we will not be released for six to seven years and will be bound to suffer hardships.' Military service was three, rather than six years, but it still stung. Additionally, numerous exemptions existed, including the option to pay your way out of service, an unfair practice that the government finally terminated in 1889.

In early Meiji years, rural riots proved endemic, a barometer measuring the rising social pressures of Meiji reforms. In 1868 alone, some 180 disturbances erupted over various grievances, including taxation, conscription, outcaste liberation, introduction of Christianity, and cholera inoculations. In 1873, the same years as the Mimasaka Rebellion, 300,000 people rioted in Fukuoka on the southern island of Kyushu because they understood high food prices to have been caused by hoarding, a classic Tokugawa-era suspicion of wealthier farmers. The government dispatched troops and successfully quelled the uprising, and executed or imprisoned many of the ringleaders. Farmer protests in Mie prefecture turned violent in 1876 when the government levered excessive land taxes, well above the market value. The protests quickly spread throughout central Japan, but the government successfully suppressed them as well. In the end, the government fined or punished some 50,000 people for their involvement in this particular episode. In 1877, as marginalized former samurai fought Meiji conscript troops in the Satsuma Rebellion, ending in the dramatic ritual suicide of Saigô Takamori (1828–77), farmer riots in the countryside finally began to subside. However, rural poverty lingered. In 1881, with the deflationary policies of Finance Minister Matsukata Masayoshi (1835–1924) rural poverty continued grinding at Japan's countryside. In 1883, farmers lost some 33,845 rural households to bankruptcy, while that number increased to 108,050 only two years later.

The Matsukata deflationary policies (1881–85) ravaged many rural communities. One wealthy farmer and community leader wrote that, in Kanagawa prefecture, farmers are 'unable to repay their debts because of declining prices and the depressed state of the silkworm business and the textile industry in general'. He continued, 'People are being crushed underfoot by the usurers as if they were ants.' He warned that, without relief, farmers could turn violent; but the government ignored his pleadings. Consequently, in 1884, disruptions erupted throughout central and eastern Japan, culminating in the Chichibu Uprising (1884). That year, raw silk prices dropped 50 per cent and, the next year, crops failed, throwing farmers into abject penury. Moneylenders subjected Chichibu farmers to brutal collection tactics, and attempts by farmers to negotiate relief of debt failed. In response, farmers and local political activists formed the Poor People's Party, which demanded a moratorium on debt collecting and other forms of financial relief. In Chichibu, members of the Jiyûtô (Liberal Party), a national political party committed to the Popular Rights Movement, were among supporters of the Poor People's Party, which endorsed the overthrow of the Meiji government.

The Liberal Party was a product of the revolutionary fires of Meiji political change. Its founders, Itagaki Taisuke (1837–1919) and Gotô Shôjirô (1838–97), influenced by the English philosopher John Stuart Mill, called for the establishment of a 'national assembly'. In doing so, they echoed Sakamoto Ryôma's (1836–67) late-Tokugawa 'Eight-point Plan', which advocated the creation of national legislative bodies, along with a restoration of power to the imperial court. In October 1881, Itagaki and others formally established the Liberal Party, which remained committed to the Popular Rights Movement and the creation of a 'national assembly'. At least in part, the Popular Rights Movement and the Liberal Party were driven by newly imported Western philosophies of 'natural rights', ones confuting traditional Confucian hierarchies and Meiji oligarchical rule. In the early Meiji years, a flood of Western ideas saturated the Japanese intellectual landscape, highlighted by notions of 'natural rights' as articulated in Mill's *On Liberty* (1860) and Jean-Jacques Rousseau's *The Social Contract* (1762). Two prominent thinkers, Ôi Kentarô (1843–1922) and Ueki Emori (1857–92), through the *Liberal Newspaper* and other publications, began the process of disseminating these Western notions of 'natural rights' in the countryside. They advocated land and tax reform, and insisted that ensuring 'individual liberty' and the 'freedom to act' served as the principal 'duties' of any enlightened government, which the Meiji purported to be. Importantly, both men visited Fukushima and Chichibu only months before both areas broke out in violent rebellion.

In Chichibu, however, the Liberal Party distanced itself from the Poor People's Party, which they accused of being helmed by 'extremists'. There is some truth to the claim: in 1884 a plot to assassinate government officials was uncovered and, before the government could take action, the Poor People's Party announced the beginning of their rebellion at Mount Kaba in Ibaraki prefecture. Clearly influenced by 'natural rights', their manifesto read, 'Of primary importance in creating a nation is ensuring a fair distribution of the wealth and rights that heaven has bestowed on each individual ... It appears that our wise and virtuous emperor has neglected to realize that this is not the time to make heavy demands of people who are walking the road to starvation.' They assembled at Mount Kaba to 'fight for revolution and to overthrow the despotic government'. The Poor People's Party began assembling a peasant army led by a Robin Hood-like gang boss named Tashiro Eisuke (1834–85). 'It is my nature to help the weak and crush the strong', he once said. In November 1884, Tashiro's 'revolutionary army' marched on the county capital, Ômiya, while vandalizing the houses of moneylenders and public buildings. Once the 'revolutionary army' had reached Ômiya, its ranks had swelled to some 8,000. They proclaimed the creation of a 'revolutionary government', with Tashiro as the prime minister. Eventually, authorities brought the rebellion under control, but only after capturing some 3,000 rebels and arresting Tashiro, who was sentenced to death.

In the end, the Chichibu Uprising did little to divert attention to Japan's neglected countryside. By the early twentieth century, the difference between life in Japan's cities and countryside was stunning. Whereas the cities featured Western hairstyles and restaurants, theatres, trains, gaslights (eventually electric lights), telegraphs, newspapers, ballroom dancing, and a host of other civilized pastimes, the countryside remained mired by squalid conditions. In 1874, the ever observant Fukuzawa Yukichi wrote, 'The purpose [of government] seems to be to use the fruits of rural labour to make flowers for Tokyo.' Another writer who worked as a doctor's assistant observed

> There is no one as miserable as a peasant, especially the impoverished peasants of northern Japan. The peasants there wear rags, eat coarse cereals, and have many children. They are as black as their dirt walls and lead grubby, joyless lives that can be compared to those insects that crawl along the ground and stay alive by licking the dirt.

The importation of Western civilization opened a gaping chasm between town and country, between educated and uneducated, between connected and unconnected, and above all between the rich and poor. Nowhere were Japan's growing pains felt more sorely than in the countryside, where the weight of Meiji reforms crushed many farmers, who enjoyed few of the fruits of Japan's nineteenth-century enlightenment. In large part, the situation persisted until the abolishment of the tenancy system and the dramatic reforms initiated during the US occupation.

MODERN EXTINCTIONS

But it was not just farmers who were crushed by Meiji reforms. By the time Japan entered the twentieth century, Meiji policies had placed severe pressure on Japan's wildlife. In early modern Japan, Shintoism and Buddhism had viewed wildlife as invested with spiritual life, either embodying *kami*, deified essences, or serving as divine messengers. With Buddhism, the continuum of life and the transmigration of the soul meant that any ancestor's soul might inhabit the body of a non-human animal, so people often treated them compassionately. With early Buddhist theologians, forests and mountains, and the plants and animals that lived there, took on increasing importance as divine spaces. For the monk Ryôgen, to take one example, the life-cycle of plants paralleled the Buddhist process of enlightenment. He mused that, 'The sprouting forth of a plant is really the mode by which it bursts forth its desire for enlightenment; its residing in one place is really undertaking of disciplines and austerities; its reproduction of itself is its attainment of enlightenment.' It is not surprising that Shinto shrines, with their *torii* gates, often sat at the forest's edge. Because Shintoism saw wildlife as embodying *kami*, some animals, such as foxes, were wrapped up in specific forms of religious practice such as Inari worship. Many Japanese believed that foxes, as well as raccoon-dogs, known as *tanuki*, had the ability to metamorphose into other forms and, when they did, often took the form of mischievous tricksters, or beauties who seduced woodsmen.

Although deified non-human animals could be powerful, it is not true that their internal *kami* immunized them from exploitation.

Even under the Tokugawa shoguns, consumers bought vast quantities of wild game from urban butchers. As one European observer wrote, at some Edo butchers customers bought 'rabbits, hares, wild boar and deer' in abundance. Edo cookbooks also contained recipes for wild boar stew, as well as a variety of other wild-game cuisine. Even wildlife extermination was not beyond the early modern Japanese imagination. In 1700, on the island of Tsushima, located between Kyushu and the Korean peninsula, local domain officials initiated a nine-year boar extermination programme that led to the near annihilation of these tenacious hoofed-omnivores. During this extermination campaign, domain officials fenced the island into sections and eliminated the boar population one section at a time. With the exception of some hogs in Nagasaki, where Chinese influence was strongest because of their trading compound, Japan had relatively little animal husbandry under Tokugawa rule. In large part, the high premium on labour, including non-human labour, determined the absence of livestock for human consumption in pre-Meiji Japan. This mixture of labour and compassion for animals can be seen in the farming memoirs of Katayama Sen (1859–1933). A prominent socialist, he wrote of farming with animals in the pre-Meiji years, 'I was born in a farmhouse, and I worked as a farmer. The family ox was absolutely necessary for ploughing, and we loved him as one of ourselves. I followed behind him working, and I made money on his labour. I had so many memories of the animal that I would have never wanted to eat meat.'

With the advent of Meiji industrialization and economic development, wildlife habitat came under increasing pressure, leading to the diminution of sensitive species. The fate of Japan's two subspecies of wolf, the Japanese wolf and the Hokkaido wolf, best exemplifies the pressures that Meiji economic expansion placed on wildlife throughout Japan. Early on, the wolves of Japan had been integrated into sacred traditions. The *Man'yôshû* poetry collection, for example, contains poems that refer to the 'plains of the Large-Mouthed Pure God', an image that conjured the divine lair of the wolf. The Japanese name for wolf, *ôkami*, can be phonetically understood as 'great deity', and many Shinto shrines in Japan celebrated traditions of wolf worship. The Shinto deity

Daimyôjin of the Ôkawa Shrine, in Kyoto prefecture, used the wolf as a divine messenger, while at the Mitsumine Shrine, in Saitama prefecture, the two traditional guardian deities at the entrance of the shrine were replaced by two guardian wolves. Interestingly, Mitsumine's history parallels the waxing and waning of Buddhism and Shintoism over the course of Japanese history. Early in its history, Mitsumine incorporated esoteric Tendai and Shingon Buddhist elements, including those of Shugendô, or mountain asceticism; but after the Meiji Restoration, officials targeted the site as part of the 'orders to separate Buddhist and Shinto deities' and the shrine shed many of its Buddhist elements and became a Shinto shrine within the official Meiji system. Even while an official Shinto shrine, Mitsumine continued to sport its unique wolf iconography, including votive amulets and talismans with images of wolves (Figure 16).

The separation of Shinto and Buddhism proved an important part of the spread of Meiji nationalism. Shinto's *kami* became important legitimizers of the Meiji Restoration because they, as articulated by early modern nativist thinkers such as Motoori

16 A wooden votive amulet depicting wolves from the Mitsumine shrine.

Norinaga (1730–1801), were purely indigenous deities, untainted by continental influences. Meiji reformers emphasized that Japan's emperor traced his genealogy to the Sun Goddess Amaterasu Ōmikami, and that certain *kami*, according to early texts we have mentioned in previous chapters, had created the Japanese islands. Buddhist deities, these reformers argued, had defiled the native *kami*, and this thinking motivated a re-engineering of Japan's divine landscape. Meiji reformers ordered the forced separation of the previously intertwined categories of Shinto 'shrines' and Buddhist 'temples', a division that persists to this day, and thereby linked the newly formulated 'way of the *kami*', or Shinto, with the Japanese imperial state. The Meiji emperor became not only Japan's monarch, but also the chief priest of state Shinto. By way of example, after the Meiji Restoration, the tonsured priest at Mount Zōzu, on Shikoku Island, shed his Buddhist connections and renamed the local deity Kotohira Ōkami, a distinctly Shinto name, solidly affiliating the religious complex with state Shinto. As such, the Kotohira Shrine disseminated Shinto teachings designed to combat foreign religions and celebrated the imperial state.

Though farmers and others had worshipped Japan's wolves at shrines blending Shinto and Buddhism, and placed wolf talismans around their fields to protect them from the voracious appetites of deer and boar, the Meiji government's commitment to scientific agriculture, including livestock ranching, demoted the wolf to a 'noxious' animal. Even before the Meiji Restoration, Japanese farmers in the northeast, who raised prized samurai mounts, had undertaken some wolf hunts because of predation on valued ponies and the eighteenth-century spread of rabies, which had turned wolves into potentially dangerous animals. But hunting wolves is different than eradicating wolves, and the latter was a product of Meiji policies, largely introduced to Japan by agricultural advisers from the US who had considerable experience killing wolves.

Edwin Dun (1848–1931) was one such adviser. Dun came to Japan in 1873 from Ohio, at the recommendation of cattle brokers there. Under the direction of the newly created Kaitakushi (Hokkaido Development Agency), Dun was hired to oversee development of a livestock industry on Hokkaido (formerly the territories of Ezo examined in previous chapters). Known as 'the father of Hokkaido agriculture', Dun fastened Hokkaido's future to sheep, horses, and cattle, representing a radical departure from Japan's grain-farming past. Under Tokugawa Neo-Confucian ideologies, Japanese believed that, as philosopher Kumazawa Banzan (1619–91) had written, the 'treasure of the people is grain', while all other elements of the economy are merely 'servants of grain'. But the Meiji commitment to livestock farming and other elements of Western scientific agriculture shifted Japanese attention to non-human animal production, which reconfigured the place of wolves in the Japanese imagination. As one ministry report noted, when Japan entered the twentieth century, the modern nation had experienced a 'revolution in the butcher business', with some 1,396 slaughterhouses built throughout the country. Between 1893 and 1902, slaughterhouse employees dispatched some 1.7 million cattle to fuel the new modern bodies of Meiji Japan. Given the commitment to livestock and the bodybuilding meat it produced, wolves were no longer the 'Large-Mouthed Pure Gods' that patrolled grain crops looking for deer and boar, but 'noxious animals' slated for extermination. Meiji modernization had completely reconfigured the way that Japanese viewed wildlife, in particular wolves.

Highlighting the environmental transformations wrought by Meiji reforms, the disappearance of deer, an important prey species for wolves, proved one reason wolf predation on horses became so severe on Hokkaido. Between 1873 and 1881, hunters exported some 400,000 deer pelts from Hokkaido, nearly eliminating the main source of food for wolves. Instead, wolves turned to horses, which served an important military purpose in the emerging Japanese empire. Subsequently, the Hokkaido Development Agency oversaw wolf and bear hunting at a pace designed to erase these animals from Hokkaido. Within the third decade of the Meiji period, hunters, many of them Ainu, had harried the Hokkaido wolf to extinction. Importantly, the cultural and ecological implications of wolf extinction on Hokkaido, as well as mainland Japan, cannot be underestimated. In Japan, ancient chronicles and poetry anthologies had intertwined the wolf with imperial rule and Confucian culture, while on Hokkaido, Ainu believed themselves descended from the union of a wolf and a mythical princess. In the Meiji context, wolf hunting and eventual extinction around the turn of the century represented a form of mythological patricide, in which reformers, through an imperial bounty system and other eradication techniques and technologies, killed earlier animistic deities and replaced them with a renewed imperial institution. For Ainu, the Japanese emperor represented the new deity for their colonized world. The last mainland Japanese wolf was killed in 1905, after decades of successful eradication campaigns. Meiji reforms had not just transformed Japanese politics, economics, and society, but remade the very ecological fabric of the country. The landscape had become modernized, where cattle and horses, engineered to serve industrial human needs, had replaced the worshipped wildlife of earlier centuries. Though earlier agriculture certainly contributed, wolf extinctions were among the first signs of Japan's contribution to the Anthropocene, a geologic epoch characterized by a reconfiguration of Earth's surface by human hands to service human needs, and also characterized by what is often called the 'sixth extinction'.

MINING THE NEW ENERGY REGIME

Wolf killing represented not merely a radical remaking of Japan's national ecosystem, but also of Earth's basic biodiversity. Similarly, the Meiji shift to a fossil fuel economy represented one of the most important transitions in Japanese history. It represents an important shift in global history, too, and even recent geological time, because of the link between fossil fuels and climate change. Prior to the Meiji Restoration, Japan depended on charcoal and wood, renewable energy resources extracted from more or less carefully managed forests. As we have seen, early modern *daimyô*, within their domain forests, often practised rational silviculture in order to protect forests from unauthorized logging. They also controlled firewood collecting for the charcoal industry and protected wildlife reserves for hunting. Castles and Buddhist temples required timber, as did castle town building, and domain lords profited from lumber exports to such places as the capital of Edo. Renewable fuel such as wood and hydropower, along with the sinewy power of human and non-human muscles, powered Japan's proto-industrial economy.

After 1868, Japan began switching to coal in a concerted effort to industrialize. Implicit in this energy transition were revolutions in Japanese political structures and a radical reconfiguration of geographic space, as newly engineered vertical geographies tapped stored carbon energy from deep underground. In many respects, the Meiji story is about energy transitions: industrialization required reconfigurations of human energy, in the form of new labour practices; feeding more people with less farm labour required new scientific farming practices, producing more caloric energy; and fuelling industrial Japan required tapping into Earth's non-renewable fossil fuels.

This energy transition is critical for several reasons: for the first time in a millennium, Japan's history started taking place underground. Up to 1868, Japan's history had flowed horizontally, atop domestic and imperial landscapes; after 1868, however, it began thrusting downward vertically. Moreover, in Japan as elsewhere around the world, the age of fossil fuels created new forms of mass politics. Coal extraction and transportation workers were among the first to organize into militant unions; through the threat of general strikes, these same workers slowly democratized political practices in one country after another. In Japan as elsewhere, coalmines became important sites for often-violent protests, development of a unionized labour force, and, in the long run, the broadening of political participation. It is unsurprising that such activists as Ishimoto Shidzue, whom we met in the introduction, and her first husband, the progressive Baron Ishimoto Keikichi, started cutting their political teeth at Kyushu coalmines. Indeed, as much as the adoption of Western political philosophies, it was Japan's recruitment of fossil fuels that enabled democratization in the first place.

Japan's national coal production numbers reflect this modern energy transition. In 1874, the national yield was 208,000 tons, but by 1890 that number had increased to upwards of 3 million tons. By 1919, Japan's coal production had reached 31 million tons. Reliance on stored non-renewable solar energy has its limits, however. To begin with, coal and oil supplies on Earth are finite, including the rich seams once mined in northern Kyushu and Hokkaido, the locations of Japan's best coalfields. Modern Japan's fossil fuel civilization is thus term-limited by physical and geologic realities. Moreover, the climate change resulting from burning fossil fuels has transformed human societies into geologic agents. Basically, the geology-altering process of climate change can be dated to 1874 and James Watt's (1736–1819) steam engine; this allowed miners to pump water out of mineshafts and vastly increase stores of accessible coal. In this respect, the steam engine, which signalled the birth of the industrial age, serves as a watershed for both historical and geological transformations: the Industrial Revolution and the birth of the Anthropocene Epoch. Geology is no longer simply the result of natural plate tectonics, volcanism, and erosion, but value-driven human decisions as well. This includes the values inherent in the Meiji Restoration. The coalmines that thrust Japan into the age of fossil fuels developed with astonishing speed in the decades bracketing the turn of the twentieth century. But this growth also brought long-term dangers in its train.

In the early Meiji years, the state controlled many coalmines, such as the Miike mine on Kyushu. Starting in 1873, prison labour worked many of the Miike coal seams, even after Mitsui bought the mine in 1888 as part of Finance Minister Matsukata's scheme to sell off government-owned industries, creating Japan's giant *zaibatsu*. Only in 1933 did prison labour discontinue at the Miike mine. Women also worked Japan's coal seams. One female Miike worker recalled that, 'You were in constant danger of losing your life. A cave-in might occur at any moment. There were times when gas came out. Then a blue ball of fire would shoot through the mines. The sound was loud enough to burst your eardrums.' Miike blew up in 1963, killing 458. The largest coalmining accident on Japanese soil occurred earlier in 1914, in northern Kyushu, when the Hôjô colliery exploded, killing 687 people.

The case of Hôjô encapsulates the new dangers inherent in this vertical, subterranean landscape. The main coal vein at Hôjô had been discovered in 1897. Over the course of the next decade, engineers laid railway tracks to the mine and installed the mineshaft cage that lowered miners hundreds of feet beneath the surface in a few ear-popping seconds. By 1913, the Hôjô mine had produced some 230,000 tons of high quality bituminous and anthracite coal annually. More broadly, the Chikuhô region, where the Hôjô Colliery was located, produced some 10 million tons of coal that year, nearly half of Japan's entire coal production. The vertical Hôjô mine became central to Japan's sprawling surface empire, because it fuelled the ships and trains that facilitated Japanese expansion. The coal in the Nanaheda and Tagawa coal seams at Hôjô produced the formidable power of 7,353 calories per ton, which proved critical for Japan's move into the age of fossil fuels.

By the early twentieth century, coalmining accidents in Fukuoka prefecture, including cave-ins, chemical explosions, flooding, suffocation, and gas or coal dust explosions, had dramatically increased, claiming hundreds of lives. In the Chikuhô region, coal dust and gas explosions killed 210 miners at the Hôkoku mine in 1899 and later, at the same mine, 365 in 1907. They also killed 256 miners at the Ônoura mine in 1909 and then 365 at the same mine just eight years later. Hence the explosion at the Hôjô Colliery was hardly isolated or anomalous, and neither was the cause of the explosion that shattered this fragile subterranean environment.

An intrepid prefectural official, following his official investigation, determined that the coal dust explosion had been ignited by a faulty safety lamp. After analysing the trace patterns of the coke and other burned matter in the shafts, he determined that the ignition occurred near the junction of the '7½ incline' and the '16th side'. From this point, violent explosive waves cascaded through the mineshafts; most miners were burned alive, while others suffocated when the intense flames sucked every last molecule of oxygen out of the shafts. The prefectural official discovered small traces of coke dust on the inside of the gauze mesh of one safety lamp. The mesh is designed to let oxygen in, but not such combustibles as coal dust or methane gas. The faulty safety lamp belonged to Negoro Yôjirô, a Hiroshima man who laboured at the mine with his wife, Shizu, and his eldest daughter, Hatsuyo. On a map produced after the explosion, there are six bodies represented at the intersection of the '7½ incline' and the '16th side'. Two of them were most certainly Yôjirô and his wife, who died at his side. Unlike hard-rock mines, where superstitions regarding 'mountain deities' kept women on the surface, both men and women worked coalmines, often as teams. Despite the inherent dangers of Japan's subterranean empire of inclines and shafts, coal extracted from

Hôjô and elsewhere built modern Japan, just as petroleum continues to do in the present day.

MODERN METALS

Hard-rock mining at Ashio was also central to Japan's industrialization. Originally, two peasants had discovered copper at the site north of Edo and reported the discovery to Nikkô Zazen'in, a Buddhist temple. Shortly thereafter, the Edo *bakufu* took an interest in the copper. Throughout the seventeenth and eighteenth centuries, rice paddies and hard-rock mines buttressed Tokugawa power, and the shoguns exported thousands of tons of copper to China and the Netherlands. Between 1684 and 1697, some 55,000 tons of copper left Japan. After the Meiji Restoration, copper, and the electrified technologies it wired, became bound up in Japan's industrialization. Following the establishment of the Industry Ministry in 1870, Itô Hirobumi (1841–1909) wrote that the purpose of the ministry was to 'make good Japan's deficiencies by swiftly seizing upon the strengths of the Western industrial arts; to construct within Japan all kinds of mechanical equipment of the Western model, including shipbuilding, railway, telegraph, mines and buildings; and thus with one great leap to introduce to Japan the concepts of enlightenment'. For Itô and many other Meiji reformers, the key to Japan's 'enlightenment' was the 'mechanical equipment' that facilitated industrialization, and copper wiring proved critical to that endeavour. By 1895, some 4,000 miles of copper transmission lines bound Japan tightly to its new modern enlightenment.

In part, the entrepreneur Furukawa Ichibei (1832–1903) had made this possible when he purchased the Ashio copper mine in 1877. After the discovery of rich copper veins in 1884, Ashio produced over 25 per cent of Japan's copper, a number that continued to grow. However, paralleling the increases in copper production was evidence of environmental destruction and the dangerous consequences for human health surrounding the mine site. Birth rates plummeted in areas polluted by the Ashio copper mine's erosion and toxic tailings: in unpolluted Tochigi prefecture, birth rates hovered around 3.44 per one hundred people, while in polluted parts of Tochigi that number fell to 2.80. Similarly, Tochigi residents experienced 1.92 premature deaths in the unpolluted sections, and over double that number, or 4.12 incidents, in the polluted parts of the prefecture. Moreover, it was not long before mothers in Tochigi complained of lactation deficiencies and other problems related to toxins in the environment. Such bodily portents served as vivid reminders that, even in Japan's increasingly industrialized landscape, human bodies were inextricably tied to the environments around them, especially those downstream from active mines.

The Watarase River, which flowed through the Ashio mine site, started to turn a 'bluish white' colour, and locals reported dead fish floating down the river. Children who played or waded in the river observed red festering sores on their legs. Fishery stocks plummeted, hurting the local economy; nearby mulberry plantations, grown as silkworm nurseries, wilted under the acid rain produced by Ashio's smelting operation. Japanese copper deposits are notoriously sulphuric, with sulphur comprising upwards of 30–40 per cent of the ore. Ashio smelters released heavy doses of sulphur dioxide into the atmosphere, bathing thousands of hectares in acid rain. Meanwhile, the Watarase River became a highly efficient transporter of arsenic from the mine. When the river flooded in 1890 and 1891, and then again in 1896, it drenched even more farmland in a stew of toxic chemicals, covering thousands of hectares with sulphuric and arsenic-laden silt. The flooding left a moon-like terrain in its wake, and farmers likened their new industrial landscape to a 'Buddhist hell'.

But if the Meiji enlightenment produced its champions, such as the intrepid Fukuzawa Yukichi or the energetic Ishimoto Shidzue, it also produced critics, early harbingers of a global environmental movement. Tanaka Shôzô (1841–1913) was one such man (Figure 17). In Tanaka's thundering speeches in the Diet, Japan's new National Assembly, one detects the kernels of a powerful and enduring critique of Japan's modernization, one that after the 11 March 2011 'triple disaster' has recaptured the nation's attention. As Japan's history attests, many human casualties occurred as a result of Meiji Japan's rapid industrialization.

At the dawn of the twentieth century, Tanaka perceived these environmental threats to Japan. He was born in the Watarase River Basin, where the land had turned to a 'Buddhist hell', and witnessed

翁 造 正 中田

17 Portrait of Tanaka Shôzô.

first-hand the devastation wrought by the Ashio copper mine. In 1890, during Japan's first parliamentary elections, Tanaka represented Tochigi prefecture in the Diet. One year later, on the floor of the Diet he berated the Meiji government for not suspending

Ashio's operations owing to the horrible pollution. In a thunderous tone, he exclaimed, 'The poisonous effluent from the copper mine at Ashio ... has been allowed to inflict heavy losses and hardship each year since 1888 on villages in every district on either side of the Watarase River.' Portending the diseased bodies that would haunt Japan's twentieth-century industrial experience, he continued, 'With fields being poisoned, drinking water contaminated, and even the trees and grasses living in the dykes being threatened, no one can tell what disastrous consequences the future may hold.' By 1897, the situation downstream from the Ashio copper mine had deteriorated causing Uchimura Kanzô (1861–1930), the celebrated Christian humanist, to muse, 'Ashio pollution is a stain on the Japanese empire. If we do not remove it, there is no glory or honour in all our Empire.' Tanaka also ramped up his rhetoric against the Meiji oligarchy. He compared the Agriculture and Commerce Ministry to a 'club of criminals in the pay of Furukawa'; he scolded the Home Ministry as a 'pack of hobgoblins'. Hearkening to a past when, as Neo-Confucian Kumazawa Banzan wrote, the 'treasure of the people' was grain, Tanaka was targeting the owner of the Ashio mine, Furukawa Ichibei, explaining that the Meiji government was 'run by traitors who could decorate Furukawa while allowing him to ravage the fields that gave the nation its very life'.

After severe flooding in 1902, the Meiji government proposed levelling several villages, including Yanaka in Tochigi prefecture, in order to build a giant sediment basin. Subsequently, after cooling his heels in a Tokyo jail for 'behaviour insulting to an official', Tanaka relocated to Yanaka to fight the forced removal and destruction of the village. He reflected, 'it's been inevitable that I should come here, the natural thing'. Yanaka became the symbolic centre for Tanaka's fight against the Meiji government. When the government began 'compulsory purchases' in Yanaka, Tanaka concluded that the 'government was at war with its own people'. But it was during the fight for Yanaka that he condensed his philosophy into the phrase 'care for mountains and forests, care for rivers and streams', predating the 'thinking like a mountain' of Aldo Leopold (1887–1948) by decades. Tanaka wrote, 'To care for mountains, your heart must be as the mountains – to care for rivers, your heart must be as the rivers.' It was a lone call for an environmental consciousness amidst the clanking machines, belching smokestacks, and raking steam shovels of industrializing Meiji Japan, but one that anticipated the need for environmental protection in the coming century. Tanaka came to link his own life with the life of Japan's environment. 'If they die', he said of Japan's mountains and rivers, then 'so must he', referring to himself. He continued in the third person in a letter to friends, 'When he fell, it was because the rivers and forests of Aso and Ashikaga are dying, and Japan herself [*sic*], too ... If those who come to ask after him hope for his recovery, let them first restore the ravaged hills and rivers and forests, and then Shôzô will be well again.'

CONCLUSION

The Meiji Restoration brought 'civilization and enlightenment' to Japan, rapidly advancing the country by virtually all modern or industrial metrics, but it also exacted serious short- and long-term costs. New political systems, manners of funding the state, rapid industrialization, and elaborate development schemes placed a heavy burden on Japan's most vulnerable people, as well as its environment. Meiji reforms squeezed Japan's rural populations, in particular, sparking instances of murderous violence between former 'honourable peasants' and 'non-human' outcastes after the latter's 'liberation' and the establishment of the 'commoner' class, which encompassed most rural inhabitants. Other short-term costs included local environment destruction, such as in the Watarase River Basin's degradation as a result of the Ashio copper mine. Tailings from the mine, as well as erosion and toxic flooding, turned once-rich farmland into a veritable moonscape. But it is the long-term environmental costs of Japan's modernization that have started to attract the most attention.

Energy – lots of energy – proved the key to industrialization and producing modern lifestyles, and Japan's transition to fossil fuels was, after the Meiji Restoration, immediate and widespread. The advent of industrial economies and widespread burning of greenhouse gas-producing fuels has caused anthropogenic climate change, which in turn has prompted such basic geologic changes as melting glaciers and rising sea levels, resculpting the basic face of

Earth. As an island nation with extensive coastal development, Japan has much to lose from rising sea levels, particularly from storm surges and tsunami, a topic we will return to in the final chapter. But any history of a highly industrialized nation must take into account the long-term environmental consequences of the transition to fossil fuels, because even though all organisms will share the deleterious effects, the responsibility for anthropogenic climate change is shared by only a handful of industrialized economies – and Japan is one of them.

11

The Birth of Japan's Imperial State, 1800–1910

Historians often observe that post-Meiji forces shaped the direction of Japanese empire, and for the most part this assertion is correct. Meiji policy-makers learned, through encounters like the 'black ships' and through international agreements like the 'unequal treaties', that empire building was an integral part of Western modernity, particularly the fostering of economic strength. Empire was a characteristic the Great Powers all shared and if Japan were to ever join their ranks, the island nation needed to construct an empire of its own. To be sure, this lesson was not entirely a new one for Japanese policy-makers. Japan had undertaken earlier colonial experiments, ones not necessarily forged in the crucible of encounters with the West, but rather ones born from encounters with Okinawans to the south and Ainu to the north. Satsuma domain had conquered the Ryukyu Kingdom (Okinawa) in 1609, turning the archipelago into a kind of protectorate. To the north, Tokugawa officials had justified the slow and incremental colonizing of southern Hokkaido not with the language of international agreements and global commerce, but with the language of Confucian customs and, more importantly, the necessity of trade. Eventually, the entanglement of early modern and modern forces provided the justification for Japanese expansion onto the continent and the creation of the 'Greater East Asian Co-prosperity Sphere', where Japan's imperial interests would clash with those of the US and its European allies.

NORTHERN COLONIZATION

During the final decades of the Edo *bakufu*, Japan embarked on its experiments with colonizing. In 1802, after two centuries of rule by Matsumae domain, the *bakufu* established the Hakodate magistracy, basically a northern viceroy, and Edo began determining the affairs of the northern region and its Ainu inhabitants. In part, Russian encroachment through Sakhalin Island and the Kuril Islands had forced Edo to assert more central authority over the north. After the Treaty of Nerchinsk (1689) between Russia and China, Russian fur trappers had moved into the Kuril Islands in search of valuable pelts and, by century's end, established an outpost on the Kamchatka Peninsula. From Kamchatka, Russian trappers collected pelts from local Kamchadal and Kuril Ainu, which the Czars viewed as 'tribute' from the 'obedient conquered people' of the North Pacific. Ainu were not always submissive participants, however. In 1770, during the 'Iturup Incident', Russians killed several Ainu who refused to pay tribute to their new masters. The next year, Ainu retaliated by ambushing Russian traders on Iturup Island, in the Kuril archipelago, killing at least ten Russians in the process. During the incident, Ainu fighters chased Russians back to their ships, climbed the gunnels, and attacked them with poisoned arrows and clubs. Despite such moments of stubborn resistance, with the dawning of the eighteenth century, Russian traders and explorers had become a permanent fixture on Japan's northern border.

In 1778, for example, two Russians landed in eastern Hokkaido seeking to open trade with Japan. In eastern Hokkaido they encountered a local Matsumae official who told them that, because of the Edo *bakufu*'s maritime prohibitions, it was best that they leave rather than be caught by intolerant *bakufu* representatives. Before the two Russians left, however, they presented Matsumae officials with Russian-manufactured gifts that would, when word of them reached Edo, ignite heightened suspicion that the northernmost domain was, contrary to the shogun's wishes, clandestinely trading with Russia. In time, the *bakufu* dispatched official Satô Genrokurô to determine the extent of this illicit Russian trade. In the interrogation of a local fishery overseer, Satô became aware of ongoing trade between Ainu and Russians and that the bulk of this trade was conducted in the Ainu language, which some Russians had learned. Satô also learned that Russian-manufactured cloth and other products had changed hands as far as Edo. Although Japanese traders in eastern Hokkaido proved tight-lipped regarding the illicit trade, Ainu chiefs told of the 'beautiful silks, the calico and cotton textiles, as well as sugar, and medicine' that Ainu obtained from Russian traders for furs. In response to the Russian trade and other Matsumae violations, the *bakufu* seized control of Ezo in the beginning of the nineteenth century.

Similar to Anglo-American settler justifications for the conquest of Native American lands, or the so-called 'white man's burden' of European empires, Japanese projected the conquest of Ainu lands through the lens of Confucian 'benevolent rule', or the need to rescue Ainu from their disease-ridden lives. Indeed, providing medical assistance to Ainu proved one manifestation of Japanese control over Hokkaido. This culminated in 1857 with Edo dispatching physicians to provide Ainu with smallpox vaccinations. Through their encounters with Ainu bodies, physicians such as Kuwata Ryûsai began the process of mapping out the new boundaries of Japan's body politic. Cultural frameworks proved important as well: Ainu understood smallpox to be a deity, and the fact that Japanese could vanquish the divine airborne killer with the prick of an arm surely destabilized the Ainu pantheon. Japanese officials also encouraged Ainu to assimilate to Japanese life, including learning the Japanese language. In sum, by the early nineteenth century, Japan started to cut its colonial teeth on the northern island, paving the way for its formal incorporation under the Hokkaido Development Agency after the Meiji Restoration.

Japanese control over the Ainu altered course in the powerful currents of Meiji initiatives to modernize and better insinuate the state into the lives of its subjects. Japanese policy shifted from Confucian 'benevolent care' to the colonial 'protection' of evolutionarily lagging Ainu. Throughout the twentieth century, Japanese imperial expansion was often cloaked in the language of extending 'civilization', whatever its definition at that historical moment, and providing economic and other benefits to the colonized. This involved, for example, the forced adoption of Japanese names by subject peoples.

This transition to 'protecting' Ainu signalled the beginning of policies designed to transform them – up to this point hunters, gatherers, and traders – into small-scale farmers. The Meiji policies of paternalism culminated in the 'Hokkaido Former Aborigine Protection Act' of 1899, which distributed five-hectare (12 acre) agricultural plots to Ainu. Essentially, the Meiji government sought through this policy to break down Ainu cultural autonomy and after 1878 make them subjects called 'former aboriginals', just as outcastes had been re-designated 'new commoners'. Kayano Shigeru (1926–2006), an Ainu activist who served in the Diet, summarized Meiji assimilation policies in this matter-of-fact manner:

> Laws like the Former Hokkaido Aborigine Protection Act restricted our freedom first by ignoring our basic rights, as a hunting people, to hunt bear and deer or catch salmon and trout freely, anywhere and any time, and then by compelling us to farm on inferior land the Japanese 'provided'. In 'providing' land, the Japanese also legitimated their plunder of the region.

On Hokkaido, the Development Agency, which oversaw colonization of the island between 1872 and 1882, mainly concerned itself with agricultural and industrial development, inviting, as we have seen, such foreign experts as Edwin Dun and his wolf-killing expertise to the northern frontier. But the Development Agency also attempted to ban such Ainu cultural practices as facial and hand tattooing by women, earring wearing by men, burning homes after deaths, traditional greeting ceremonies, and the use of traditional hunting practices such as poisoned arrows. The Meiji regime also continued the earlier Tokugawa policy of encouraging the Ainu to learn Japanese, and even sent thirty-five Ainu, including a handful of women, to Tokyo in 1878 to receive an education at an agricultural college.

Under experts, such as the geologist Benjamin Lyman (1835–1920), the agricultural college president William Smith Clark (1826–86), cattleman Edwin Dun, German-educated brew-master Nakagawa Seibei (who founded Sapporo Beer in 1876), and a host of others, Hokkaido became a proving ground for empire creation, an area where the fledgling Meiji government strengthened its ability to control foreign territories. Meanwhile, the Ainu, their population in shambles from smallpox, measles, influenza, and, after the Meiji Restoration, tuberculosis, became a miserable people in desperate need of colonial care and civilizing. As Horace Capron (1804–85), a Civil War veteran and foreign overseer of the development effort on Hokkaido, remarked in a letter to his Japanese counterpart Kuroda Kiyotaka (1840–1900): 'It would seem that the same difficulties are to be encountered in efforts to civilize these people [Ainu] which are met in similar attempts with the North American Indians. The Aino [Ainu], however, possesses more amiable and attractive traits of character than the Indian, and greater capacity to appreciate the advantages of higher civilization.' Capron's frame of reference for interpreting Hokkaido was the American West. In Hokkaido, Lyman and other foreign experts assisted with identifying and surveying coal and other mineral deposits, as well as killing countless bears, crows, and wolves in bounty programmes, turning Ainu hunters into farmers, exploiting fisheries, and denuding hillsides. Much like colonial frontiers around the globe and their relationship to political and economic centres, Hokkaido was exploited, often ruthlessly and violently, by the resource-hungry regime in Tokyo, a precedent that would be applied throughout Japan's modern empire in the years to come.

THE KOREA QUESTION

After the experience on Hokkaido, Japan witnessed a convergence of historical forces that propelled the country towards building an Asia-Pacific empire of its own, much like the Great Powers it emulated during the Meiji period. One important marker of the move towards imperialism was a transformation of China's traditional place in the Japanese political imagination. Early modern thinkers envisioned China as an exalted place that evoked powerful moral and cultural associations as the 'Middle Kingdom' or, even more illustrious, the 'central florescence'. For those who advocated Zhu Xi Confucianism in the seventeenth and eighteenth centuries, China evolved into a de-historicized political abstraction, one associated with moral order and the benevolent ancient sage kings that Japan's leaders sought to emulate. As we have seen, nativist scholars had challenged China's moral centrality in the final decades of the Tokugawa period by arguing that Japan, rather than China, was the 'central florescence' based on the longevity of the imperial institution. As Motoori Norinaga (1730–1801) emphasized, China's history, unlike Japan's, was replete with disorder and political illegitimacy. Similarly, Ôkuni Takamasa (1791–1871) pointed out that it was Japan that had enjoyed direct and unbroken rule by the imperial family, not China, which he referred to not as the 'central florescence' but rather with the pejorative name 'Shina'. Famously, Satô Nobuhiro (1769–1850), in a text that articulated a secret strategy for expansion, spun Japanese moral superiority into an expansionist dialogue when he pushed for Japan's military conquest of Manchuria. Essentially, even before the collapse of the Edo *bakufu*, China and Manchuria had come to occupy the crosshairs of Japan's imperial imagination.

Initially, however, interest in continental expansion focused on affairs in Joseon Korea (1392–1897), which at the end of the nineteenth century found itself inextricably lodged between two incompatible worlds: the traditional confines of Qing China's tributary order, wherein Chinese officials viewed the peninsular country as a tributary state, and Meiji Japan's modern imperial ambitions. The intractability of the situation was made clear when, after the Meiji Restoration, Japanese diplomats sent the Joseon court a formal announcement of the founding of Meiji imperial rule. But because the 'imperial decree' contained language used only by the Chinese emperor, and thus placed Japan on parity with China, the Koreans refused to recognize it. There was also the Un'yô Incident (1875), when a Korean coastal garrison on Ganghwa Island, on edge after having just defended itself from French and US intruders, fired on a Japanese ship. As a result, just as Commodore Perry had 'opened' Japan with his 'black ships' in 1852, eventually establishing commercial and diplomatic ties with the once-closed Japan in the 'unequal treaties', Japan returned the imperial favour in Korea when Hanabusa Yoshitada (1842–1917) travelled to Busan to begin 'opening' Korea to Japanese diplomatic and commercial interests with the 'Japan–Korea Treaty of Amity' (1876). Much as the 'Harris Treaty' (1858) between the US and Japan had accomplished, the 'Japan–Korea Treaty' opened Korean trading ports, approved diplomatic relations, allowed Japan to make coastal surveys, and specified the 'independent status of Korea', detaching Korea from its former tributary obligations to China. Japan's East Asian imperial adventure had begun, and it was largely modelled after the country's gunboat encounter with the West.

Fukuzawa Yukichi, with flawless nineteenth-century imperial pragmatism, articulated the necessity of Japanese expansion into Korea in the context of experiences with US and European empires. It is no wonder that the 'Japan–Korea Treaty' so closely resembled the 'US–Japan Treaty' of nearly two decades earlier. In his famous 'Datsu-A-ron' (Disassociation from Asia) treatise, which first appeared in the widely circulated *News of the Times* in 1885, Fukuzawa laid it out plainly: either Japan colonize Asia, or be colonized by the Great Powers. An outspoken proponent of Westernization, he argued that, after the Meiji Restoration, Japan had adopted 'contemporary Western civilization in all things, official and private, across the entire land'. Unlike its Asian neighbours, specifically Korea and China, 'Japan is alone in having freed itself from old ways, and it must move beyond all Asian countries by taking a "disassociation from Asia" as the keynote of a new doctrine.' In his mind, Japan needed to distance itself from its East Asian neighbours.

For Fukuzawa, the Meiji Restoration represented a cultural transcendence of Japan's own historical and geographic origins. 'Although Japan lies close to the edge of Asia', he wrote in a historically revealing assertion, 'the spirit of its people has transcended Asian conservatism and moved towards Western civilization'. Japan's diplomacy in Korea proved one example of that move. Because of Korea and China's 'affection for convention and antiquated custom', he observed, 'it appears inevitable that they will lose their independence' through colonization, 'divided amongst the civilized nations of the world'. Fukuzawa asserted that, rather than extend Korea and China special privileges, 'we should deal with them just as Western nations do'. Still smarting from the 'unequal treaties', Japan understood exactly how Western nations dealt with Asian ones. This colonize or be colonized mentality, implicit in Japan's nineteenth-century experience, proved a major driver in the eventual creation of the 'Greater East Asian Co-prosperity Sphere'.

With the Meiji government plotting a course for an imperial future, Japan's focus on Korea inevitably led to a confrontation with China. While Japan ramped up its interest in Korea, it signed the Tientsin Convention with Qing China in 1885. Signed by Itô Hirobumi (1841–1909) and Li Hongzhang (1823–1901), the convention sought to defuse tension after the Gapsin Coup in Korea in 1884, when Kim Ok-gyun (1851–94) and Pak Yonghyo, members of the pro-Japan Enlightenment Party, precipitated a three-day *coup d'état* designed to overthrow the Joseon court. When the coup failed, the perpetrators fled to Japan, and Chinese troops occupied much of Korea. In response, the Tientsin Convention agreed that both countries would withdraw their forces from Korea, and that neither side would dispatch troops to Korea without alerting the other. Contrary to the agreement, when the pantheistic Donghak Peasant Rebellion broke out in 1894, the Joseon court requested military assistance from China, which dispatched troops without alerting the Japanese. Donghak rebels made the situation even more volatile when they burned Japan's legation in Seoul.

With War Minister Yamagata Aritomo (1838–1922) applying considerable pressure, Tokyo dispatched 1,500 troops to Incheon near Seoul to guard its commercial and diplomatic interests. It was not long before clashes erupted between Japanese and Chinese forces. Within days Japan, equipped with its newly trained Western-style military, seized Pyongyang and, within three months, controlled territory well inside China and Manchuria, including the strategically critical Port Arthur. By March 1895, China sued for peace and dispatched Li to Japan to negotiate an armistice.

Patriotically elated by its victory, Japan demanded land and an indemnity from the Qing dynasty. But Germany, Russia, and France intervened and denied Japan the spoils of war in a 'Triple Intervention'. Russia had its own designs on the Korean peninsula and, furthering those ends, concluded a treaty of their own with the Qing dynasty in 1898. Japan countered with an agreement with England in 1902. When the Russians opted against recognizing Japanese interests in Korea the two countries went to war in 1905. Once the conflict was under way, General Nogi Maresuke (1849–1912) laid siege to the Russian fortress at Port Arthur for 156 days before forcing a Russian surrender. When Admiral Tôgô

Heihachirô (1848–1934) spectacularly sank much of the Russian Baltic fleet at the Battle of Tsushima Straits, the Czar sued for peace. Japan's victory sparked another exuberant patriotic outpouring from all quarters. At the Treaty of Portsmouth (1905) Japan won a handful of important concessions; but Tôyama Mitsuru (1855–1944), a right-wing political leader, and opposition leader Kôno Hironaka, both claimed Japan had settled for a humiliating compromise, given the high human and monetary costs of the conflict. Indeed, it is estimated that the Japanese lost some 70,000 men, including deaths from disease and wounds. Nonetheless, buoyed by military success against a European power and strident domestic patriotism, Japan had exploded onto the global scene at the dawn of the twentieth century.

JAPAN AT THE DAWN OF EMPIRE

While Japan expanded its influence in Korea and beyond, domestically the country underwent important changes. Meiji economic policies led to the early twentieth-century ascendancy of Japan in key areas, including cotton and silk textile production. Many of the first large-scale Meiji-sponsored interests were textile companies, and they benefited from the government's generous subsidies. By the 1880s, manufacturers had created the Japan Cotton Spinners' Association, which facilitated the creation of some of Japan's legendary labour efficiency techniques. As late as 1935, cotton textile production accounted for 26 per cent of all Japanese exports, and nearly 15 per cent of all industrial production. In the late Meiji period and after, textiles represented an industrial colossus in Japan. Importantly, Japan was prepared not only to compete on the geopolitical stage of colonial gamesmanship, but in the realm of global manufacturing and trade as well.

Even though Japan had produced silk in the early modern period, Western models drove the modern silk textile industry, as was typical of most Meiji initiatives. In 1870, European specialists travelled to Japan to assist with the building of an industrial silk textile mill. Two years later, the Meiji government opened a 'model factory' in Tomioka, which other silk manufacturers around the country emulated with astonishing success. In 1868, at the time of the Meiji Restoration, Japan exported 1 million kilograms (2.2 million pounds) of silk. By 1893, as Japan ramped up its imperial efforts in Korea, it also ramped up silk production to 4.6 million kilograms (10 million pounds) exported. Two years after the conclusion of the Sino-Japanese War (1895), Japan produced some 27 per cent of the world's raw silk. By 1913, at the dawn of the First World War, no fewer than 800,000 Japanese workers, and countless silkworms, laboured in Japan's silk industry. Ironically, Japan's dominant Meiji industry, the centrepiece of its modern industrial complex, was built on an age-old symbiotic relationship between humans, known as 'factory girls' in this context, and their traditional insect ally, *Bombyx mori*.

Factory girls were the thousands of young women that companies or professional recruiters enticed to labour in Japan's textile mills. Most of these 'factory girls', as a 1927 survey concluded, endured the dank, horrific conditions in the textile mills to contribute to their family's finances. One woman recalled:

> When I went home with a year's earnings and handed the money to my mother, she clasped her hands and said, 'With this, we can manage through the end of the year'. And my father, who was ill, sat up in his bed and bowed to me over and over. 'Sué', he said, 'it must have been difficult. Thank you ... Thank you ...' Then we put the money in a wooden box, and put the box up on the altar and prayed ... Whenever I thought of my mother's face then, I could endure any hardship.

For factory girls, working in the brutal textile mills served as one way to fulfil enduring Confucian filial obligations. Initially, when the model factory opened in Tomioka, the industry, because of its connections to Western-style industrialization, carried a glamorous appeal, and 40 per cent of the 371 woman employed hailed from former samurai families. Eventually, the industry came to require more 'docile and obedient' country daughters, and farmers often leapt at the opportunity to improve their financial lot and replace the wooden taste of old daikon radishes with the delicate taste of polished white rice.

Conditions inside the silk mills were brutal and the air filled with lint. For proprietary reasons, the cocoons needed to be soaked in scalding water and steamed before the thread could be removed and, as a result, condensation accumulated on factory ceilings and throughout the day fell on workers like rain showers. In the winter, women often caught colds or influenza from these pervasive moist conditions. The industry also exposed woman to a host of lung diseases, including tuberculosis. Tuberculosis is often called the 'modern epidemic' because of its association with industrial settings, where the manufacturing process crowded people together in environments where the tubercle bacilli were easily exchanged between already immunologically compromised bodies. Tuberculosis is debilitating and deadly: the bacilli are not toxic themselves, but the body's robust immunological response to them causes tubercles to form in the lungs. These caseous areas in the lungs, identified by an unhealthy cheesy consistency, leave cavities, and when cavities form near pulmonary blood vessels they cause haemorrhaging, or the bloody coughs called haemoptysis often associated with the disease. These factories, quite literally warm and moist bacilli incubators, multiplied throughout the Meiji period; about 90 per cent of the workforce were women, mostly under the age of twenty-five.

Tuberculosis and other pulmonary diseases quickly emerged as mass killers. In 1903, the Meiji government commissioned a study of the textile mills, titled 'The Condition of Factory Workers', and of 689 workers dismissed from work for health problems between 1899 and 1902, half were dismissed for 'respiratory disease', and half of these for tuberculosis, even though doctors rarely diagnosed tuberculosis because of the social stigma attached to the disease. Dangerous to family reputations, tuberculosis was rumoured to be hereditary until quite late. Other surveys conducted by physicians concluded that 50 per cent of the women dying in the silk textile industry died of tuberculosis, which they identified as the textile industry's, and perhaps even industrial Japan's, most serious health challenge. In a 1913 speech before the National Medical Society, one doctor implicated the textile industry in the spread of tuberculosis because factory owners, to deal with the problem, simply dismissed workers back home once ill. This effectively created vectors to spread the disease throughout the country and caused a national epidemic. Along with beriberi, a nutritional disease caused by thiamine deficiency, which often killed as many soldiers and sailors as war, tuberculosis was emerging as Meiji Japan's national disease.

One factor that facilitated the spread of tuberculosis nationally is that many women suffering from the disease kept it a secret, or referred to it by a host of pulmonary-disease pseudonyms. In large part, because many viewed it as hereditary, the disease could bring misfortune and shame on an entire family, or at a minimum ruin marriage prospects. This delicate theme was explored in Tanizaki Jun'ichirô's (1886–1965) masterpiece, *Sasameyuki* (The Makioka sisters, 1948). In the novel, a well-heeled Japanese family, represented by the Makioka sisters, tries to find a suitable husband for the third-oldest sister, Yukiko. On one occasion, a potential suitor requests that Yukiko get a chest X-ray because of her frail, sickly physique. The results turned up negative for tuberculosis but, in the meantime, the sisters find fault in the suitor's background, specifically the decade-long insanity of the gentleman's mother, and the engagement is terminated. Later, when a wealthy Nagoya man courts Yukiko, he hires a private investigator to conduct a background check on the Makioka family. When he discovers that the Makioka mother had died of tuberculosis at the age of thirty-six, the man terminates the engagement. As the novel suggests, the social stigmatic and hereditary rumours of tuberculosis persisted well after German scientist Robert Koch (1843–1910) discovered the tubercle bacilli in the 1880s.

Much like the Prussian government that funded Koch's research, the Meiji government proved intensely interested in tuberculosis and its possible cure, given how the epidemic plagued industrial, urban, and military settings where crowds of people could easily spread the disease. It makes sense that in 1890, when Koch presented his preliminary report for a tuberculosis cure in Berlin, Kitasato Shibasaburô (1853–1931) (Figure 18), a prominent medical scientist, immediately forwarded the presentation to a leading Japanese medical journal. The Meiji government had sent Kitasato, an aspiring bacteriologist working for the Home Ministry, to Berlin in 1885 to study under Koch, who quickly came to view the thirty-two-year old as one of his favourite students. Kitasato had proven instrumental in the discovery. In 1889, for example, Kitasato successfully cultured a pure sample of the tetanus bacilli and, while working with Emil von Behring (1854–1917), another German scientist, uncovered many of the mysteries of anti-toxic immunities. Not surprisingly, Kitasato

18 Bacteriologist Kitasato Shibasaburô.

assisted Koch extensively in his laboratory. After Home Ministry bureaucratic regulations threatened to bring him home, the Meiji emperor intervened and Kitasato was allowed to stay in Berlin to continue his prestigious work with Koch.

By March 1891, the first shipments of tuberculin, Koch's cure, arrived in Japan, and the army, Japan Health Society, and Tokyo University began conducting clinical trials. In the end, tuberculin had mixed results, and a true cure for tuberculosis remained years away; the discovery, however, facilitated a bacteriological revolution in Japanese science and medicine. Illustrating this, by 1891, not a single microscope could be found on store shelves in all of Tokyo prefecture, with two shops having sold 170 instruments between them. That same year, the Meiji government opened its Tokyo Microscopy Centre, which conducted bacteriological analysis of tuberculosis and other micro-organisms. Eventually, industry and government refocused on prevention, but tuberculosis remained a killer in Japan for decades.

PUBLIC DISCIPLINE

The attempts by the Meiji state to control Japanese subjects had become stifling by 1910. With the emergence of the Japanese empire, the Meiji state actively strove for the 'reform of body and soul', as one slogan trumpeted, in order to withstand the threat of Western empire and create a new Japanese one. Reform was accomplished through control over the human body and sexuality in ways never seen before in Japanese history. If the early modern state had concerned itself with control over the status system, by monitoring haircuts and other social customs that identified status boundaries, the Meiji state sought to discipline the body through hygiene and control over sexuality, as the creation of the Central Sanitation Bureau (1872), the school hygiene system (1898), and various laws requiring health checks exemplified. Like so much in the Meiji period, the focus on sanitation and hygiene required a whole new language and level of intrusiveness by the state. During the Iwakura Mission (1871), Nagayo Sensai (1838–1902) had been impressed by medicine and sanitation in Germany and the Netherlands, and created the new Japanese word for hygiene (*eisei*) based on the German word. He founded the Bureau for Hygiene in 1874, which was eventually folded into the Home Ministry. The bureau monitored the hygienic state of the nation and the emerging empire.

Similarly, Gotô Shinpei (1857–1927) was influenced by European theories of hygiene and medicine and projected sanitation and hygiene concerns onto the fledgling Japanese empire. Part of a growing contingent of thinkers who, influenced by German thought, viewed the nation as a body or organism, Gotô drew on Rudolf Virchow's (1821–1902) 'social medicine' and Otto Von Bismarck's (1815–98) 'social policy'. In his 'state as human body' analogy, the army served as the teeth and claws of the body, and hygiene and health policies as its immune system. Such 'state as human body' metaphors became increasingly common as Japan inched towards the Pacific War and developed nascent fascist policies at home.

Meiji officials believed that health threats such as tuberculosis, or even insanity, were contagious and malignant and could metastasize from the individual to the entire national body. Reflecting this view of the state, Ôkuma Shigenobu (1838–1922) remarked: 'Insanity occasionally becomes infectious. This infection can be terrible, spreading ceaselessly among the people. A society, or even a state, can eventually become morbid.' Armed with such hygienic philosophies, in the early twentieth century Japanese policy-makers sought to 'improve the race' and 'improve society' through strict health-related policies. In 1902, the Meiji government hired thousands of physicians to work in schools and inspect children for such maladies as scrofula (a form of tuberculosis affecting the lymph nodes), chronic diseases, and nervous disorders. Often, Japanese doctors linked symptoms such as exhaustion to masturbation, which was viewed as a social malady resulting from improper sex education. Some policy-makers advocated 'sexual pedagogy' based on the German model, in order to inoculate the national body from widespread masturbation and venereal disease. Girls' schools and textile factories also became the foci of hygiene policies, some of which sought to reform 'factory girl' dormitory habits so as to not threaten the moral constitution of Japan's national body. Importantly, as Japanese policy-makers and intellectuals drew on German thought and used the analogy of the body to describe the nation, any social discord or political opposition came to be viewed as a threatening disease, portending Japan's slide into fascism decades later.

Finally, using the body as an analogy to describe the nation also shaped Japanese natural sciences, particularly the development of ecological thought. Drawing on ecological thinking from Germany and a handful of US universities, Japanese thinkers began to participate in discussions about the role of societies in driving evolution, not just the individual, as Charles Darwin (1809–82) had suggested. Reflecting Japan's Confucian milieu, humans could be viewed not just as individualistic creatures, as Western liberalism suggested, but rather as a highly social species, one in which group evolutionary success outweighed that of individuals. Imanishi Kinji (1902–92), an important Japanese evolutionary biologist, anticipated the importance of social evolution over a half century ago.

In *Seibutsu no sekai* (The world of living things, 1941), he first proposed the existence of the 'specia', or the holistic, socially evolving species-society. He demoted the individual organism in evolution, a hallmark of Darwinism, and elevated the social whole. Imanishi wrote, 'members of a species can be understood as being linked by kinship and territorial relations and which share the same life form'. Just as the subject is nothing more than a constituent of the imperial nation, Imanishi, though no fascist himself, argued that the individual organism is 'nothing more than a constituent of the species' and that society is a 'place of shared living' where the 'individual reproduces and sustains itself'. Whereas Darwin had identified in the *Origin of Species* (1859) inherited 'individual differences' as of the 'highest importance' because they 'afford materials for natural selection', Imanishi viewed evolution as occurring at the social level through affinities that transcended the individual. Though not necessarily the product of fascist thinkers, such ecological theories bolstered the basic idea that social groups, including nations, constituted natural bodies that needed to be strengthened through state hygiene and other policies.

CONCLUSION

Although Japan learned many of its colonial strategies from the tough experiences gained in its own 'unequal treaties' with the US and European nations, Japanese colonialism was not exclusively a product of cultural borrowing from the West. Whether in Okinawa or Hokkaido, Japan had early learned indigenous lessons in conquering and colonizing other peoples and their lands, lessons that policy-makers transported across the seas to their new East Asian colonial frontiers. Reflecting the Confucian milieu that birthed them, such indigenous Japanese tactics were largely cultural in nature, operating under the ancient Confucian principal that peripheral 'barbarians' could be incorporated through adopting the civility of the centre. Hence, Japanese forced Ainu to speak Japanese and to abandon hunting to become farmers; they forced Ainu to take Japanese names and worship according to Japanese belief systems; they forced Ainu to see the Japanese emperor as their new patriarchal leader. To greater and lesser degrees, Koreans were the recipients of similar soft colonial tactics, as well as harder tactics of sheer violence. By the early twentieth century, Japan was well on the road to empire creation, a road that in many respects came to dominate its twentieth-century story.

12

Empire and Imperial Democracy, 1905–1931

In the first half of the twentieth century, empire stood squarely at the centre of Japanese life: competition with European and US powers in the Asia-Pacific region, the need for natural resources, working distant fishing grounds to regenerate revenue and feed hungry mouths, and other forces all drove empire building. In the end, however, Japan's 'China policy' served as the spark in the dry tinderbox that eventually led to the Pacific War. Japan's 'special interests' in China challenged US and European access to Chinese manufactures and markets, and placed Japan on a collision course with the Great Powers. Japan's foreign policy was designed to protect its economic and military investments in China, the most important of which revolved around the South Manchurian Railroad, leased to Japan after the Russo-Japanese War (1905).

But other subsurface forces propelled Japan towards 'total war' in Asia. In the US, a half-century's worth of racially charged immigration legislation and antagonistic foreign policy disillusioned many Japanese diplomats and policy-makers who set an increasingly autarkic course towards empire. After the dual victories of the Sino-Japanese (1895) and Russo-Japanese (1905) wars, the Great Powers conspired to deprive Japan of its war spoils, chiefly territory in northern Korea and China. Clearly, no place setting remained at the table of the Great Powers for the up-and-coming Asian nation. In this context, Japan increasingly pursued an alternative form of modern nationhood, one that wove the legitimacy of an empire in East Asia from the threads of modernization and 'pan-Asianism'.

Rhetorically, Japan sought to defend its Asian brothers and sisters from Western imperial aggression and encroachment. It is no secret that race served as a powerful driver in the events leading up to the Pacific War.

MAKING JAPANESE EMPIRE

The Russo-Japanese War had been a savage conflict, with both sides suffering heavy losses at Mukden and other major engagements. Meeting in Portsmouth, New Hampshire, with US mediation Japanese and Russian diplomats agreed to recognize each other's colonial holdings on the continent, including the deployment of small police forces to guard their respective interests. Significantly, Russia relinquished its lease over the South Manchurian Railway to Japan, a concession that later proved instrumental in the outbreak of the Pacific War. Originally, Russia had laid the rail line at the close of the nineteenth century as part of the China Eastern Railway, but then lost the southern portion of the railway from Harbin to Port Arthur. The Japanese government founded the generously capitalized South Manchuria Railway Company in 1906, and charged it with developing economic assets along the railway's zone, basically 62 metres (203 feet) on either side of the track for a distance of approximately 1,100 kilometres (683 miles). The railway linked over twenty towns and cities, in which Japanese stationed coal, electrical equipment, and other supplies necessary for keeping the trains moving (Figure 19). Gotô Shinpei (1857–1929), the former governor of Taiwan and an individual we have met before, served as the first president of the company, which Japanese officials headquartered in Dalian on the Liaodong peninsula.

The railroad proved the linchpin of Japanese holdings in East Asia and the defining feature of Japan's economic investments in resource-rich northeastern China and Manchuria. In its first twenty-five years, company assets for the railway rose from ¥163 million to over ¥1 billion, amounting to a 20–30 per cent annual rate of growth. It became not only Japan's largest company, but for many years the most profitable as well. Moreover, as a result of the lease, Japan's economic and personal entanglements in China increased steadily throughout the early twentieth century. In

19 Loading coal from the Fushun mine in 1940.

1900, before Japan gained the lease, only about 3,800 Japanese resided in China. In 1910, five years after the Treaty of Portsmouth, that number had increased to 26,600. By 1920, that figure reached 133,930. Most Japanese resided in Manchuria, but some had started to settle in such southerly cities as Shanghai, as a result of the expanding textile industry. Japan benefited in several ways from the First World War, which preoccupied the Great Powers. In 1914, as the 'war to end all wars' broke out in Europe, Japan's foreign trade with China stood at ¥591 million. By 1918, that number had soared to ¥2 billion. In 1895, immediately after the Sino-Japanese War, Japan's foreign trade constituted about 3 per cent of the Chinese market; that number had increased to 30 per cent by 1920, demonstrating Japan's ability to take advantage of the First World War.

Provocative colonial policies accompanied Japan's increasing economic presence in China and Manchuria. In 1915, while the Great Powers laid razor wire and carved trenches across the European continent, Prime Minister Ôkuma Shigenobu (1838–1922) and Foreign Minister Katô Kômei (1860–1926, aka Katō Takaaki) tried to force the notorious 'Twenty-one Demands' on the dysfunctional Chinese government, recently sundered by the rise of warlord

Yuan Shikai (1859–1916). Briefly, the Qing dynasty had fallen in 1911 after the Wuchang Uprising, when revolutionaries elected Sun Yatsen (1866–1925) as their provisional president. However, Sun turned over the fledgling republican government to Yuan in exchange for his arranging the abdication of the Qing child emperor Puyi (1906–67), who later became the puppet emperor of Japan-controlled Manchukuo (1932). The young Chinese republic also sought the support of the Beijing military, which Yuan commanded. In 1913, when China held elections for the new National Assembly, the Guomindang (Nationalist Party) won an overwhelming victory. The Guomindang's brightest light was Song Jiaoren (1882–1913), who, while travelling with friends, was killed on a train station platform by an assassin probably working for Yuan. Immediately after, Yuan cracked down on the fledgling Guomindang and declared himself emperor of China. At this moment, the new emperor, reigning over a fragile and restive China, received Japan's secret 'Twenty-one Demands', and was forced to agree to almost all of them, though many were retracted.

Brazen in nature, the 'Twenty-one Demands' sought to expand Japan's economic interests and influence throughout China. As a reward for siding with the Allies during the First World War, Japan acquired German colonial holdings on the Shandong peninsula, as well as the region's valuable railways. China recognized Japan's 'special rights' in Manchuria and Inner Mongolia, and a joint Sino-Japanese company received mining monopolies along the Yangzi River. Japan also attempted to restrict the ability of European powers to lease bays and harbours along China's coast, and acquired a broad mandate to build railroads throughout China. Even more controversially, Japan sought to deploy its own police throughout the country, as well as insisting that 50 per cent of China's military purchases come from Japan and that China employ Japanese military advisers.

In sum, Japanese asserted wide-ranging colonial demands on China at a time when the US and European powers were preoccupied. For the US, the 'Twenty-one Demands' flew in the face of the 'open door policy', which insisted no one country had 'special rights' in China. In 1899, US Secretary of State John Hay (1838–1905) had dispatched a diplomatic note to the imperial players, including Japan, setting out the 'open door policy'. In essence, Hay asserted that all powers had rights to Chinese ports within their respective colonial spheres of interest, as well as commensurate access to Chinese markets. This fundamental disagreement between the 'special rights' of Japan and the 'open door policy' of the US and its allies became a major source of friction propelling the two Pacific powers towards war.

Contention over the 'open door policy' was not the first dispute that arose between the two countries. In the US, a series of discriminatory policy decisions had alienated Japan and Japanese immigrants, putting the two countries on a collision course. In 1906, the San Francisco School Board announced that, 'to save white children from being affected by association with pupils of the Mongolian race', Asian youngsters would be separated from white students in schools. In 1913, the 'California Alien Land Law' prohibited 'aliens ineligible for citizenship' from owning land in the Pacific coast state. The law impacted Chinese, Korean, and Indian immigrants, but it was principally aimed at the Japanese. The Japanese government responded by explaining that the law was 'essentially unfair and inconsistent ... with the sentiments of amity and good neighbourhood which have presided over the relations between the two countries'. The law was designed to curtail Japanese immigration and created a hostile environment for those Japanese already living and farming in California. Then, in 1922, the US Supreme Court held that Japanese were ineligible for citizenship. In *Takao Ozawa* v. *United States*, the Supreme Court ruled that Ozawa was a member of an 'unassimilable race' and therefore could not be naturalized as a US citizen. In a final insult, the 1924 'Immigration Bill' effectively prohibited Japanese from immigrating to the US because they were now ineligible for citizenship.

US racism also affected international negotiations. In the 1919 negotiations for the Treaty of Versailles, the Japanese delegation sought to affirm Japanese control over former German holdings on the Shandong peninsula, which they achieved. They also sought to have explicit language guaranteeing 'racial equality' placed in the founding documents of the League of Nations. But US President Woodrow Wilson (1856–1924) and others successfully scuttled this effort. To the Japanese delegation, most rhetoric of 'racial equality' in the new post-First World War international order proved to be empty rhetoric indeed. Three years later, at the Washington Naval Conference (1922), Japan begrudgingly submitted to a '5–5–3 ratio' for warship tonnages, placing the young Asian empire at a disadvantage vis-à-vis the US and Great Britain. Increasingly, Japan began to realize that the new international order was a racially dominated one, and the fledgling Japanese empire would struggle to find a seat at the table of the Great Powers.

In some respects, these international events precipitated a China pivot, wherein Japan began to redouble its focus on the continent by articulating new connections to its Asian neighbours. Ever since the Russo-Japanese War, Japan had become a model for independence in Asian nationalist circles. Regarding the critical naval engagement of the Russo-Japanese War, one London diplomat observed, 'The battle of Tsushima is by far the greatest and most important naval event since Trafalgar.' In the US, President Theodore Roosevelt (1858–1919) called the stunning defeat of Russia 'the greatest phenomenon the world has ever seen'. But more important than Western observations were those of Japan's Asian neighbours, who had long chafed under colonial rule. The Japanese victory prompted Jawaharlal Nehru (1889–1964), the future first Prime Minister of India, to fantasize about 'Indian freedom and Asiatic freedom from the thraldom of Europe'. In South Africa, a young Mohandas Gandhi (1869–1948) was likewise inspired: 'When everyone in Japan, rich or poor, came to believe in self-respect, the country became free. She could give Russia a slap in the face ... In the same way, we must, too, need to feel the spirit of self-respect.' Even Mao Zedong (1893–1976), whose Chinese Communist Party later gained popularity fighting the Japanese, remembered that, 'At that time, I knew and felt the beauty of Japan, and felt something of her pride.' Japan had become a beacon of hope in Asia, a fact that precipitated and fuelled Japan's China pivot.

Chinese revolutionaries such as Sun Yatsen were thus lured to the rising Asian beacon of freedom. His 'Revolutionary Alliance' was largely founded while he studied in Japan. As party politics grew and diversified in Japan in the 1920s in what is often called 'Taishô democracy', a similar democratization occurred in China during the May Fourth Movement (1919), in which students expressed anger over China's capitulation in the Treaty of Versailles. Some in Japan, such as the journalist and politician Ishibashi Tanzan (1884–1973), advocated a 'small Japan' policy, where Japan would abandon its Manchurian holdings. In 1918, the prominent literary figure Tanizaki Jun'ichirô (1886–1965) toured Korea, northern China, and Manchuria. In 1922, the 'Institute for Oriental Culture' was established at Tokyo Imperial University, and a decade later the 'Concordia Society' similarly promoted harmony between the five ethnic groups coexisting in Manchuria. As late as 1941, the 'Concordia Society' disseminated leaflets in Manchuria encouraging racial equality and disavowing the racism of Nazi Germany. Japan's China pivot proved instrumental in strengthening ties to its Asian neighbours, even though all of those ties would be destroyed by Japanese conduct during the Pacific War. The China pivot also legitimized, in a cultural sense, Japan's expansion into China and the wider Asia-Pacific sphere.

PELAGIC EMPIRE

Paralleling the early terrestrial successes in empire building were maritime feats. Japan's succession of territorial gains was impressive for a country the size of Montana: the Ryukyu Islands in 1871, the Bonin and Kuril Islands in 1875, Taiwan in 1895, southern Sakhalin Island and parts of the Liaodong peninsula in 1905, the annexation of Korea in 1910, Micronesia after the First World War, and Manchuria after 1931. The Pacific War began with the Marco Polo Bridge Incident of 1937, leading to an invasion of China and Southeastern Asia. But Japan's fluid maritime empire, what one historian has labelled Japan's 'pelagic empire', paralleled and underpinned these dramatic terrestrial gains. Just as Japan sought natural resources throughout Asian lands, such as coal in Manchuria or rubber in Southeast Asia, the empire also sought marine resources throughout its pelagic empire, exploiting offshore fisheries throughout much of the Pacific Ocean.

Pelagic conquest was a critical part of Japan's late nineteenth- and early twentieth-century ascendancy. The Treaty of St Petersburg in 1875 allowed Japanese to fish in Russia's North Pacific waters, and fishermen wasted little time establishing operations throughout the

Okhotsk littoral. In 1875, the number of Japanese fishing vessels in the area was 300, but by 1904, on the eve of the Russo-Japanese War, the region had witnessed a tenfold increase. Meanwhile, Russian fishermen in the area remained around 200. When it came to exploiting fishing grounds, Japan stood at the cutting edge of technological innovation, as they do to this day. In 1908, Japan commissioned its first 'otter trawler', a fishing boat designed in Britain, and five years later some 100 of these plied the seas around the Japanese archipelago. Japan also commissioned motorized tuna boats in 1906, which allowed Japanese fishermen to harvest skipjack near the Bonin Islands, nearly 700 miles away from the main islands. While trawlers plied waters north and south of the main islands, Japanese troops earned international attention for their gains in wars against China and Russia.

Hunger for natural resources fuelled the terrestrial conquest of Manchuria. As Japan's population grew, planners viewed Manchuria as fertile ground for increasing agricultural output in order to feed hungry mouths. In the mid-1930s, one ministry oversaw experimental agriculture settlements in Manchuria in an attempt to increase agricultural productivity. In four years, planners mobilized some 321,882 farmers from many Japanese prefectures to participate in the programme. Driven by social scientific research, planners hoped to eventually relocate roughly one third of Japan's rural population to 1.6 hectare (4 acre) plots located in colonial Manchuria. There, they would become yeoman farmers, producing food for the hungry empire. With rural Japan depopulated, planners hoped that independent (not tenant) farmers would emerge on the main islands. In the end, retrograde technologies and a poor understanding of the land stymied many Japanese farmers in Manchuria, but the linkages between empire and expansion of natural-resource bases remained an important one. Planners viewed Japan's pelagic empire in a similar fashion. As one ministry official explained:

> With the steady increase of population . . . the demand for fishing products is showing a striking advance, a condition still further accelerated by the increased demand from abroad. Under these circumstances the fishermen can no longer remain satisfied with coastal work alone, but are obliged to a greater extent than ever before to venture into the open sea and even to the distant coasts of Korea and the South Sea Islands.

In other words, just as Japanese farmers could no longer be content to hoe the rows of Japan's main islands, fishermen needed to expand their spheres from mere coastlines to include the 'open sea'. Many Japanese heeded this call: armadas of crabbers, for example, expanded Japan's take of crab to 407,542 cases of canned crab in 1931, or eight times what they produced a decade earlier. Life on one of these industrial crab boats became the material for one of Japan's great proletarian novels, *Kanikôsen* (Factory ship, 1929) by Kobayashi Takiji (1903–33), who would be arrested, stripped naked in the winter, and beaten to death by Japan's notoriously brutal thought police.

Though planners often explained that Japan needed marine products to feed a growing population, much of the fish was actually canned and sold in Western markets in order to keep wartime resources, such as oil, rubber, and iron ore, flowing. To do so, every aspect of Japan's pelagic fishing fleet grew. In 1930, Japan accounted for only 1 per cent of worldwide whale catches, but by 1938 that had increased to 12 per cent. Now, Japan is nearly synonymous with whaling. In this regard, Japan's pelagic empire evolved much as its terrestrial one did. Manchuria strengthened Japan's economy by serving as an important market, causing one Osaka businessman to remark in 1933: 'Manchuria has recently become an incredible boom area as a consumer market for Japanese goods; this year's exports have approached 300,000 yen, more than ten times what they were only a few years ago, and far surpassing exports to China.' Similarly, as one booster of Japan's pelagic fishing industry noted in 1940, 'The fishing industry serves Japan as an important source of foreign exchange. Her exports of marine products amount annually in value to between ¥150,000,000 and ¥160,000,000 and thus rank third after raw silk, and cotton yarn and piece-goods exports.' Evidencing the importance of the pelagic empire to Japan's broader imperial ambitions was state-sponsored exploration of potential new fisheries. Japan probed nearby waters in the South China Sea, the Sea of Japan, and the Bering Sea, as well as waters further abroad near Mexico's Pacific coast, Argentina's Bay of La Plata, and the Arabian Sea. Japanese trawlers often displaced local fishermen, as they did Chinese yellow croaker fishers in the East China

Sea. By the 1930s, Japan was able to draw heavily from its terrestrial and pelagic empires to gear up for total war.

Commensurate with the expansion of Japan's pelagic fishing fleet was the increasing identification of Japan as an 'ocean empire'. One author explained that, 'From the Ages of the Gods, Japan has been a kingdom of fisheries.' Folklorist Yanagita Kunio (1875–1962), who sought to understand the origins of the Japanese people, argued at one point that the Japanese came from the South Pacific, birthing a wartime obsession with taking the region known as 'Nan'yô'. Many suggested that Japan's military ambitions should be extended south into Micronesia rather than the barren grassy steppes of Northeast Asia, where Japan's Kwantung Army became mired. In 1941, on the eve of Japan's naval attack on Pearl Harbor, the government proclaimed 'Marine Memorial Day' as a national holiday in order to 'give thanks for the blessings of the sea and pray for the prosperity of maritime Japan'. Within such a cultural milieu, oceans were easily integrated into Japan's wartime 'Greater East Asian Co-prosperity Sphere'. Although the war effort drafted and ultimately sacrificed Japan's impressive fishing fleet, the notion of a pelagic empire continued to be a driving force in Japanese imperial ambitions.

The legacies of Japan's pelagic empire are not insignificant in world history. The island country pioneered many of the fishing techniques and technologies that today have reduced the world's commercial fish populations to near extinction. Drift nets, or 'walls of death' as they are often called, a technology Japanese perfected in the 1970s, kill countless whales, dolphins, sea turtles, sharks, and other marine life. In 1990, scientists estimated that drift nets annually killed between 315,000 and one million dolphins alone. At their height, world drift-netters set enough nets nightly to wrap round the Earth one and a half times, with monofilament mesh to spare. Meanwhile, monofilament long-lines, dragging the carcasses of waterlogged albatrosses and leatherback turtles, not to mention both species of bluefin tuna and other commercial fish they are designed to snare, stealthily cruise the world's oceans as automated killers. Globally, Japan's long-liners set some 107 million hooks annually, killing some 44,000 albatrosses each year as 'bycatch'.

In 1971, approximately 1,200 Japanese long-liners worked the Southern Ocean around Australia, each baiting millions of hooks. Because of these efforts, bluefin catches peaked at more than 20,000 tons of fish in 1982. In 1991, however, scientists estimated that Southern Ocean bluefin numbers had decreased by 90 per cent since 1960, and overfishing threatened them with extinction. But the stakes are high in the tuna industry. In 2001, one bluefin, caught off the coast of Aomori prefecture, fetched $173,600 in a Tsukiji auction, or a staggering $391 per pound for the 444-pound giant. Today, the flesh of the bluefin tuna, prized in sushi bars around the world, represents the new precious metal in our modern oceanic bonanza. Realizing that tuna populations face impending commercial extinction under such pressure, Japanese outfits have started 'tuna ranching' around Port Lincoln, Australia, catching juvenile fish, raising them, and finally killing them for sushi markets in Japan. In this industry, 'tuna cowboys' wrestle live tuna from enclosures onto the decks of fishing boats, where they are dispatched with metal rods to the brain and back. They are then flown to Tsukiji. In Mediterranean tuna ranches, by contrast, where the fish grow much larger, the bluefin are herded to a corner of the pen and shot with rifles from boats. Most of this fish is for Japanese markets, or European sushi markets.

As of this writing, Japan's so-called 'research' vessels still pursue and kill whales in the North and South Pacific with explosive tipped harpoons in an industry fuelled less by economics, subsistence, or marine science than by invented traditions and misplaced anti-Western nationalism. Pro-whaling advocates insist that, 'we have been making food of them [whales] since more than a thousand years ago', but this claim ignores the fact that whaling was never a significant part of Japanese subsistence or economic practices. Other pro-whaling advocates conjure debates over 'food lifestyles' as the cause of the whaling controversy. 'The eating culture of Japanese, who use whale meat as a source of animal protein, must be respected', one newspaper editorial submitted. 'Europeans and Americans are pressing their own food culture and ethical views [on Japan] in saying that it is all right to eat cow meat and pig meat, but unacceptable to eat whale meat.' During one recent demonstration, a pro-whaling protester, with a classic yakuza perm and dark sunglasses, proudly held a sign aloft that said, 'Don't fuck with the Japanese!!' Most of Japan remains against whaling, and seldom if ever eats whale meat, but the industry remains adequately fuelled by many of the country's darker constituents. For the moment, their voices have proved louder than others', and Japan continues to pursue its 'scientific' whaling programme at the expense of its international reputation.

THE NEW MIDDLE CLASS

Japan's political experiences in the 1920s and 1930s are bracketed by the decay of 'Taishô democracy' and the rise of the early Shôwa 'national emergency'. Japan's economy ebbed and flowed over this time period, moreover, causing social disparities and political turmoil. During the First World War, not only did Japan's economic involvement with China increase, but its overall industrial output also increased. With the US and Europe bogged down, this was a key opportunity for the expansion of Japan's economy. Between 1914 and 1918, Japan's industrial output increased nearly sevenfold from ¥1.4 billion to ¥6.8 billion, with cotton exports alone growing by 185 per cent. With a scarcity of industrial workers, wages rose handsomely, but so did the prices of consumer goods, and crippling inflation blunted any popular benefit from the economic growth. Consequently, profound economic disparity characterized this period, with Japan's industrial nouveaux riches rising to prominence. According to one source, between 1915 and 1919 the number of 'millionaires' in Japan increased 115 per cent. In these gilded years, Japan's newly wealthy flourished, but in 1920 the country experienced a devastating banking crisis. Industries dismissed workers as they reeled through painful downturns. By the following year, the economy had started to show signs of recovery, but then the 'Great Kantô Earthquake' suddenly turned much of Tokyo, Japan's political and economic hub, into rubble and ashes. Once more, within two years, some signs of recovery were evident, but Japan experienced another banking crisis in 1927 that plunged the country headlong into the worldwide Great Depression. Major banks collapsed, including such prominent colonial institutions as the Bank of Taiwan, and Japan sank deeply into economic doldrums. The effects of these tumultuous years stretched further than mere economic concerns: they also served to undermine the legitimacy of democratic politics by associating party politicians with industrial fat cats, and increasing the military's involvement in domestic politics, principally through political assassinations and overseas adventurism.

Japan's economic successes during the 1920s did lead to the rise of widespread consumerism and the emergence of a Japanese middle class. The leisure associated with Japan's new economic prominence led to new pastimes such as 'Ginza cruising', where smartly attired dandies and their ladies perused department stores, such as Mitsukoshi, and visited coffee shops and expensive restaurants. Middle-class women thumbed through the pages of *Fujin no tomo* (Women's friend), a popular women's magazine about home-making and middle-class lifestyles that reached a circulation of three million copies in the 1920s. The magazine promoted an image of modern women as both loving mothers and devoted home-makers, individuals who nurtured their own domestic talents. In 1925, radio stations began broadcasting in Japan's large cities. The next year, the government combined three independent stations to create Japan's national broadcaster, NHK, which monopolized the airwaves for years. With just under 1.5 million radios in the country, Japanese middle-class families could huddle around their receivers to listen to Western music, comedic novels and other stories. Movies also became popular. The medium arrived in Japan at the turn of the century with importation of the Edison Vitascope and Cinématographic Lumière, but truly blossomed with the emergence of Japan's middle class. The 1924 classic *Nichiyôbi* (Sunday) poked fun at middle-class, white-collar jobs, much in the spirit that later films, such as *Shall we Dance?* (1996), a Japanese remake of the 1937 US classic, did a half-century later.

In the 1910s, moreover, 'salaryman' first appeared as a description of urban middle-class men dressed in Western clothing and toting *bentô* lunch boxes as they went to their offices. 'Salaryman' became a characterization of urban middle-class workers that persists to this day. With the expansion of the new middle class, women's roles and identities shifted dramatically. As we have seen, the Meiji state had expressed great interest in women, passing regulations and policies such as proscribed hairstyles that positioned women as repositories of Japanese tradition. But the 'modern girl' of the mid-1920s challenged those proscriptions. Some historians see the 'modern girl' as a feminist icon, others see her as a consumer waif, but either way she was a product of her times and she symbolized the manner in which Japan's new consumer culture transformed the fabric of society.

The 'modern girl' cruised the Ginza wrapped in her tight knee-length dress, glistening sheer stockings, and high-heeled shoes, which had the effect of accentuating her voluptuous buttocks. Influenced by US film stars such as Clara Bow (1905–65) and Gloria Swanson (1899–1983), she covered her short bobbed hair with a soft-brimmed hat, provocatively concealing her liberating hairstyle. The bobbed hairstyle was fashionable and politically volatile because it flew in the face of the 1872 Meiji ordinance that forbade short hair. 'Modern girl', as a descriptor, first appeared in a 1924 article, which explained that 'young men are enamoured of girls who speak their minds instead of always being humble and never voicing their opinions'. Bobbed hair pushed the boundaries of acceptable behaviour. When one woman returned from Europe and decided to cut her hair, her mother was outraged and accused her of injuring the reputation of the family. 'You must be crazy! If you go out, everyone will call you one of those new women', her mother excitedly pronounced. Conversely, poet and feminist Takamure Itsue (1895–1964) saw the 'modern girl' (and all things 'modern' for that matter) as nothing more than a product of facile US 'hedonism'. She observed, 'The birthplace of modern hedonism, or modernism, is America, where all the wealth of the world is concentrated. The concentration of wealth is the motivating force behind amusements and entertainment.' Whether an activist feminist or shallow fashion diva, the 'modern girl' remained a powerful symbol in Japan prior to the Great Depression, and it was not long before she was accompanied by the 'modern boy' while cruising the Ginza district of Tokyo.

The rise of the middle class came at the expense of others, however. The tumultuous economic and social environment provoked greater social and economic inequality in Japanese society. In the 1920s, for example, union membership grew from 103,412 to 354,312 members, with many prominent strikes threatening to slow Japan's modern industrial engine. In 1921, women workers at the Tokyo Muslin Company walked off the job demanding better pay, an eight-hour day, and better food in the corporate dormitories. That same year, 30,000 skilled industrial workers from the Kawasaki and Mitsubishi shipyards in Kobe stopped work in order to demand better wages and working conditions. In 1927, thousands of workers at the Noda Soy Sauce Company, maker of the Kikkôman brand, went on strike. The strike turned violent when the company fired the striking workers and hired scabs, who were then attacked by picketing workers. One scab even had acid thrown in his face, and police responded by beating strikers. Eventually, famed industrialist Shibusawa Eiichi (1840–1931) mediated talks between the two sides, effectively ending the strike.

As workers struggled for a greater share of the Taishô economic pie, other marginalized groups continued their quests for access. Left riddled with disease and mired in poverty after the Meiji period, many characterized the Ainu of northern Japan as a 'dying race'. To combat such perceptions, in 1930 a handful of activists created the 'Ainu Society', which still lobbies for better treatment of Ainu. In many respects, the effort represented an attempt to fully assimilate Ainu into mainstream Japanese society. Others tried to elevate the stature of Ainu culture. The young Chiri Yukie (1903–22), before she died tragically at nineteen, compiled oral tales for 'Song of the Owl God', which celebrated the disappearing oral traditions of Ainu villages. Like the Ainu, Japanese outcastes also sought equal treatment in the 1920s. Constituting about 2 per cent of the Japanese population, outcastes continued to be associated with 'pollution', and struggled to find jobs and integrate into mainstream Japanese society. In 1922, young outcaste activists formed the 'Levellers' Society', and devoted themselves to achieving 'total liberation by our own efforts'. They undertook a nationwide 'denunciation campaign' in an attempt to garner apologies from people who had discriminated against them in the past and prevent future prejudice.

IMPERIAL DEMOCRACY

Alongside the emergence of a new middle class and consumer identities Japan's new democratic politics also paralleled the country's economic rise. Prior to the promulgation of the Meiji Constitution, 'elder statesmen' had handled Japan's affairs of state. Appointed by the Meiji emperor, such men as Itô Hirobumi (1841–1909) and Kuroda Kiyotaka (1840–1900) oversaw the Meiji government. Throughout the first decades of the Meiji period, a small handful of men, largely from Chôshû and Satsuma domains, circulated between powerful cabinet positions. Japanese male voters visited the polls for the first time in July 1890 and elected 300 men for the new House of Representatives. The results excited democratic activists in Japan because such parties as Ôkuma Shigenobu's (1838–1922) Shinpotô (Progressive Party) and Itagaki Taisuke's (1837–1919) Jiyûtô (Liberal Party) won a majority of seats. At the end of the nineteenth century, it appeared that parliamentary democracy had arrived on the shores of Japan. But party politicians soon irritated the 'elder statesmen' with their incessant bickering, posturing, and debating, inviting accusations that they only served their own 'narrow, self-serving agendas'. In the later Meiji period, the fear of self-serving party politicians led to the emergence of 'transcendental cabinets', statesmen that, as Kuroda Kiyotaka trumpeted, could 'always steadfastly transcend and stand apart from the political parties, and thus follow the path of the righteous'. Fearing the international repercussions of scuttling democratization, Itô abandoned the idea of the 'transcendental cabinet' and made Itagaki his Home Minister in 1896. The appointment of other party politicians followed.

The most prominent politician of the early 1920s was Hara Kei (1856–1921, aka Hara Takashi) (Figure 20), who, with his Rikken Seiyûkai (Friends of Constitutional Government Party), consolidated the first effective party government in Japanese history. Hara was the first major politician in Japan to come from a commoner background, but this did not compromise his hunger for law and order and economic growth. In 1920, for example, Hara deployed the military to suppress a steel workers' strike and, in doing so, earned the admiration of such old military hands as

20 Portrait of Hara Takashi.

Yamagata Aritomo, who long served as elder statesman in the political establishment. Yamagata remarked, 'Hara is truly remarkable! The streetcars and steel mills have settled down. Hara's policies are remarkable.'

Hara's legacy is a mixed one: he failed to exploit his majority to push through universal suffrage legislation, much to the ire of his socialist and democratic critics. Defending his inaction, Hara argued, 'It is too soon. Abolition of property tax [voting] restrictions, with the intent to destroy class distinctions, is a dangerous idea.' In 1919, Hara did finally modify property tax voting requirements, increasing Japan's electorate from 3 million men to some 5 per cent of the population. Moreover, modifying the 1900 Meiji legislation, the government granted women limited rights to attend political meetings. Hara also made Japan a founding member of the League of Nations.

Between 1918 and 1931, Japan's party political system created a revolving door for prime ministers and their governments: eleven prime ministers formed cabinets, all from the Rikken Seiyûkai, Kenseitô (Constitutional Party), and Rikken Minseitô (Constitutional Democratic Party). Increasingly, party politics in Japan became associated with greed and corruption, angering right-wing ultranationalists and creating what one US observer described as 'government by assassination'. Illustrating the political volatility of the age, a nineteen-year-old railway switchman stabbed Hara to death in 1921. The 1920s and 1930s proved dangerous times for Japan's party politicians and industrialists. Ultranationalists condemned industrialists and their party lackeys for undermining the empire with their narrow self-interests, and took matters into their own hands. In 1930, for example, ultranationalists attacked Prime Minister Hamaguchi Osachi (1870–1931), and he died of his wounds nine months later. In 1932, some members of the ultranationalist Blood Brotherhood shot Inoue Junnosuke (1869–1932), former governor of the central Bank of Japan, and one month later, other members shot Dan Takuma (1858–1932), director-general of the Mitsui *zaibatsu*, as he left his office. The Blood Brotherhood blamed these men for Japan's economic hardships during the Great Depression. Then, naval cadets assassinated Prime Minster Inukai Tsuyoshi (1855–1932) in his residence, after the leader of Japan's civilian government had timidly challenged the Kwantung Army's continued military vigilantism in Manchuria. The cadets also tossed hand grenades into several other government and political party offices, as well as the Mitsubishi Bank headquarters in Tokyo. Judging from their targets, ultranationalists had come to view Japan's major industrialists and their party patrons as the reasons for the nation's social, economic, and foreign policy ills.

Such men as Dan Takuma, who graduated from the Massachusetts Institute of Technology, proved consistent advocates of democracy and liberal economic policies. In 1921, he had travelled with business leaders to the US and Europe and sought closer relations with the Great Powers, a choice that, in the eyes of ultranationalists, warranted his death. To such young men, he had betrayed the legacy of the Meiji Restoration, or what was often called the 'pride of Meiji'.

By the early 1930s, civilian government had become more fragile than ever and right-wing criticism more vociferous. For example, the founding document of another ultranationalist group formed in 1930, the Cherry Blossom Society, expressed these right-wing concerns concisely: 'As we observe recent social trends, top leaders engage in immoral conduct, political parties are corrupt, capitalists and aristocrats have no understanding of the masses, farming villages are devastated, unemployment and depression are serious.' In essence, under the democratic-party system, 'The positive enterprising spirit that marked the period following the Meiji Restoration has completely faded away.' The shadows of the Meiji period loomed large as the doldrums of the late 1920s and early 1930s ground slowly onward. Young officers in the military and other ultranationalists leveraged the imperial nationalism of the late Tokugawa and Meiji periods, contrasting the purity of imperial rule to the greed and self-interest of party politics. Hence, the Cherry Blossom Society could contend: 'The people are with us in craving the appearance of a vigorous and clean government that is truly based upon the masses, and is genuinely centred around the Emperor.' For this Society, founded by a lieutenant-colonel, the military under exclusive command of the emperor in accordance with the Meiji Constitution could play a decisive role in restoring a 'clean' government, where the corruption of party politics could be washed away. 'Although we, as military men, certainly should not participate directly in government', the Society continued, 'our devotion to serve the country, at times and as the occasion demands, could reveal itself and work for the correction of rulers and expansion of national power'.

Though progressive in a limited sense, Japan's party governments of the 1920s also proved capable of political violence. In

1920, Hara's suppression of a strike at Japan's largest steel mill proved brutal and decisive. Three years later, in the aftermath of the Great Kantô Earthquake, government forces tolerated and even encouraged violence against 'Bolsheviks' and 'Koreans', while the political parties turned a blind eye. Two weeks after the temblor, police murdered feminist social critic Itô Noe (1895–1923) and her lover, anarchist Ôsugi Sakae (1885–1923), along with his nephew. They also murdered a prominent union leader. In 1925, under the Kenseitô, the government passed the Orwellian 'Public Security Preservation Law', which made critiques of the emperor and the system of private-property ownership punishable by death. It was under the Public Security Preservation Law that in 1928 police rounded up thousands of Communist Party members. The government also strengthened the activities of the secret thought police who weeded out political dissent, principally from communists. It is estimated that between 1925 and 1945 government police arrested some 70,000 people under the law. It proved a notorious symbol of Japan's 'dark valley' during the 1920s and 1930s.

From this unstable political environment new voices began to emerge, ones that fail to fit squarely within either left- or right-wing categories. Kita Ikki (1883–1937) was one such voice. He became interested in socialism at the age of fourteen, and at seventeen published articles in a local newspaper criticizing Meiji political theories regarding Japan's 'national essence'. The articles earned him a police investigation, but nothing further came of the matter. In 1904, Kita moved to Tokyo where he entered into socialist circles, only to become disillusioned with these shallow 'opportunists'. In fact, Kita's socialist political theories possessed few Marxist traces, more resembling the National Socialism of Germany, minus the anti-Semitism. Kita spent several years in China involved with the overthrow of the Qing dynasty, and then returned to Japan in 1919 where he became involved with radical ultranationalist politics. He first published his *Nihon kaizô hôan taikô* (Plan for the reorganization of Japan) that year, which outlined the need for an Asia liberated from the shackles of Western imperialism. A reinvigorated Japan promised to lead Asia out from the darkness of Western oppression. 'Truly, our seven hundred million brothers in China and India have no path to independence other than that offered by our guidance and protection', he wrote. Japan needed to become a charismatic authoritarian state led by the emperor, fulfilling what Kita called the 'Shôwa restoration'. By suspending the Meiji Constitution, Japan could avoid the 'malign influence' of the Diet and self-interested political parties. Kita's ultranationalist, anti-democratic, anti-party voice became increasingly influential as Japan entered the 1930s. Most importantly, it gained traction with a large number of young officers in the military, who increasingly believed they needed to take matters into their own hands.

An obscure event illustrates the minefield of navigating imperial Japanese politics at this juncture. In 1936, a handful of Okinawan martial arts masters gathered in Naha, Okinawa, to discuss how to better integrate the Okinawan fighting styles into the martial arts and athletic clubs of imperial Japan. Traditionally, Okinawans knew their martial art form as *tôdi*, which can alternatively be read as *karate*. The *kanji* meant 'Chinese hands', and the word made sense because the fighting techniques had originally been imported through China, where practitioners knew them as *quanfa*. The Ryukyu Islands, before becoming Okinawa prefecture in 1879, had served as a major conduit for goods, medicines, and ideas coming from China. But the political climate in 1936 meant that the Okinawan masters changed the *kanji* of their traditional martial arts in order for it to be included alongside activities such as judo and kendo. Eventually, they changed the *kanji* for karate from 'Chinese hands' to 'empty hands', denoting the weaponless fighting style. The important point is that this quintessentially Japanese martial art actually came from China through Okinawa where masters, in order to preserve their cultural heritage, had to carefully negotiate the imperial politics of the 1930s, where China's stock had fallen considerably in the Japanese imagination. Once the birthplace of Confucianism and 'exalted goods', China was now being erased, literally, from Okinawan traditions as it was assimilated into the Japanese empire.

CONCLUSION

In October 1929, the New York Stock Exchange crashed. As with many nations, the Great Depression hit Japan hard, although it was statistically less damaging than the financial meltdown in the US. The Great Depression hit Japanese tenant farmers and city shop-keepers hard, but unemployment statistics never equalled those of the US or parts of Europe. But the Great Depression undermined what little support party politics still possessed in Japan. The dry kindling of Japan's domestic environment was easily ignited by international events, particularly those in north China and Manchuria. In the midst of the economic crisis, Manchuria seemed to hold great promise for helping Japan rescue itself from the economic doldrums. Young officers, brimming over with the ideals of Kita Ikki and weary of self-interested party politics, began taking matters into their own hands. Strategic assassinations proved one ingredient to the emergence of ultranationalism and fascism in Japan, but so did vigilante military actions in Manchuria. In 1931, young officers in the Kwantung Army manufactured the events that precipitated the Pacific War. In their minds, igniting a 'final war' with the US would purge self-interested liberal economics from Japan with ascendant imperial fascism. The fate of the world, many believed, swayed in the balance.

13

The Pacific War, 1931–1945

In the 1930s, Japan's culture of fascism shaped its politics, culture, and foreign affairs. Military adventurism in Manchuria and political assassinations at home led to the fall of party politics and the rise of military governance, wherein generals, admirals, and their lieutenants occupied top cabinet posts. After 1931, the Kwantung Army conquered much of Manchuria and Tokyo eventually accepted these territorial gains as *fait accompli*. The birth of Japan's autarkic empire (Map 3) paralleled these military victories; incensed with irksome diplomacy, Japan withdrew from the League of Nations and most of its international agreements. With a full-fledged invasion of China after 1937, Japan waged the so-called 'Greater East Asian War', eventually attacking Pearl Harbor (1941) and drawing the US into the conflict. For both sides, racism, cultural misunderstanding, and sheer mercilessness characterized the fighting. The historical currents that led to the dramatic collapse of party politics and the rise of militarism had their roots in imperial nationalism and the Meiji Constitution, which had isolated the military from the turgid malaise of parliamentary politics. Japan's military always stood beyond the political fray and in the popular imagination easily transcended the corruption of liberal economics and politics, which became strongly associated with the excesses of US individualism and greed.

The Pacific War exacted a heavy toll on all involved. Millions died in the Pacific theatre as a result of Japanese expansionism;

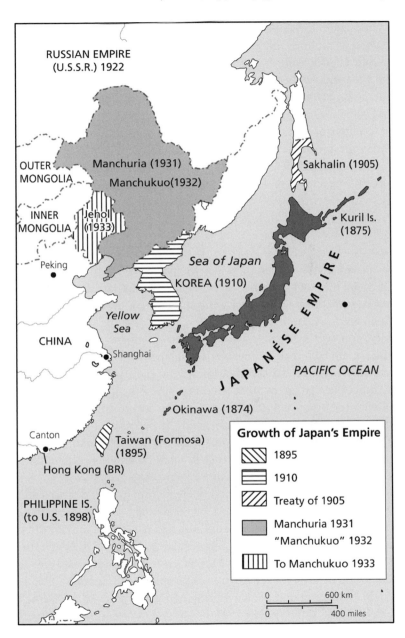

RUSSIAN EMPIRE
(U.S.S.R.) 1922

OUTER
MONGOLIA

Manchuria (1931)
Manchukuo(1932)

Sakhalin (1905)

INNER
MONGOLIA

Jehol
(1933)

Kuril Is.
(1875)

Peking

Sea of Japan

KOREA (1910)

JAPANESE EMPIRE

*Yellow
Sea*

CHINA

Shanghai

PACIFIC OCEAN

Okinawa (1874)

Canton

Taiwan (Formosa)
(1895)

Hong Kong (BR)

PHILIPPINE IS.
(to U.S. 1898)

Growth of Japan's Empire

1895

1910

Treaty of 1905

Manchuria 1931
"Manchukuo" 1932

To Manchukuo 1933

0   600 km
0   400 miles

3 Japan's empire, 1874–1945

domestically the Japanese, though initially enthralled with the exuberant culture of total war, began suffering through the so-called 'dark valley' as defeat loomed on the horizon. By 1945, the US and its Allies had crippled Japan's domestic industrial and military machinery, and with the atomic bombing of Hiroshima and Nagasaki, Japan 'unconditionally surrendered'. The seven-year US occupation of Japan that followed the war witnessed profound and widespread changes in Japanese political institutions, law enforcement and defence, education, economics and popular culture, the legacies of which have shaped Japanese society throughout the post-war years.

MANCHURIAN INCIDENT

Kwantung Army officer Ishiwara Kanji (1889–1949), architect of the Manchurian Incident (1931), believed that Japan and the US were destined for a massive Pacific showdown, or what he called a 'final war'. At stake, he submitted, was nothing less than the 'salvation of the world'. Like so many idealistic young military officers, he champed at the bit for an incident that would spark war in Manchuria. 'When the military preparations are completed we do not need to go to great lengths to find the motive or occasion; all we need to do is pick the time and proclaim to the world our absorption of Manchuria', he argued. 'If necessary the Kwantung Army could create the occasion for this with a plot and force the nation to go along.' This is precisely what he and his collaborator, Itagaki Seishirô (1885–1948), did in September 1931.

The Kwantung Army had tried to create and exploit disturbances in Manchuria before. In 1928, for example, its forces blew up Manchurian warlord Zhang Zoulin's (1875–1928) train car. On a return trip from Beijing, Zhang's train had passed through the Japanese-controlled South Manchurian Railroad, where a Kwantung Army officer had planted explosives. Japanese officers would later claim that the Kwantung Army was angered by Zhang's inability to slow Chiang Kai-shek's (1887–1975) Northern Expedition (1926–8), the Guomindang's (Nationalist Party) attempt to unify China under a single national authority. The Japanese had thrived in China's vulnerable and decentralized political environment, and the Guomindang's attempts to unify the country threatened their colonial enterprise. But it is also true that the Kwantung Army, by killing Zhang, had sought to spark a broader Manchurian conflict that could create the *raison d'être* for widening the north China war and outflanking the bumbling party politicians in Tokyo.

The 1928 killing of Zhang had failed to broaden the conflict, but the 18 September 1931 Manchurian Incident had the desired effect. Under cover of darkness, members of the Kwantung Army tried to blow up a section of the South Manchurian Railroad. The Kwantung Army immediately blamed the blast on Chinese bandits and, within days, occupied Mukden and Changchun. With lightning speed, the Kwantung Army entered Jilin (22–23 September), Qiqihar (20 November), southwestern Manchuria (31 December), and Harbin (5 February). Fed up with Tokyo's foot-dragging, Kwantung Army officers forced Tokyo's civilian government to accept the *fait accompli*, with the cabinet of Prime Minister Wakatsuki Reijirô (1866–1949) reluctantly approving the conquest of Jilin. Prime Minister Wakatsuki later resigned after the taking of Qiqihar, and Inukai Tsuyoshi (1855–1932), Japan's last civilian prime minister until the post-war period, took the reins until his assassination in 1932 by ultranationalists. In 1932, under Inukai, Japan established Manchukuo, which became the empire's protectorate.

In December 1931, the League of Nations commissioned the 'Lytton Report' to determine what had actually happened in Manchuria. When the report was finally published in October 1932, the matter of who precipitated the incident was left largely unexamined. But the report was critical of the Kwantung Army's supposedly 'self-defence' driven actions following the incident, in particular the invasions of major Manchurian cities. When the League of Nations raised a motion to condemn Japan as an 'aggressor' in Manchuria, Japan's flamboyant Ambassador Matsuoka Yôsuke (1880–1946) walked out. Japan formally withdrew from the League of Nations the following month. After this withdrawal, Japan began withdrawing from other international agreements, such as the 1911 Fur Seal Convention, thereby creating an autarkic empire largely divorced from international law.

Japan's military actions in Manchuria continued to transform politics and culture at home, leading to the rise of a fascist state. Reports from Manchuria flooded Japan's news media, with newspapers and radios bringing Manchuria into household living rooms. More households than ever listened to war reports, including live coverage from the front. In 1932, the most popular books in Tokyo included *Understanding New Weapons* and *The Army Reader*, testimony to the militarized culture that consumed mainstream Japan. Magazines focused attention on the 'Manchurian problem', with special editions flying off newsstand shelves. Patriotic war songs began replacing the freewheeling jazz of a decade earlier, with 'Ah, Our Manchuria!' among the public's favourites; stage productions, such as *The First Steps into Fengtian – South Manchuria Glitters Under the Rising Sun*, topped Tokyo's billings. Many stage productions promoted a mythos of sacrifice, with the 'three human bullets' topping the list. In the mid-1930s, most Japanese found the prospect of total war in Manchuria exhilarating, and Manchuria became the dominant concern of news and entertainment.

Not all Japanese bought into the exhilarating culture of war, however. The same year as the Manchurian Incident, Japanese secret police arrested some 10,422 leftists, with 13,938 and 14,622 leftists finding their way behind bars in the following two years, respectively. The government viewed the left as dangerously subversive to Japan's *kokutai*, or 'national essence'. The government also took aim at scholars, including constitutional expert Minobe Tatsukichi (1873–1948). Minobe had submitted in his 'emperor-organ theory' of government that the imperial institution was just one of a handful of governing 'organs', the Diet and bureaucracy being two others. His theories implicitly limited the centrality of the emperor in Taishô and Shôwa politics, arousing the ire of ultranationalists. As one patriotic organization complained, 'emperor-organ theory is contrary to the essence of our unparalleled national polity and blasphemes the sacredness of the throne'. In 1937, the Education Ministry articulated the idea of Japan's 'unparalleled national polity' in the *Kokutai no hongi* (Cardinal principles of the national polity), mentioned briefly in Chapter 2, which linked Japan's 'beautiful nature not seen in other countries' to its unique 'national essence'. Offering comparative examples, the *Kokutai no hongi* explained: 'Natural features overpower India, and in the West one senses that man subjugates nature, and no deep harmony is found between man and nature as in our country. On the contrary, our people are in constant harmony with nature.' The natural environment became tied to its 'unparalleled national' character. In this context it is unsurprising that, in the 1930s, Japan established its first national parks as an attempt to preserve elements of this awe-inspiring natural environment.

During the dramatic 'Two Twenty-Six Incident', the patriotic thinking regarding Japan's 'unparalleled' national polity, emperor, and military found frightening expression in the streets of downtown Tokyo. On 26 February 1936, twenty-one young officers from the accomplished First Division roused some 1,400 troops out of their Tokyo barracks in an attempt to overthrow the government. On that snowy February morning, the capital rang out with gunshots signalling another round of political assassinations. Military zealots killed Finance Minister Takahashi Korekiyo (1854–1936), former Prime Minister Saitô Makoto (1858–1936), and others. Prime Minister Okada Keisuke (1868–1952) escaped assassination only after his wife smuggled him from their home dressed as a woman. By noon the coup leaders were largely in control, with the Diet and military headquarters surrounded. Kita Ikki's right-wing political philosophy had inspired the perpetrators, who sought to 'awaken the people and bring about a Shôwa Restoration'. Basically, the coup leaders sought to 'remove the barriers which have separated the people from the emperor' by nationalizing major industries, helping tenant farmers, and removing corrupt political parties from power. Eventually, however, the takeover crumbled when Emperor Hirohito (1901–89) turned against the perpetrators, and ten battalions moved into Tokyo and surrounded rebel positions. By 29 February, the episode had ended; the military pardoned most of the non-commissioned officers and soldiers, but executed by public firing squad thirteen junior officers, as well as the intellectual figurehead of the coup, Kita Ikki. The 'Two Twenty-Six Incident' proved the last serious challenge to the government's authority during these stormy years, in large part because the country was faced with the daunting prospect of total war in China.

GREATER EAST ASIAN WAR

In July 1937, Japan and China plunged into total war after the seemingly trivial 'Marco Polo Bridge Incident'. Under the Boxer Protocol (1901), Japan had stationed troops near Beijing. While conducting night exercises near the ornate Marco Polo Bridge, Chinese soldiers apparently responded to Japanese blank cartridges with live rounds, and a Japanese soldier went temporarily missing. Military officials in Tokyo and on the scene in China immediately sought to de-escalate the situation. Even the architect of the Manchurian Incident, Ishiwara Kanji, whom officials had transferred to headquarters in Tokyo, sought to defuse the incident. Ishiwara, like many of his colleagues, had by this time come to believe that the Soviet Union, not China, was Japan's most immediate strategic threat in the region. With a keen knowledge of military history, Ishiwara likened Japan's potential involvement in mainland China to Napoleon's involvement in Spain, seeing it as a 'slow sinking into the deepest sort of bog'. Following the military's lead, Prime Minister Konoe Fumimaro (1891–1945) reiterated Tokyo's commitment to 'non-expansion' and 'local settlement' of what increasingly came to be known as the 'China problem'. Although Chinese and Japanese military commanders successfully hammered out a local settlement, Chiang Kai-shek refused to accept it. The Guomindang had become increasingly powerful in northern China after the 1928 establishment of the Nationalist regime in Nanjing, and Chiang began channelling the sentiments of nationalists who harboured an intense antipathy towards Japan. Carefully navigating the political landscape, Chiang instructed local Chinese military commanders to reject the settlement. He then relocated his four best divisions to Hebe province in violation of earlier Sino-Japanese agreements.

Ten days after the Marco Polo Bridge exchange, Chiang pronounced, 'If we allow one more inch of our territory to be lost, we shall be guilty of an unpardonable crime against our race.' Chiang successfully elevated the Marco Polo Bridge Incident out of the hands of local commanders and into the arena of geopolitical manoeuvrings. Japan answered Chiang's rhetoric with sabre rattling of its own, and dispatched three divisions to China, under the advice of General Tôjô Hideki (1884–1948). Some twenty days after the original exchange at Marco Polo Bridge, Japan's China Garrison Army successfully occupied Beijing: the 'China problem' had thus become the China war. Violence soon erupted in Shanghai, which had witnessed cruel struggles between Chinese nationalists and communists in April 1927, and where Japanese forces were thin compared to the roughly 100,000 Guomindang soldiers. Once again, Prime Minister Konoe let rhetorical bombs fly when he stated that China had assumed an 'arrogant and insulting' attitude towards Japan, one that required 'resolute action'. Then, Chinese bombers struck Japanese naval installations in Shanghai, and Chiang ordered China's complete mobilization for war. He explained, 'China is duty bound to defend herself and her national existence.' The fighting in Shanghai proved savage, with troops engaged in hand-to-hand combat in the streets for months. Though Japanese troops ultimately took Chiang's capital of Nanjing and Canton, by 1938 the war had bogged down into a stalemate, much as Ishiwara had earlier prophesied it would.

Japan's rhetoric remained lofty and resolute as it enumerated its geopolitical goals in East Asia. After the fall of Canton, Prime Minister Konoe explained, 'What Japan seeks is the establishment of a new order that will insure the permanent stability of East Asia. In this lies the ultimate purpose of our present military campaign.' Towards those ends, in August 1940, Foreign Minister Matsuoka announced the formation of the 'Greater East Asian Co-prosperity Sphere', a cooperative area encompassing the puppet state of Manchukuo and China, as well as French Indochina and the Dutch East Indies. Prime Minister Konoe proclaimed that the nations of the 'Great East Asian Co-Prosperity Sphere' would be united as 'eight crown cords, one roof', a reference from the eighth-century *Nihon shoki* (Chronicles of Japan, 720) describing the extension of Emperor Jinmu's dominion over the ancient realm. In its twentieth-century incarnation, 'eight crown cords, one roof' suggested a family of nations led by Japan's imperial benevolence. It served as the ultimate culmination of pan-Asianism, where every nation could find 'its proper place in the world' under Japanese paternalism. In order to deflect a US response to the move into Southeast Asia, Foreign Minister Matsuoka signed the 'Tripartite

Pact' with Nazi Germany and fascist Italy the next month, cementing Japan into a security alliance with the European belligerents. In December 1941, he concluded the 'Thai–Japan Alliance', in which the two countries promised 'close and inseparable relations', including in the event of an attack. In April 1941, Matsuoka travelled to Moscow where he concluded the 'Soviet–Japan Neutrality Pact', securing Japan's northern borders in Manchukuo. In July, after Matsuoka's whirlwind diplomacy, Japanese troops moved into French Indochina.

The US responded to Japanese belligerence in East and Southeast Asia with sanctions, limiting Japan's ability to acquire resources badly needed for its war effort. The sanctions began in October 1937, when President Franklin Roosevelt (1882–1945) delivered a thundering speech condemning a global 'epidemic' of 'terror and international lawlessness', in a not so subtle reference to Japan and Nazi Germany. As Japan acquired more territory, the US broadened the extent of its sanctions. In 1939, Roosevelt extended the sanctions to include aluminium, molybdenum, nickel, and tungsten. The next year, sanctions encompassed aviation fuel, lubricating oil, and other necessities of Japan's war machine. In 1941, after the Japanese entered French Indochina, Roosevelt froze Japanese assets in the US and imposed a complete oil embargo. In 1941, Roosevelt named General Douglas MacArthur (1880–1964) commander of the Far East, strengthening the US military posture in Asia. Finally, that same year, Winston Churchill (1874–1965) and Roosevelt signed the 'Atlantic Charter', calling for internationalism and the disarmament of nations that demonstrate 'aggression outside their frontiers'. These moves failed to deter Japan. With war with the US looming on the horizon, Japan began planning for invasions of the Philippines, Malaya, Burma, and, under the auspices of Admiral Yamamoto Isoroku (1884–1943), the US naval base at Pearl Harbor. With the latter, Yamamoto sought to achieve for Japan a rapid, decisive strike against the US Pacific Fleet and establish dominance in the Pacific theatre.

In October 1941, as the US and Japan careened headlong towards war, Emperor Hirohito named General Tôjô the new prime minister in order to diplomatically 'wipe the slate clean'. Japan's navy was burning '400 tons of oil an hour', the Navy Chief of Staff cautioned, and Japan needed to end the diplomatic stalemate with the US. Working closely with military advisers, Prime Minister Tôjô formulated two proposals, both of which ultimately proved unacceptable to US Secretary of State Cordell Hull (1871–1955). Essentially, the US refused to recognize Japan's 'Greater East Asian Co-prosperity Sphere', while Japan rejected a US presence in Asia it found dangerous to its economic and security interests. At the beginning of December 1941, Tôjô told confidants that he had 'exhausted every means at his disposal', and that the US refused to budge. Japan's President of the Privy Council summarized Japanese anxieties at this juncture when he intimated that the US sought to destroy Japan's modern accomplishments and undermine the legacies of the Meiji period. 'But it is clear that the existence of our country is being threatened', he announced, 'that the great achievements of the Emperor Meiji would all come to naught, and that there is nothing else we can do. Therefore, I believe that if negotiations with the United States are hopeless, then the commencement of war is inevitable.' At the very moment these thoughts were being aired, Yamamoto's fleet steamed headlong towards Pearl Harbor and war between the two Pacific adversaries.

On 7 December 1941, when crack Japanese pilots dropped the final bombs on Pearl Harbor, eight US battleships and 200 planes had been damaged or destroyed, and nearly 4,000 US servicemen killed. A scribe on Admiral Yamamoto's flagship remembered that, after the attack, 'Telegrams of celebration and congratulations poured in from the entire nation addressed to Admiral Yamamoto Isoroku personally ... I took care of them, opening every letter and handing them over to the Admiral personally.' The Admiral responded with humility and knowledge that the war would be a long one. 'I swear I shall conduct further strenuous efforts and shall not rest on this small success in beginning the war.' Five days later, the Japanese government proclaimed the beginning of the 'Greater East Asia War', which now included the US and the other ABCD Powers (a reference to America, Britain, China, and the Dutch).

With blistering speed, Japanese troops entered Hong Kong (25 December), Manila (2 January 1942), Singapore (15 February), Jakarta (5 March), and Rangoon (8 March). However, by the summer of 1942, the seemingly invincible Japanese war machine found itself on the defensive. In the Battle of Midway, the US navy sent four of the six Japanese carriers involved in Pearl Harbor to the bottom of the Pacific Ocean. Moreover, the landing of US marines at Guadalcanal forced an eventual Japanese evacuation after ferocious jungle fighting. The Battle of Midway was not the first major engagement between the US and Japanese navies, but it proved the most decisive. In May 1942, at the Battle of the Coral Sea, US and Japanese carriers had squared off in the first such maritime exchange; both limped away severely wounded, though the Japanese had destroyed more US vessels. By 1943, the US and its Allies had handed the Japanese military several major defeats, including downing Admiral Yamamoto's transport plane and killing him. After a series of stinging defeats, Tôjô cryptically informed the Diet that, 'The real war starts now'. In October 1944, Fleet Admiral Chester Nimitz (1885–1966) and MacArthur converged at Leyte Gulf, in the Philippines, sinking six Japanese carriers, irreversibly crushing the once-proud Japanese navy. With the loss of the Philippines, Japan's war effort became more desperate, with *kamikaze*, or 'divine wind', pilots hurling themselves at the approaching US navy throughout early 1945. Despite such suicidal tactics, the US occupied Iwo Jima (March 1945) and then Okinawa (April 1945) on their approach towards the Japanese homeland.

Nearing Okinawa, US forces first landed on the smaller island of Tokashiki, about twenty miles west from the main island of Okinawa. When US forces landed there in late March 1945, under military orders euphemistically called 'crushing of jewels', Japanese on Tokashiki began committing mass suicide, often killing family members with their own hands: rumours had spread that US forces mutilated the bodies of captured Japanese. Huddled in a cave on Tokashiki, one man remembered, 'We knew that if we were captured we'd be chopped to pieces. They'd cut off our noses, our ears, chop off our fingers, and then run over our bodies with their tanks.' Frightened and desperate, he and his brother dutifully killed their mother by bludgeoning the poor woman's head with stones. They also killed their younger brother and sister. Once the battle reached Okinawa, the fighting proved ferocious (Figure 21). A Japanese garrison of 110,000 men died defending the island; some 50,000 US servicemen died taking it. With racist propaganda saturating

21 The *Yamato*, pride of the Japanese navy. The heaviest battleship of her day, she was commissioned in December 1941 and sunk near Okinawa in April 1945.

both sides of the Pacific, Japanese and US servicemen waged a savage and merciless war. As US reporter Ernie Pyle (1900–45) observed, 'In Europe we felt that our enemies, horrible and deadly as they were, were still people ... [But in the Pacific] I soon gathered that Japanese were looked upon as something subhuman and repulsive; the way some people feel about mice and cockroaches.' It was not by chance that US servicemen viewed Japanese as 'subhuman'; years of government propaganda, often portraying Japanese as monkeys or lice, deeply embedded itself in the mindset of US soldiers, turning farm boys into battlefield killers.

In contrast, rather than dehumanizing US servicemen, Japanese propaganda elevated the racial purity of the Japanese, turning the 'Greater East Asia War' into a moral struggle against ABCD imperialism. Indeed, as the Japanese government trumpeted during the conflict:

> We, the Yamato race, are presently spilling our blood to realize our mission in world history of establishing a Greater East Asian Co-prosperity Sphere. In order to liberate the billion people of Asia and also to maintain our position of leadership over the Greater East Asian Co-prosperity Sphere forever, we must plant the blood of the Yamato race in its soil.

Despite the lofty rhetoric, Japanese had waged a merciless war of their own, symbolized by the 'Nanjing Massacre' (December 1937) and other well-documented atrocities, such as the biological warfare and cruel human experimentation conducted by Unit 731. Sadly, the observations of Lewis Smythe (b. 1901), a Christian missionary, became commonplace in Nanjing as Japanese commanders lost control of their soldiers. 'Last night, on December 15, Japanese soldiers entered a Chinese house . . . and raped a young wife and took away three women. When two husbands ran, the soldiers shot both of them.' Later, in 1946, the District Court of Nanjing estimated that Japanese forces had killed nearly 300,000 men, women, and children in the massacre.

ENVIRONMENTAL FOOTPRINTS OF WAR

It is well known that total war exacted a horrific toll from the human population of the Japanese islands and the Pacific theatre. After the war, Japan was left in ruins. Tokyo lost about 50 per cent of its houses to fire bombings; nationally, the war left some 8 million people without homes. Over 80 per cent of Japan's shipping was destroyed and over 30 per cent of its industrial capacity. Some 2.1 million Japanese perished in the conflict. More broadly, the United Nations estimated that 18 or 19 million people died in the sphere of Japanese military activities. The Pacific War had been nothing less than catastrophic for the Asia-Pacific region.

Less well known, however, is the cost the war extracted from Japan's natural environment. Environmental damage and human casualties were often intertwined. In March 1945, the 'great Tokyo air raid' burned nearly 44 square kilometres (17 square miles) of the nation's capital and killed 80,000 people. During the bombing raids of 1944 and 1945, nearly one quarter of Japan's total housing was destroyed, burned, or demolished, leaving some 30 per cent of the Japan's population homeless. In total, US bombing killed hundreds of thousands of Japanese. In many ways, even though Tokyo had been largely rebuilt in 1923 after the Great Kantô Earthquake, the city was a tinderbox. Largely constructed of wood, many Japanese cities proved easy targets for incendiary bombs. As one French journalist prophetically observed of Tokyo just prior to the fire bombings:

The capital stirred in its filth. A Japanese house rots in twenty years. So does a city. Tokyo, rebuilt in 1923 after the big earthquake, was rotten ... You could imagine no way to save this capital from crumbling in rot and ruin except some catastrophe that would again compel rebuilding – a purifying fire, for example, that would destroy it all.

In March 1945, during 'Operation Meetinghouse', US B-29 'Super-fortress' high-altitude bombers dropped thousands of incendiary bombs on the city.

The natural world proved surprisingly resilient in the aftermath of bombing raids, however, even after the US dropped atomic bombs on Hiroshima and Nagasaki. After the twin atomic bomb-ings of August 1945, residual radiation at the hypocentres dissi-pated quickly, and plant and animal life returned to the burned-out cities. The rats and insects of Hiroshima, for example, emerged relatively unscathed from the bombings, as did much of the plant life. When Japanese scientists collected insects from around the hypocentre of the Hiroshima blast, they detected no genetic abnor-malities. Within the ruined cities, plants began to colonize once inhabited spaces, with most floral malformations disappearing within two or three years. One year after the blast, over twenty-five types of weeds had colonized Hiroshima's hypocentre, many of them formerly rare plants. Plants grew in such abundance that one Western observer wrote, 'It actually seemed as if a load of sickle senna seed had been dropped along with the bombs.' In other words, the burning of major Japanese cities, whether from incendi-ary or atomic bombs, cleared space for colonizing plants and animals, even though human inhabitants, once the war ended, quickly recolonized their built environments.

Prior to and during the war, Japanese economic activity trans-formed the natural environment. As mentioned, the Japanese gov-ernment sought to build up foreign currency reserves prior to the outbreak of total war, and expanding the available fisheries pro-vided one way to accomplish this fiscal goal. In the 1930s, when Japanese fishermen began exploring beyond Japan's coasts, they did so to provide canned fish for US markets. Japan also ramped up its pelagic whaling, becoming the globe's third largest whaling nation by 1938. By the 1930s, Japan had leveraged the environ-ments of its empire in order to fuel its war effort. Korea began raising rice for Japanese consumers, while in Manchuria soybeans became the crop of choice. Meanwhile, Japanese farmers raised more wheat to export to Manchuria in exchange for the soybeans. When crop failures occurred in Korea, which was badly suited for rice monoculture, food shortages hit Japan, hindering self-sufficiency during the war years and undermining the autarkic imperial philosophy.

In general, Japanese agriculture underwent massive convulsions during the war years. Before the war, Japan was noted for its intensive use of chemical fertilizers, but when company officials diverted production at nitrogen fixation facilities, such as the Chisso plant at Minamata, to generate chemicals for the war effort, fertilizer production tapered off. Moreover, the government had suspended all imports of phosphate and potash, which farmers had historically used for fertilizer. As a substitute, farmers started scouring the forest for mulch and other organic debris that could be used instead. Consequently, forests were injured and tree growth was stunted; erosion intensified and sedimentation of waterways occurred at an alarming pace. Many farmers returned to the earlier practice of using night soil, but often in the form of untreated and un-composted raw sewage. As a result, raw sewage often tainted water supplies, and parasites and bacteriological infections flourished during the war years. Farm animals virtually vanished from Japanese farms because the military drafted most horses for duty in Manchuria and elsewhere. Most large pets, such as dogs, had long since been sacrificed to feed Japan's increasing number of hungry human mouths. Songbirds became scarce as hunting them became a 'patriotic duty' in order to supply food. Hunters killed some 7.5 million thrushes, grosbeaks, finches, siskins, and buntings each year for human consumption.

The killing of the large animals at the Tokyo Imperial Zoo proved by far the most dramatic example of animal slaughters during the war. In the late nineteenth and early twentieth centuries, the zoo had become a popular Tokyo stage for exhibiting empire, part of the wartime euphoria described earlier. In 1897, the Imperial Household Ministry approved an exhibition of 'animal war trophies', and the zoo became a centre of imperial culture. A wild boar that had been trapped in Korea while Japanese troops were on 'safari' was enclosed next to continental deer; three Bactrian camels captured from Chinese troops at Port Arthur in 1894 also became 'new guests' at the zoo, as did a spotted leopard that a Manchurian unit had kept as a mascot. Children could feed warhorses or draft animals that had served on the front. The Meiji emperor paid for the imperial exhibition out of his own imperial coffers. Once the 'Greater East Asian War' was under way, officials mobilized the zoo to fuel the cultural requirements of total war. 'Military animal' exhibits became commonplace, featuring elephants, camels, yaks, mules, donkeys, pigeons, dogs, and horses deployed in the campaign. Because of the zoo's wild popularity among Japanese, and its use as imperial and wartime propaganda, the decision to kill the zoo animals in the summer of 1943 was all the more dramatic. The slaughter, nominally to conserve scarce food, happened under the cover of darkness; carcasses of the zoo's most celebrated inhabitants were hauled out the service entrance in covered wheelbarrows. Zoo trainers and officials killed some twenty-seven animals by starvation, poison, hammer blows, and sharpened bamboo spears. Shooting them would have attracted too much attention. Two Abyssinian lions received as a gift by Emperor Hirohito from the emperor of Ethiopia were among the victims, as were three performing elephants and the Manchurian spotted leopard. In many ways, the killing of the zoo animals paralleled other dramatic actions taking place within Japan, as the country entered a 'critical phase' in the war effort. Zoos in London and Berlin had killed animals as well, but the Buddhist ceremony surrounding the killings, the 'Memorial Service for Animal Martyrs' held in early September, betrayed that even in death the zoo's animals served as valuable propaganda for Japan's war effort.

Japan not only lost many of its animals, but also many of its trees. Increasingly, Japan felled its forests in order to cut timber imports; by the late 1930s, it even sold its timber on international markets to build foreign currency reserves. During the war, loggers felled many of Japan's most stately timber stands. The numbers are staggering: between 1941 and 1945, loggers cut some 15 per cent of Japan's forests for the war effort, and the vast majority of that was clear cut. In 1951, one US forester in Japan observed that, 'The accessible forests have been reduced to a depleted condition from poor forest management, prolonged over-utilization, insufficient reforestation, soil erosion and depredation by insects.'

Japan's 'pine oil project' also contributed to this rampant deforestation. After the US oil embargo, petroleum reserves dried up and by 1944 Japanese researchers sought alternative sources of energy to fuel Japan's war machine. For many, pine oil became the answer to Japan's fuel shortages, but extracting the new motor fuel proved laborious and highly destructive to the natural environment. Despite the daunting human energetic and environmental sacrifices required to make the fuel, Japanese subjects, reeling from years of total war, built 34,000 stills in order to extract 70,000 barrels of pine oil crude from the remaining forests. As one observer wrote, 'Monumental piles of roots and stumps lined many of the roadways. Mountainsides were stripped bare of every tree and sapling.' Ironically, precious little of the pine oil ever burned in the engines of Japan's fighter planes or warships because scientists never perfected the refining methods. The final nail in the coffin of Japan's forests was a pine bark beetle infestation caused by rapacious wartime forestry practices. Foresters estimated that by 1946 some 600,000 hectares (1.5 million acres) of coniferous forest was infested by the hungry chafers.

In the industrial realm as well, preparations for war led to environmental problems. At the turn of the century, Mitsui's Kamioka mine in Toyama prefecture had transitioned from silver and copper mining to lead and zinc extraction, critical metals in war making. In doing so, the mine released hundreds of metric tons of highly pulverized cadmium into the Jinzû River drainage. The cadmium poisoned thousands of farmers, predominantly women, with 'it hurts, it hurts disease'. Japan needed lead for batteries and bullets; munitions plants used zinc in brass shell casings and shipyards used it in galvanizing naval warships. An intricate web of historical circumstances had led to the emergence of cadmium poisoning in the 1950s, but use of the Potter pulverization method, a mining separation technology, contributed to making cadmium waste highly bioavailable in nearby rice plants. Kamioka's pulverized ore, which by the 1920s could be reduced to 0.18 mm particles in order to be floated in separation vats, oxidized and ionized as it washed down streams and rivers, easily making its way up the stalks of rice plants in low-lying paddies. Imperial labour practices also contributed to pollution and diseased bodies. In 1941, before significant numbers of Korean prisoners and downed US pilots worked at Kamioka, zinc recovery percentages stood at near 90 per cent, and workers released some twenty tons of cadmium into the environment. After 1943, when untrained Koreans, brought basically as slaves, constituted nearly 50 per cent of the miners, they extracted less zinc and the amount of cadmium discarded tripled. The enduring footprint of the Pacific War in Toyama was cadmium pollution and poisoning, where, well after the war's conclusion, women continued to suffer from the debilitating environmental contamination caused by Japan's war effort. The bodies of these women are not enshrined at Yasukuni as martyrs; but they, too, need to be included as victims of the 'Greater East Asian War'.

HIROSHIMA AND NAGASAKI

By 1945, the grinding hum of B-29s had come to terrorize Japanese civilians and soldiers alike. The Boeing-made 'Superfortresses' brought havoc and wanton destruction wherever they targeted. Virtually nothing remained of the city of Toyama; much of Tokyo, as mentioned, had been reduced to ashes. On 6 August 1945, the B-29 *Enola Gay* dropped its atomic payload 'Little Boy' over Hiroshima, which detonated just under 2,000 feet over the city. The bombing of Nagasaki followed three days later. At Hiroshima, the X-ray-heated air that exploded from the hypocentre moved concentrically outward at the speed of sound, reducing to ashes most everything flammable in its path. The fireball birthed by 'Little Boy' was 370 metres (1,200 feet) in diameter and produced surface temperatures reaching 6,000 degrees centigrade (10,830 Fahrenheit). Within minutes after the blast, 'Little Boy' released a firestorm some 3.2 kilometres (2 miles) in diameter. The fifteen-year old Yamaoka Michiko remembered the moment the bombs exploded: 'Nobody there looked like human beings. Until that moment I thought incendiary bombs had fallen. Everyone was stupefied. Humans had lost the ability to speak. People couldn't scream, "It hurts!" even when they were on fire. People didn't say,

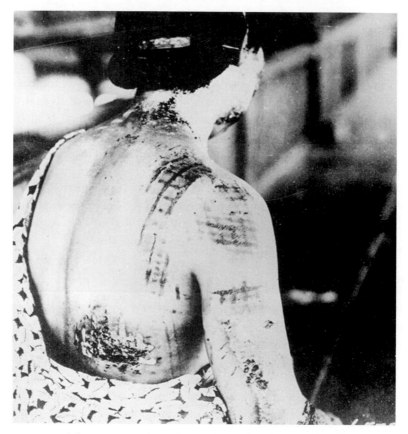

22 A burns victim from the atomic bombing of Hiroshima.

"It's hot!" They just sat catching fire' (Figure 22). Some 66,000 citizens of Hiroshima died directly from 'Little Boy', while 'Fat Man' claimed 73,883 Nagasaki lives. Of course, thousands more died of radiation sickness over the coming months and years. President Harry Truman (1884–1972) articulated US vengeance when he explained the use of the new weapon: 'Having found the bomb we have used it', he stated. 'We have used it against those who attacked us without warning at Pearl Harbor, against those who have starved and beaten and executed American prisoners of war, against those who have abandoned all pretence of obeying international laws of warfare.'

On 15 August 1945, Japan surrendered. At noon on that day, Japanese gathered around their radios to hear, for the first time, the shaky voice of Emperor Hirohito explain the decision. Obfuscating his considerable role in starting, waging, and prolonging the war, Hirohito claimed that he surrendered to save 'human civilization' from 'total extinction', creating a 'grand peace for all generations to come'. Even as Japan's cities burned, Hirohito explained, 'Let the entire nation continue as one family from generation to generation, ever firm in its faith of the imperishability of its divine land, ever mindful of its heavy burden of responsibilities, and of the long road before it.' It was this war-ravaged divine land that General MacArthur faced when he de-planed at Atsugi air force base on 28 August 1945.

CONCLUSION

Japan lives uncomfortably with the historical legacies of its twentieth-century imperial aggression to this day. Many young people have started to explore more apologetic narratives, such as Kobayashi Yoshinori's (b. 1953) controversial graphic history *Sensôron* (On war, 1998). Speaking directly to a generation of young people born after the war, Kobayashi's critique of the idea that Japan waged a 'war of aggression', rather than pursued legitimate foreign policy goals prior to and during the Pacific War, gained considerable traction when it first appeared, much to the consternation of Japan's neighbours. The Pacific War remains the defining experience of twentieth-century Japan. Illustrating other legacies of the Pacific War, many, such as post-war Prime Minister Nakasone Yasuhiro (b. 1918), insist that Japan's post-war Constitution 'smells like butter' and have sought to rewrite it to reflect Japanese values, including revamping language related to the emperor and 'Article Nine'. Nakasone once observed that, 'As long as the current constitution exists, the state of unconditional surrender persists.'

Whether Japan still lives in a condition of 'unconditional surrender' is a matter of political perspective, but Japan's need to rebuild after the war was imperative. With the conclusion of the US occupation in 1952, Japan began the work of rebuilding its economic, social, and political infrastructure. At this task Japan proved remarkably successful, but not without enduring national costs. As Japan began to emerge as a world economic leader for a second time, during its 'miraculous' post-war recovery, the environmental implications of an unbridled prioritization of economic growth began to sicken some of Japan's most vulnerable communities.

14

Japan's Post-War History, 1945–Present

Japan emerged from the Pacific War in tatters, but the small island country, showing Meiji-era resolve and with US support, quickly began rebuilding. By the 1950s, Japan had entered the era of 'high speed growth' and washing machines, refrigerators, and televisions, the 'three sacred jewels' of post-war consumerism, started to inhabit most Japanese homes, or at least most consumer imaginations, brightening once-glum lives. Government agencies, working in tandem with corporations and labour, and sheltered by the US security umbrella, orchestrated the economic recovery that birthed such global powerhouses as Toyota Motor Corporation and Sony. Politically, the conservative Liberal Democratic Party dominated the Diet for decades. It revised US occupation reforms and later pushed for constitutional changes, as well as further privatization of the economy. But as Japan entered the 1970s, environmental pollution tainted its celebrated economic success. Although the 'big four' pollution cases of Niigata and Minamata methyl-mercury poisoning, Yokkaichi asthma, and cadmium poisoning in Toyama stole most national and international headlines, smaller, equally devastating pollution problems occurred wherever industrial development went unchecked. In the name of the post-war economic recovery, which preoccupied Japanese politics for decades, the nation appeared willing to poison its most vulnerable people and environments.

If Japan's manufactured exports, ranging from the Toyota Corona to the Sony Walkman, characterized the decades after the

Pacific War, pop culture exports have characterized recent decades. Whether in the urban exploits of Godzilla or the animated films of Miyazaki Hayao (b. 1941), Japan's cultural production reflects many Japanese anxieties about nuclear warfare and industrial pollution. But Japan has emerged as a major exporter of culture. Today, the island nation is as much celebrated for its graphic novels as it is for the 'sacred war' it fought against the US and its staggeringly successful post-war economy.

THE OCCUPATION AND REVERSING COURSE

Japanese and Allied representatives signed the instrument of surrender on 2 September 1945, aboard the USS *Missouri*. There was little fanfare during the sombre occasion, but the two US flags aboard the *Missouri* had been carefully selected. Officials had flown the first flag at the White House on the morning of the 'day of infamy' at Pearl Harbor; the other, a thirty-one star Old Glory, had flown on Commodore Matthew C. Perry's flagship when he 'opened Japan' nearly a century earlier. On signing, Japan surrendered unconditionally. According to a US statement to General MacArthur, 'Our relations with Japan do not rest on a contractual basis, but on an unconditional surrender. Since your authority is supreme, you will not entertain any question on the part of the Japanese as to its scope.' MacArthur perceived his 'scope' in Japan to be comprehensive. In his words, he sought to 'bring Japan abreast with modern progressive thought and action'. The Japanese, in turn, embraced defeat, strategically following MacArthur's lead and, immediately after the US occupation (1945–52), reforming policies and priorities as necessary. As his memoirs attest, MacArthur's occupation policies were profoundly ambitious: 'First destroy the military power. Punish war criminals. Build the structure of representative government. Modernize the constitution. Hold free elections. Enfranchise women. Release political prisoners. Liberate the farmers. Establish free and responsible press. Liberalize education. Decentralize the political power. Separate church and state . . .' At a certain level, he sought to revisit Japan's Meiji experience and put the country back on a democratic trajectory, one closely modelled after the US.

Although many Japanese anticipated the occupation with trepidation, anxiety soon turned to excitement when it became evident that US servicemen did not plan to transform Japan into a colossal amusement park, as had been rumoured, with a handful of enslaved Japanese women working the concession stands. Many Japanese embraced their US occupiers because they had liberated them from the militarized state that dominated Japan for decades. As one reporter observed after the war:

> It appears that the reason young people consider Tokyo to be a delightful place is because they were liberated from the oppressive forces by America. The police could no longer strut around arrogantly, neither could the teachers and principals. The young could behave as freely as they desired so long as they did not break the law. The pleasures of youth and freedom – Tokyo now seems ready to freely grant these to them.

Viewed from this popular vantage point, the US occupation liberated the Japanese from their militarized selves.

In this sense, an atmosphere of liberation existed not only throughout the former 'Greater East Asian Co-prosperity Sphere', but also in Japan itself, where the defeat of the fascist military government had liberated average Japanese from a succession of war prime ministers and cabinets. But as many have pointed out, this sense of domestic liberation has also served to obviate a sense of popular responsibility for Japan's wartime atrocities, placing the blame squarely on the backs of a handful of military leaders such as General Tôjô Hideki. As we have seen, however, in the early years national exuberance for total war had extended far beyond the small cadre of generals, as many Japanese eagerly consumed war movies, war radio programming, war novels, and visited 'military animals', from heroic horses to patriotic pigeons, exhibited at Tokyo's Imperial Zoo. Herein lie some of the contemporary Korean and Chinese critiques of Japan's unwillingness to accept wartime responsibility. Whereas the wages of guilt in Germany have been widely distributed to the population through education initiatives, in Japan there has never been a thorough national reckoning of responsibility for wartime atrocities such as the Nanjing Massacre (1937). The weary ghosts of General Tôjô and thirteen of his 'Class A' criminal colleagues continue to shoulder that national burden at Tokyo's Yasukuni shrine, where the souls of Japan's war dead are interred.

In part, this inability to accept national responsibility has opened the door for lively debates within Japan regarding war guilt and atrocities. The debate started when historian Ienaga Saburô (1913–2002) published *Shin Nihonshi* (New Japanese history, 1947), and was subsequently approached by a major Tokyo publisher to revise the book into a high-school text. Because of the highly centralized structure of the Japanese education system, the textbook would likely have been used throughout the country. Throughout the 1950s, however, Ienaga struggled with the Education Ministry's textbook authorization procedures, which consistently found fault with Ienaga's interpretations of key wartime events. Starting in 1965, Ienaga initiated three lengthy lawsuits against the government over the unconstitutional nature of textbook authorization protocols, which he claimed violated his free speech rights, as codified in the post-war Constitution (promulgated March 1946). He won partial victories over the years; more importantly, however, he brought controversies regarding interpretations of the Pacific War into an international spotlight. Since then, such conservative historians as Hata Ikuhiko (b. 1932) have challenged mainstream interpretations of wartime atrocities such as the Nanjing Massacre. In several scholarly books, Hata has consistently revised the number of Chinese civilians killed at Nanjing (his estimates lower the number from approximately 300,000 to 40,000, in large part by excluding Chinese soldiers). Several of Hata's books have been translated into Chinese, and the consequent historical controversies continue to incense Japan's neighbours. Graphic novelist Kobayashi Yoshinori's (b. 1953) strategy has been slightly different. Rather than engage the tweed-wearing 'uncool men' that generally interpret the past, Kobayashi, in his wildly popular graphic history *Sensôron* (On war, 1998), sought to write 'something that intellectuals cannot write – something that young people find pleasure to read and get completely absorbed in, and yet is not light but deep'. In this graphic history, Kobayashi argues that Japan did not fight a war of aggression, but rather a justified war to liberate Asia from 'white' Western imperialism. Further, he asserts that the denigration of Japan's war heroes is a

US plot to 'brainwash' young Japanese and steer them away from a healthy love of their country. Through his work, Kobayashi has sought to awaken the 'unconscious nationalism' alive in all Japanese through his retelling of the saga of the 'Greater East Asian War'. Kobayashi's major departure from mainstream histories is to treat Japan's soldiers, including many war criminals, as war heroes, which historically revises one of the more high-profile undertakings of the occupation: the International Military Tribunal for the Far East, which sought to bring to justice those Japanese who had committed 'crimes against peace'. Of the twenty-eight men charged as 'Class A' war criminals the most notorious was General Tôjô, who, after MacArthur had landed at Atsugi, tried to commit suicide but was heroically resuscitated by US doctors only to be hanged by the neck after the tribunal three years later. Other tribunals convicted thousands of men of Class B and C offences and many of them later served in the post-war government. MacArthur appointed twelve jurists to oversee the tribunal, and most came from nations that had signed the 'instrument of surrender' at the conclusion of the war. Indian Jurist Radhabinod Pal (1886–1967) offered the only dissenting opinion: 'I sincerely regret my inability to concur in the judgment and decision of my learned brothers', he explained. Judge Pal basically accused the US and its Allies of victor's justice when he wrote, 'belligerents, who during war succeed in winning victories and getting prisoners of war, are liable to be credited with cruelties of the character alleged in the present indictment and, if ultimately defeated, their very defeat as it were establishes their most devilish and fiendish character'. Regardless of Judge Pal's opinion, of the twenty-eight 'Class A' criminals, one was found unfit for trial and two died during the proceedings; of the twenty-five who survived the ordeal, seven were hanged by the neck and sixteen were sentenced to life in prison.

The decision to not try Emperor Hirohito proved the most controversial. MacArthur wrote that when Washington, DC appeared to be moving in the direction of trying the emperor (largely because of pressure from the Russians and British), 'I had advised that I would need at least one million reinforcements should such action be taken. I believed that if the Emperor were indicted, and perhaps hanged, as a war criminal, military government would have to be instituted throughout all Japan.' The occupation thus began the business of rewriting Japanese history to exonerate the emperor from any war responsibility. At the end of 1945, the head of Civil Information and Education Section for the Supreme Commander of Allied Powers (SCAP) wrote a series of articles that were translated into Japanese by Japan's official news agency. Symbolically, the first instalment appeared on 8 December 1945, and included the following sentence: 'Recently, the emperor himself said that it had not been his wish to attack Pearl Harbor without warning, but the military police exerted every effort to prevent [this statement] from reaching the people.' Emperor Hirohito was a peace-loving man, in other words; the campaign to resculpt the emperor as a champion of non-belligerent democracy had begun. In the end, the Allies spared the emperor, but they did oversee the renunciation of his divine status. In a radio address to the nation on 1 January 1946, Emperor Hirohito explained that, 'The ties between us and our people have always stood upon mutual trust and affection. They do not depend upon mere legends and myths. They are not predicated on the false conception that the Emperor is divine and that the Japanese people are superior to other races and fated to rule the world.' Just as the Meiji emperor transformed from his traditional garb to a Prussian field marshal when required, Emperor Hirohito dismounted from his white wartime horse, changed out of his military uniform, and became the benign symbol of a democratic nation until his death in 1989.

US occupation reforms were truly widespread and transformative. The occupation oversaw the advent of a new education system, widespread '*zaibatsu* busting', a new decentralized police force, and the crafting of a progressive Constitution. Initially, SCAP officials tapped legal scholar Matsumoto Jōji (1877–1954) to write the new Constitution; but MacArthur proved dissatisfied with the results. In Matsumoto's rendition, sovereignty still resided with the emperor rather than with the people. Eventually, SCAP officers simply drafted a Constitution of their own. In it the emperor became a 'symbol of the state and the unity of the people', no longer the centre of state sovereignty. Unlike the Meiji Constitution (1889), the document was not a 'gift' from a divine ruler nor did sovereignty emanate from him; rather, the Constitution came from a small cohort of New Deal officers serving in Japan during the occupation. In the Constitution, 'Article Nine' renounced Japan's 'right of belligerency' in resolving international disputes. The controversial article read, 'Aspiring sincerely to an international peace based on justice and order, the Japanese people forever renounce war as a sovereign right of the nation and the threat or use of force as means of settling international disputes.' The US occupation, led in large part by New Dealers, was remaking Japan into a progressive, pacifistic, democratic society from the ground up.

Despite the liberal New Deal tenor of the first two years of the occupation, however, signs of change were evident by 1948. In large part, SCAP's attitudes and policies towards Japan's highly activist labour unions constitute a significant bellwether of shifting attitudes and priorities, as the US pivoted for the coming Cold War with the Soviet Union. Before the war, Japanese labour had rapidly shifted from predominantly female textile mill workers to men working in heavier industries. As a consequence, labour unions became more assertive in the immediate post-war environment because of their importance to Japan's economic recovery. Socialist and communist politicians also began aiding labour unions with their organizational prowess. Although MacArthur was himself politically conservative, SCAP had granted labour unions a relatively long leash, finding them a useful club with which to coerce a Japanese government keenly anxious about the spread of communism after the war. In 1945, SCAP prodded the Diet into passing the 'Trade Union Law', which was modelled after the progressive Wagner Act of 1935 in the US. The increasingly progressive 'Labour Relations Adjustment Law' (1946) and the 'Labour Standards Law' (1947) soon followed. In sum, this early legislation ensured the right to organize, engage in collective bargaining, and strike, as well as standardized work hours, vacations, workplace safety and sanitation, and included restrictions on female and child labour. By 1948, however, the labour unions started running afoul of SCAP. Mainly, SCAP viewed labour union tactics as threatening the economic recovery that the US so desired. Occupation officials also became perplexed at the strident political activism of Japan's unions, who behaved differently than relatively docile US labour organizations.

In February 1947, SCAP started cracking down on Japan's labour unions by cancelling a general railway strike. From this point forward, union leaders found themselves confronting Japanese police supported by US combat troops, sometimes with tanks conspicuously placed in rear positions. By 1949, the Diet, under the influence of SCAP, abandoned the progressive philosophy of the Wagner Act (1935) for the more conservative Taft-Hartley Act (1947). Stunned by SCAP's reversal, Japan's labour movement became increasingly suspicious of the US and its designs in Japan. It was also at this time (February 1949) that banker Joseph Dodge (1890–1964) arrived in Japan to serve as economic adviser to SCAP. In the 'Dodge Line', SCAP coerced the Diet into promoting fiscal austerity, balancing the budget, establishing a single foreign exchange rate, and further privatizing the Japanese economy, all reversals of the statist 'political economy' of the Meiji years. In short, Japan was increasingly becoming less of an experiment in New Deal democratization than a capitalist bulwark in Asia for the coming Cold War.

POST-WAR POLITICS

At this critical juncture, Japan's pre-eminent post-war politician arrived on the scene in the person of the conservative Yoshida Shigeru (1878–1967). Yoshida was anything but new to Japan's government: he had served as ambassador to Italy and the UK during the tumultuous 1930s. Because of his prominent place in Japan's empire, US authorities had briefly imprisoned him in 1945; however, on his release he quickly became a central figure in post-war politics. SCAP officials approved of Yoshida because of his explicit desire to align Japan economically and militarily with the US. In what became known as the 'Yoshida Doctrine', the prime minister prioritized economic recovery along liberal Western lines, while relying on the military protection of the US, which became a key ingredient to Japan's post-war economic success. In essence, Japan could rebuild without exorbitant defence bills. In order to accomplish these goals and banish the spectre of unconditional surrender, Yoshida signed the San Francisco Peace Treaty and the US–Japan Security Treaty, formally ending the war in April 1952 and setting up Japan's security arrangements with the US. With the occupation finally laid to rest, Japan's post-war period had begun. Throughout the 1950s, Yoshida and other conservative politicians sought to blunt or modify many of the more progressive SCAP reforms. In the arena of education, for example, SCAP had ordered the government to liberalize education and weed out militaristic and nationalistic elements from school curricula. Under Shidehara Kijûrô (1872–1951), the prime minister when Japan surrendered, the Japanese government balked at such reforms, citing a need to combat the 'root of our recent moral decay'. Prime Minister Shidehara supported an emphasis on the Meiji Imperial Rescript on Education (1890), the document recited in Japanese schools that taught traditional Confucian patriarchy and emperor worship. Needless to say, MacArthur rejected these concerns, insisting that school curricula be revised to harmonize with 'representative government, international peace, the dignity of the individual, and such fundamental rights as the freedom of assembly, speech and religion'. More controversially, SCAP turned over control of school curricula to elected prefectural boards, as well as gave them the authority to approve textbooks. SCAP had gutted the central authority of the Education Ministry, particularly in the arena of approving textbooks, in favour of decentralized US educational models.

Such reforms alarmed the conservative-minded Yoshida, however, who was concerned about the 'decline in public morals, the need for curbing excesses arising from a misunderstanding of the meaning of freedom, the neglect into which respect for the nation and its traditions had fallen due to mistaken ideas of progress'. Immediately after the war, the moral health of the people became a preoccupation of Japanese conservative politicians; they even used it to explain the exhausted nation's defeat. On 28 August 1945, for example, Prime Minister Higashikuni Naruhiko (1887–1990) had identified the decay of public morality as one reason why Japan lost the war. 'We have come to this ending because the government's policies were flawed', he explained at his first press conference. 'But another cause [of the defeat] was a decline in the moral behaviour of the people.' In order to reverse SCAP reforms and thus combat the country's moral decay, in 1954 the Diet introduced changes that weakened Japan's Teachers' Union and, eventually, began recentralizing control of education.

SCAP's reforms of Japan's police force are also instructive. Similar to its education reforms, SCAP had decentralized Japan's police force along US lines. During the war, the Home Ministry had directed policing, including the nefarious activities of the secret police; under the US model, municipalities and prefectures now handled law enforcement. But as with educational reform, starting in 1951 and ending with the 1954 Police Reform Bill, the Diet abolished municipal police in favour of a prefectural police force under the control of the National Public Safety Commission. Moreover, in the context of the Cold War and the outbreak of the Korean War (1950–3), Asia had become increasingly volatile, particularly after the founding of the People's Republic of China (1949). In response, Prime Minister Yoshida began the process of beefing up Japan's defensive capabilities, even within the framework of the non-belligerent 'Article Nine'. In 1950, Japan created the National Police Reserve, designed to replace the 75,000 US troops that had left Japan for the Korean theatre. Following the 'Treaty of Mutual Cooperation and Security between the US and Japan' (1952), the National Police Reserve morphed into Japan's Self-Defence Forces in 1954, which continue to serve Japan's defensive security interests. Originally, Japan's Self-Defence Forces were confined to the Japanese islands, but in recent decades Japan has started deploying the Self-Defence Forces on peacekeeping operations. Strategically, in the twenty-first century, the Self-Defence Forces have begun focusing on China with the emergence of the Senkaku/Diaoyu Islands dispute and other neighbouring hotspots. Testifying to its importance, in 2013 Japan had the fifth-largest defence budget, even though its military is exclusively for self-defence.

As of this writing, the Senkaku Islands have become a dangerous flashpoint for Sino-Japanese relations. Composed of eight islets with a combined area of 6.3 square kilometres (2.5 square miles), the Senkaku Islands have rekindled discussions in Japan about the role of the Self-Defence Forces and the need to modify 'Article Nine' of the Constitution. The history of the islands is as follows: in 1895, after the Sino-Japanese War, Japan had laid claim to the islands and, shortly thereafter, Japanese entrepreneurs built fish processing plants there. These failed in 1940, and, though privately owned by Japanese citizens, the islands have remained deserted ever since. In 1945, the US government assumed control of the islands; the US then relinquished that control in 1971, with the 'Okinawa Reversion Treaty'. The next year, both the People's Republic of China and the Republic of China (Taiwan) laid claim to the islands, after the United Nations Economic Commission for Asia and the Far East identified oil and gas reserves nearby. Since then, the rivalry between the two Asian giants has intensified. In October 2012, as China became more vocal about its claims to the Senkaku Islands, Prime Minister Noda Yoshihiko (b. 1957) announced that Japan had 'unwavering resolve to defend its territorial lands and waters'. In an unusual display of muscle, Japanese Coast Guard cutters have played cat and mouse with Chinese surveillance ships; they have also attempted to prevent Japanese ultranationalists from swimming ashore to plant Japanese flags on the islands. In the face of confrontational posturing from China over the Senkaku/Diaoyu Islands, Korea over the Takeshima/Dokdo Islands, and the threat of North Korea's nuclear weapons and missile programmes, Japan has been forced to re-evaluate the place of the Self-Defence Forces in its own geopolitical posturing.

Throughout the majority of the post-war years, Japan has been governed by the Liberal Democratic Party (1955), relying on a triangulation of power between conservative Diet politicians, government bureaucrats, and corporate executives. The LDP governed Japan between 1955 and 1993, with fifteen different men serving as prime minister during that time. Japan's post-war politics have often resembled musical chairs. One exception was the charismatic Nakasone Yasuhiro (b. 1918), a contemporary and ally of his conservative US counterpart, President Ronald Reagan (1911–2004). Nakasone served as Prime Minister between 1982 and 1987. Notably, as a staunch conservative and nationalist, Prime Minister Nakasone was the first Japanese head of state to visit the Yasukuni Shrine after fourteen 'Class A' war criminals had been reinterred there in 1978. Infamously, Nakasone caused a diplomatic stir between the US and Japan in 2001 when he identified racial homogeneity as the root of Japan's excellent educational test scores. As for the US, Nakasone explained that, 'There are many blacks, Puerto Ricans and Mexicans in America. In consequence the average score over there is exceedingly low.' He then sought to clarify his remarks: admittedly, the US has 'great achievements', but 'there are things the Americans have not been able to do because of multiple nationalities there'. Showing how hard some attitudes die, Nakasone then explained, 'On the contrary, things are easier in Japan because we are a mono-racial society.' Nakasone's remarks were cast as his alone, but it is clear that, among LDP conservatives, such wartime ideas regarding Japan's racial purity continue to resonate. He also privatized key components of the Japanese economy, including the tobacco industry in 1985, which the government had monopolized since 1898, and the Japanese National Railways, replaced in 1987 by seven private companies known as the 'JR Group'. The mantra of privatization became the hallmark of conservative LDP rule in post-war Japan.

THE SECOND ECONOMIC MIRACLE AND ITS DISCONTENTS

Within a decade of the US occupation, the Japanese economy began to recover. Immediately after the war, the main purpose of economic planning was keeping people from starving to death; but by 1955, Japan was entering the era of 'high speed growth', where economic expansion became Japan's main priority. In the 1960s, Japan's economic growth mesmerized the world; on average, its Gross National Product (GNP) grew 10 per cent a year, surpassing West Germany and every other capitalist country in the world except for the US. In large part, Japan's economy revved up with lucrative US procurements for the Korean War. By 1955, after the US had spent some $2 billion on Japanese goods, economic conditions in Japan had improved to the point where many people possessed the resources to purchase household durable goods. In the early 1970s, Japan's economy slowed slightly when the Organization of Petroleum Producing Countries raised oil prices; but following that brief contraction, Japan resumed staggering growth in GNP for decades, often 3.5 to 5.5 per cent per year. In 1987, Japan's economy overtook the US in per capita GNP. In part, such government agencies as the Ministry of International Trade and

Industry (1949) and the Economic Planning Agency (1955) orchestrated much of the industrial planning that led to Japanese success. Unlike during the Meiji period, when reforms benefited cities, Japan's 'high speed growth' spread material benefits to the countryside as well. By the 1970s, household incomes in the countryside stood some five times higher than they had in the 1950s; and these households purchased the same 'three sacred jewels' (washing machines, refrigerators, and televisions) as their city counterparts. The post-war recovery thus embraced most levels of Japanese society.

Many pre-war industries thrived in the post-war environment. In 1937, for example, Toyoda Loom Works began its transformation into the Toyota Motor Company. The son of the founder, Toyoda Kiichirô (1894–1952), built an elaborate production facility near Nagoya and began to surround himself with experts, including engineers and physics professors. The production complex encompassed some seventeen different facilities, ranging from metal casting and panel pressing to welding and painting. Between 1937 and 1940, utilizing its new Nagoya facility, Toyota's vehicle production expanded from 4,013 to 14,787 annually. As a result of the Second World War, Toyota and other major firms were forced to become less dependent on foreign technologies and more reliant on developing their own. When Toyota developed its own Institute for Physical and Chemical Research, the company explained:

> Now that we are facing a second Great War in Europe it has become extremely difficult to import Western knowledge, and as the Allies have closed their research sections to outsiders it has become very hard to gain information on their research successes. In such a climate it is more and more urgent that we ourselves should conduct independent and self-directed research and should establish research institutions to open up our own path to progress.

US bombs destroyed most of Toyota's facilities; the company recovered, however, particularly after it received handsome procurements to fabricate parts for US military vehicles in Korea. In the 1950s, Toyota, as well as its competitor Nissan, began automating assembly lines with robots and improving production processes, leading to the introduction of such popular models as the Toyota Corona (1957). As a result of these innovations, Japan's automobile industry experienced dramatic expansion: in 1953, Japan manufactured 49,778 automobiles and exported none; by 1983, Japan manufactured over 11 million automobiles and exported over half of them.

The success of such companies as Matsushita (National and Panasonic) and Sony also demonstrate the diversity of Japan's economic growth in the post-war years. Take the latter company, Sony Corporation, founded in 1946 by Ibuka Masaru (1908–97) and Morita Akio (1921–99). In 1950, under Ibuka's engineering prowess, Japan built its first tape recorders. In 1953, Sony perfected the transistor radio, revolutionizing the consumer electronics industry. If Ibuka was the engineering genius behind the operation, Morita provided the international marketing muscle, and in 1970 Sony became the first Japanese company to find its name listed on the New York Stock Exchange. Under Sony, the label 'Made in Japan' began to signal quality and high technology, rather than poorly made Asian imports. Like Toyota, Sony continually sought to improve its products, even ones that had been initially developed abroad. Sony televisions serve as an interesting example: conventionally, in the 1960s, televisions were valve-operated sets, but Sony introduced transistor-operated sets that made it possible to manufacture a smaller television more suitable to Japanese homes. In doing so, Sony spearheaded the commitment to electronic miniaturization, which eventually became the gold standard in the personal and home electronics industry.

Japan's myopic quest for industrial expansion and economic growth came at a high environmental and human cost, however. During the post-war recovery, four high-profile pollution cases destabilized Japan's total commitment to economic growth and forced the Diet, in the form of concrete legislation, to take action to clean up Japan's polluted air, water, and soil. Now famous, the 'big four' pollution cases were Minamata methyl-mercury poisoning (Kumamoto prefecture), Niigata methyl-mercury poisoning (Niigata prefecture), Yokkaichi asthma (Mie prefecture), and cadmium poisoning (Toyama prefecture). In the early 1970s, photographer W. Eugene Smith (1918–78) brought international attention to bear on 'Minamata disease' with his photographs of the diseased fishing communities of the Shiranui Sea. He documented their valiant effort to receive justice from the national government and the Chisso Corporation, which had dumped mercury into nearby waters. Chisso had roots in the early twentieth century: Noguchi Shitagau (1873–1944) had founded the company in 1908, during a time when scientists were pushing for advancements in electrochemistry, specifically nitrogen fixation technology for producing fertilizer.

Quickly, Chisso became a leviathan in twentieth-century Japanese industry, producing calcium carbide and nitrogenous products. Fertilizer had become critical in industrial development because as more farmers left their fields to labour in factories, the land needed to be more productive. But Japan's war effort provided another market for Chisso's chemicals, in particular the weapons industry. Like many of Japan's industrial giants, Chisso became intimately involved with Japan's total war. In 1929, for example, it built a sprawling fertilizer plant in Hungnam, in northern Korea, transforming a small fishing village into a sprawling industrial city of 180,000 people. Elsewhere in Japan's newly acquired empire, Chisso built hydroelectric facilities on the Pujon, Changjin, Honchon, and Yalu rivers. The company also expanded its munitions manufacturing to Taiwan. In 1932, an engineer at Chisso developed the 'reaction liquid circulation method', which blew acetylene gas over mercuric sulphate in order to produce acetaldehyde. Then, in 1951, Chisso engineers replaced manganese with nitric acid as the oxidizer in the manufacturing of acetaldehyde; they then drew brackish water from the nearby estuary, producing a highly soluble type of methyl-mercury. It easily absorbed into ecosystems and bodies, whether shellfish, cats, or local fishermen. At Chisso, these technological advancements boosted production and profits; but they also polluted the nearby marine environment in complex ways. In the end, Chisso killed thousands.

Between 1930 and the 1960s, Chisso dumped as much as 600 tons of mercury into Minamata Bay. As methyl-mercury nefariously travelled up the marine food chain of the Shiranui Sea, it eventually came to rest at the pinnacle of local trophic ladders: the human foetus. Because of the lipid solubility of methyl-mercury, it easily penetrated the placenta; later tests demonstrated that mercury levels in women's umbilical cords measured higher than in the same women's blood. Basically, the mother's body was unknowingly shunting mercury to the foetus, interrupting critical neurological phases in foetal organogenesis. Some of the first signs that methyl-mercury had penetrated the ecosystem were Minamata's 'dancing cats', basically careening and dying wharf cats, their brains marinated in mercury; these cats had once kept coastal rat populations down. Human victims followed, however, and 'Minamata disease' became characterized by the painfully clenched hands, rolled-back eyes, drooling mouths, slurred speech, and quaking bodies of children who had contracted the disease congenitally. When fishermen sought justice, their 'selfish demands' were shot down because they threatened to slow Japan's post-war recovery and destroy badly needed jobs. In March 1973, in a landmark ruling, Judge Saitô Jirô found Chisso guilty of 'corporate negligence', and victims and perpetrators have battled in courtrooms ever since. Tens of thousands of people have sought certification for having the disease, but as of 2001 only some 2,265 victims had been recognized (many more received some form of compensation), and most of them have died. For Minamata fishermen and their families, the human costs of Japan's post-war recovery were excruciatingly high.

Sulphur dioxide poisoning at Yokkaichi is another example of the high environmental price paid for Japan's post-war recovery, a burden always felt disproportionately by the most impoverished communities. In 1955, during the era of 'high speed growth', the government had selected Yokkaichi as a site for a sprawling petrochemical complex. Before the war, the site had served as a deepwater port, so it was ideally suited for the large tankers that transported oil to Japan. With oil being critical to Japan's postwar recovery, construction started in Yokkaichi in 1956, reclaiming wetland marshes and the bombed-out rubble of earlier oil refineries. Industrial planners referred to their overall vision for Yokkaichi as a *konbinato*, a Japanized version of the Soviet word *kombinat*, referring to a large industrial campus comprised of clusters of related industries. By 1958, tankers regularly tied up at Yokkaichi's Showa Oil Refineries docks, where engineers refined the oil into gasoline, kerosene, and naphtha. But in nearby Isozu, a small fishing village, air quality was becoming intolerable as pollution engulfed the area; the Tsukiji fish market, moreover, rejected their catches as being unhealthy, sending their fragile livelihoods into a death spiral. In April 1964, the first casualty of what became known as 'Yokkaichi asthma' died. Many others followed. In order to provide gasoline for cars, kerosene to heat homes, and naphtha to make plastics, industrial Japan proved once again willing to kill its most vulnerable people.

In response, the Diet passed the 'Basic Law for Pollution Control' in 1967. At the most basic level, the law sought to 'combat environmental pollution' and ensure 'protection of the people's health and the conservation of their living environment'. The law also defined technical terms, such as *kōgai*, the Japanese word for environmental pollution, as 'any situation in which human health and the living environment are damaged by air pollution, water pollution, soil pollution, noise, vibration, ground subsidence, and offensive odours, which arise over a considerable area as a result of industrial or other human activities'. Everything from the noxious polluted airs of Yokkaichi to the deafening noise at Osaka Airport, where complaints over noise pollution raged in the 1960s, were encompassed by the new legislation. Consequently, in December 1969, with the Basic Law for Pollution Control on the books, citizens in the vicinity of Osaka's Itami Airport filed a lawsuit in the District Court seeking damages for the alarming noise pollution. The lawsuit kicked around for a decade, with various courts finding in the plaintiffs' favour; in November 1975, the courts finally issued an injunction halting flights at the airport between 9:00 p.m. and 7:00 a.m. The case eventually made it to the Supreme Court of Japan, one of the most conservative supreme courts in the world, which, after six years of deliberation, ruled that the injunction was illegal, but that victims remained entitled to settlements. Regardless of the constitutional debates, Osaka's Itami Airport remains tightly regulated.

In 1970, shortly after the passage of the Basic Law for Pollution Control, what many called the 'Pollution Diet' passed some fourteen pieces of environmental legislation. Moreover, the 'big four' pollution cases were settled within several years after the law being passed: Niigata methyl-mercury poisoning in 1971, Yokkaichi asthma in 1972, Toyama cadmium poisoning in 1972, and Minamata methyl-mercury poisoning in 1973. Then in 1971 the government established the Environment Agency, which was promoted to the Ministry of Environment in September 2001. At this time, lawmakers purged industry-friendly language, mainly verbiage that sought to 'harmonize' pollution control with economic growth, from the 1967 law. Many environmental challenges still exist in Japan, but the late 1960s and early 1970s witnessed a strong backlash against the unchecked industrialization of the decades following the Pacific War.

NEW CULTURAL EXPORTS

Today, Japan is known as much for its pop culture exports as for its industrial manufacturing, particularly after the bursting of the Japanese 'bubble economy' in 1991, which initiated what many have called the 'lost decades'. The first such popular culture icon exported was the indefatigable Godzilla, who first debuted on Japan's movie screens in the 1954 film, *Gojira*. Honda Ishirô (1911–93) directed the film; the Tôhô Company, one of Japan's largest film companies, invested some ¥60 million in the film's then cutting-edge special effects (Figure 23). Movie star Shimura

23 Godzilla throttles Japan's Self-Defence Forces in Tokyo.

Takashi (1905–82), who that same year became famous for his leading role in Akira Kurosawa's (1910–98) *The Seven Samurai* (1954), played the leading human role. Godzilla appeared in the same year as the 'Lucky Dragon Incident', when in March 1954 US nuclear testing on Bikini Atoll accidentally exposed fishermen aboard a Japanese tuna boat to nuclear fallout. Less than seven months later, the boat's radio operator had died from acute radiation syndrome. Godzilla emerged from these same waters of nuclear testing as a pop-culture protest against nuclear testing and warfare. Director Honda once explained, 'We had no plans for a sequel and naively hoped that the end of Godzilla was going to coincide with the end of nuclear testing.' Not only did Godzilla not disappear in 1954, but rather the adorable eater of trains became among the most enduring serials in Japanese movie history. Only in July 1995, with the epic *Gojira tai Desutoroia* (Godzilla versus Destroyer), did Tôhô pull the plug on the movies. 'Because the Godzilla movies are serialized, some constraints came to be imposed on the character of Godzilla and the background story', conceded one Tôhô executive. 'That's why we decided to end the series.'

Since Godzilla made his debut on US movie screens in 1956's *Godzilla, King of the Monsters*, many other Japanese pop-culture exports have found their way around the world. Unlike the serious radioactive post-war waters in which Godzilla swam, Japan in the 1980s was characterized by an inexplicable pursuit of 'cuteness'. In Tokyo and other cities, some adult women could be seen dressed as grade school girls, with fuzzy baby animals dangling from pink sweaters or from the zippers of handbags. Women, in particular, sought to look 'eighteen going on twelve', as one observer wrote. As products of this cuteness milieu, such female vocalists as Seiko Matsuda (b. 1962) made a killing, particularly among young Japanese men, when she dressed up as Little Bo Peep for concerts or television appearances. Hundreds of thousands of *burikko*, or women who charmed men by re-enacting their adolescence, paraded across the cities of Japan. But a more enduring product of Japan's cuteness phase was the Sanrio creation Hello Kitty, which debuted in 1974. Though on the surface just a cute tote bag motif, Sanrio gave Hello Kitty a cosmopolitan biography: 'Hello Kitty was born in London, England, where she lives with her parents and her twin sister, Mimi. Both Hello Kitty and Mimi are in the third grade ... Her hobbies include music, reading, eating the cookies her sister bakes, and best of all, making new friends.' Hello Kitty even had her own newspaper, *Ichigo shinbun* (Strawberry news). Sanrio describes its product as 'social communication gift goods', and they appear to be working, judging from profits. In 2010, with US personalities such as Lady Gaga adorning themselves in Hello Kitty handbags, less for the cuteness, one presumes, than its naughty irony, Sanrio profits rose to nearly ¥10 billion.

Even Japanese media have achieved popularity around the world, including *manga* (graphic novels) and *anime* (animated films). Although Japanese read *manga* prior to the war, and the genre probably has cultural roots that stretch back to the woodblock prints of the early modern period, the modern form of *manga* blossomed after the US occupation. Today, the genre encompasses everything from serious conservative critiques of Japanese attitudes towards the Pacific War and steamy S&M pornography to economic treatises and science fiction stories. The artist and storyteller who propelled *manga* to its dominant place in Japanese post-war popular culture is Tezuka Osamu (1928–89), known as the 'god of *manga*'. Tezuka held a medical degree but never practised; he was also an amateur entomologist, who held a keen interest in the insect world: his *nom de plume* was Osamushi, a reference to a kind of ground beetle. In his *manga*, Tezuka tackled a number of weighty topics, including stories of tarnished, fallible heroes grappling with intractable issues. Because of the weighty nature of his topics, Tezuka made it acceptable for adults to read *manga*, which, as anybody who has commuted by train in Japan knows, they do in droves. Tezuka grew up in Takarazuka, home of the gender-bending Takarazuka Revue Company, where he was mesmerized by movies, particularly Walt Disney (1901–66) animated films. He once said he watched *Snow White* and *Bambi* some eighty times, until he had virtually memorized every frame. For the post-war generation, Tezuka's most celebrated manga is *Tetsuwan Atom* (Astro Boy), which ran between 1951 and 1969. Today, *manga* is among the more important Japanese cultural exports, and the genre has become widely popular outside of Japan.

Manga is closely related to *anime*, or animated films, which have also gained international popularity. Unlike Tezuka, who worshipped Disney films as a youth, Japan's premier *anime* creator, Miyazaki Hayao (b. 1941), never cared much for classic Disney films, often finding them trite. Miyazaki and his collaborator, Takahata Isao (b. 1935), together formed Studio Ghibli, which has become a juggernaut in the animated film industry. Miyazaki first gained international acclaim for his 1984 *Kaze no tani no Nausicaä* (Nausicaä of the valley of the wind), one of many films that explore the intersections of human behaviour, particularly commercial greed, and the frail and mutating natural world. In this fantastic eco-drama, Nausicaä, a sensitive young girl, struggles to survive in a post-apocalyptic, toxic world inhabited by warring tribes of mutant insects. The main character resembles the Heian princess in *Mushi mezuru himegimi* (The princess who loved insects, twelfth century); she was also based on the character Maryara, from the US illustrator Richard Corben's (b. 1940) *Rowlf* (1971). Other eco-fables produced by Studio Ghibli include the 1994 film *Heisei tanuki gassen ponpoko* (Heisei badger wars), the story of a tribe of shape-shifting raccoon-dogs that draw on their fabled metamorphic powers to fight the development of the Tama New Town. The 'Operation Ghost' scene, where the shape-shifting badgers conjure a menagerie of Japanese ghosts and cultural icons to frighten the new inhabitants of Tama New Town, is visually stunning. Miyazaki followed *Heisei tanuki gassen ponpoko* with *Mononokehime* (Princess Mononoke, 1997), the story of a young girl raised by a pack of godlike wolves, ones reminiscent of Japan's real-life wolves, once worshipped but hunted to extinction in the Meiji period. The main character is a young Emishi prince named Ashitaka, who finds himself embroiled in a struggle between the industrializing Iron Town and nearby forest animals and the Great Forest Spirit. In some respects, the film explores the death of nature; as human industrialization and exploitation of the natural world intensifies, animals lose their subjective, or godlike existence, and become unintelligent objects for human exploitation. Over the course of the film, as the natural world is exploited by Iron Town, animals increasingly lose their ability to speak, symbolizing their objectification in the human imagination.

Clearly, if industrial growth and environmental collapse characterized the post-war years, then those historical trends were paralleled by a cultural exploration of those same themes. From the
radioactive Godzilla to the wolf princess, Japanese popular culture
has continued exploring the theme of the modern human place in
the natural world.

CONCLUSION

In 1991, Japan's 'bubble economy' burst with a muffled pop. The
bursting was not an immediate event, but rather a slow deterior-
ation of the economic boom triggered by real estate and stock price
inflation. In 1985, for example, Tokyo residential land prices leapt
by 45 per cent, to ¥297,000 per square metre; in 1990, at the
bubble's peak, that same square metre of residential real estate
was worth an astonishing ¥890,000. Basically, with such elevated
real estate prices the economy overheated, which also caused
uncontrolled money supplies and credit expansions. After the Bank
of Japan tried to cool the economy down with a succession of
monetary tightening protocols, in 1991 stock and asset prices
plummeted, sending Japan into the 'lost decades'. For a new generation of Japanese, the prosperous 1980s, with their inflated real
estate and stock prices, are a distant memory; many Japanese never
experienced them at all. Combined with the triple disaster, Japan
entered the twenty-first century as vulnerable as ever, as a series of
new 'black ship' challenges have confronted the resourceful island
nation.

15

Natural Disasters and the Edge of History

In the nineteenth century, when Meiji reformers set in motion Japan's rapid industrialization, they recognized only its obvious economic and military benefits, ones ruthlessly demonstrated by Western imperialism. Since then, Japan has become part of a community of wealthy nations who have, through the burning of fossil fuels, slowly undermined the relatively stable climate that has insulated human civilizations. Since the Meiji transition to nonrenewable energy, Japan has become a major global contributor to climate change, with carbon dioxide equivalents, or greenhouse gases, at 1,390 megatons in 2005, more than Germany or the UK. One consequence of Earth's changing climate is sea level rise, which poses serious challenges to many island nations in the Pacific, including Japan. The link between Japan's nineteenth-century industrialization and the reality of rising oceans is unequivocal and has placed Japan on a precarious historical precipice. For all the benefits of nineteenth-century 'civilization and enlightenment', and the economic growth they offered, within a handful of generations it has come to threaten Japan at a fundamental level. Japan's climate, topography, and biodiversity are in the thrall of dramatic changes, and therefore so is the nation that this physical environment supports. As one historian has observed, the 'discipline of history exists on the assumption that our past, present, and future are connected by a certain continuity of human experience', but climate change threatens those continuities. In the case of Japan, climate change has underwritten a tumultuous half-century, in which natural forces, from seismic events to Pacific super storms, interface with unnatural ones, such as coastal settlement patterns and land reclamation, to set the tone for Japan's twenty-first century prospects.

SHIFTING NATURES

In Japan, centuries of philosophical rumination have sought to discern how the country's island nature drives its culture. In the early twentieth century, the most influential voice in this discussion was the philosopher Watsuji Tetsurô (1889–1960). Responding to such European giants as Martin Heidegger (1889–1976), Watsuji, in his masterpiece *Fûdo* (Climate and culture, 1935), sought to link geographic space with historical time as critical co-determinants in the development of national cultures. Watsuji sought to reconstruct Japanese culture from its natural foundations, emphasizing the interplay between climate and human communities. Watsuji assumed that people never transcend their environments, and that topography, climate, soil, water, plants, and animals synchronize to shape a nation's cultural evolution. It was not just about time, as Heidegger had suggested in his influential *Sein und Zeit* (Being and time, 1927), but about the basic material nature of place. Early on, Watsuji had concluded that, 'all inquiries into the culture of Japan must in their final reduction go back to the study of her nature'.

But the climatological constant of Watsuji's philosophy is upended by 'climate change' and rising sea levels. Globally, sea levels have started rising because of both thermal expansion (water expands when it warms) and the melting of terrestrial water reservoirs (such as glaciers, ice caps, and ice sheets), changing the actual volume of ocean waters. Local processes, such as ocean circulation and atmospheric pressure, as well as tectonic movement and subsidence and sedimentation, exaggerate ocean-volume increases to further alter sea levels. In part, such climatologic transformations underpin the birth of the Anthropocene Epoch, where man-made forces outweigh natural forces in creating features on Earth's dynamic surface.

Using tide gauges and satellite altimetry, scientists have tracked recent changes in sea levels that have paralleled the industrialization of Japan and other nations. It appears that for much of human history to 1900 CE, ocean levels remained relatively stable, making it possible for such philosophers as Watsuji to link cultural development to a relatively unchanging topography and climate. Prior to that time, during the Pleistocene Epoch (approximately 2,588,000 to 11,700 YBP), sea levels fluctuated wildly, rising some 120 metres. By the mid-Holocene Epoch (11,700 YBP), however, sea levels stabilized, in large part because of the broader climatological stability that made agriculture and the development of human civilizations possible. But industrialization destabilized the Holocene climate bubble. After 1900 CE, because of thermal expansion and glacial melting, sea levels have risen discernibly, increasing as industrialization spread around the globe. Between 1900 and 1993, sea levels rose on average 1.7 millimetres per year. After 1993, that number increased to 3 millimetres per year. Scientists for the Intergovernmental Panel for Climate Change (IPCC) speculate that by 2090 that number will increase to 4 millimetres per year.

More devastating than 'mean' sea level changes are 'extreme' ones because they exaggerate the destructive capabilities of natural disasters, events to which Japan is prone. Extreme sea level events are generated by tsunami, which are not directly related to climate change but rather tectonic shifts and storm surges generated by typhoons and other storms. The frequency and intensity of such extreme sea level events parallel the increase of the mean sea level. In other words, as the average sea level has increased during the twentieth century, so has the frequency and intensity of extreme storm surges and the devastation caused by tsunami, which are made more dangerous as sea levels increase. As IPCC scientists observe, 'climate change may be perceived most through the impacts of extremes', including the ferocity of Pacific storms. Since the 1950s, western North Pacific storms, those that impact Japan directly, have almost doubled their power dissipation index (PDI) value, with an increase of about 30 per cent in the number of Category 4 and 5 storms since 1990. Rising ocean temperatures, caused by global warming, influence El Niño southern oscillation (ENSO) to further exacerbate storm intensity. In the second half of the twentieth century, Japan has witnessed an increase in extra-tropical cyclones, as well as dangerous tropical storms and hurricanes. During this time Japan's 1000 mm to 2000 mm (40–80 inches) average annual rainfall has not changed dramatically, but the pattern of that precipitation has changed. Since the times of the Heian courtiers, Japan's predictable 'plum rains' have provided timely precipitation and shaped the rhythms of Japanese aesthetics, much as Watsuji insisted it did. But now Japan's rainfall is far more variable and harder to predict, meaning that the 'climate' of Watsuji's philosophy is no longer a constant. Rather, it is transforming, paralleling changing natural and historical landscapes.

Rising sea levels have the potential to cause economic damage and loss of life in some of Japan's most populated areas, including some twenty-three wards in metropolitan Tokyo, which engineers constructed on low-lying land. Industrial sectors ranging from manufacturing and energy production to fishing and recreation are focused along Japan's low-lying coastal areas, making the threat of sea level rise potentially catastrophic to Japan's economy. On its own, Tokyo boasts about 28 per cent of Japan's industrial output, 39 per cent of its wholesale businesses, nearly half of Japan's college students, 85 per cent of its foreign companies, and over half of the total employees in Japan's information industry. If Nagoya and Osaka, major cities also built on low-lying coastal areas that have been shaken by earthquakes and swept by tsunami in the past, are included in these statistics, the economic percentages are overwhelming. The bulk of Japan's industrial sector resides in coastal areas vulnerable to sea level increases.

Japan has a long coastline when compared to the country's total land size, some 34,390 kilometres (21,369 miles), making it particularly vulnerable to rising sea levels, extreme weather events, and tsunamis. Of the total land size, some 72 per cent of the country is a mountainous spine, meaning that Japan's population tends to be concentrated on the flatlands near the coast. Presently, about 11 million people, or about 10 per cent of the total population, live in flood-prone areas. The majority of Japan's coastline is a built environment, some of it characterized by sea walls, breakwaters, and other forms of protection, but much of it is completely exposed to surrounding seas. In industrial areas the numbers are staggering: 95 per cent of Osaka Bay, for example, is artificial, with only small pockets of the once-celebrated white sand and pine beaches, such as around Suma. Japan's coasts are predominantly built environments.

THE ARTIFICIAL NATURE OF EXTREME EVENTS

One historian has observed that not only do so-called 'natural disasters' bear overwhelming man-made components, but that politicians and planners 'view these events as purely natural in an effort to justify a set of responses that has proved both environmentally unsound, and socially, if not morally, bankrupt'. It is a harsh indictment, but certainly this reasoning echoes the Japanese government's response to the triple disaster – the earthquake, tsunami, and nuclear meltdown on 11 March 2011 – where the natural and unforeseeable aspects of the calamity, the ones that made it a 'thousand-year disaster', are used to justify not only government ineptitude, particularly with regards to oversight of the nuclear power industry, but also to legitimize further expansion of nuclear power in Japan. However, natural disasters do not 'just happen', and they are not disinterested, 'morally inert' catastrophes. Rather, they are historically constructed on several levels, and with climate change and sea level rise, the nature of the super storms themselves bears the human fingerprints of past choices and policy decisions.

As IPCC scientists demonstrate, extreme coastal events, including super storms and tsunami, parallel mean sea level increases. As the average sea levels increase, so do the power of storms, storm surges, and waves to flood, kill, and endanger property and other economic assets. Moreover, these same scientists have demonstrated that since the 1950s, western North Pacific storms have increased their PDI values, a trend that parallels climate change. Such storms have intensified with sea level changes, and they will only become more ferocious in the future as oceans continue to warm and sea levels rise. Scientists estimate that, in Japan at present, some 861 km² (332 square miles) of land are below the mean high water level, with about two million inhabitants and ¥54 trillion in assets in these vulnerable low-lying areas. When sea levels rise one metre, as they are predicted to do by century's end, land below the mean high water level will increase to 2,340 km²

(903 square miles) or nearly triple its present size. The population of this area will increase to over 4 million with assets estimated at ¥109 trillion. Furthermore, the flood-prone areas of Japan will increase from 6,270 km² (2,420 square miles) to 8,900 km² (3,436 square miles) with more than 15 million people in danger. With tsunami, waves can reach more than 20 metres (65 feet) in height depending upon local conditions, meaning that the mischief from sea level rise would be amplified even further in cases of offshore earthquakes.

When it comes to storms, serious ones have names of their own and therefore, as historical actors, require some biographical exploration. In Earth's conditions during the Anthropocene Epoch, sea level rise, ocean warming, and coastal development have combined to exaggerate storm intensities, and the damage caused by storm surges, torrential rains, and high winds has been exacerbated as well. The decade after the Pacific War witnessed several major typhoons, but two storms in particular, Typhoon Ida (better known as Typhoon Kanagawa in Japan) and Typhoon Vera, contained barometric pressure, wind velocity readings, casualties, and property damage that were reflective of the super storms of the Anthropocene Epoch.

On the nights of September 26 and 27, 1958, Typhoon Ida (Figure 24) pounded Japan near the town of Kanagawa with 190 km/h (118 mph) winds, gusting to 258 km/h (160 mph), and the accompanying heavy precipitation caused destructive mudslides throughout central Japan. The storm had formed in the western Pacific near Guam, and then gathered strength as it moved across warm waters towards Japan. On 24 September, when Hurricane Hunter aircraft used dropsonde (an expendable weather-measuring device designed by the US National Center for Atmospheric Research) to take measurements, they read a barometric pressure of 877 mb (millibars), or 25.9 inHg (inches of mercury), as well as estimated peak winds of 325 km/h (200 mph). These readings made Typhoon Ida the strongest storm on record. Typhoon Ida hit Japan with a hard wallop. Once the Kano, Meguro, and Arakawa rivers spilled over their banks, some 2,118 buildings were destroyed or washed away. One-metre tide surges flooded more than 48,562 hectares (120,000 acres) of rice paddies in the area,

24 The eye of Typhoon Ida.

causing widespread destruction. Typhoon Ida dropped almost
430 mm (17 inches) of rainfall on Tokyo, which was the highest
daily total since recordkeeping began in 1876. In the end, the storm
claimed some 1,269 lives, left tens of thousands of people homeless,
and caused $50 million in damages. It was the first of twin super
storms that initiated Japan to the extreme weather of the
Anthropocene Epoch.

Exactly one year later, Typhoon Vera savaged Ise Bay in central
Japan, near the highly industrialized city of Nagoya. When Vera
made landfall, its winds exceeded 193 km/h (130 mph), and the
twelve inches of rain per day caused widespread mudslides, which
crushed or washed away over 36,000 buildings. A six-metre (17
foot) storm surge inundated Ise Bay, and washed ashore seven
ships, including a formidable 7,412-ton British freighter. Thirty-
foot waves sank some twenty-five fishing boats that attempted to
ride out the storm, killing nearly fifty seafarers. In the end, Typhoon
Vera claimed 5,159 lives and left one million homeless. Damages

were estimated at $2 billion, making Vera the most destructive storm in modern Japan's history. Storm surges contributed much of the destructive power of both these super storms, as did the warming oceans that caused the storms to intensify as they moved towards Japan.

Not just storms, but also tsunami stand to be influenced by sea level changes. As we have seen, Japan is a seismically active piece of real estate, and the nineteenth and twentieth centuries have seen their share of destructive earthquakes, many of them with accompanying tsunamis. The best-documented earthquakes remain the Ansei quake (1854–55), the Nôbi quake in central Japan (1891), the Meiji-Sanriku quake (1896), the Great Kantô earthquake (1923) of Yokohama and Tokyo, and the Great Hanshin-Awaji earthquake of 1995. Because the Ansei temblor occurred during the Tokugawa period (1603–1868), the records for this disaster took the form of hundreds of woodblock prints depicting a catfish with merchants and government officials balanced on its slippery back. When the catfish writhed and swung its tail, the Earth shook, often relieving the wealthy of their riches, depicted in the form of gold coins falling from the sky. In the tumultuous times of the mid-nineteenth century, when, as we have seen, 'pressure from abroad and disorder from within' had weakened the Edo *bakufu* to the point of collapse, such earthquakes and their social interpretation, seen as a redistribution of wealth by many, proved threatening to Tokugawa legitimacy. The three successive quakes caused massive tsunami, fires, and mayhem, resulting in some 17,000 deaths; but the political resonances might have been the real legacy of the Ansei quake, as the Tokugawa regime fell about a decade later.

The Nôbi earthquake occurred during the Meiji period. The quake measured at a magnitude 8.0, making it the largest inland earthquake in Japanese history. It claimed around 7,000 lives, and demolished many of the modern brick buildings so carefully erected by Meiji reformers. In Osaka and elsewhere, most of the traditional wooden houses withstood the 28 October 1891 temblor, but the Naniwa cotton mill, a 'three-storey red brick building in the usual English factory style', as one newspaper described it, totally collapsed, the only building in Osaka to do so. The building, which had 'only been standing a few months', crushed twenty-one people when it collapsed. As reported, it was not only the Naniwa cotton mill that collapsed, but also 'all the other foreign-built factories were more or less damaged', as were many of the brick homes in the foreign concessions. Similarly, as another newspaper reported, in Nagoya, the 'magnificent brick buildings', such as the Nagoya Post Office, crumbled, but the traditional Japanese wooden ones survived. That foreign brick buildings collapsed in this seismic disaster exposed the man-made elements of the natural event.

On 1 September 1923, when the Great Kantô Earthquake turned much of Tokyo and Yokohama to burning rubble, the shifting seismic fault lines exposed jarring social divisions within Japan's new imperial order, resulting in racial violence throughout the Tokyo area. The resourceful Gotô Shinpei (1857–1929), a man who cut his teeth as a colonial administrator in Taiwan and as mayor of Tokyo, oversaw the post-disaster recovery, which, with the help of the imperial army, proceeded quickly and efficiently, even if the military was brandished unnecessarily. Originally Gotô, with the help of US historian and urban planner Charles A. Beard (1874–1948), had sought to transform Tokyo's burned-out areas into a model modern built environment, but political opponents foiled his ambitions. Regardless, the quake exposed the underbelly of imperial Japan. The day after the quake, a Tokyo newspaper reported that, 'Koreans and socialists were planning a rebellious and treacherous plot. We urge the citizens to cooperate with the military and the police to guard against Koreans.' Simultaneously, the imperial navy moved warships to the Korean peninsula. With Japan's ethnic nationalism and racial anxieties fanning the flames, Japan's 1923 seismic disaster quickly transformed into a social one. For the next several days, after rumours spread of Koreans setting fires and poisoning the city's water supply, vigilantes roamed the streets of Tokyo, dispatching 'Koreans' and 'Bolsheviks'. Despite moments of international cooperation and goodwill, the legacy of the Great Kantô Earthquake marks the rise of Japanese militarism, as much as the rhetoric of social renewal and recovery. The natural disaster portended for many the need for change in the unnatural world of human civilization. As the Taishô emperor (1879–1926) pronounced in the aftermath of the Great Kantô Earthquake, 'In recent years much progress has been made in science and human wisdom. At the same time frivolous and extravagant habits have set in ... If [they] are not checked now, the future of the country, we fear, is dark, the disaster that has befallen the Japanese people being severe.'

Historically, most of Japan's major earthquakes have occurred offshore and hence have generated tsunami. The Tônankai earthquake of 7 December 1944, caused extensive damage along the coast of Wakayama prefecture and the Tôkai region. Some 1,223 souls lost their lives in the temblor and the accompanying 8-metre (26 feet) tsunami, which also washed away, destroyed, or badly damaged 73,000 homes. Then, on 20 December 1946, the magnitude 8.1 Nankaidô quake shook the region around southern Honshu and Shikoku Islands. Its tsunami reached maximum heights of 6 metres (20 feet), killing thousands of people and destroying 36,000 homes. Many of Japan's most devastating off-shore temblors have occurred east of the Sanriku coast of north-eastern Japan, along the Japan trench subduction area. The Japan trench is created as the Pacific plate subducts underneath the Okhotsk plate off the Sanriku coast, a movement that causes most of northeastern Japan's worst quakes and tsunami. In the Meiji period, the Sanriku earthquake of 15 June 1896 signalled the devastation that northeastern shakers could potentially cause, par-ticularly with their accompanying tsunami. The quake possessed a magnitude of 8.5 and generated tsunami with peak heights of 25 metres (80 feet), some of which even reached the California coast. Some 22,000 people died as a result of the quake and tsunami, and it destroyed 10,000 homes, leaving scores without shelter. Then, on 2 March 1933, another Sanriku earthquake rocked the northeastern coast. This one possessed a magnitude of 8.4 and the accompanying tsunami washed away thousands of homes. The maximum tsunami height was 28.7 metres (94 feet), and caused damage as far away as Hawai'i.

Both of these Sanriku quakes, devastating as they were, paled in comparison to the 11 March 2011, mega-quake, with its magnitude of 9.0. Thrust faulting near the Japan trench subduction zone caused the disaster, which was the worst on record in a country frequently visited by seismic disasters. The important point is that super storms and seismic events, with their accompanying tsunami, have been an important part of Japan's modern experience. As Japan turns to face a future characterized by climate change and sea level rise, the unnatural violence of such natural disasters only promises to become more severe.

On 9 March 2011, two days before the Great Eastern Japan Earthquake struck, several unnerving foreshocks jolted such northern cities as Sendai, one of them registering magnitude 7.2. On 11 March, several more powerful foreshocks jolted northeastern Japan until the main mega-thrust shook the region fifteen minutes before three o'clock in the afternoon. Hundreds of brutal aftershocks followed the massive earthquake, continuing for years following the disaster. Geologically, as a result of the mega-thrust, Japan's main island of Honshu moved east 2.4 metres (8 feet), and the quake actually shifted Earth's axis by as much as 25 centimetres (10 inches). It was the most powerful earthquake ever recorded in Japan and the fifth most powerful in the world since modern recordkeeping started in 1900. The epicentre of the mega-thrust originated near the Japan trench, where the Pacific plate subducts under Japan's main island of Honshu, some 72 kilometres (45 miles) east of Miyagi Peninsula; the hypocentre, basically the earthquake's 'ground zero', was at a relatively shallow depth of 32 kilometres (20 miles). As a result of the temblor, tsunami waves of over 40 metres (133 feet) made landfall at Iwate prefecture and, in some instances, travelled as far as 10 km (6 miles) inland to wreak extensive havoc in low-lying communities.

All these geological and seismic factors contributed to the natural capacity of the Great Eastern Japan Earthquake (Map 4). Other than the effect that sea level increases might have had, the earthquake and tsunami originated beyond the hands of people. The earthquake was naturally occurring. But once the waves of shaking earth and the colossal tsunami's wall of water reached the eastern coast of Japan, the natural disaster immediately became a man-made one, destroying or washing away economic development schemes, class divisions, sea walls, retail stores, public schools, subsidized fishing ports, greenhouses, and other artefacts of

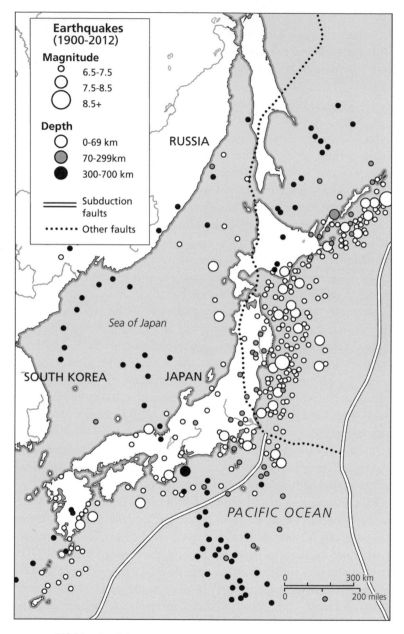

4 USGS seismicity map, 1900–2012

Japanese policies and decision-making. Irrigation canals, ports, parking lots, and streets all channelled the water once it made landfall. The local ancestors of some northeastern communities, such as those of Yoshihama village in Iwate prefecture, had relocated their village from low-lying areas to higher ground after the previous northeastern tsunami disasters of 1896 and 1933. Instead of train stations, schools, and houses, all of which Yoshihama villagers relocated to higher ground, the raging tsunami met paddy lands, which replicated natural marshlands and mitigated the tsunami's damage. Consequently, only one person in the village died on 11 March 2013. But such lessons were hard learned. In 1896, Yoshihama had lost some 204 inhabitants, most of them swept away as they attended a wedding ceremony in the low-lying coastal areas. Following 1896, the Yoshihama headman incentivized building homes in the surrounding hills, at higher elevation, which paid off in 1933 when only seventeen people perished as a result of that disaster. In other nearby villages, many folks, their memories too short, had started encroaching on low-lying lands, building houses near paddy fields as the 1896 and 1933 tragedies sank below a generational horizon. Unfortunately, these villages paid a heavy toll on 11 March 2011 (Figure 25).

One such village was Minami Sanriku, which stood directly in the path of the 2011 tsunami. Twelve-metre (40-foot) waves pummelled the town, nearly completely destroying it and washing away almost a tenth of its inhabitants. What was once a fishing town had been laid waste by the tsunami. One of the most enduring images from the tsunami is the mayor of Minami Sanriku clinging to the top of the government building, one of the ten out of 130 people in the building who survived the thrashing waves and flood surge. The tsunami had devastated a 500-kilometre (310-mile) stretch of the Japanese coast, obliterating many communities and killing close to 20,000 people. When the wave came ashore, it savaged a part of Japan already reeling from neglect and depopulation. Some experts estimated that the northeast stood to lose as much as 20 per cent of its population by 2025. Grimly, the tsunami accelerated the depopulation process by washing nearly 20,000 people out to sea.

25 Little girl returns to the site of her home after the 11 March 2011
tsunami.

As it turned out, the earthquake and tsunami were only the
beginning of Japan's 11 March nightmare. Three nuclear reactors
melted down at the Fukushima Daiichi complex run by Tokyo
Electric Power Company (TEPCO), and saturated nearby communities with dangerous levels of radiation, rendering many of them
uninhabitable for generations. To put this in the perspective of
Japan's nuclear experiences, the Japanese government estimated
that the meltdown had produced 170 times more cesium 137 and
twice the amount of strontium than the US military released over
Hiroshima in the closing days of the Pacific War. Within days after
the earthquake and tsunami, Japanese became familiar with specialized units of measurement, such as microsieverts and bec-
querels, as well as such dangerous material as cesium and
strontium. Most of the 110,000 people whom the government
evacuated from the area own homes that would sicken them if
they ever decided to return. The radioactive material has turned
up everywhere: in water supplies, day care centres, breast milk,
baby formula, lake smelt, beef, and green tea. Fukushima radiation
permeated Japan's national food chain, and it was not long before
government officials had detected radiation in every Japanese

prefecture, including distant Okinawa. Some half of the children in Fukushima had internal radiation, threatening serious health problems, including dangerous cancers. Within two years after the triple disaster, physicians had already detected higher than normal rates of thyroid cancer in Fukushima's children, with nearly half of them showing evidence of thyroid cysts (though some of this evidence is disputed).

In some respects, the government responded quickly. Immediately, it established a Crisis Management Centre and Disaster Countermeasures Headquarters and prefectural governors rapidly requested aid from Japan's Self-Defence Forces (SDF). Prime Minister Kan Naoto (b. 1946) also assumed control of TEPCO for limited periods, when the giant utility failed to report the hydrogen explosion at the Fukushima complex. He mobilized the SDF to the 'maximum level', and within three days some 100,000 Japanese troops, about half of Japan's standing military, were engaged in search and rescue operations throughout the northeast. SDF distributed nearly 5 million meals and 30,000 tons of water, as well as gathered the corpses of more than 8,000 fellow citizens.

But there were also massive failures, and a chorus of voices criticized Prime Minister Kan as 'reckless' and 'incompetent' after he failed to convene the National Security Council or include military officers in his emergency management centres. Japanese officials estimated that the cost of the disaster was ¥16.9 trillion, while Standard & Poor's put the number closer to ¥50 trillion. The Japanese economy felt the disaster in a number of ways. For example, the automaker Toyota suspended production in the US and Europe, and its 2011 sales declined by over 30 per cent. More broadly, as a result of the triple disaster the Japanese economy declined by nearly 4 per cent in the first quarter of 2011 and then an additional 1.3 per cent in the second quarter. Fearing radiation-saturated Japanese food products, many foreign countries restricted Japanese imports, and Japanese food exports consequently declined by over 8 per cent. But that did not stop foreign nations, many of them neighbours, from dispatching aid and relief teams. China had accepted Japanese aid, including from the SDF, after a devastating 2008 earthquake in Sichuan, and returned the favour in 2011 by dispatching a fifteen-person rescue team and a pledge of $4.5

million in assistance. The people of South Korea also responded quickly, with the Korean Red Cross generating some $19 million for victims in the northeast. Taiwanese charities raised $175 million in assistance. In the immediate aftermath of the triple disaster, some of Japan's most sensitive regional rivalries were set aside to assist the reeling island nation.

The US sent around $630 million in aid to northeastern Japan's disaster victims, while the US military played a prominent support role immediately after the disaster. When the quake and tsunami struck, the Nimitz-class carrier USS *Ronald Reagan* had been holding joint exercises with South Korea, but it was quickly redeployed to northeastern Japan. It hovered off the coast on 13 March, where it served as a forward base for relief efforts, including transporting and refuelling SDF units. In what came to be named 'Operation Tomodachi (Friendship)', the US military provided radiation-immune robots to assess the damage at the Fukushima Daiichi nuclear plant. But there were also critics of the US response, including the right-wing cartoonist Kobayashi Yoshinori (b. 1953). He pointed out that 'Operation Tomodachi' cost only a small fraction of the 'Host Nation Support' that the US receives from the Japanese government for military bases. He also characterized the US as a 'heartless friend' when he learned that the *Ronald Reagan* had relocated to safety after the hydrogen explosion at the Fukushima Daiichi reactor.

To many, the triple disaster signalled the need for a Japanese awakening after the 'lost decades' of recession and disaffection. Recall from Chapter 3, Kamo no Chôme, the medieval hermit, who described an earthquake and tsunami so savage that the 'sea surged up and overwhelmed the land'. Placing the natural disaster in the unnatural context of his age, he concluded that, in the wake of the temblor, the people became 'convinced of the impermanence of all earthly things', and started to 'talk of the evil of attachment to them, and of the impurity of their hearts'. His thoughts represented a Buddhist understanding of earthquake and tsunami, one in which, as he concluded, 'all the difficulties of life spring from this fleeting evanescent nature of man and his habitation'. Similarly, as conservative Tokyo governor Ishihara Shintarô (b. 1932) explained, the triple disaster served as an opportunity to 'wash away the greed' of contemporary Japanese society, while left-leaning scientists viewed the disaster as the 'beginning of a new chapter in Japanese history'. Immediately, the rhetoric of disaster and recovery became palpable in Japan. As Social Democrat Abe Tomoko (b. 1948) explained, 'all of Japan, not just Tohoku – needs a recovery'. Not only do natural disasters frequently have man-made attributes, but they also signal crises in the world of men.

At least one government official has described Japanese political and economic institutions as afflicted with a 'geriatric disease', and observed that disaster recovery offered an opportunity to 'generate a new nation'. A professor in Tokyo viewed the triple disaster as an opportunity to 'change our thinking, our civilization'. Philosopher Umehara Takeshi (b. 1925), a prominent Japanese essentialist, mobilized the triple disaster to moralize about the need for Japan to return to a simpler manner of living, one reminiscent of the Jômon hunting cultures discussed in the first chapter. He referred to the triple disaster as a 'civilizational disaster', one that exposed the limits of the European Enlightenment and the commensurate 'arrogant' war against nature. Harkening back to a mythologized past, Japan needed to 'return to coexistence with nature', he explained, one rooted in Buddhist altruism. Local leaders evoked the triple disaster when they beseeched communities to establish 'bonds' of 'human contact' that could engender 'solidarity'. In some respects, it was not surprising when the head abbot of the Kiyomizu Temple in Kyoto chose 'bond' as the *kanji* character of the year in 2011. Heroes also played a role in re-establishing a lost sense of community in Japan. Prominent were the 'Fukushima Fifty', workers who, risking their own health, returned to the Fukushima Daiichi reactor to limit the potential damage. One newspaper report claimed, 'bearing the burdens of uncertainty, they continue to battle an unseen enemy'.

Immediately after the triple disaster, the term that came to characterize discussions of the event was 'unimaginable'. Like using 'natural' to describe disasters, 'unimaginable' served to place the earthquake and tsunami, and more importantly, the meltdown at Fukushima Daiichi, outside of Japanese decision-making regarding energy choices. As one TEPCO manager explained, the 'accident at

Fukushima Daiichi was caused by a tsunami far beyond the design basis'. He characterized the event as an 'unforeseeable accident'. One Tokyo University professor, who specialized in fields he labelled 'dangerology' and 'failureology', criticized experts for constantly evoking the term 'unimaginable' to describe the triple disaster. 'Imagining disasters is the responsibility of experts', he insisted. Yosano Kaoru, a former government official and nuclear industry employee, explained of the triple disaster that 'there is no explaining God's work' and insisted nuclear power is safe. He charged that it was 'unjust' to make TEPCO pay for an 'abnormal' natural disaster. 'Because the incident was well beyond any scientifically anticipated scale', he reasoned, 'there is no merit in reflecting on it'.

But some did start reflecting on the triple disaster, particularly those in Japan's lively anti-nuclear movement. In the post-war years, Japan had steered a course towards a nuclear future, even as memories of Hiroshima and Nagasaki were still quite fresh. In 1954, the Liberal Democratic Party had approved the first atomic power budget of ¥250 million. Although this initial budget proved modest, throughout the post-war years Japan continued to spend more and more on nuclear power. Between 1970 and 2007, the Japanese government spent ¥10 trillion on nuclear power, approximately one third of all public-sector energy spending and 95 per cent of the national budget for energy research and development. The Ministry of International Trade and Industry had established 'public policy companies' to help private firms develop nuclear power, in effect socializing the heavy cost of starting nuclear power plants. Toshiba worked with General Electric, for example, while Mitsubishi worked with Westinghouse. By the mid-1980s, all of Japan's utilities, with the exception of Okinawa Electric Power Company, operated nuclear power plants. Prior to the triple disaster, nuclear power plants generated about 30 per cent of Japan's electricity, slightly less than liquefied natural gas. But after 2011, critics renewed their attacks on the reeling industry. Among the many problems they identified was the disposal and storage of spent fuel. Already by the 1970s, Japanese nuclear reactors produced more spent fuel than they could reprocess.

One byproduct of uranium reprocessing, plutonium, has proven particularly dangerous and difficult to store, and can also be turned into weapons-grade material. Recently, Japan has faced international pressure over its eight tons of separated plutonium stored at the Rokkasho reprocessing plant in Aomori prefecture, representing enough to make some 1,000 nuclear warheads (although 315 kilograms [700 pounds] of weapons-grade plutonium was returned to the US in 2014). Rokkasho, at ¥2.2 trillion and counting, has proved an enormous money sink, but to many energy experts the financial risk is acceptable given that the reprocessed uranium and plutonium promises to fuel Japan's nuclear power plants until the middle of the twenty-first century. Japan Nuclear Fuel Limited (JNFL) operates Rokkasho, and the largest shareholder for JNFL is TEPCO, the operator of the polluting Fukushima Daiichi plant. Rokkasho's main purpose is to make MOX fuel (mixed oxide fuel), often consisting of a plutonium and uranium blend that experts hope can be used in a new generation of heavy water reactors. However, adequate technology has proven elusive, as has the public appetite for nuclear energy, leaving Japan with dangerous stores of plutonium that threaten to proliferate. As of this writing, all but two of Japan's nuclear reactors remained shut down, so the future of the entire Rokkasho project is in doubt.

Mistakes and mishaps also riddled Japan's nuclear power industry. By 2007, Japan's utilities reported that ninety-seven mishaps had occurred, including critical accidents at the Fukushima Daiichi plant in 1978 and 1989. In 1995, a sodium leak occurred at a reactor operated by the Power Reactor and Nuclear Fuel Corporation. Four years later, a nearly daylong critical accident occurred at a reactor in Tôkai, during which two workers died of radiation exposure. Protesters have become brazen in their not-unreasonable demands. Galvanized by safety concerns after the triple disaster, Fukushima parents, while protesting against the Education Ministry decision to raise the maximum allowable radiation exposure for schoolchildren by 2,000 per cent, dumped bags of playground sand on the desks of officials. They enquired whether they would let their children play in it. In September 2011, Nobel Laureate Ôe Kenzaburô (b. 1935) led a large protest at the Meiji Shrine in Tokyo, where demonstrators paraded signs that read, 'Sayonara Nuclear Power'. Later, in July 2012, an anti-nuclear demonstration in Yoyogi Park, Tokyo, attracted about 170,000 people. Clearly, the triple disaster had galvanized anti-nuclear sentiments in the one country that has experienced the destructive power of nuclear weaponry.

EPILOGUE

Japan faces many challenges today. Some of them, such as foreign policy challenges vis-à-vis China and Korea, are rooted in historical decisions about the conduct of war and the framing of peace. Japan and its neighbours still struggle with the legacies of the Pacific War, even though the generation that fought it is largely gone. In 2014, after Prime Minister Abe Shinzô (b. 1954) visited Yasukuni, the Tokyo shrine interring Japan's war dead, including fourteen 'Class A' war criminals, the Chinese foreign minister responded by explaining that Abe was not welcome to visit China anymore. He continued, 'Abe's hypocrisy in his claims of prioritizing relations with China and hopes for dialogue with the Chinese leaders has been fully revealed.' Of the war criminals interred at the Yasukuni shrine, the minister explained, 'Their hands are covered with the blood of the victimized peoples. They are fascists. They are the Nazis of Asia.' As these comments illustrate, tensions over Japan's 'Greater East Asian War' continue to torture relations between Japan and its Asian neighbours, defining politics and foreign relations in this volatile part of the world.

Like all life on Earth, Japan also faces challenges regarding climate change and rising sea levels. As of this writing, as Earth's climate warms as a result of greenhouse gases trapped in the atmosphere, the future of the entire globe, including its human and non-human inhabitants, is united by a common threat, making energy-related chapters in any industrial nation's history important ones. According to the US Environmental Protection Agency's (EPA) climate change projections, depending on future levels of greenhouse gases, Earth's global temperatures could rise 11 degrees by 2100. This means that from the vantage point of 2014, within about the same time that elapsed between the Meiji Restoration and the atomic bombing of Hiroshima and

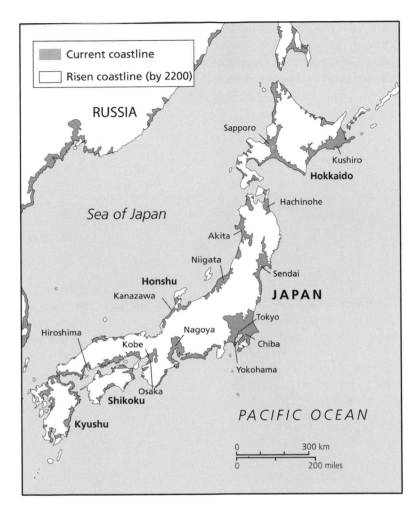

5 The effect of rising sea levels on Japan by century's end

Nagasaki, it is likely that humans will cause catastrophic damage to the planet because of the turn to non-renewable fossil fuels. For Japan, or any industrialized nation for that matter, any historical policies or decisions that facilitated increasing greenhouse gases require analysis, because melting icecaps and glaciers seriously threaten Japan's heavily populated coastlines. Nearly 100 million people, or about 80 per cent, of Japan's present population is considered coastal, making any discussion of sea level change an important one (Map 5).

How Japan will face these multiple challenges is still unknown. But the island country's actions will be important because they will serve as a bellwether for all of us as we navigate the choppy waters of the twenty-first century.

GLOSSARY

Amaterasu Ômikami 天照大御神:	The Sun Goddess that served as the tutelary deity of the imperial household.
Anthropocene Epoch:	The geologic epoch following the Holocene Epoch, characterized by the overwhelming presence of litho-stratigraphic and bio-stratigraphic signatures of human beings, rather than naturally occurring forces. The advent of the Anthropocene coincides with the Industrial Revolution.
bakufu 幕府:	Literally 'tent governments', this term refers to samurai governments in Kamakura, Kyoto, and Edo.
chonmage 丁髷:	A common samurai hairstyle of the Edo period.
daimyô 大名:	A samurai lord of the Edo period who oversaw a domain.
dogû 土偶:	Earthenware figurines from Jômon archaeological phase.
Emishi 蝦夷:	Also read 'Ezo', this term referred to Epi-Jômon groups in northeastern Japan that existed outside the sphere of the establishment of imperial government in western and central Japan.
fumie 踏み絵:	'Stepping on the image' was a technique used by Edo officials to ferret out Christians from villages by making suspected Christians step on a sacred image.
gekokujô 下克上:	The 'low rising against the high' is a reference to the social and political turmoil of the Warring States period.

gun'eki 軍役: The theoretical early modern conscription military system wherein domain lords pledged men and weapons in relation to the projected yield, gauged through cadastral surveys, of their cultivated land.

haiku 俳句: A form of seventeen-syllable poetry, usually in 5–7–5 order, made popular by Matsuo Bashô in the early modern period.

hakama 袴: Traditional Japanese pants.

Inari shrine 稲荷神社: Inari shrines and the accompanying Inari *kami*, often embodied by a red fox, represent a variety of Shinto that revolves around agriculture and industry. Inari shrines are often placed near agricultural fields.

Jimintô 自民党: The conservative 'Liberal Democratic Party', formerly established in 1955, governed Japan throughout the post-war period, with the exception of eleven months in 1993–4 and 2009–12.

jitô 地頭: Medieval stewards who governed *shôen* estates at the behest of the Kamakura and Ashikaga *bakufu*.

Jiyûtô 自由党: The 'Liberal Party', formally established in 1881 by Itagaki Taisuke and Gotô Shôjirô. It emerged from the Popular Rights Movement and called for the establishment of a National Assembly.

Jômon culture 縄文: An archaeological phase that occurred on the Japanese archipelago between 14,500 and 300 BCE and is designated by cord markings on pottery and hunting and gathering subsistence patterns.

kaikoku 開国: The 'open the country' position pursued by the Edo *bakufu* following the arrival of Matthew C. Perry in 1853. The 'open the country' position contrasted with the 'revere the emperor, expel the barbarian', or *sonnô jôi*, slogan expounded by imperial loyalists.

kana かな: Japanese vernacular syllabic script developed predominantly by women in the Heian period and used in such classical poetry styles as *waka*. Today, *kana* takes the form of *katakana* and *hiragana* scripts.

kanji 漢字: Chinese syllabic script comprised of pictographs and ideographs and today used with *katakana* and *hiragana* in Japanese writing.

kanpaku 関白:
The executive imperial adviser, the emperor bestowed the 'regent' title on some of the most powerful men in the realm, including Fujiwara no Michinaga and Toyotomi Hideyoshi.

karate 空手:
Literally 'empty hands', the term denotes a traditional Okinawan martial arts form imported from China. In Okinawa, the characters for the fighting form had been *tôdi* 唐手, but imperial Japanese found the association with China unpalatable so the *kanji* was changed to reflect the weaponless combat technique.

Kenseitô 憲政党:
The 'Constitutional Party', which was established in 1898 after the merger of the Shinpotô and Jiyûtô political parties.

kôbugattai 公武合体:
The 'union of imperial court and Edo *bakufu*' policy pursued after the Sakuradamon Incident and the assassination of Ii Naosuke.

Kofun 古墳:
An archaeological phase that occurred on the Japanese archipelago between 250 and 700, after the Yayoi phase, and designated by the emergence of large burial tombs.

kôgai 公害:
Literally 'public damage', this is the common term for all forms of environmental pollution. Defined in 1967 as 'any situation in which human health and the living environment are damaged by air pollution, water pollution, soil pollution, noise, vibration, ground subsidence, and offensive odours, which arise over a considerable area as a result of industrial or other human activity'.

kokutai 国体:
Nationalistic terminology that refers to the 'national essence of Japan'. Nativist scholars of the early modern period pushed the concept, as did later modern nationalists who described the unique qualities of the Japanese imperial state. The *kanji* characters literally mean 'national body'.

kurobune 黒船:
'Black ships' refers to the steam-powered vessels of Commodore Matthew C. Perry's East India Squadron during his expedition to Japan in 1853.

Nanbanjin 南蛮人:
A reference to sixteenth-century Portuguese and other Europeans who arrived in southern Japan. The term means 'Southern Barbarians'.

*Nihon*日本: The Japanese name for Japan (the formal is
                            Nippon), the term means 'originated in the sun'
                            and references the role of Amaterasu Ômikami,
                            the Sun Goddess, and the mythical founding of
                            the country.

ofudafuri 御札降り: When Ise shrine talismans reportedly fell from the
                            sky in the nineteenth century, portending the fall of
                            the Edo *bakufu* and the imperial restoration.

ôkimi 大王: Regional kings, sometimes called *daiô*, that
                            governed the provinces during the Yamato
                            confederacy.

Rikken Minseitô   The 'Constitutional Democratic Party', founded in
立憲民政党: 1927 by a merger of the Kenseitô and Seiyu Hontô
                            political parties.

Rikken Seiyûkai   The 'Friends of Constitutional Government Party',
立憲政友会: established by Itô Hirobumi in 1900.

ritsuryô 律令: Imperial 'penal and administrative' bureaucratic
                            government imported from China's Tang dynasty
                            during the Yamato and Nara periods.

sakoku 鎖国: Reference to Japan as a 'closed country' following
                            the maritime prohibitions of the early seventeenth
                            century, which forbade contact with European
                            countries, with the exception of the Netherlands.
                            Under maritime prohibitions, Japan continued to
                            have diplomatic and commercial ties with other
                            Asian countries.

sankin kôtai   In 1635, the 'alternate attendance' policy, or some-
参勤交代: times the 'hostage system', required early modern
                            daimyô to keep residences in Edo, where they spent
                            every other year. When not in Edo, the policy
                            required that they keep wives and eldest sons in
                            the capital as hostages, lest they entertain forming
                            alliances against the Edo *bakufu*.

seii taishôgun   Literally 'Barbarian Subduing General', the
征夷大将軍: emperor gave this title to the head of samurai
                            bakufu governments.

shiki 職: Court authorization that described rights of an
                            aristocratic family or Buddhist monastery to
                            develop *shôen* estates.

Shinpotô 進歩党: The 'Progressive Party', originally established by
                            Ôkuma Shigenobu in 1896.

shishi 志士:	'Men of high purpose' were samurai who embraced the 'revere the emperor, expel the barbarian', or *sonnô jôi*, slogan and sought to overthrow the Edo *bakufu* in the mid-nineteenth century.
shôen 莊園:	Estates that the court authorized aristocratic families or Buddhist monastery to develop for revenue purposes. Originally, under the 'equal field' system, these estates were exclusively imperial holdings, but over the course of the Heian period they came to resemble private holdings.
shugo 守護:	Medieval provincial governors appointed by the Ashikaga *bakufu* to oversee the provinces.
sonnô jôi 尊皇攘夷:	The slogan 'revere the emperor, expel the barbarians' that rallied imperial loyalists in the final years of the Edo *bakufu* and facilitated the imperial restoration of 1868. This rallying cry contrasted to the 'open the country', or *kaikoku*, policy initially pursued by the Edo *bakufu*.
waka 和歌:	A classical form of thirty-one syllable poetry using *kana* script and popular in the Heian period.
Yayoi culture 弥生:	An archaeological phase that occurred on the Japanese archipelago between 300 BCE and 300 CE and is designated by the emergence of wetland paddy agriculture and social specialization.
yûgen 幽玄:	An aesthetic notion popular in the medieval period that denotes a deep grace, one connected to Buddhist ideas of the unfathomable and distant.
zaibatsu 財閥:	A financial and industrial conglomerate, such as Mitsubishi or Sumitomo corporations, that controlled much of the Japanese economy between the late Meiji period and 1945.

FURTHER READING

INTRODUCTION: WRITING JAPANESE HISTORY

Benedict Anderson, *Imagined Communities: Reflections on the Origin and Spread of Nationalism* (New York: Verso, 1991)

Edward B. Barbier, *Scarcity and Frontiers: How Economies Have Developed through Natural Resource Exploitation* (Cambridge University Press, 2011)

David Christian, *Maps of Time: An Introduction to Big History* (Berkeley and Los Angeles: University of California Press, 2004)

Prasenjit Duara, *Rescuing History from the Nation: Questioning Narratives of Modern China* (University of Chicago Press, 1995)

Carolyn Merchant, *The Death of Nature: Women, Ecology, and the Scientific Revolution* (San Francisco: Harper & Row, 1980)

Tessa Morris-Suzuki, *Re-Inventing Japan: Time, Space, Nation* (Armonk, NY and London: M. E. Sharpe, 1998)

John F. Richards, *The Unending Frontier: An Environmental History of the Early Modern World* (Berkeley and Los Angeles: University of California Press, 2003)

Will Steffen, Paul J. Crutzen, and John R. McNeill, 'The Anthropocene: Are Humans Now Overwhelming the Great Forces of Nature?', *Ambio* 36.8 (December 2007)

Anne Walthall, *Japan: A Cultural, Social, and Political History* (Boston and New York: Houghton Mifflin Company, 2006)

Max Weber, *The Religion of China: Confucianism and Taoism*, trans. Hans H. Gerth and intro. C. K. Yang (New York: Macmillan Company, 1964).

1. THE BIRTH OF THE YAMATO STATE, 14,500 BCE – 710 CE

Delmer M. Brown, *The Cambridge History of Japan,* Volume 1: *Ancient Japan* (Cambridge University Press, 1993)

William Wayne Farris, *Japan to 1600: A Social and Economic History* (Honolulu: University of Hawai'i Press, 2009)

Charles Holcombe, *The Genesis of East Asia, 221 BC–AD 907,* Asian Interactions and Comparisons (Honolulu: University of Hawai'i Press, 2001)

Mark J. Hudson, *Ruins of Identity: Ethnogenesis in the Japanese Islands* (Honolulu: University of Hawai'i Press, 1999)

Keiji Imamura, *Prehistoric Japan: New Perspectives on Insular East Asia* (Honolulu: University of Hawai'i Press, 1996)

J. Edward Kidder, Jr., *Himiko and Japan's Elusive Chiefdom of Yamatai: Archaeology, History, and Mythology* (Honolulu: University of Hawai'i Press, 2007)

Herman Ooms, *Imperial Politics and Symbolics in Ancient Japan: The Tenmu Dynasty, 650–800* (Honolulu: University of Hawai'i Press, 2009)

Joan R. Piggott, *The Emergence of Japanese Kingship* (Stanford University Press, 1997)

Brett L. Walker, *The Lost Wolves of Japan,* foreword by William Cronon (Seattle: University of Washington Press, 2005).

2. THE COURTLY AGE, 710–1185

Robert Borgen, *Sugawara no Michizane and the Early Heian Court* (Honolulu: University of Hawai'i Press, 1986)

The Diary of Lady Murasaki, trans. Richard Bowring (New York: Penguin Books, 1996)

William Wayne Farris, *Japan to 1600: A Social and Economic History* (Honolulu: University of Hawai'i Press, 2009)

William Wayne Farris, *Population, Disease, and Land in Early Japan, 645–900* (Cambridge, MA: Council on East Asian Studies, Harvard University, and the Harvard-Yenching Institute, and distributed by Harvard University Press, 1985)

The Gossamer Years: A Diary by a Noblewoman of Heian Japan (Tokyo and Rutland, VT: Charles E. Tuttle Co., 1973)

Charles Holcombe, *The Genesis of East Asia, 221 BC–AD 907* (Honolulu: University of Hawai'i Press, 2001)

Ivan Morris, *The World of the Shining Prince: Court Life in Ancient Japan,* intro. Barbara Ruch (New York and Tokyo: Kodansha International, 1964)

Nihongi: Chronicles of Japan from the Earliest Times to AD 697, trans.
W. G. Aston, intro. Terence Barrow (Rutland, VT: Charles E. Tuttle
Company, 1972)

The Pillow Book of Sei Shônagon, trans. Ivan Morris (New York: Penguin
Books, 1967)

Haruo Shirane, *Japan and the Culture of the Four Seasons: Nature, Literature, and the Arts* (New York: Columbia University Press, 2012)

Haruo Shirane, ed., *Traditional Japanese Literature: An Anthology, Beginnings to 1600* (New York: Columbia University Press, 2007)

Brett L. Walker, *The Conquest of Ainu Lands: Ecology and Culture in
Japanese Expansion, 1590–1800* (Berkeley and Los Angeles: University of California Press, 2001)

Mimi Hall Yiengpruksawan, *Hiraizumi: Buddhist Art and Regional Politics in Twentieth-Century Japan* (Cambridge, MA: Harvard University
Asia Center and distributed by Harvard University Press, 1998).

3. THE RISE OF SAMURAI RULE, 1185–1336

William Wayne Farris, *Heavenly Warriors: The Evolution of Japan's
Military, 500–1300* (Cambridge, MA: Council on East Asian Studies,
Harvard University, 1995)

William Wayne Farris, *Japan to 1600: A Social and Economic History*
(Honolulu: University of Hawai'i Press, 2009)

William Wayne Farris, *Population, Disease, and Land in Early Japan,
645–900* (Cambridge, MA: Council on East Asian Studies and
Harvard-Yenching Institute Monograph Series 24, Harvard University, 1985)

Karl F. Friday, *Hired Swords: The Rise of Private Warrior Power in Early
Japan* (Stanford University Press, 1992)

Andrew Goble, *Kenmu: Go-Daigo's Revolution* (Cambridge, MA: Council
on East Asian Studies, Harvard University, 1996)

Eiko Ikegami, *The Taming of the Samurai: Honorific Individualism and the
Making of Modern Japan* (Cambridge, MA: Harvard University Press,
1995)

*In Little Need of Divine Intervention: Takezaki Suenaga's Scrolls of the
Mongol Invasions of Japan*, trans. and interpretative essay by Thomas
D. Conlan (Ithaca: East Asia Program, Cornell University, 2001)

Pierre François Souyri, *The World Turned Upside Down: Medieval Japanese
Society*, trans. Käthe Roth (New York: Columbia University Press, 2001)

The Ten Foot Square Hut and Tales of the Heike, trans. A. L. Sadler
(Rutland, VT & Tokyo, Japan: Charles E. Tuttle Company, 1972)

Paul Varley, *Warriors of Japan, As Portrayed in the War Tales* (Honolulu: University of Hawai'i Press, 1994).

4. MEDIEVAL JAPAN AND THE WARRING STATES PERIOD, 1336–1573

Mary Elizabeth Berry, *The Culture of Civil War in Kyoto* (Berkeley and Los Angeles: University of California Press, 1994)

Thomas Donald Conlan, *State of War: The Violent Order of Fourteenth-Century Japan* (Ann Arbor: Center for Japanese Studies, University of Michigan, 2003)

Andrew Edmund Goble, *Confluences of Medicine in Medieval Japan: Buddhist Healing, Chinese Knowledge, Islamic Formulas, and Wounds of War* (Honolulu: University of Hawai'i Press, 2011)

John Whitney Hall, Nagahara Keiji, and Kozo Yamamura, eds., *Japan Before Tokugawa: Political Consolidation and Economic Growth, 1500–1650* (Princeton University Press, 1981)

Lynn Margulis and Dorion Sagan, *Microcosmos: Four Billion Years of Microbial Evolution* (London: Allen & Unwin, 1987)

John F. Richards, *The Unending Frontier: An Environmental History of the Early Modern World* (Berkeley and Los Angeles: University of California Press, 2003)

Pierre François Souyri, *The World Turned Upside Down: Medieval Japanese Society*, trans. Käthe Roth (New York: Columbia University Press, 2001)

Conrad Totman, *The Green Archipelago: Forestry in Pre-Industrial Japan*, foreword by James L. A. Webb, Jr. (Berkeley and Los Angeles: University of California Press, 1989; reprint, Athens: Ohio University Press, 1998)

H. Paul Varley, *The Ōnin War: History of Its Origins and Background – With a Selective Translation of the Chronicle of Ōnin* (New York and London: Columbia University Press, 1967).

5. JAPAN'S ENCOUNTER WITH EUROPE, 1543–1640

Michael Cooper, S.J., comp., *They Came to Japan* (Berkeley and Los Angeles: University of California Press, 1965)

Ann Bowman Jannetta, *Epidemics and Mortality in Early Modern Japan* (Princeton University Press, 1987)

Robert B. Marks, *The Origins of the Modern World: A Global and Ecological Narrative from the Fifteenth to the Twenty-first Century* (New York and Oxford: Rowman & Littlefield, 2007)

Kenneth Pomeranz and Steven Topik, *The World that Trade Created: Society, Culture, and the World Economy, 1400 to the Present*, 2nd edition (Armonk, NY and London: M. E. Sharpe, 2006)

John F. Richards, *The Unending Frontier: An Environmental History of the Early Modern World* (Berkeley and Los Angeles: University of California Press, 2003)

Timon Screech, *The Lens Within the Heart: The Western Scientific Gaze and Popular Imagery in Later Edo Japan* (Honolulu: University of Hawai'i Press, 2002)

Gregory Smits, *Visions of Ryukyu: Identity and Ideology in Early-Modern Thought and Politics* (Honolulu: University of Hawai'i Press, 1999)

Masayoshi Sugimoto and David L. Swain, *Science and Culture on Traditional Japan, AD 600–1854* (Cambridge, MA: MIT Press, 1978)

Ronald P. Toby, *State and Diplomacy in Early Modern Japan: Asia and the Development of the Tokugawa Bakufu* (Stanford University Press, 1991).

6. UNIFYING THE REALM, 1560–1603

Mary Elizabeth Berry, *Hideyoshi* (Cambridge, MA: Harvard University Press, 1982)

John Whitney Hall, Nagahara Keiji, and Kozo Yamamura, eds., *Japan Before Tokugawa: Political Consolidation and Economic Growth, 1500–1650* (Princeton University Press, 1981)

Jeroen Lamers, *Japonius Tyrannus: The Japanese Warlord Oda Nobunaga Reconsidered* (Leiden: Hôtei Publishing, 2000)

Conrad Totman, *Early Modern Japan* (Berkeley and Los Angeles: University of California Press, 1993)

Conrad Totman, *The Green Archipelago: Forestry in Pre-Industrial Japan*, foreword by James L. A. Webb, Jr. (Berkeley and Los Angeles: University of California Press, 1989; reprint, Athens: Ohio University Press, 1998).

7. EARLY MODERN JAPAN, 1600–1800

Mary Elizabeth Berry, *Japan in Print: Information and Nation in the Early Modern Period* (Berkeley and Los Angeles: University of California Press, 2006)

Matsuo Bashô, *The Narrow Road to the Deep North and Other Travel Sketches*, trans. Nobuyuki Yuasa (New York: Penguin Books, 1966)

Susan Hanley, *Everyday Things in Premodern Japan: The Hidden Legacy of Material Culture* (Berkeley and Los Angeles: University of California Press, 1997)

David L. Howell, *Capitalism from Within: Economy, Society, and the State in a Japanese Fishery* (Berkeley and Los Angeles: University of California Press, 1995)

David L. Howell, *Geographies of Identity in Nineteenth-Century Japan* (Berkeley and Los Angeles: University of California Press, 2005)

Eiko Ikegami, *Bonds of Civility: Aesthetic Networks and the Political Origins of Japanese Culture* (Cambridge University Press, 2005)

Tetsuo Najita, ed., *Tokugawa Political Writings* (Cambridge University Press, 1998)

Tetsuo Najita, *Visions of Virtue in Tokugawa Japan: The Kaitokudô Merchant Academy of Osaka* (University of Chicago Press, 1987)

Herman Ooms, *Tokugawa Ideology: Early Constructs, 1570–1680* (Princeton University Press, 1985)

Luke S. Roberts, *Mercantilism in a Japanese Domain: The Merchant Origins of Economic Nationalism in 18th-Century Tosa* (Cambridge University Press, 1998)

Thomas C. Smith, *The Agrarian Origins of Modern Japan* (Stanford University Press, 1959)

Thomas C. Smith, *Native Sources of Japanese Industrialization, 1750–1920* (Berkeley and Los Angeles: University of California Press, 1988)

Conrad Totman, *Early Modern Japan* (Berkeley and Los Angeles: University of California Press, 1993)

Brett L. Walker, *The Conquest of Ainu Lands: Ecology and Culture in Japanese Expansion, 1590–1800* (Berkeley and Los Angeles: University of California Press, 2001)

Brett L. Walker, 'Mamiya Rinzô and the Japanese Exploration of Sakhalin Island: Cartography, Ethnography, and Empire', *Journal of Historical Geography* 33.2 (April 2007)

Marcia Yonemoto, *Mapping Early Modern Japan: Space, Place, and Culture in the Tokugawa Period (1603–1868)* (Berkeley and Los Angeles: University of California Press, 2003).

8. THE RISE OF IMPERIAL NATIONALISM, 1770–1854

Susan L. Burns, *Before the Nation: Kokugaku and the Imagining of Community in Early Modern Japan* (Durham, NC and London: Duke University Press, 2003)

H. D. Harootunian, *Things Seen and Unseen: Discourse and Ideology in Tokugawa Nativism* (Chicago and London: University of Chicago Press, 1988)

H. D. Harootunian, *Toward Restoration: The Growth of Political Consciousness in Tokugawa Japan* (Berkeley and Los Angeles: University of California Press, 1970)

Donald Keene, *The Japanese Discovery of Europe, 1720–1830* (Stanford University Press, 1952)

J. Victor Koschmann, *The Mito Ideology: Discourse, Reform, and Insurrection in Late Tokugawa Japan, 1790–1864* (Berkeley and Los Angeles: University of California Press, 1987)

Tetsuo Najita, *Japan: The Intellectual Foundations of Modern Japanese Politics* (Chicago and London: University of Chicago Press, 1974)

Hitomi Tonomura, Anne Walthall, and Wakita Haruko, eds., *Women and Class in Japanese History* (Ann Arbor: Center for Japanese Studies, University of Michigan, 1999)

Conrad Totman, *The Collapse of the Tokugawa Bakufu, 1862–1868* (Honolulu: University of Hawai'i Press, 1980)

Stephen Vlastos, *Peasant Protests and Uprisings in Tokugawa Japan* (Berkeley and Los Angeles: University of California Press, 1986)

Bob Tadashi Wakabayashi, *Anti-Foreignism and Western Learning in Early Modern Japan: The 'New Theses' of 1825* (Cambridge, MA: Council on Easy Asian Studies, Harvard University, 1991)

Anne Walthall, ed. and trans., *Peasant Uprisings in Japan* (Chicago and London: University of Chicago Press, 1991)

Anne Walthall, *The Weak Body of a Useless Woman: Matsuo Taseko and the Meiji Restoration* (Chicago and London: University of Chicago Press, 1998)

George M. Wilson, *Patriots and Redeemers in Japan: Motives in the Meiji Restoration* (Chicago and London: University of Chicago Press, 1992).

9. MEIJI ENLIGHTENMENT, 1868–1912

The Autobiography of Yukichi Fukuzawa, trans. Eiichi Kiyooka (New York: Columbia University Press, 1960)

W. G. Beasley, *The Meiji Restoration* (Stanford University Press, 1972)

Daniel V. Botsman, *Punishment and Power in the Making of Modern Japan* (Princeton University Press, 2005)

Albert M. Craig, *Chôshû in the Meiji Restoration* (Cambridge, MA: Harvard University Press, 1961)

Albert M. Craig, *Civilization and Enlightenment: The Early Thought of Fukuzawa Yukichi* (Cambridge, MA: Harvard University Press, 2009)

T. Fujitani, *Splendid Monarchy: Power and Pageantry in Modern Japan* (Berkeley and Los Angeles: University of California, Press, 1996)

Carol Gluck, *Japan's Modern Myths: Ideology in the Late Meiji Period* (Princeton University Press, 1985)

Jeffrey E. Hanes, *The City as Subject: Seki Hajime and the Reinvention of Modern Osaka* (Berkeley and Los Angeles: University of California Press, 2002)

David L. Howell, *Geographies of Identity in Nineteenth-Century Japan* (Berkeley and Los Angeles: University of California Press, 2005)

Douglas R. Howland, *Translating the West: Language and Political Reason in Nineteenth-Century Japan* (Honolulu: University of Hawai'i Press, 2002)

Marius B. Jansen, *Sakamoto Ryôma and the Meiji Restoration* (New York: Columbia University Press, 1961)

Marius B. Jansen and Gilbert Rozman, eds., *Japan in Transition: From Tokugawa to Meiji* (Princeton University Press, 1986)

Masao Miyoshi, *As We Saw Them: The First Japanese Embassy to the United States* (New York and Tokyo: Kodansha International, 1979)

Sir Ernest Satow, *A Diplomat in Japan: An Inner History of the Japanese Reformation* (Rutland, VT and Tokyo: Charles E. Tuttle Co., 1983)

Sharon L. Sievers, *Flowers in Salt: The Beginnings of Feminist Consciousness in Modern Japan* (Stanford University Press, 1983).

10. MEIJI'S DISCONTENTS, 1868–1920

Roger W. Bowen, *Rebellion and Democracy in Meiji Japan: A Study of Commoners in the Popular Rights Movement* (Berkeley and Los Angeles: University of California Press, 1980)

Irokawa Daikichi, *The Culture of the Meiji Period*, trans. Marius B. Jansen (Princeton University Press, 1985)

Mikiso Hane, *Peasants, Rebels, and Outcastes: The Underside of Modern Japan* (New York: Pantheon Books, 1982)

David L. Howell, *Geographies of Identity in Nineteenth-Century Japan* (Berkeley: University of California Press, 2005)

James Edward Ketelaar, *Of Heretics and Martyrs in Meiji Japan* (Princeton University Press, 1990)

Kenneth Strong, *Ox Against the Storm: A Biography of Tanaka Shôzô, Japan's Conservationist Pioneer* (New York: Routledge, 2005)

Sarah Thal, *Rearranging the Landscapes of the Gods: The Politics of a Pilgrimage Site in Japan, 1573–1912* (Chicago and London: University of Chicago Press, 2005)

Brett L. Walker, *The Lost Wolves of Japan*, foreword William Cronon (Seattle: University of Washington Press, 2005)

Brett L. Walker, *Toxic Archipelago: A History of Industrial Disease in Japan*, foreword William Cronon (Seattle: University of Washington Press, 2010).

II. THE BIRTH OF JAPAN'S IMPERIAL STATE, 1800–1910

James R. Bartholomew, *The Formation of Science in Japan* (New Haven and London: Yale University Press, 1989)

Gail Lee Bernstein, ed., *Recreating Japanese Women, 1600–1945* (Berkeley and Los Angeles: University of California Press, 1991)

Sabine Frühstück, *Colonizing Sex: Sexology and Social Control in Modern Japan* (Berkeley and Los Angeles: University of California Press, 2003)

Fumiko Fujita, *American Pioneers and the Japanese Frontier: American Experts in Nineteenth-Century Japan* (Westport, CT: Greenwood Press, 1994)

Sheldon Garon, *Molding Japanese Minds: The State in Everyday Life* (Princeton University Press, 1997)

A Japanese View of Nature: The World of Living Things by Imanishi Kinji, trans. Pamela J. Asquith, Heita Kawakatsu, Shusuke Yagi, and Hiroyuki Takasaki (London: RoutledgeCurzon, 2002)

William Johnson, *The Modern Epidemic: A History of Tuberculosis in Japan* (Cambridge, MA: Council on East Asian Studies, Harvard University Press, 1995)

Kayano Shigeru, *Our Land Was a Forest: An Ainu Memoir*, trans. Kyoko Selden and Lili Seldon (Boulder: Westview Press, 1980)

Richard Siddle, *Race, Resistance and the Ainu of Japan* (London and New York: Routledge, 1996)

E. Patricia Tsurumi, *Factory Girls: Women in the Thread Mills of Meiji Japan* (Princeton University Press, 1990)

Brett L. Walker, 'The Early Modern Japanese State and Ainu Vaccinations: Redefining the Japanese Body Politic, 1799–1868', *Past and Present* 163 (May 1999).

12. EMPIRE AND IMPERIAL DEMOCRACY, 1905–1931

W. G. Beasley, *Japanese Imperialism, 1894–1945* (Oxford: Clarendon Press, 1987)

Richard Ellis, *The Empty Ocean* (Washington, DC: Island Press/ Shearwater Books, 2003)

Richard Ellis, *Tuna: A Love Story* (New York: Alfred A. Knopf, 2008)

Sheldon Garon, *The State and Labor in Modern Japan* (Berkeley and Los Angeles: University of California Press, 1987)

Andrew Gordon, *Labor and Imperial Democracy in Prewar Japan* (Berkeley and Los Angeles: University of California Press, 1991)

Andrew Gordon, *A Modern History of Japan: From Tokugawa Times to the Present* (New York and Oxford: Oxford University Press, 2009)

Michael Lewis, *Rioters and Citizens: Mass Protest in Imperial Japan* (Berkeley and Los Angeles: University of California Press, 1990)

Yoshihisa Tak Matsusaka, *The Making of Japanese Manchuria, 1904–1932* (Cambridge, MA: Harvard University Asia Center, Harvard University Press, 2001)

James L. McClain, *Japan: A Modern History* (New York: W. W. Norton, 2002)

Micah S. Muscolino, *Fishing Wars and Environmental Change in Late Imperial and Modern China* (Cambridge, MA: Harvard University Asia Center, Harvard University Press, 2009)

Tetsuo Najita, *Hara Kei in the Politics of Compromise, 1905–1915* (Cambridge, MA: Harvard University Press, 1967)

Gregory M. Pflugfelder and Brett L. Walker, *JAPANimals: History and Culture in Japan's Animal Life* (Ann Arbor: Center for Japanese Studies, University of Michigan, 2005)

Carl Safina, *Song for the Blue Ocean* (New York: John Macrae Books/ Henry Holt and Company, 1997)

William Tsutsui, 'The Pelagic Empire: Reconsidering Japanese Expansion', in *Japan at Nature's Edge: The Environmental Context of a Global Power*, ed. Ian Jared Miller, Julia Adeney Thomas, and Brett L. Walker (Honolulu: University of Hawai'i Press, 2013)

Koryu Uchinada, *Ancient Okinawan Martial Arts*, trans. Patrick McCarthy (Rutland, VT and Tokyo: Tuttle Publishing, 1999)

Louise Young, *Japan's Total Empire: Manchuria and the Culture of Wartime Imperialism* (Berkeley and Los Angeles: University of California Press, 1998).

13. THE PACIFIC WAR, 1931–45

Alexander Bay, *Beriberi in Modern Japan: The Making of a National Disease* (Rochester, NY: University of Rochester Press, 2012)

Herbert Bix, *Hirohito and the Making of Modern Japan* (Tokyo: Harper-Collins, 2000)

Timothy Brooks, ed., *Documents on the Rape of Nanking* (Ann Arbor: University of Michigan Press, 1999)

Haruko Taya Cook and Theodore F. Cook, *Japan at War: An Oral History* (New York: The New Press, 1992)

John W. Dower, *War Without Mercy: Race & Power in the Pacific War* (New York: Pantheon Books, 1986)

Tsuyoshi Hasegawa, *Racing the Enemy: Stalin, Truman, and the Surrender of Japan* (Cambridge, MA: Belknap Press, Harvard University Press, 2005)

James L. McClain, *Japan: A Modern History* (New York and London: W. W. Norton, 2002)

Ramon H. Myers and Mark R. Peattie, eds., *The Japanese Colonial Empire, 1895–1945* (Princeton University Press, 1984)

Ian Jared Miller, *The Nature of the Beasts: Empire and Exhibition at the Tokyo Imperial Zoo* (Berkeley and Los Angeles: University of California Press, 2013)

Mark R. Peattie, *Ishiwara Kanji and Japan's Confrontation with the West* (Princeton University Press, 1975)

Ienaga Saburô, *The Pacific War, 1931–1945* (New York: Pantheon Books, 1968)

Julia Adeney Thomas, *Reconfiguring Modernity: Concepts of Nature in Japanese Political Ideology* (Berkeley and Los Angeles: University of California Press, 2001)

Brett L. Walker, *Toxic Archipelago: A History of Industrial Disease in Japan* (Seattle and London: University of Washington Press, 2010)

Louise Young, *Japan's Total Empire: Manchuria and the Culture of Wartime Imperialism* (Berkeley and Los Angeles: University of California Press, 1998).

14. JAPAN'S POST-WAR HISTORY, 1945–PRESENT

John W. Dower, *Cultures of War: Pearl Harbor, Hiroshima, 9–11, Iraq* (New York: W. W. Norton, 2010)

John. W. Dower, *Embracing Defeat: Japan in the Wake of World War II* (New York: W. W. Norton, 1999)

J. W. Dower, *Empire and Aftermath: Yoshida Shigeru and the Japanese Experience, 1878–1954* (Cambridge, MA: Council on East Asian Studies, Harvard University Press, 1979)

Timothy S. George, *Minamata: Pollution and the Struggle for Democracy in Postwar Japan* (Cambridge, MA: Harvard University Asia Center, Harvard University Press, 2001)

Andrew Gordon, *A Modern History of Japan: From Tokugawa Times to the Present* (New York and Oxford: Oxford University Press, 2009)

Andrew Gordon, ed., *Postwar Japan as History* (Berkeley and Los Angeles: University of California Press, 1993)

James L. McClain, *Japan: A Modern History* (New York: W. W. Norton, 2002)

Gavan McCormack, *The Emptiness of Japanese Affluence*, revised edition, foreword by Norma Field (New York and London: M. E. Sharpe, 2001)

Ishimure Michiko, *Paradise in the Sea of Sorrow: Our Minamata Disease*, trans. Livia Monnet (Ann Arbor: Center for Japanese Studies, University of Michigan, 2003)

Tessa Morris-Suzuki, *The Technological Transformation of Japan: From the Seventeenth to the Twenty-first Century* (Cambridge University Press, 1994)

Mark Schilling, *The Encyclopedia of Japanese Pop Culture* (New York: Weatherhill Inc., 1997).

15. NATURAL DISASTERS AND THE EDGE OF HISTORY

Gregory Clancey, *Earthquake Nation: The Cultural Politics of Japanese Seismicity, 1868–1930* (Berkeley and Los Angeles: University of California Press, 2006)

Peter Duus, 'Dealing with Disaster', in *Natural Disaster and Nuclear Crisis in Japan: Response and Recovery after Japan's 3-11*, ed. Jeff Kingston (London: Nissan Monograph Series, Routledge, 2012)

Kerry Emanuel, 'Increasing Destructiveness of Tropical Cyclones over the Past 30 Years', *Nature* 436 (4 August 2005)

Tetsushi Furukawa, 'Watsuji Tetsurô, the Man and His Work', in Watsuji Tetsurô, *Climate and Culture: A Philosophical Study*, trans. Geoffrey Bownas (Tokyo: The Hokuseido Press, Ministry of Education, 1961)

David Longshore, *Encyclopedia of Hurricanes, Typhoons, and Cyclones*, new edition (New York: Facts On File Inc., 2008)

Gavan McCormack, *The Emptiness of Japanese Affluence*, revised edition, foreword Norma Field Armonk (New York and London: M. E. Sharpe, 2001)

Nobuo Mimura, Masahiro Isobe, and Yasushi Hosokawa, 'Impacts of Sea Level Rise on Japanese Coastal Zones and Response Strategies', in *Intergovernmental Panel on Climate Change: Climate change 1995: The Science of Climate Change* (Cambridge University Press, 1996)

S. Solomon, D. Qin, M. Manning, Z. Chen, M. Marquis, K. B. Averyt, M. Tignor, and H. L. Miller, eds., *Contribution of Working Group I to the*

Fourth Assessment Report of the Intergovernmental Panel on Climate Change: The Physical Science Basis (Cambridge University Press, 2007)

Ted Steinberg, *Acts of God: The Unnatural History of Natural Disasters in America* (Oxford University Press, 2000)

Julia Adeney Thomas, *Reconfiguring Modernity: Concepts of Nature in Japanese Political Ideology* (Berkeley: University of California Press, 2001)

Evaggelos Vallianatos, 'The Nuclear Meltdown at Fukushima: Danger, Deception and Betrayal', *The Huffington Post* (11 November 2013)

P.J. Webster, G.J. Holland, J.A. Curry, and H.R. Chang, 'Changes in Tropical Cyclone Number, Duration and Intensity in a Warming Environment', *Science* 309 (16 September 2005).

INDEX